**Aubrey Malone** has published numerous anthologies of quotations, including *The Cynic's Dictionary*. He lives in Dublin.

# THE MAMMOTH BOOK OF

# IRISH HUMOR

## Aubrey Malone

RUNNING PRESS
PHILADELPHIA · LONDON

Constable & Robinson Ltd
55–56 Russell Square
London WC1B 4HP
www.constablerobinson.com

First published in the UK by Robinson, an imprint of Constable & Robinson Ltd, 2012

A copy of the British Library Cataloguing in Publication
Data is available from the British Library

UK ISBN: 978-1-78033-797-5 (paperback)
UK ISBN: 978-1-78033-798-2 (ebook)

1 3 5 7 9 10 8 6 4 2

First published in the United States in 2013 by Running Press Book Publishers,
A Member of the Perseus Books Group

US ISBN: 978-0-7624-4808-1
US Library of Congress Control Number: 2012942532

9 8 7 6 5 4 3 2 1
Digit on the right indicates the number of this printing

Running Press Book Publishers
2300 Chestnut Street
Philadelphia, PA 19103–4371
Visit us on the web!
www.runningpress.com

Printed and bound by CPI Group (UK) Ltd, Croydon, CR0 4YY

# CONTENTS

Contents    vii

x   Contents

# INTRODUCTION

Niall Toibin once said that only those without humour analyse it. Perhaps. Nonetheless, there are certain things that need to be said – not least the fact that humorists often have dark sides (including Toibin himself) and often they're their own worst analysts. "Comedy is no laughing matter" as the cliché goes, and this is particularly relevant to the Irish psyche, which is noted for wild bursts of manic energy and also, perhaps as an inevitable offshoot, a form of whistling in the metaphorical graveyard.

The Irish are noted for the gift of the gab, if not the grab – and for shooting from the lip (if not the hip). Both qualities are in evidence in some quantity in these pages. Ireland is also a country that has produced some of the liveliest word-smiths in the world, and their heady loquaciousness is on display here too, though I've done my best to capture the national spirit in more bite-sized chunks.

Part of the charm of Irish wit is its lunacy. For this we defer to the likes of Flann O'Brien, aka Myles na gCopaleen and Brian O'Nolan (when somebody has three names, you know something funny – both ha-ha and peculiar – is going on). It's also innocent, which has perhaps given rise to the "Irish joke", a phenomenon which doesn't always flatter the teller, but certainly entertains the person being told. The Irish joke is a byword for serendipity, contradiction, a curious lack of logic and a strange, unpredictable profundity (if you're patient enough to wade through the nonsense). Spike Milligan put it well when he said, "I'm Irish. We think sideways."

It may be microscoped in the anecdote of the traveller who asks for directions on the road from a rustic gent and receives the reply, "If I was you I wouldn't start from here." (There's no answer to that.) This is perhaps suspiciously close to an "Irish" joke – which subsequently morphed into a Kerry joke, a Polish joke or whatever you're having yourself.

I've included a few of these in the book, not to illustrate
ignorance so much as ingenuity. (Witness the young boy
having trouble with maths in the "Potatoes" section, courtesy of Paddy Crosbie.)

There are also some Paddy (not Crosbie) jokes in the
"Drink and Drinking" section – this was too hard to resist –
and other examples of "Oirish" humour, which may be of
interest to folklorists today more from a sentimental purview
than anything else. As Frank McNally put it, Ireland has gone
from being an island of saints and scholars to one of limousines and lapdancers. (That was before the recession. The
limos have now become broken-down Datsuns and most of
the lapdancers have gone back to Eastern Europe.)

Like many formerly colonized nations, Ireland's humour is
often iconoclastic. It rebels not only politically but also in
other walks of life – philosophy, ethics, music, clothing,
language. The humour is frequently prickly, with an under-
tow of darkness. This sometimes conduces to ambiguity or
downright unfathomability. Irony can be a first cousin of
such strains. So can black comedy, as when the Irish republican prisoner Wolfe Tone said, *apropos* of unsuccessfully
trying to cut his throat prior to being executed, "I find I am
but a bad anatomist." (He had severed his windpipe instead
of his jugular.) This is, literally, gallows humour. The Irish are
good at it, all the way from George Bernard Shaw ("If you
cannot get rid of the family skeleton, you may as well make
it dance") to Samuel Beckett ("When you're in the last ditch,
the only thing left is to sing").

Considering the fact that iconoclasm is so prevalent in the
Irish mindset maybe I should have included a "Non-conformity"
section; but of course non-conformity is present in almost
every page of the text, whether overtly or covertly. That's
epitomized by Brendan Behan's classic comment, "The first
item on every Irish agenda is The Split." Or his brother Brian's
declaration that he was once expelled from the Anarchist
Party.

We can even see it in the humorous anecdote by John
Sheahan who, shortly after joining the folk group The
Dubliners in the 1960s, got a shock when he witnessed the
band members telling each other what to do with

themselves one night in a pub, having imbibed overmuch (as was their wont). He felt that was effectively that as far as his musical future was concerned, but a few nights later Ronnie Drew, the lead singer, rang him to ask him if he was "all right for Friday". Sheahan told Drew he'd heard everyone disbanding (literally) in the pub and Drew consoled him with, "Oh for fuck's sake, don't take any notice of that kind of thing. It happens every week." It's probably significant to note that Drew got married in a pub, O'Donoghue's in Merrion Row. Since he was spending more of his time there than anywhere else, both gigging and boozing, it seemed to make sense.

Fintan O'Toole sees the iconoclasm another way – as a kind of contrariness, or moral greyness. The Irish "only enjoy something when we feel we're not entitled to it", he believes. It all goes back to the Forbidden Fruit syndrome. David Slattery talks about Irish people "running around the streets in a panic on Good Friday, gasping for an illegal drink", this being the only day of the year when Irish pubs are closed, "despite their own stockpiles at home". Delving into these would be too easy; we prefer the nudge-wink excitement of finding an alehouse where we can get in the back door for a guilty pleasure. Such pleasures form part of the hallowed tradition of drinking in Ireland. There's a famous story of a Garda (i.e. an Irish policeman) raiding a pub after hours in the middle of nowhere, only to find our former Taoiseach (Prime Minister) Charlie Haughey drinking there with some friends. Haughey is alleged to have said to the Garda, "Do you want a pint or a transfer?"

With regard to phraseology, some terms (like the above two) may prove incomprehensible to British and American readers so I've explained them wherever necessary. Other phrases like "crack" (also spelled "craic" and meaning "fun" rather than anything to do with substance abuse) have recently found their way into the British vernacular. So also has "feck", as a milder form of abuse than the better-known "F" word. This is largely due to its frequent use on *Father Ted*, a series ironically rejected by RTE, Ireland's flagship TV station, before becoming a huge success on Channel 4 and then, with typical Irish logic, being bought back by RTE afterwards. We might also consider the fact that Brendan Behan had his first stage success "across the pond".

However, as George Bernard Shaw once reflected, Ireland and America are two countries divided by a common language, and so also are Ireland and Britain in many ways even yet. Some readers may not know that, up until recently, Fianna Fáil was Ireland's leading party in government, or that the seat of government is called The Dáil, or that Irish politicians are called TDs, or that our aforementioned Taoiseach is pronounced "Tee-shock". Jack Charlton, Ireland's erstwhile football manager and near-adoptive Irishman, preferred to say "Teashop". (Which was pretty good for him considering he often had difficulty pronouncing even some of his own players' names.)

These, and others, are Gaelic terms. Or, as the Irish would say, "Irish" terms. In Ireland we would never dream of calling Gaelic "Gaelic" any more than we would dream of calling Ireland "Eire". Only foreigners (particularly the British) do that.

When I was training to be a teacher many years ago I betook myself to the Conradh na Gaeilge club on Stephen's Green, an Irish-speaking establishment where they served after-hours drink (I was more interested in the latter activity than the former). One night I went up to the bar and ordered a Pionta Cláirseach, "Pionta" being the Irish (sorry, Gaelic) for "pint" and "Cláirseach" for Harp, our home-brewed beverage. The barman said to me, "You're obviously not a native speaker. A native speaker would have said 'Piont Harp'." In other words the "a" of "pionta" would have been dropped to make it sound more English, and "Harp" would have been preserved for the same reason.

The cult of bilingualism (popular because it's believed it sexes up the language, which is dying on the vine in most areas of the country) goes even further. Residents of Gaeltachts (i.e. Gaelic-speaking districts) will say things like "Thit me as mo bhicycle" ("I fell off my bicycle") instead of "Thit me as mo rothar", "rothar" being the Irish for "bicycle" and therefore not as "sexy". The "h" after the "b" is curious. It's a Gaelic aspiration (which used to be signalled by a dot over the letter when I was young) on an English word so the two languages are mixed. The aspiration changes the pronunciation of the "b" of "bicycle" — into "wycycle" if one is from the country, or, if one is from Dublin, into "vycycle". I hail from the West of Ireland so I would say "wycycle" but I taught in a Dublin school so had to learn "vycycle" instead. At this point things get a mite complicated. Irish-American comedian Des Bishop has done a hilarious study of the absurdities inherent in the language, and even brought out a DVD of it called *In the Name of the Fada*, a pun on the title of Jim Sheridan's movie *In the Name of the Father*, "fada" being an Irish accent which caused Bishop much confusion.

I've quoted Bishop extensively in the book as he's been living in Ireland for most of his adult life and has immersed himself in the culture more than most natives. In general I've tried to feature as many modern personages as I could turn up, though the "usual suspects" of yore are also here, letting us see where we've come from and where the influences for the contemporary "stand-up" have their roots. Those with a tenuous (or further back) Irish lineage appear less frequently. I've occasionally included people from other countries if they're speaking of things Irish.

Traditional Irish wits were undoubtedly gentler than the modern breed of "alternative" comedians, whose penchant for *Schadenfreude* (and indeed Freud) is usually present and correct. But then all humour has an element of cruelty in it, going back to the slapstick idea of laughing at someone who slips on a banana skin, or the clown who sticks his foot into a can of paint. As the actor Dan O'Herlihy once put it, "To err is humour."

With the emergence of Tommy Tiernan, who's always skated very close to the wind with his incendiary material, we saw a new type of humour making itself apparent, which probably reflects a seismic shift in the minds of his audiences, and the Irish psyche in general, which would probably cause no small degree of chagrin to people like Oscar Wilde or George Bernard Shaw were they to be reincarnated. Diehards tell us that "Alternative Comedy", as the expression goes, is often little more than an alternative *to* comedy. So be it. Every genre, even (especially?) *avant garde*, has its blind spots and I've sat through many purgatorial evenings listening to contemporary stand-up comics dying on their feet as I pined silently for the "shaggy dog stories" of the wits of yesteryear, who knew how to tell a joke without being precious about it, or pretentious, even if it wasn't wildly original.

Tiernan has outraged as many people as he's entertained over the years, poking fun at handicapped people and going beyond the pale with his sacrilegious quips and anti-Semitic rants. He sees this as testing the waters of public tolerance, and in the process digging deep into his own reserves of inspiration.

Dara O'Briain is more user-friendly, if not cuddly, in his embracing of British culture. O'Briain has lived in England for a number of years now and has even gone on the record as saying he'd cheer if his son scored a goal for England against Ireland in World Cup soccer. He's been tagged with what we might call the "Terry Wogan" sin of treachery to his own but he still manages to pull in large audiences when he performs in Dublin so feelings are divided about him, as they are about most comedians here.

In general, the goalposts have shifted significantly as regards what constitutes usable material for Irish comedians, the whimsicality of such as Noel V. Ginnity and Hal Roach having given way to the edgier material of Tiernan, Jason Byrne, David McSavage, Dylan Moran, P. J. Gallagher and a host of other "new wave" comics — though Brendan Grace can still market DVDs featuring the drunken man at the wedding, that old staple of "Oirish" humour. Sex also plays a large part in the modern comic routine, which means that themes only hinted at in the old days are given full vent now, often to the extent of turning off audiences of "a certain age". We've certainly come a long way from Oliver Flanagan's pronouncement that "There was no sex in Ireland before television" (which makes one wonder how he himself was conceived).

Where will things go from here? Ireland has now become poor again after a decade or so of affluence during the hey-years of the Celtic Tiger, and to many that has meant a return to more traditional values before the country, as they say, "lost the run of itself". So will we see a return to traditional comedy, to the hoary old yarns that cabaret performers like Jimmy O'Dea and Maureen Potter specialized in?

Hardly. The toothpaste is now out of the tube and most things are up for grabs. There are few sacred cows left, and few targets safe from the scabrous pens and tongues of our latterday satirists. Conservative audience members tell us that expletives are the sign of a poor vocabulary. Whether this is so or not, they're as much part of the modern "act" as its iconoclasm.

The other main development in the humour gene is the phenomenon of "observational" wit, whereupon comedians, almost like the stand-up equivalent of method actors, dig deep into their neuroses in order to express themselves, in marked contrast to the "chicken and chips" type of comic that used to proliferate at cabaret clubs and trade quips willy-nilly. This phenomenon, which takes an idea and runs with it (or, in the case of the failed *nouvelle vague* would-be wit, *walks*) would seem to wage war against the idea of the oneliner. How many times have we seen stand-up comics almost apologize for "cracking a joke" in their routines, as if this is the one remaining taboo for the creative artist: the oneliner?

Tiernan has spoken of jokes as the bane of the stand-up comedian, something he should avoid like the plague for fear it will kill his stream of consciousness. This chimes with the oft-held belief that the main difference between Irish and British humour is that Irish humour is in the telling whereas the British prioritize the punchline. This is a facile generalization but it has a grain of truth. (Which reminds me of the "backlash" Paddy quip: Why are Irish jokes so simplistic? So the English can understand them. Boom boom.)

Oneliners, in any case, are the business of the anthologist, and I've featured as many of them here as I could find, even if they've been told reluctantly by Tiernan and his fellow revisionists who prefer to say things funny than say funny things, which at its worst can mean that the humour of a situation is lost in transit between the stage and the page — an occupational hazard for any anthologist.

The other quality we may discern in our present-day humorists is something we might describe as the disease of cleverosity, i.e. a sense of "Oh, aren't we all very trendy and streetwise here". This is apparent in the work of everyone from Colin Murphy to Andrew Maxwell to Ed Byrne, who cut their comedic teeth in Dublin's Laughter Lounge and, to a lesser extent, on the television show *The Panel*, which was hosted by the aforementioned O'Briain. Their personas stand out in marked contrast to more "retro" talents like Jon Kenny and Pat Shortt of D'Unbelievables, who tend to give more of a "Simple Joe" vibe (while still remaining riotously funny). Set against the wilfully cruel and sexually outrageous new breed, Kenny, Shortt, Grace, Fox, Ginnity, Roach & Co. come across as positively quaint, even when they're giving the wicked eye, or gag.

The bottom line, of course, is whether they make us laugh or not. Whether comedy is clever or dumb, whether it celebrates traditional values or contemporary ones — or indeed no values at all — we should reserve the right to judge it on whether it tickles our funnybone. At the end of the day the clown sticking his foot into the can of paint may cause as many bellylaughs as the Tommy Tiernans of this world trying to reinvent the wheel, or push himself into areas light years away from his forebears with post-Lenny Bruce-style grossness or outrage. In such circumstances, discussions of whether someone has breached bad taste or gone a bridge too far may be less relevant than whether a joke "works" or not. And that's something nobody can predict, because, as everyone from Tony Hancock to Bob Monkhouse would observe, "It's the way you tell 'em."

The decision of whether that chemistry has successfully travelled from stage to page will rest with whatever readers this volume will find.

# ABSENTEEISM

I joined a health club last year which cost me a fortune but I still didn't lose any weight. Apparently you have to turn up. *Hal Roach*

When I was playing for Manchester United I used to go missing a lot: Miss America, Miss Uruguay, Miss Peru . . . *George Best*

A clergyman in Portadown told his congregation, "If you'd been here this morning to see the empty seats you'd have been ashamed of yourselves for staying away." *Tony Butler*

Absence makes the heart go wander. *Bill Kelly*

It's surprising how relatively few brides and grooms fail to turn up at their weddings, but these days it's probably easier to go through a divorce than to work out what to do with the presents. *David Slattery*

My university career was over. It had been shortened somewhat by my failure to register for any course, a fact which had upset the bureaucrats. *Ian MacPherson*

Ireland is overrun by absentee landlords. *Sir Boyle Roche*

I only use my sick days for hangovers and soap opera weddings. *Kate O'Brien*

# ABSURDITY

The definition of absurdity is an elephant hanging off a cliff with his tail tied to a daisy. *Jack Cruise*

The visitor complained of the long muddy avenue to the hotel. "Well now," soothed the proprietor, "if it was any shorter it wouldn't reach the house." *Tony Butler*

After my grandfather died, my grandmother came to live with us. Which came as a bit of a shock to me, because she's married to my other grandfather – who's still alive. *Michael Redmond*

I'm thinking of setting up an Association for Non-Members. It'll have no rules and won't meet once a month. People will ring us and ask us for our reaction to the news of the day and we'll say, "No comment, but don't quote us on that." *Kevin Marron*

All wooden gates in Ireland should be made of iron. *Sir Boyle Roche*

# ABUSE

Why don't you suck Cameron's rod, you non-Irish cunt. *Tweet directed at Dara O'Briain as a result of his perceived "treachery" towards the Irish after he moved to Britain*

If you think the EU is going to be sorted out by dozy Sarkozy and his gang of snail-guzzling simpletons, you'd blinkin' well believe the moon is made of Three Counties cheese. That frog-chomping bargain basement Napoleon is about as useful as a half-baked baguette in a swordfight with the Three Musketeers. *Mick the Maverick*

A man said to me, "Come here, Shit-for-Brains." I said, "Are you offering to swap?" *Michael Mee*

In Ireland a man may be called a "fucker", a "right fucker" or a "bad fucker". A "right fucker" is usually worse than a "fucker" but don't get alarmed if your friends call you one. The likelihood is that they're just taking the piss out of you. *Tadhg Hayes*

Larry Gogan: "What 'S' is a native of Liverpool?"
Contestant: "Scumbag!"
*Exchange on Gogan's* **Just-a-Minute Quiz**

The hierarchy of abuse in Ireland is like a freemasonry. Admission to this select group is normally at the level of "Bollocks". Once you are dubbed a bollocks, it is then a straightforward ascent through the ranks. You become a "Big Bollocks", an "Ignorant Bollocks" and so on, until you reach the penultimate level: a "Complete Bollocks". There is only one step up from here and few people can aspire to achieve it: "Bollocks of the Highest Order". *Frank McNally*

# ACCENTS

The main reason English people get on well with the Irish is because they're never quite sure from their accents whether they're posh or common. *Terry Wogan*

It is absurd to say there are neither ruins nor curiosities in America when they have their mothers and their accents. *Oscar Wilde*

Terry Wogan took on a British accent when he went to England, but it was an Irish British accent. Now you have British people trying to imitate him. An Irishman started by imitating the English and now you have the English trying to imitate an Irishman trying to imitate the English. *Shaun Geoghegan*

Somebody should clip Sting around the head and tell him to stop using that ridiculous Jamaican accent. *Elvis Costello*

English women are mad about Irish men. When you ask them why, the answer is always the same: our accent. For some reason, they don't really go for the pasty skin, the Guinness belly or the flamingo legs. *Keith Farnan*

He should be indicted for crimes against the Dublin accent. *Myles Dungan on Kevin Spacey in* **Ordinary Decent Criminals**

I once auditioned for the part of an Irish priest and was told that my Irish accent wasn't appropriate for someone from Ireland. *Malachy McCourt*

When I speak in England and the English people hear my Irish accent they think of me as the sort of man who would be delivering their laundry. **Brian Moore**

There's no Irish accent. Each county has a different one. **Sean O'Casey**

I even put on an accent when I'm impersonating myself. **Des Bishop**

With a Geordie accent you sound just the same after a stroke as before one. **Neil Delamere**

# ACCIDENTS

I had a bad accident the other night. I was climbing over my wife to get into bed and I broke my arse on the lightbulb. **Gene Fitzpatrick**

"Officer, I've just been knocked down by my friend."
  "What gear was he in?"
  "The usual woolly jumper and Nike runners."
**Liam O'Mahony**

I once got hit by a Volkswagen. I had to go to the hospital to have it removed. **Pat McCormick**

My father always used to say "Whatever doesn't kill you makes you stronger" – until his accident. **Jimmy Carr**

Every day of our lives we hear of cyclists being involved in accidents of one sort or another on our roads. Well I had a eureka moment the other day. All of a sudden it came to me: why don't they leave their bikes at home and get the bus? **Paddy Murray**

The biggest mistake Bill Clinton ever made was not getting Teddy Kennedy to drive Monica Lewinsky home. **Denis Leary**

A Norwich Union customer collided with a cow. The questions and answers on the claim form were as follows:
Q. What warning was given by you?
A. Horn.
Q. What warning was given by the other party?
A. Moo.
*Insurance company report*

Mr Hughes, I hear you've been in a lot of plane crashes. Is it true you're held together with wire and string? *Maureen O'Hara to Howard Hughes*

The *Evening Herald* says a man is knocked down by a car every three hours. He must be getting fed up of it. *Shaun Connors*

My wife told me she had some good news and some bad news for me the other day. I asked her to tell me the good news first. She said, "The air bag on the BMW works." *Dusty Young*

Alex Higgins tried to perfect the art of freefall parachuting without a parachute. *Declan Lynch on Higgins' drunken fall from a window*

Girl 1: "I crashed my car yesterday."
Girl 2: "Where?"
Girl 1: "On the road."
*Overheard in Dublin*

O'Hara fell from the scaffold and dropped two storeys. His fellow workers gathered around him and the foreman asked him, "Did the fall hurt you?" The victim felt his aching bones. "It wasn't the fall that hurt me. It was the sudden stop." *Joan Larson Kelly*

# ACHIEVEMENTS

She didn't know it couldn't be done so she went ahead and did it. *Bridget O'Donnell*

One of the most pleasing experiences of my life was writing "Yeats" and "fuck" in the same sentence. *Joe O'Connor*

Everybody sets out to do something and everybody does something but no one does what he sets out to do. *George Moore*

As far as I can gather, Lady Diana's only remarkable achievement was to get herself killed while in a tearing hurry to enjoy a night of leg-over with the upwardly mobile son of a Knightsbridge huckster. *Hugh Leonard*

I got a 155 once. It was a bus to Ilford. *Snooker ace Ken Doherty*

An Irishman would have been the first to climb Everest but he ran out of scaffolding. *Noel Purcell*

I made my film debut in *Excalibur*. My main achievement there was raping King Arthur's mother in a full suit of armour. *Gabriel Byrne*

# ACRONYMS

FAI stands for "Find an Irishman". *Paddy Mulligan*

It's just as well they weren't called Pat and Rick. *Joseph Dunne on John and Edward Grimes, aka Jedward*

I used to be known as BOC, my initials. I had a brother called Finbar, who did even worse. Thank God I didn't have one called Conor. *Brendan O'Carroll*

Brian Cowen is called Biffo because it's an acronym for Big Ignorant Fucker from Offaly. *Paul Byrne on Ireland's former Taoiseach*

# ACTORS AND ACTING

People tell you acting is an easy life. Not really, because every eight weeks or so you're basically back on the dole. *Brendan Gleeson*

I was useless at every job I did before acting. Some people say I'm useless at that too. *Gabriel Byrne*

The trouble with him is that he is in love with his wife and an actor can only afford to be in love with himself. *George Bernard Shaw on an acquaintance*

There was some evidence Jennifer Lopez could act in the early days, but then they started giving her lines and ruined it all. *Brendan O'Connor*

There's nothing duller than a respectable actor. Actors should be rogues, mountebanks and strolling players. *John Huston*

I would like to amend the old acting adage "Never work with children or animals" to "Never work with children, animals or Denholm Elliott". *Gabriel Byrne*

Most of the best acting we do in life is off-screen. *Cyril Cusack*

My most enjoyable acting experience was portraying Liz Hurley as a sexually-confused smalltown girl of thirty-three who still lives at home with the mammy, coaches the local ladies football team and plays bass in the AC/DC tribute band, 50–50. *Katherine Lynch*

Those whom the gods wish to punish they make mad – or actors. *Donal McCann*

Acting with Jeff Chandler was like acting with a broomstick. *Maureen O'Hara*

I never knew that cunt could act. *John Ford on John Wayne after seeing* **Red River**

She had many qualifications for an acting career. She was superficial, she had an excess of stupid vanity, and most of all she knew nothing about dramatic literature. *Patrick Kavanagh*

Acting is largely a matter of farting about in disguise. *Peter O'Toole*

I always admired you as an actor before you became a film star bollox. *Flann O'Brien to James Mason*

I'm paid to make an eejit of myself. **Pat Shortt**

Every now and then Arnold Schwarzenegger, the man once memorably described as looking like a condom stuffed with walnuts, does something to surprise us. Like acting. **Ian O'Doherty**

Rock Hudson knew as much about acting as a monkey did about chopping onions. **Lee Dunne**

Your best performances lie in the filing cabinets of therapists. **Richard Harris to Marlon Brando**

Look into the eyes of some Hollywood actresses and there's no one home. God help us, it's like looking at an unlit lamppost. **Peter O'Toole**

The suggestion that Michael Caine will live in legend is tantamount to prophesying that Rin Tin Tin will be solemnized beyond the memory of Marlon Brando. **Richard Harris**

Actresses start off as Cinderella and end up as the stepmother in *Snow White and the Seven Dwarfs*. **Dervla Kirwan**

If she were cast as Lady Godiva, the horse would steal the show. **Patrick Murray on a poor actress**

Acting isn't about acting. It's about *not* acting. **Jack MacGowran**

People don't really notice when you're bad. When you think you're terrific, that's when they say they didn't like it. **Stephen Rea**

I've played everything but a harp. **Lionel Barrymore**

Actors are born with the rise of the curtain and we die with its fall. Every night in the presence of our patrons we write our new creation and every night it is blotted out forever. What use is it to say to the audience, "Ah but you should have seen me last Tuesday"? **Micheál MacLiammóir**

Actors are crap. **John Ford**

# ADAM AND EVE

When Eve asked Adam "Do you love me?" he answered, "Who else?" *Clare Boylan*

If Adam was an Armagh footballer, he'd still be in Paradise. He would have refused the apple from Eve, seeing as it wasn't on the diet sheet, and settled for a banana instead. *Colm O'Rourke*

The main reason Adam and Eve were so happy in the Garden of Eden was because Adam didn't have to listen to Eve prattling on about all the other men she could have married. *Frank Hall*

Adam and Eve ate themselves out of house and home. *Frankie Blowers*

Man came first. They usually do. *Cliodhna O'Flynn*

Adam was the world's first book-keeper. He turned over a leaf and made an entry. *Sean Kilroy*

# ADDICTIONS

I'm on the see-food diet. Whenever I see food, I eat it. *Derek Davis*

When I was an altar boy as a child I became addicted to congealed candle grease. I used to slug it down with altar wine and Communion hosts. *Gabriel Byrne*

I have a drink problem. I can't get enough of it. *Christy Brown*

It's official: Nicorette is the best cure for nicotine addiction. Just put a patch over each eye and you won't be able to find your cigarettes. *Brendan O'Carroll*

"Golf, golf, golf," she wailed to her husband as he started to throw the clubs into the old Merc last Sunday. "I really believe

I'd drop dead if you spent one weekend at home." "Now dear," he answered, "bribery will get you nowhere." *James N. Healy*

Before I got into crocheting I learned to knit. Crack cocaine had nothing on the addictive powers of knitting for me. I'd have got up in the middle of the night to knit. And did. *Terry Prone*

# ADVERTISEMENTS

If I were Ikea's marketing department I would use the slogan "More shit than you actually need" on all promotional material. Because that is exactly what Ikea is. *Fiona Looney*

For Sale. Beautiful Wedding Dress. Only Worn Twice. *Ad in Roscommon Herald*

Janet Reno inserted an advert in the classifieds: "Husband wanted". The next day she received a hundred letters. They all said the same thing: "You can have mine". *John Scally*

Young lady required to work in accounts office. Previous experience not essential, but must be able to type. *Ad quoted by Patrick Myler*

Gentleman requires first-class accommodation, full board, in quiet guesthouse in seaside resort where he can put up with his wife for the first two weeks in August. *Ad quoted by Patrick Myler*

Datsun Saloon 120Y for immediate sale. Body in terrible condition. Front seating most uncomfortable. Would make ideal chicken coop. Also suitable for bringing turf from the bog. *Car ad in Kerry's Eye*

A tailor's advertisement making sentimental remarks to a milliner's advertisement in the middle of an upholsterer's and decorator's advertisement. *George Bernard Shaw on a typical play in the 1890s*

I've been asked to come up with an advertising slogan for Guinness. I've just thought of a good one: "It makes you drunk". *Brendan Behan*

The best part of American TV is the ads. *Nuala O'Faolain*

I lost my dog so I put an ad in the paper. I wasn't sure how to word it so I just wrote "Here, boy". *Frank Carson*

Black sheep disappointed in life would marry scapegoat with troubled past. *Ad spotted by Samuel Beckett in Paris in 1953*

For Sale: Austin 1972 Hearse. Body In Good Condition. *Belfast Telegraph*

I saw this advert in an Irish paper: "Before using your hair tonic I had three bald patches. Now I have only one." *Kevin Murtie*

# ADVICE

I always remember the advice I got from my Career guidance teacher. I asked him, "How do I get into medical school?" He said, "Donate your body to science." *Dan O'Dowd*

Never take Ecstasy when you're visiting a Holocaust museum. *Sean Hughes*

Don't ask an Irish person how many drinks he's going to have on a given night. He wouldn't understand the question. *Tommy Tiernan*

A good man giving bad advice is more dangerous than a nasty man giving bad advice. *Conor Cruise O'Brien*

My mum told me the best time to ask Dad for anything was during sex – not the best advice I've ever been given. I burst in through the bedroom door saying "Can I have a new bike?" and he was very upset. But his secretary was surprisingly nice about it. *Jimmy Carr*

When facts conflict with the legend, print the legend. *John Ford*

Al Pacino told me, "Don't sleep with your co-stars." I think it's a bit late for that. **Colin Farrell**

If people keep pushing tradition on you about your impending marriage, tell them you've decided to adopt the ancient one of the Aztecs where they sacrificed the bride's family's first-born son and ate his liver over the wedding altar. **Peter Downey**

If your girls are not in at the hours appointed, lay the lash upon their backs. That was the good old system and it should be the system today as well. **Directive to parents from the Bishop of Galway in 1927**

The world is only a blue bag. Knock a squeeze out of it when you can. **Eric Cross**

Surprise the woman in your life. Marry her sister. **Foggy Spellman**

"Live every day as if it's your last," my grandma used to say to me. I can still feel the soft skin of her hands around my neck. **Kevin McAleer**

My mother had a way of giving advice that made her sound like a cross between Lady Bracknell and the Delphic oracle. It wasn't the word of God. It was the word of God's superior. **Terry Prone**

Don't touch a woman's knee at the table. She has an instinctive knowledge of whether a man who does this is caressing her or only wiping his greasy fingers on her stocking. **George Moore**

When passing for Irish, you're advised to go easy on the deodorant and the shampoo. Dandruff is de rigueur. **Sean Kelly**

Never make a promise you can't break. **Gene Kerrigan**

If you need time to think, ask the questioner to ask the question again. Then pretend not to understand it. **W. B. O'Carolan**

To drink gin properly you have to be female, forty-five, and sitting on the stairs. **Dylan Moran**

Never take anyone's advice. **George Bernard Shaw**

# THE AFTERLIFE

I'm an agnostic. I believe there's something, but I don't believe it's the one where we all either go to hell or shake hands with God in heaven, sit down for porter and meet our Uncle Jack. *Ronnie Drew*

I'm an atheist, but I'd love to be proved wrong. I'd love to wake up somewhere floating or whatever in a place where nothing happens – a permanent sense of being slightly pissed with your friends. *Roddy Doyle*

Them that does all the talk about how nice it is in the next world, I don't see them in any great hurry to get there. *Brendan Behan*

I don't think much of this one! *James Joyce's response when asked what he thought of the next world*

My theory about Judgement Day is that life is hard enough. If the first words out of God's mouth when I meet him aren't "Well done, you came through that" I'm going to go for the fucker. *Tommy Tiernan*

The first thing I'd say to God if I met him in the next world would be, "I've been dying to see you." *Ben Dunne*

On the off-chance that there's no hereafter, won't the goodie-goodies get a terrible kick in the arse. *Charlie McCreevy*

I couldn't tell you where Dermot Morgan is now, but wherever it is, Dermot didn't believe in it. *Peter Howick on the late star who played Father Ted*

Is there an afterlife? There should be, because there's an afterbirth. *Kevin McAleer*

I once had this great idea that in the afterlife I could ask dead people so many questions. I'd ask Hitler's mother if she ever heard of contraception, Lee Harvey Oswald how much the CIA had promised him, the guy who invented football if he hates Man United as much as the rest of us, William Tell's son if he was to do it all again would he not use a large melon, and the people of Pompeii what the hell they were thinking of building there. **Tom Reilly**

# AGE

Remember when grooving out at a Bob Dylan gig was a way of showing you were hip? Now it's a way of showing your replaced hip. **Pat Fitzpatrick**

This little boy is crying. A man says to him, "What's your problem?" The boy says, "I don't know what age I am." The man says, "Are you interested in sex, drugs and money?" The boy says, "No." "Then you're three," the man tells him. **Noel V. Ginnity**

Alice Cooper identified the biggest problem with being an ageing rocker: It's hard to sing songs about hating your parents when you hit fifty. So he threw in the towel and turned to golf. **Pat Fitzpatrick**

Thirty-five is a very attractive age. London society is full of women of the very highest birth who have, of their own free choice, remained thirty-five for years. **Oscar Wilde**

I've hit that age now where I'm too old to be young and too young to be old. It's the age when you start getting invited to dinner parties. **Sean Hughes**

It's hard for boybands to realize that the vast majority of their audience are probably seven or eight years of age. **Paul Keogh**

I wish I could tell you my age but it keeps changing. **Greer Garson**

If you're going to lie about your age, do it in the opposite direction than most people. If you're thirty-nine, tell them you're fifty-five and they'll think you look brilliant. **Frank Hall**

Some people react to the ageing process by back-combing what is left of their hair, wearing suede denims and discovering that the young woman with whom one had a rapport at that dimly lit party last night is in fact one's daughter's schoolmate. *Hugh Leonard*

When I became middle-aged, for the first time in my life I felt I had something of value to say. The problem was, by now nobody wanted to hear it. *Mary McEvoy*

Children are growing up too fast nowadays. I met a ten-year-old girl at a party the other day. She said, "You do your hair and put on make-up but nobody knows the real you. Get me a Martini." *Dylan Moran*

If fifty is the new forty, does that mean that when you're twelve you're still looking for your soother? *Stephen Byrne*

# AIRLINES

I want to play football for Ireland. I qualify because I flew Aer Lingus once. *Jimmy Greaves*

I used to think cunnilingus was an Irish airline until I discovered Smirnoff. *Bernard Manning*

Ryanair trips to Luton are cheap, but make sure you check beforehand if you're allowed to bring a suitcase, and if the plane has actual wings. *Joe O'Connor*

I refuse to travel on Virgin Airlines. I don't like planes that don't go all the way. *Conal Gallen*

I don't know why they call it Virgin airlines. I've seen the air hostesses. They all have mattresses strapped to their backs. *Brendan O'Carroll*

People ask me how we can have such low fares in Ryanair. I tell them our pilots work for nothing. *Ryanair boss Michael O'Leary*

Ryanair gets us all eventually. I will be late. I will have no ID. I will forget the email confirmation. The check-in queue will be too long. I will not have shaved. They won't like my jumper. *Paul Kilduff*

Yes, Ryanair is cheap, but now they're talking about charging you to use the loo. It's only a matter of time before we'll be asked to bring our own parachutes. *Damien Tiernan*

Do we carry rich people on our flights? Yes. I flew on one this morning and I'm very rich. *Michael O'Leary*

It isn't terrorism that bothers me when I fly, it's Ryanair. They're talking about getting rid of seats and tickets now. Pilots will be the next thing to go. They'll just get these giant catapults and fire people in the general direction of their destination. *Ardal O'Hanlon*

The emblem of the New Zealand air force is a kiwi. Kiwis can't fly. *Neil Delamere*

# ALCOHOL

Paddy said he couldn't go to the party because he had a bad case of laryngitis. His friend said, "Come on, they'll drink anything there." *Jack Cruise*

The problem with Ireland and drink is that we don't have a problem with having a problem with it. If other people have a problem with it, that's their problem. *Deirdre O'Kane*

On a recent visit to my sister in Brighton I tried an ale called Old Speckled Hen. Warmed-up baby puke, says you. OK, but as warmed-up baby puke vomit goes, it was very tasty. *Pat Fitzpatrick*

# ALIMONY

Alimony is proof that you pay for past mistakes. And pay. And pay. And pay . . . *Peter O'Toole*

I was once so drunk I proposed marriage to a man. He should have accepted. I pay very good alimony. *Richard Harris*

# THE ALPHABET

Because I came from a poor area, my school had a small budget and was unable to teach the second half of the alphabet. So, to me, anything past the letter "m" is pretty much a mystery. *George Carlin*

# AMBITIONS

If I ruled Ireland for a day I'd make Roscommon into a handball alley. *Katherine Lynch*

Ambition is a dirty word in my family. You get told, "Stop showing off. Jaysus, I could act better meself with a fucking bag over me head." *Aidan Quinn*

My greatest ambition is to marry the Pope, have 2.7 kids, divorce him on grounds of mental cruelty, win custody of the two older kids and leave him to change the nappy on the remaining point seven. *David Norris*

Ideally I'd like to spend two evenings a week talking to Proust, and another conversing with the Holy Ghost. *Edna O'Brien*

I'd love to shoot the Pope because I know he'd forgive me. *Tommy Tiernan*

I'd like to be a pop singer, and if not, a cash register. *Caller to 5–7 Live radio show*

The lecturer was proud of his ancestry and didn't conceal it from his County Cork audience. "I was born an Englishman," he said, "I live as an Englishman and I hope to die an Englishman." "Yerra," came a voice from the back of the hall, "have ye no ambition in ye at all?" *Doug Anderson*

I'd like to get married and have four children one day. Then I'd do something else the next day. *Michael Redmond*

When I die I want to decompose in a barrel of porter and have it served in all the pubs in Dublin. *J. P. Donleavy*

My burning desire is to be a monk. I've had enough women in my life to know that lurking under that Helena Rubinstein exterior is a very vicious animal. *Richard Harris*

I have no ambition. I used to be ashamed of that, but then I came across the word in an old dictionary and looked up its etymology. It comes from the Latin *ambitio* which means "Walking around looking for votes". *John McGahern*

As a child I dreamed of jumping trains in the US dustbowl like Woody Guthrie. But then I got to my teens and it was, "I'll take the 7.15 to Portarlington, please." *Tommy Tiernan*

Yeats' occult mission, it seemed, was to celebrate the wedding of Madame Blavatsky and Finn MacCumhaill. *Frank O'Donnell on Yeats' simultaneous espousal of theosophy and Ireland's folk history*

When I die I think I'd like to get scattered partially from the power station in Aghada (high, stripy, near the sea) and partially into a tray of freshly baked raspberry scones (delicious, warm, buttery). *Maeve Higgins*

When I was twelve I decided I was going to be a writer. I told a friend and he said, "You'll have to go to university first." So I abandoned the idea for a couple of years and went back to thinking I might make a go of killing people. *Dermot Bolger*

My ultimate vocation in life is to be an irritant. *Elvis Costello*

# AMERICA AND AMERICANS

Americans are crazy people. They treat cigarette smokers like villainous carriers of the Black Death, and yet every home is a virtual arsenal, bulging with handguns. Babes from birth suck on the teated muzzles of .38 revolvers and are trained to perforate anyone who might call to the wrong address after nightfall. *Hugh Leonard*

The 100 per cent American is 99 per cent idiot. *George Bernard Shaw*

George Bush was the man who put the "er" back into America. *Joe O'Connor*

Americans believe in life, liberty and the pursuit of par. *David Robbins*

An American was crossing Murphy's field and said to him, "Is the bull safe?" Murphy replied, "He's a lot safer than you are." *Hal Roach*

They say anyone in the US can become President. Maybe that's the problem. *Brian Moore*

There are two kinds of people in America: fat fuckers and fit fuckers. *Tommy Tiernan*

Americans will go on adoring me until I say something nice about them. *George Bernard Shaw*

I sometimes think people flock to America because nobody dies there. Everyone passes on, passes away, goes to their eternal rest, breathes their last or shuffles off the mortal coil. But die? Not on your Nellie. *Malachy McCourt*

Ireland has everything in common with America today – except language. *Oscar Wilde*

Americans are so thick they couldn't tip shite off a welling-ton boot if the instructions weren't on the heel. *Patrick Kielty*

Americans are like a broken bicycle saddle. They give you a pain in the arse. **Brendan Behan**

America is air-conditioned land-cruisers drenched in muzak, with Coca-Cola available from a tap in the dashboard. **Patrick Campbell**

Only 20 per cent of Americans possess passports so we must be grateful for small mercies. **Paul Kilduff**

America is a country that has leapt from barbarism to decadence without touching civilization. **John O'Hara**

America is a place where most people believe professional wrestling is real but 9/11 was faked. **Michael Cullen**

Visiting America was like falling asleep in your local cinema while watching a film and waking up to find that you were actually in it. **Jimmy Higgins**

# THE ANGLO-IRISH

An Anglo-Irishman only works at riding horses, drinking whiskey and reading double-meaning jokes at Trinity College. **Brendan Behan**

In Ireland we have two types of Irish. We have "Irish" and we have "Anglo-Irish". You can always tell the Anglo-Irish because they wear tweeds and carry shotguns and they live in London. **Dave Allen**

An Anglo-Irishman is a Protestant on a horse. **Brendan Behan**

Ireland is a product of the Anglo-Saxon imagination. **Brendan Behan**

# ANIMALS

The black dog was the only intelligent member of the family. He was poisoned, and no one will convince me it wasn't suicide. *Hugh Leonard*

I never really liked Cheetah the chimp in the Tarzan films. He didn't like me either, or any girls. He adored Johnny Weissmuller but was terribly jealous of me. *Maureen O'Sullivan*

A tenant complained to a landlord about the profusion of mice in his flat. "There isn't a single mouse in that flat," the landlord protested. "I know," said the tenant, "they're all married with large families." *Jimmy O'Dea*

Two dinosaurs were dating one another for two hundred years, after which they began holding hands. After another two hundred years, the male dinosaur asked the female if he could sleep with her. "I'd love to," she replied, "but I'm having my decade." *Foggy Spellman*

Why do we call them guinea pigs when they're not pigs and they don't come from Guinea? *Josef Locke*

If one person calls you a donkey, ignore him. If two people do it, buy a saddle. *Austin O'Malley*

The safari park had a notice that said, "Elephants: Please Stay In Your Car". *Spike Milligan*

If you crossed a chicken with a zebra, would you get a four-legged chicken with its own barcode? *Archie Hughes*

All the animals in the world went into Noah's Ark in pairs but the worms went in apples. *James McKeon*

The English country gentleman galloping after a fox: the unspeakable in pursuit of the uneatable. *Oscar Wilde*

I never thought much of the courage of a lion-tamer. In the cage he is at least safe from people. *George Bernard Shaw*

Two lions were walking through O'Connell Street at a weekend. One turned to the other and said, "Quiet today, isn't it?" *Val Doonican*

When I was a kid, the idea of having a pet really appealed to me but we never had one. My parents said the road we lived on was too busy and it might get run over. This was a bit rich given that we played football on it all summer long and cars were so rare that when one went by you wanted to photograph it. *Dave Fanning*

When a lion escapes from a circus in Africa, how do they know when they've caught the right one? *George Carlin*

# ANONYMITY

There was once an Irishman who sent a cheque to his aunt as a birthday gift but he didn't sign it as he didn't want her to know who sent it. *Peter Hornby*

Anyone who would stoop so low as to write an anonymous letter should at least sign his name to it. *Sir Boyle Roche*

# ANTI-CLIMAXES

All he said to me was "Do you like truffles?" "Yes," I replied, "I am very fond of truffles." *James Joyce on a meeting with Marcel Proust*

I'm a terrible lover. The best I can give a woman is an anti-climax. *Des Sheehy*

What if we simply altogether stopped having erections? Enough sperm floating about the place. *Samuel Beckett*

Once after sex I lit the cigarette and said, "You were great," and she shouted, "You can put it in now, Sean." *Sean Hughes*

Life is a long rehearsal for a play that's never produced. **Micheál MacLiammóir**

Sky TV has devoted such resources to the build-up, it seems a shame to spoil it all with the actual competition, which is bound to be an anti-climax. **Declan Lynch on the 2006 Ryder Cup**

They say he has sex nearly every night of the week. Nearly on Monday, nearly on Tuesday, nearly on Wednesday ... **Hal Roach**

The highlight of our stay in Cayenne, French Guinea, was the time we saw a dog crossing the street. We still talk about it. **Hector O'hEochagáin**

# APATHY

Neil Jordan is the master of the mutter, the Fellini of pained indifference. Getting him to be open is rather like trying to persuade Greta Garbo to go ice-skating in the nude with you in broad daylight. **Barry Egan**

I don't give a shite if anyone likes me or not. **Ryanair boss Michael O'Leary**

A foreign correspondent once asked why political candidates in Ireland "stood" for office while in the United States and Britain they "ran" for it. The answer of course is that you can't run for anything with your head in the sand. **Dick Walsh**

If I've ever offended anyone in any of my acts I'd like to say from the bottom of my heart ... I couldn't give a fuck. **Brendan O'Carroll**

Pierce Brosnan is so laid-back you almost want to check him for a pulse. **Ciara Dwyer**

What's the difference between ignorance and apathy? I don't know and I don't care. **Dominic Behan**

I once became a sleeping partner in a wine business. Someone unkindly said I was sometimes more of a comatose one. **George Best**

The vodka malaise is the one that imbues the sufferer with such apathy that if the world were coming to an end it would merely be welcomed. **Tom Galvin**

So little time, so little to do. **Samuel Beckett**

# APHRODISIACS

I find financial insecurity a great aphrodisiac. **Marian Keyes**

The Irish G-spot is guilt. **Cliodhna O'Flynn**

"Well, luv, did ye give him the ten oysters before going to bed to get him goin' like I told ye?"
　"Indeed I did, luv, but I think only five of them worked."
**Paul Ryan**

# APOLOGIES

I was asked to speak at a screening of The Commitments in Amherst once and only one guy turned up at the lecture. He apologized on behalf of the entire population of America. **Roddy Doyle**

I had sex for five hours once, but four and a half was apologizing. **Conan O'Brien**

Alex Higgins was very good at apologizing, but then he had a lot of practice. **Dennis Taylor**

The "could have been worse" apology is where you grovel for murdering my budgie but draw my attention to the fact that my goldfish are still circling their bowl whereas you could have had them for an appetizer. **Terry Prone**

# APPEARANCE

A man carved from a turnip looking out from astonished eyes. **W. B. Yeats on George Moore**

W. B. Yeats looked like an umbrella left behind at a picnic. **George Moore in retaliation**

Kitty Brucknell looks just like Charlize Theron...from *Monster*. **Katherine Lynch**

Why don't you start neglecting your appearance? Then maybe it'll go away. **Cecil Sheridan**

Have you ever seen a picture of a murderer and thought: He's actually really good-looking? **Sharon Horgan**

Jo O'Meara looks uncannily like the bastard child of Pat Butcher and Vinnie Jones. **Ian O'Doherty**

Possibly as a result of my rugby-ball-shaped head, I have been informed that I am not unlike one of Tony Soprano's henchmen. **Dara O'Briain**

Now that Kiefer Sutherland has shed the two tons of playdough that used to be his face, he's beginning to look eerily like his father. **John Boland**

Liza Minnelli's last husband was a boiled egg in sunglasses. **Graham Norton on David Gest**

Doctor: "I don't like the look of your husband."
Woman: "Neither do I, doctor, but he's kind to the children."
**Laura Stack**

All my mother's family have that "taxi driver from Tel Aviv" look. **Bono**

I saw Lee Majors the other day. He looked a million dollars — he's really let himself go. **Eddie Bannon**

I once saw an Argentinian lapdancer whose unrestrained bosom hopped around like the balls in a Lottery machine. She had what a friend of mine calls a BOBFOC — Body Off Baywatch, Face Off Crimewatch. *Philip Nolan*

John Daly has one of the worst haircuts I've ever seen. He looks like he has a divot over each ear. *David Feherty*

It is only shallow people who do not judge by appearances. *Oscar Wilde*

When I played Rashers Tierney in *Strumpet City* I looked like a slightly depressed hyena. *David Kelly*

The Virgin Prunes looked like a bunch of pre-Raphaelite serial killers. *Ferdia MacAnna*

Des Lynam is a mythical creature, half man and half moustache. *Martin Kelner*

Amy Winehouse looked like a poster for neglected horses. *Michael Cullen*

Madeleine Stowe's freakishly huge lips are pumped so full of collagen, they now resemble a Salvador Dalí sofa. *Donald Clarke*

I'm not saying she's ugly, but one night she walked into a bar and seven men took the pledge. *Hal Roach*

One look at Wayne Rooney tells you he's a product of the Irish vegetable gene pool, with a potato for a face, a turnip in his skull and a vermilion carrot in his trousers. One look at Peter Crouch tells you he's a true son of England, with a sheep skull where his face should be, a mangel-wurzel where most people keep their frontal lobe, and a purple cucumber down below. *Kevin Myers*

# APPLES

There was a time when an apple a day kept the doctor away. Now it's malpractice insurance. *Malachy Smyth*

With a bagful of apples you can have a great time with the doctor's wife. *Frank Carson*

It wasn't the apple on the tree but the pair on the ground, I believe, that caused the trouble in the Garden of Eden. *M. D. O'Connor*

# ARCHITECTURE

The Colosseum is a wreck. They should have employed Irish builders. *Tony Cascarino*

The city manager and his assistants regard me as a prick in the fat arse of municipal pretension. *Environment campaigner Frank McDonald*

Rome wasn't built in a day, but then I wasn't on that job. *Brian Behan*

All modern architects should be pulled down and redeveloped as car parks. *Spike Milligan*

The most famous building in the heart of Dublin is the Abbey Theatre, once the city morgue and now entirely restored to its original purpose. *Frank O'Connor*

I have a theory about architecture in Los Angeles. I think all the houses came to a costume party and they all came as different countries. *Michael O'Donoghue*

Galway is a victim of some of the worst architectural planning since the bombing of Dresden. *Tommy Tiernan*

Dublin's inner-city architecture is like a lady in the morning without her make-up on. *Jim Tunney*

Dublin's Temple Bar was a shithole in the mid-nineties and since then, year on year, it's become even shitholier. *Michael O'Doherty*

# ARGUMENTS

A woman has the last word in every argument. Anything a man says after that is the beginning of a new argument. *Paul O'Farrell*

Never argue with a woman when she's tense — or relaxed. *Frank Kelly*

They say never go to bed mad. With this in mind, my wife and I once stayed up for six months. *Brendan Grace*

The best way to win an argument with a woman is to say the three little words every woman always wants to hear: "You are right". *John D. Sheridan*

There's no arguing with Johnson for when his pistol misses fire he knocks you down with the butt end of it. *Oliver Goldsmith on Samuel Johnson*

My last relationship was one big argument. The only reason I stayed in it was to win the argument. *Ed Byrne*

# ARMS

Armpits lead lives of quiet perspiration. *Patrick Murray*

I wouldn't worry too much about that weakness in your arm. It will do you no harm. My brother Liam Shaun had it for years, the Lord have mercy on him. *Tony Butler*

I was both surprised and delighted to take the armband for both legs. *Irish soccer international Gary O'Neill*

# THE ARMY

The Irish army were out on reconnaissance, and the sergeant and corporal fell into conversation about a new recruit.

"I wonder what O'Hara did before he enlisted," said the sergeant.

"Why?" asked the corporal.

"Well," the sergeant explained, "every time he fires a shot, he takes out a hankie and wipes his fingerprints off the rifle." *Frank Hall*

At an army medical examination the doctor said to me, "Get your clothes off." I said, "Shouldn't you take me out to dinner first?" *Spike Milligan*

The Irish militia are useless in times of war and dangerous in times of peace. *The Duke of Wellington*

Women want men in uniforms. You can say what you like about the Nazis but those guys knew how to turn heads. *Dylan Moran*

A sentimental Irishman once enlisted in the 75th Regiment to be near his brother, who was in the 76th. *Joan Larson Kelly*

I have half a mind to join the British army. They tell me that's all I'll need. *John Linehan*

The rain in Ireland actually saves many lives. It makes all the ammunition wet. *Dave Allen*

# ART AND ARTISTS

The perfect aesthete logically feels that the artist is strictly a Turkish bath attendant. *Flann O'Brien*

Monet began by imitating Manet, and Manet ended by imitating Monet. *George Moore*

Critics talk about significance; artists about turpentine. **Sean Keating**

The best way to tell if a modern painting is completed is to touch it. If the paint is dry, it's finished. **Graham Knuttel**

Only in Ireland would it be seen as a mark of civilization that artists don't have to pay tax. **Carlos Gebler**

William Orpen never got under the surface till he got under the sod. **Oliver St John Gogarty**

It goes without saying that the true artist must have time to chew the cud of his thoughts. To this end he should drink only sufficient alcohol to merit the prefix "tortured". **Ian MacPherson**

Every artist is an unhappy lover. **Iris Murdoch**

I'm a bad Catholic. It's the religion of all great artists. **Brendan Behan**

I used to think Hertz Van Rental was a Dutch artist. **Graffiti spotted on the toilet door of the National Art Gallery**

Don't ask me about art. I make pictures to pay the rent. **John Ford**

It doesn't matter how badly you paint as long as you don't paint badly like other people. **George Moore**

I have several original Mona Lisas in my house, all painted by that great artist, Mr Kodak. **Spike Milligan**

An Irish intellectual has been defined as one who goes to an art gallery when it isn't raining. **Peter Hornby**

An Irish Arts Centre used to mean a whitewashed basement where you might be able to buy freshly brewed coffee and some woman might know where you could go to get an abortion. **Graham Norton**

The true artist will let his wife starve, his children go barefoot and his mother drudge for his living at seventy sooner than work at anything but his art. **George Bernard Shaw**

Back in the mid-sixties music wasn't considered a career opportunity, but these days it wouldn't be strange to see an ad in the Job Centre announcing "Pop Star Wanted". I realize I'm being snobbish, but you don't get any old git knocking up a painting and having it hung in the Tate. *Boy George*

The true artist is a mad man who tries to appear sane: the phoney one is a sane man trying to appear mad. *Bryan MacMahon*

When having my portrait painted I don't want justice, I want mercy. *Billy Hughes*

The wonderful thing about art is that it's completely useless. *John Banville*

After art, let me assure you, there is nothing. *Iris Murdoch*

# ATHEISTS

When I told the people of Northern Ireland I was an atheist I was asked if I was a Catholic or a Protestant one. *Quentin Crisp*

I'm a lapsed atheist. *John Waters*

Irish atheists have started a Dial-a-Prayer service. When they phone, nobody answers. *Hal Roach*

If God existed he'd probably be an atheist. *Peter DeRosa*

I hope God doesn't find out I'm an atheist. *Rory McGrath*

I would no more believe in God than I would in the existence of James Stewart's six-foot-tall phantom rabbit friend in the 1950 film *Harvey*. Decent movie, by the way. *Dave Fanning*

You don't have to be Albert Einstein to figure out why Albert Einstein rejected the idea of a personal God. *Trevor White*

An Irish atheist is a man who wishes to God he could believe in God. *J. P. Mahaffy*

Atheism is an affectation of the college classes. *Eoghan Harris*

An agnostic is just an atheist without balls. *Stephen Colbert*

No man is an atheist on the approach to Heathrow. *Hugh Leonard*

# ATHLETICS

Running is good. It comes in handy when you are about to miss the bus, or when the girlfriend's husband comes home unexpectedly. *Richard O'Connor*

What's wrong with drugs in sport? If someone wants to run the 100 in half a second, let him. It's only a programme on the telly. What I want to see is him trying to slow down as he gets to the bendy bit. *Tommy Tiernan*

The best way for athletes to disguise the fact that they're on anabolic steroids is to run slower. *George Carlin*

Sonia O'Sullivan probably wouldn't have to run so fast if she left the house earlier in the morning. *Jimmy Magee on the Cork athlete*

I take athletics very seriously indeed as they seem to produce more bad feeling, bad manners and international hatred than any other popular movement. *George Bernard Shaw*

Joggers are basically neurotic, bony, smug types who could bore the paint off a DC-10. It's a scientifically proven fact that having to sit through a three-minute conversation between two of them will cause your IQ to drop thirteen points. *Rick Reilly*

In my younger days it was not considered respectable to be an athlete. An athlete was a man that was not strong enough to work. *Finley Peter Dunne*

I run like a sloth in slow motion. *Mary McEvoy*

# ATTRACTION

Most men are only attracted to women whose IQ is twice their age, which explains why women over forty-five have trouble attracting one. **Pat Fitzpatrick**

I'm attracted to thin, good-looking men who have one common denominator: they must be lurking bastards. **Edna O'Brien**

Edward Martyn started the Pro-Cathedral choir not because he liked choirs but because he liked choirboys. **George Moore**

W. H. Auden didn't love God; he just fancied him. **Micheál MacLiammóir**

When I went to dances and sat in the corner petrified, I used to think that maybe I could turn my petrification into some kind of sexual allure. I was hoping some girl would say, "God, who's that incredibly interesting guy over there in the corner who doesn't say anything? Maybe he's somebody I could get off with." But they never said that. They just said, "Jaysus, who's that bore over there in the corner? Make sure you don't get caught." **Gabriel Byrne**

If you still haven't found what you're looking for, Bono, try looking behind the drumkit. **Boy George on his fascination with Larry Mullen**

# AUSTRALIA

There used to be a joke about Aussie Rules commentators. When things got heavy in a match, one would say to the other, "OK, you call the game and I'll call the fight." **Gerry O'Carroll**

We used to send our convicts to Australia. Now we send Ronan Keating and Bryan McFadden. **Louis Walsh**

I've never understood the point of Australia. It's only three-quarters of a mile from the surface of the sun. All you can do there is either fry yourself or go swimming. *Dylan Moran*

Do Australians call the rest of the world "Up Over"? *Dusty Young*

# AUTOGRAPHS

I changed my name from Brian to Bryan so I wouldn't have to lift the pen off the page when I was signing autographs. *Bryan McFadden, formerly of Westlife*

Dear Sir, I never send autographs. Yours sincerely, Daniel O'Connell. *O'Connell giving an unexpected boon to an aspirant autograph-seeker*

# AUTOPSIES

He looked better at the autopsy than he did when he was alive. *Brinsley MacNamara*

The Michael Jackson autopsy found four possible causes of death: sunshine, moonlight, good times and boogie. *Sharon Mannion*

# AVERSIONS

My pet hate is people who ask me what my pet hate is. *Mike Murphy*

I don't like the Sign of Peace handshake at Mass. How do you know where the hand you're shaking has been? It might have been up somebody's nose. They might have been scratching their backside with it. *David Norris*

What do I think of agents? Dogs. Worms. Vermin. *Joe Kinnear*

I could instance a load of fuckers whose throats I'd cut and push over a cliff. *Charlie Haughey in an infamous interview in 1984*

People like to hate him in instalments so it'll last longer. *Denis Franks on an unpopular acquaintance*

# AWARDS

How is it they always overlook "Anon" when they're giving out doctorates and literary awards? *John B. Keane*

Samuel Beckett got the Nobel Prize for putting a woman in a bin for two hours on a stage. *Brian Behan*

I was an English actor when I was winning awards. I was an Irish pugilist when I was getting drunk on the street. *Richard Harris*

That performance would have won him Olympic Gold in the championship four years ago, which he won anyway. *Des Lynam*

Awards are like haemorrhoids. Sooner or later every arsehole gets one. *Frank McCourt*

# BABIES

Mr O'Kelly rang the hospital to find out if his wife had the baby yet.

"Is this her first child?" the nurse enquired.

"Arrah not at all," said O'Kelly, "this is her husband." *Joe Linnane*

The doctor delivered the child safely and said to Mrs Rafferty, "Bejapers, the little whippersnapper only weighs a meagre nineteen ounces." The husband butted in, "Well what would you be expecting, Dr Douglas, and me and Maureen only wed five weeks." *Peter Cagney*

"Liam, your uncle is on the phone and he wants to know is the new child a boy or a girl."

"Well now, will you ask the poor bothered man what else it could have been." *Doug Anderson*

# BACHELORS

I'm single and it's my choice. My second choice. *Graham Norton*

Down with marriage — be a bachelor like your father was! *Spike Milligan*

The great thing about being single is that you can do what you want when you want. The bad thing is that you've got nothing to do and no one to do it with. *James O'Loughlin*

The reason I never married is because I couldn't find a woman who understood the apostrophe. You can never trust a woman who misuses the apostrophe. *Con Houlihan*

Better to have loved and lost than to have married her, had a shitload of children and been forced to attend all those PT meetings. *Joseph Glynn*

Will your wild playboy mates give you a second thought as they walk down the aisle and you're left with nothing but a second-hand Porsche and a couple of mismatched ear-rings on the back seat? *Graham Norton*

The Church is just a lot of fat Irish bachelors. *Tommy Tiernan*

# BANKS

If money doesn't grow on trees, why do banks have branches? *Jacinta O'Brien*

The Celtic Tiger was fabulous in Ireland. We all got in touch with our inner banker. *Eddie Hobbs*

My bank says it's built on trust but when you walk in the pens are glued to the desks. *Luke Kelly*

# BANS

I'm the leader of the banned. *Brendan Behan*

Ireland still goes on her Bonnie Prince Charlie way in a pietistic sense, banning book and banning play. John Charles of Drumcondra gives a faint shake of the head and Dublin is in a panic of reparation. *Sean O'Casey on Dublin's former archbishop, John Charles McQuaid*

Archbishop McQuaid banned tampons because he thought they might get women excited. *Donal O'Dea*

The smoking ban in pubs has taken away one of the greatest pleasures known to man – chasing a cigarette butt down a trough for ninety seconds while urinating. If Nintendo brought this out as a game they'd make a fortune. *Colin Murphy*

I think the smoking ban in pubs is wrong. I'm not a smoker myself but I've always enjoyed coughing. *Ardal O'Hanlon*

Oliver Cromwell's successors in Ireland banned all public practice of Catholicism and hunted down priests and executed them, which saved the locals from having to listen to hour-long sermons. *Donal O'Dea*

The best case for the banning of all poetry is the fact that it is bad. Nobody is going to manufacture a thousand tons of jam in the expectation that five tons of it may be eatable. **Flann O'Brien**

# BAPTISM

Ian Paisley was christened with a flamethrower. It was a baptism of fire. **Michael Cullen**

If baptism removes the stain of sin from all our souls, why baptize babies? Would it not be more logical to wait until people are dying? **Sheamus Smith**

# BRIGITTE BARDOT

When I'm trying to play serious love scenes with her, she's positioning her bottom for the best angle shot. **Stephen Boyd on co-starring with the famous sex symbol**

Brigitte Bardot made St Tropez famous in the film *Et Dieu Créa La Femme*, which is French for "Brigitte Bardot Capering Around with No Clothes On". **Joe O'Connor**

# BEAUTY

Did you hear about the beauty contest in Kerry? Nobody won. **Laura Stack**

You know you've had too much to drink when the ugly barmaid suddenly has two faces, and both of them are beautiful. **Dave Allen**

No woman can be a beauty without a fortune. *Robert Lynd*

Beauty is all very well at first sight, but who ever looks at it when it's been in the house three days? *George Bernard Shaw*

Two business ladies require sleeping partner for beauty salon. *Ad in* **Tipperary Star**

It's not possible for a family to be as uniformly beautiful as the Corrs. I often feel there must be a Pat Corr hidden away somewhere. A guy with sausage-like fingers who repeatedly asks to be allowed to play the mandolin and keeps getting knocked on the head and told "No!" *Jack Dee*

I never had illusions about being a beauty. I was the only seventeen-year-old character actress in the movies. *Angela Lansbury*

Keep Ireland beautiful. Shoot your mother-in-law. *Graffiti*

# BELFAST

Belfast is a hard and cruel town inhabited by people who, due to bad planning on the part of whatever passes for a Creator, happen to live next door to each other. *Gerry Anderson*

I heard of a raffle once where the first prize was a week in Belfast and the second prize was two weeks in Belfast. *James Plunkett*

They were going to get me to turn the lights on in Belfast last Christmas but they changed their minds at the last minute because when the last person called Paddy was asked to press a button in Belfast, the whole of Bedford Street went up. *Patrick Kielty*

One thing to be said in favour of Belfast: you can get out of it quickly. *Sean O'Faolain*

Buy now while shops last. *Graffiti on Belfast wall*

For God's sake bring me a large Scotch. What a bloody awful country! *Conservative Home Secretary Reginald Maudling after his first visit to Belfast in 1972*

The best way to get your rubbish collected in Belfast is to giftwrap it and put it on the back seat of your car. *Dusty Young*

If you tell people you're from Belfast they go "IRA! George Best!" That's all we're known for: fightin' and fuckin'. *Patrick Kielty*

The fastest game in the world is "Pass the Parcel" in a Belfast pub. *Brian Keenan*

A policeman found a dead horse in Chicester Street. "How do you spell Chicester?" he asked some of the people around him, but no one knew. "All right then," he said, "give me a wee hand to pull the animal over to Mary Street." *Doug Anderson*

# BELLYBUTTONS

The other day in a shop I saw that humanity had invented an electric bellybutton cleaner and I thought, "I hope aliens never land here because I'd be so embarrassed." *Sinead Murphy*

People say your bellybutton has no function but it's an ideal place to put the salt if you're having a Big Mac in the scratcher. *Shay O'Donoghue*

Blues music is about having nothing and then losing it. It's like, "I don't even have a guitar. I'm strumming my bellybutton." *Dylan Moran*

Paddy thought his navel was just a place to keep the salt when he was eating hardboiled eggs in bed. *Foggy Spellman*

Would a born-again Christian have two bellybuttons? *Eamon Lawlor*

# BERTIEISMS

*Gerry Adams is the leader of Sinn Fe´in, Ireland's Nationalist Party. (Literally this means "Ourselves Alone", though with the meltdown of the economy cartoonist Martyn Turner said "Ourselves a Loan" would probably be more applicable.) Adams coined the term "Bertieisms" to account for the adventures of* **Bertie Ahern** *(Ireland's former Taoiseach/Prime Minister) with the English language.*

I never condemn wrongdoing in any area. (He meant *"condone".*)

There are kebabs out there plotting against us. (He meant *"cabals".*)

Lehmans was a world investment bank. They had testicles everywhere. (He meant *"tentacles".*)

There have been disputes between fractions. (He meant *"factions".*)

The reason inflation is on the rise is because the boom times are getting even boomier.

At present I have my hand in a whole lot of dykes.

It is not correct. If I said so I wasn't correct. I can't recall if I did say it, but I did not say [it], or if I did say it I didn't mean to say it.

Charlie Haughey wanted to transform Temple Bar into Ireland's West Bank. (He meant "Left Bank".)

Shelving the pay increase would just be playing smoke and daggers with the public.

# THE BIBLE

The Bible says any man who sleeps with another man should be stoned. Most men would agree it definitely helps. *Michael Cullen*

The first reference to elasticity in the Bible is when Moses tied his ass to a tree and walked ten yards. *Sil Fox*

I have an aspiration that some day the Bible will be in the mythology section at the back of second-hand bookshops. *Tom Reilly*

The earliest example of swearing in the Bible was when Job cursed the day he was born. *Niall Toibin*

The reason Jesus knew the Bible so well was because his father wrote it. *Des MacHale*

The New Testament isn't new any more. It's thousands of years old. It's time to start calling it the Less Old Testament. *George Carlin*

I'm Catholic but we don't read the Bible. We pay a priest to do that for us. Man's got all week off and no wife, he can give us a forty-five-minute book report once a week. "Just weed through the crap and get to the plot, padre." *Kathleen Madigan*

I was so bored in the hotel the other night I sent down for another Bible. *Dusty Young*

I like the Ten Commandments but I have a problem with the Ninth. It should be "Thou shalt not covet thy neighbour's ox, except in Scrabble". *David O'Doherty*

David was the first blues singer. *Bono*

# BIRDS

The only living beasts on the farms of Ireland are the birds that fly over them. *Sir Boyle Roche*

A bird in the Strand is worth two in Shepherd's Bush. *Spike Milligan*

I went to a pet shop for a budgie. The owner said, "You're in luck. I've got a new lot in at the moment and they're going cheap." I said, "What do you expect them to do — bark?" I asked him how much they were and he said, "Two quid apiece." I said, "How much is a whole one?" *Jimmy Cricket*

The symbol of peace — the pigeon! *Jimmy Magee at the opening ceremony of the 1982 World Cup*

A robin that isn't a robin redbreast looks like a bank messenger in mufti. *Jack B. Yeats*

Of all the birds in the air, I hate a rat the most. *Sir Boyle Roche*

It was my uncle who taught me about the birds and the bees. He sat me down one day and said, "Remember this, George. The birds fuck the bees." *George Carlin*

# BIRTH

I've always been a rather jaded sort of individual. I came out of the womb saying, "Is that it?" *Deirdre O'Kane*

I wouldn't consider having a child after thirty. You'd be out the door with nappies. Twenty-nine of the little buggers is enough. *Katherine Lynch*

I was born with a bottle of stout in my mouth. *Eamonn Keane*

I was born at the back door of a hospital. The ambulance driver stopped when he saw the sign: Deliveries at Rear. *Frank Hall*

Because of lack of space, a number of births have been held over until next week. *Notice in the* Galway Telegraph

I came upstairs in the world for I was born in a cellar. *William Congreve*

Mrs Sarah Donnelly, a Dublin housewife who has given birth to her twelfth child, says she's had her feet in the stirrups more times than John Wayne. *Peter Cagney*

Some children are harder to bear after birth than before. *Eileen Reid*

When I was born my father gave me a funny look. As you can see, I still have it. *Maureen Potter*

"Were ye born in Dublin, son?"
  "Yeah."
  "What part?"
  "All of me."
*Paul Ryan*

The midwife said the agony of having a child could last a long time. I didn't realize she meant eighteen years. *Sinead Murphy*

There's nothing worse than a man with a cold. He thinks he's dying. I always wonder how they'd survive childbirth. *Miriam O'Callaghan*

In accordance with your request I've given birth to twins in the enclosed envelope. *Letter from Kerry mother to Social Welfare*

He was born an Englishman and remained so for years. *Brendan Behan*

To be born in a handbag displays a contempt for the ordinary decencies of family life that reminds one of the worst excesses of the French Revolution. *Oscar Wilde, from* **The Importance of Being Earnest**

I was born Catholic which came as a bit of a shock to my parents, who are both Jewish. *Michael Redmond*

# BISHOPS

Wear a Condom — Just in Casey. *Message emblazoned on T-shirts in 1992 after Bishop Eamon Casey admitted fathering a son by his lover Annie Murphy*

Eamon Casey has just invented a new game of chess. The rules are simple enough really. Bishop jumps everything! *Shay Healy*

Catholics believe you can't have sex unless you're (a) married or (b) a bishop. *Patrick Kielty*

Eamon Casey took the commandment "Love Thy Neighbour" a bit too literally. *Brian Behan*

In the old days, bishops gave us a belt of the crozier. Now they just tickle our funnybones. *Ian O'Doherty*

I'm an important Catholic. In case of accident, call a bishop. *Sean Kilroy*

Traditional wisdom has it that the poor are poor because God ordained it so, and that the special genius of women is best demonstrated in the serving of triangular salad sandwiches to visiting bishops. *Declan Lynch*

The Pope is said to have the key of heaven but it seems to me that every Irish bishop has a master key. *Sean O'Casey*

# BLOOD

When I had my liver transplant I got forty pints in ten hours. That beats my previous record by twenty minutes! *George Best*

Blood may be thicker than water but it is also a great deal nastier. *Edith Somerville*

I've always had the theatre in my veins. Blood might have been better. *Lennox Robinson*

The drunk staggered home with a small bottle of whiskey in his back pocket. Slipping on the doorstep as he tried to turn the key, he let out an expletive as he felt liquid trickling down his leg. But then came the relief. "Thanks be to Jaysus," he exclaimed. "It's only blood." *Mick Lally*

Murphy drank so much, when he donated a pint of blood last week, there was a slice of lemon in it. *Joe Cuddy*

Then there was the Irishman who was so broke he got a visit from the blood bank because his blood had bounced. *Peter Hornby*

# THE BODY

You've a grand head on your shoulders. It's a pity it isn't on your neck. *Sorcha O'Farrell*

My girlfriend has an hour-glass figure — twenty-four hours! *Frankie Blowers*

If I had the use of my body I would throw it out the window. *Samuel Beckett*

I have the body of an eighteen-year-old. I keep it in the fridge. *Spike Milligan*

A small sunburnt girl with peeling skin was overheard saying, "I'm only six years old and I'm wearing out already." *Mary Feehan*

"Chrissie, come here a minute and look at the figure on this wan."

   "Merciful hour! The last time I saw a figure like that the owner was being milked."
*Paul Ryan*

I'm a pacifist by physique. *Michael Mee*

Madonna is a gay man trapped in a woman's body. *Boy George*

My girlfriend's vital statistics are 40-34-28 but unfortunately not in that order. *Sean Kilroy*

Sometimes I feel that if I look hard enough, I'll find a "Best Before" date implanted in my nether region. My chin has already spawned a twin, those little love handles have become lifebelts, and there are already signs of snow on the roof. *Dan Buckley*

I remember the first time I made love because I was very green in that area — due to a chemistry experiment in school that went wrong. *Sean Hughes*

If I could change any part of my body I'd lengthen my spine so I could give myself a blowjob. *Brendan O'Carroll*

# BOMBS AND BOMBERS

Then there was the terrorist who lit a bomb but was too slow to let it go. He was buried with full honours . . . in Belfast and Dublin. *Henry Spalding*

A man said to me, "What's the name of that place that's always being bombed?" I said, "I don't know. It's not there any more." *Owen O'Neill*

Georgie Boy is Dirty Harry without the gift of language. At the moment he's playing Spin-the-Bottle with a world map, chanting, "Pick a country – any country". *Roisin Gorman on George Bush after his invasion of Iraq in 2004*

The Americans have a long way to go before they become as eco-friendly as al-Qaeda. The US army routinely flies troops with bombs halfway round the world while al-Qaeda source their fighters locally and walk bombs to their targets. Plus, I hate to say it, suicide bombers are a lot more bio-degradable. If you think about it, al-Qaeda is the ultimate example of "Think Globally, Act Locally". *Abie Philbin Bowman*

The great thing about the H-bomb is that it can look down on all the other little bombs. *Brendan Behan*

Being reasonable with the British means letting them know you're willing to throw an occasional bomb into one of their lorries. *Eamon de Valera*

Didn't it take Gregory Peck, one of our own, to blow the shite out of those Germans in *The Guns of Navarone*? *Joe O'Toole*

An IRA man went to heaven but when he got to the Pearly Gates St Peter told him he couldn't let him in because of his past history of bombing. "You don't understand," the IRA man said, "I don't want to go in; I'm giving you all ten minutes to get *out*." *Dermot Whelan*

The phone rang in a Ballymena pub and the owner picked it up. "This is the Provos," said a voice at the other end. "Your place is about to be bombed. You've got five minutes to get out." The owner put down the phone and went to the bar. "Last orders, everyone," he said. *Geoff Hill*

I always carry gelignite. Dynamite isn't safe. *Brendan Behan*

Londoners are brilliant at re-routing, as was apparent after the 7/7 terrorist attacks on the underground. The average response to the news that there was a bomb on the Piccadilly line was "Well I can always get the Victoria line." *Dara O'Briain*

Iraq is just the IRA with a "Q" on the end. Their specialty is suicide bombers. I remember the good old days when blowing yourself up was a mistake. *Patrick Kielty*

# BONO

The only difference between God and Bono is that God doesn't wander down Grafton Street thinking he's Bono. *Louis Walsh*

I don't write songs in English. I write them in Bongelese. *Bono*

Irish Musical Anagrams: Paul Hewson — "Halo Sewn Up". *Damien Corless*

Bono to me seems like he's looking for his inner arsehole. *David Feherty*

# BOOKS

The most important thing a writer should have is a partner with a steady income. *Clare Boylan*

I like something Rilke said: "There are certain books that must long for the death of their author so that they can assume their own lives." *John McGahern*

I don't feature sex in my books because I've never been to an orgy and I wouldn't know where the arms and legs should be. **Maeve Binchy**

There's only one thing rarer than a Ulick O'Connor first edition and that's a Ulick O'Connor second edition. **Hugh Leonard**

My books are selling like wildfire. Everyone's burning them. **Lee Dunne**

"Best-seller" really only means "good seller". There can only be one best-seller. All the rest are good sellers. Each succeeding book on the list is a better seller. **George Carlin**

With only five hundred-odd shopping days left before Christmas it's autobiography time. Terry Venables talks us through his mother's childhood. Hey, I'm not even interested in my own mother's childhood. Let's cut to the chase. Autobiographies should be brought out in pamphlet form. **Sean Hughes**

Bram Stoker's book about a man with slicked-back hair who dresses in black and sucks blood out of people is believed to be based on his experiences with South Dublin estate agents. **Paul Howard on Dracula**

I want to write a best-seller so I've decided to call my book *Harry Potter and the Da Vinci Book of Sudoku*. **David O'Doherty**

I like to read a lot. The book I always go back to is the phone directory. It was a great moment for me when I realized it was alphabetical. It takes hours off looking up numbers. **Karl Spain**

In Frankie Boyle's current book I get raped by a giant rabbit called Showbiz. **Dara O'Briain**

A man will give up on a book as rubbish if a character doesn't get killed, have sex with a stranger or show signs of having a Nazi past within the first twenty pages. Women, on the other hand, will stick with the chicklit tale of Angie, a twenty-something career girl who loves Chardonnay and saucy flings with divine stockbrokers, but longs to marry an older doctor.

If Angie dies with a swastika on her knickers, you could also nail the male market. *Pat Fitzpatrick*

When I'm in the middle of writing a book I often think: Does the world need another one? Very often the answer is no. *John McKenna*

Did you hear about the Jehovah's Witness Advent book? Every time you open it someone tells you to fuck off. *Pat Flanagan*

If you say a modern celebrity is an adulterer, a pervert and a drug addict, all it means is that you've read his autobiography. *P. J. O'Rourke*

I see my books as children — which might be why I love the bad ones more. *William Trevor*

# BOOK REVIEWS

Only a new cure for the clap can possibly justify all the circumambient peripherization of *Finnegans Wake*. It's just like one long spelling mistake. *Ezra Pound*

A bad review is less important than whether it is raining in Patagonia. *Iris Murdoch*

One must have a heart of stone to read the death of Little Nell without laughing. *Oscar Wilde on Charles Dickens'* **Little Dorrit**

Joyce talked to himself in his sleep. Hence, *Finnegans Wake*. *Oliver St John Gogarty*

If you get six out of six good reviews for a book you can ask the President of the United States to sell you the White House. *Brendan Behan*

Book reviewers are little old ladies of both sexes. *John O'Hara*

Before I became an actor I had a brief but disastrous flirtation with journalism. I was offered a book to review once. I read it twice, thought about it for three weeks, and then decided I had nothing at all to say about it. *Daniel Day-Lewis*

# BOOKSHOPS

I once went into a bookshop and asked if they stocked *The Confessions of St Augustine*. The assistant said to me, "Who is it by?" **Hugh Leonard**

Waterstones in Britain has just introduced a "Painful Lives" section in their shops. It's got to the stage when the memory of a dog peeing on your leg during your childhood, or your sister shouting at you, is enough to induce a miserabilist, million-selling memoir. **John Boland**

I like to ring bookshops. When they say "Can I help you?" I say, "It's OK, I'm just browsing." **Michael Redmond**

Murphy went into a bookshop and asked the salesgirl if she had a book called *How to Master Your Wife*. She said, "Our Fiction section is upstairs." **Hal Roach**

# BORES AND BOREDOM

If you want to bore an Irishman, introduce him to another Irishman. **George Bernard Shaw**

Samantha Cameron's memoirs will be even more boring than Anne Frank's. Excerpt: "Stayed in tonight. David cried." **Michael Cullen**

An Irishman considers a bore to be someone who keeps interrupting him. **Henry Spalding**

There's nothing more boring than listening to a drunk person who thinks he isn't boring. **Gabriel Byrne**

If well-meaning friends wanted an abstruse interpretation of some of Dylan's more obscure lines, which he had long ago forgot the meaning of himself, it wasn't long before he was on the floor wrapped up in the carpet, scratching himself like a flea-bitten hyena in paroxyms of acute boredom. *Caitlin Thomas*

Statistics show that the older you are when you get married, the more likely it is you'll stay together. Of course, because at eighty-five you can't hear how boring he is. *Christine O'Rourke*

When you're young you think of marriage as a train you have to catch. You run and run until you've caught it, and then you sit back and look out the window and realize you're bored. *Elizabeth Bowen*

It has been the kind of week during which I have been sitting around giving an imitation of an unaddressed envelope. *Hugh Leonard*

I'm not saying the game lacked atmosphere but you could hear the corpses in Glasnevin cemetery during the second half. *Damien Richardson*

He was so bored he would have attacked a nanny goat for some variety. *Brian Behan*

# BOXING

Muhammad Ali may sting like a bee but he lives like a WASP. *Eamonn Andrews*

I'm the only boxer in my family. All my ancestors were Alsatians. *Jack Doyle*

Born in Italy, most of his fights have been in his native New York. *Des Lynam*

I missed Nicky Perez with some tremendous punches. The wind from them could have given him pneumonia. *Barry McGuigan*

Dennis Taylor was the only boxer in Northern Ireland to sell advertising space on the soles of his shoes. He was once so far behind on points he needed a knock-out for a draw. *Frank Carson*

They have women boxers in Ireland now but I don't think it'll catch on. Can you imagine them at the weigh-in? "Those scales are wrong!" *Dusty Young*

The Irish referee at the big fight had to interfere when Flanagan's trainer told his man, "Look, will ye stop knocking the champ down, you fool, he's getting too much rest." *Peter Cagney*

Daniel Caruso had a strange way of preparing himself for a fight: he used to psych himself up by punching himself in the face. Before the 1992 New York Golden Gloves Championship he went too far, breaking his nose. The doctors examining him ruled that he was unfit to box. *Des Lynam*

What do the Derry football team and Frank Bruno have in common? They're both out after round one. *Pat Spillane*

# BRAS

All Women's Libbers should be kept behind bras. *Karl Spain*

When I was dating, anybody who ever got close to a bra deserved the Freedom of the City because you had to go through two or three jumpers and possibly a duffel coat. *Gerry Ryan*

I was once asked to endorse a green Wonderbra for the World Cup. *Roddy Doyle*

My wife isn't so smart. She has to reach into her bra to count to two. *Tommy Dempsey*

Elvis was pretty far gone the first time I saw him. It made sense that women threw their bras at him – he needed them. *Tom Kenny*

She told her boss her reason for being late was a severe hangover so he bought her a larger bra. *Peter Cagney*

The reason they call it a Wonderbra is because when you take it off you wonder where your tits went. *Twink*

The latest Irish soccer bra has no cups, but great support. *Philip Greene*

# BREAKFAST

Only dull people are brilliant at breakfast. *Oscar Wilde*

I eat bitches like you before breakfast. *Sinead O'Connor to Mary Coughlan*

He that looketh on a plate of ham and eggs to lust after it hath already committed breakfast with it in his heart. *C. S. Lewis*

I hate all that tycoon stuff with breakfast conferences and the like. Somebody asked me round for breakfast the other day to discuss something and I told them I only ever had a fingernail and a Gauloise for breakfast. I only make films for money and I don't care who knows it. The rest of it is rubbish. What's fame except a few bob and an entrée. *Peter O'Toole*

All marriages are happy. It's having breakfast together that causes the problems. *Dion Boucicault*

Why do the Dutch eat twenty different varieties of cheese at seven in the morning? Why do the French have nothing but tiny cups of strong coffee over and over and that's all? Why do the Germans eat slices of cucumber, tomato and cold luncheon meat roll when I eat that for lunch? Why do the Italians eat frosted chocolate cakes when I eat that for dessert? And why do the Scandinavians even bother to get up in the morning to eat small pieces of dead soused fish laid to rest on thin Ryvita crackers? *Paul Kilduff*

# BREASTS

The strangest thing about Hollywood has to be sleeping with actresses who have fake tits. It's like massaging rocks. **Colin Farrell**

A breast implant is the bust that money can buy. **Kevin Brennan**

Any woman who has breast implants should be sued under the Advertising Standards Act. **Ian O'Doherty**

There's only one sex, and that's the female one. All of us men are just deformed women. Otherwise why do we have tits? **Brendan Behan**

At the start of my life in show business I designed my own falsies. I'm very superstitious about them. I lost one once and there was a terrific panic. I was running round the theatre shouting, "Lock the doors — one of my tits is missing!" When I retire I'd like to have them dipped in gold and then auctioned off at Sotheby's. **Danny La Rue**

Golf is like an eighteen-year-old girl with big boobs. You know it's wrong but you can't keep away from her. **Val Doonican**

It is not acceptable that the Department of Health should only pay lip service to the importance of breastfeeding. **Fiona Timlin**

I've never been turned on by toplessness. I always knew women had breasts. **John Huston**

The tits of a maid from Kinsale
Were tattooed with the price of best ale.
While on her behind,
For the sake of the blind,
Was the same information in Braille.
**Old Irish limerick**

I love Dolly Parton. I don't know why. Maybe it's a subconscious desire to breastfeed. **Graham Norton**

Anyone offended by breastfeeding is staring too hard. *Dave Allen*

When I look back on my life, the fondest memory I have is not really of the Goons. It is of a girl called Julia with enormous breasts. *Spike Milligan*

# BUILDERS

Surgeons' mistakes get buried. Architects' ones get built. *Ruairí Quinn*

Those Polish bastards are stealing our work because they're not lazy fuckers like us. *Unidentified Irish builder*

The rule for meeting a potential builder for the first time is that you don't dress like an idiot. Under no circumstances should you wear anything outlandish such as a dress. In a builder's mind, anyone in a dress is an idiot. *David Slattery*

Ireland was built on specifications written on the back of fag boxes with the butty end of a pencil stuck behind a speculator's ear. *Jon Kenny*

# BURGLARS

I was out with a girl once and she got a phone call to say her house had just been burgled. She went, "Jesus, it was filthy before I left." *P. J. Gallagher*

If an Englishman catches a burglar in his house he'll say, "What do you think you're doing?" An Irishman would say, "Get out, you bastard." *Dave Allen*

If anyone ever broke into our house they'd leave a donation. *Eric Cross*

Why do people have burglar alarms? Everybody ignores them, except to utter profanities. If I were a housebreaker I would seek out houses where the alarm was going off. I'd know I was safe. *Richard O'Connor*

A burglar broke into a health shop in Killarney and stole the entire stock. Police are waiting to interview a man who lives to be 105. *Kevin Murtie*

I have a feeling we had gay burglars last night. Someone came in, rearranged the furniture, and left some quiche in the oven. *Dusty Young*

Did you hear about the burglar who broke into a bookie's and lost £20? *Josef Locke*

# BUSES

My favourite form of relaxation is wondering what happened to the number 10 bus. *Ann Marie Hourihane*

Dublin Bus has been taking out newspaper ads saying that all services would "operate normally" today. That's what I'm afraid of. *Peter Howick*

Comparing Madonna with Marilyn Monroe is like comparing Raquel Welch to the back end of a bus. *Boy George*

I got so drunk the other night I took off all my clothes and went upstairs without even saying goodnight to my wife. It was embarrassing because I was on a bus at the time. *Kevin Brennan*

Buses in Ireland tend to arrive according to some astrological calendar unknown to the rest of us. *Terry Eagleton*

Did you hear about the Irish Evel Knievel? He tried to jump over thirty-three motorcycles in a bus. *Mr O'S*

Definition of a school bus driver: Someone who thought he liked the company of children. *Hal Roach*

You know how some folk reject statistics indicating that their chances of living to a grand old age would be improved if they stopped smoking fifty fags a day, drinking eight pints a night and lying on the couch watching reality TV by saying "Sure I could get hit by a bus in the morning"? I've always felt this to be a slur on Bus Eireann. *Terry Prone*

The guy in front of me on the bus went into convulsions. He was sweating and puking and almost swallowed his tongue. His friend told me he'd been drinking for fifty-five days straight. We finally got him out and I thought: Great. *Now* who's going to drive? *Kathleen Madigan*

I was getting off the bus one day and I thanked the driver as he let me off. He replied, "It's OK, I was going this way anyway." *Overheard in Dublin*

Do you know what's come closer to breaking my spirit than polio, asthma, deafness, migraine, depression or electric shocks? Dublin fucking Bus. *Pat Ingoldsby*

The bus was crowded when an old Irish woman got on and had to stand. A polite lad stood up and asked, "Would you like my seat for a while?" "No," she said, "I daren't sit down. I'm in a hurry." *Mr O'S*

The 46A passes through Monkstown during a circuitous journey that also takes in Ayers Rock, Angkor Wat and the Puerto Moreno glacier. *Ross O'Carroll-Kelly*

# CAMELS

As the Bible says, "It's easier for a rich man to get through the eye of a needle than for a camel to get into heaven." *Andy Mulligan*

I don't trust camels or any other animal that can go without drink for a week. *Brendan Behan*

# CANADA

I went to Canada once but it was closed. *Brendan Behan*

Canada is the perpetual wallflower that stands on the edge of the hall waiting for someone to come and ask her for a dance. *Kevin Myers*

Canadians are like Americans except they don't polish their shoes as much. *Conal Gallen*

# CANNIBALS

How do cannibals behave at a wedding? They toast the bride and groom. *Dusty Young*

Did you hear about the cannibal who didn't like his mother? He left her at the side of the plate. *Bunny Carr*

And then there was the cannibal who was converted by Irish Catholic missionaries. Now he only eats fishermen on Fridays. *Kevin Murtie*

# CAPITAL PUNISHMET

There is no satisfaction in hanging a man who does not object to it. *George Bernard Shaw*

They court-martialled me in my absence and they sentenced me to death in my absence so I told them they could shoot me in my absence too. *Brendan Behan after being convicted for IRA activity*

Come closer boys and it'll be easier for ye. *Condemned republican prisoner Erskine Childers to a firing squad before his execution in 1922*

We're not going to hang anyone on the guillotine. *Bertie Ahern*

And then there was the condemned golfer who asked the hangman, "Mind if I take a couple of practice swings?" *Hal Roach*

# CARD GAMES

My father lost his hair overnight. In a poker game. *Sean Hughes*

I'm always welcome in a poker school since my face is an emotional barometer. Any good player can tell by looking at me whether I'm holding two small pairs or a broken flush. But when I look at a good poker player myself, I have difficulty in deciding whether he's alive or dead. *John D. Sheridan*

Sophia Loren is a gross card sharp. In Naples they're born with a pack of cards in their hands. *Peter O'Toole*

One should always play fairly when one has the winning cards. *Oscar Wilde*

I'd sooner live among people who don't cheat at cards than among people who are earnest about not cheating at cards. *C. S. Lewis*

I cheat at Patience and still lose. *Danny Cummins*

A man invited his friend around to see his dog. "This is the most intelligent dog in the world," he told his friend. "He can even play poker." The two men commence playing and after a few minutes the friend says, "I'm afraid I disagree with you about your dog's intelligence. Every time he gets a good hand he wags his tail." *Stephen O'Driscoll*

# CARS

My first priority is to fix the heater of the car. *John Connolly after scooping a £350,000 advance for his novel* **Every Dead Thing**

Take up car maintenance and find the class is full of other thirty-something women like me, looking for a fella. *Marian Keyes*

Most cars have one part that desperately needs to be replaced: the nut behind the wheel. *Ted Bonner*

What's the difference between a Jehovah's Witness and a Lada? It's easier to close the door on a Jehovah's Witness. *Sil Fox*

Hood ornaments were lovely and gave a sense of respect. They took them away because, "If you can save one human life" — that's always the argument — "it's worth it." Actually I'd be willing to trade a dozen human lives for a nice hood ornament. *Michael O'Donoghue*

My first car was a Talbot Horizon which was ironic because it hardly ever reached a horizon. My parents bought it from my brother-in-law's cousin who was a second-hand dealer. Within three weeks I had to replace the clutch, the gearbox and two bald tyres. *Dillie Keane*

The first commandment of life in Ireland would appear to be: Thou shalt never, under any circumstances, wash a car. *Rowan Atkinson*

All the thoroughly moral women I know have a habit of humming tunes with persistent cheerfulness in cars. *Micheál MacLiammóir*

Women are just like cars. If you want a nice comfortable ride you go for a Merc. If you want something very sexy but awkward you go for a Ferrari. If you want something easy to park you go for a Cinquecento. *Eddie Irvine*

My Mini was well ventilated. In fact if you pulled the passenger floor mat back, you could watch the road passing underneath. It was always damp inside so I grew a couple of beautiful ferns in the passenger door. Actually I didn't plant them – they just appeared. **Richard O'Connor**

# CATHOLICS

Catholics sow their wild oats from Monday to Friday and then go to Mass on Sunday to pray for a crop failure. **Tommy Makem**

One great thing about the Catholic way is that each milestone, whether it be a communion, confirmation or whatever, provided a great excuse for a party: a respectful reason for everyone to go on the piss. **Fran Cosgrave**

Whenever I hear somebody talking about a practising Catholic, I think: Why do they have to keep practising? Do they never get it right? **Hugh Leonard**

Fr Dougal: "I've heard about all these cults, Ted. People dressing up in black and saying Our Lord's going to come back and save us all."
Fr Ted: "No, Dougal, that's us. That's Catholicism."
Fr Dougal: "Oh. Right."
**Father Ted**

I once went into an Episcopal service by mistake. The reason I knew I wasn't in a Catholic church was because the priest went on for an hour without mentioning money. **John Ford**

He's such a devout Catholic he won't be satisfied until he's crucified like Jesus. **John B. Keane**

Catholicism is cheaper than Prozac, but is it good for you? **Marian Keyes**

The Catholic Church is like the Mafia. Once they have you, you're in for life. **Frank McCourt**

In Ireland there are Catholics, lapsed Catholics, non-Catholics and anti-Catholics, but there's no such thing as an ex-Catholic. **John Waters**

What they're selling in the Vatican — or the *Vatican't*, as I like to call it — is not Catholicism. ***Sinead O'Connor***

Catholicism has changed tremendously in recent years. When Communion is served now, there is also a salad bar. ***Bill Maher***

Somehow it has become acceptable to be a Catholic Who Only Believes In Some Bits Of The Religion. ***Róisín Ingle***

Being a lapsed Catholic puts you in some highly distinguished company and in some people's view comes only a little below the saints. In descending order of importance there is God, then the saints, then lapsed Catholics, then the clergy, then the simple faithful, then Protestants. But even Protestants would be Catholics if they'd stop reading the Bible. ***Terry Eagleton***

Buddhism tells us to suffer what there is to suffer and to enjoy what there is to enjoy. Irish Catholics tend to enjoy what there is to suffer and suffer what there is to enjoy. ***Mary McEvoy***

# CATS

A cat isn't fussy as long as you remember he likes his milk in the shallow rose-patterned saucer and his fish on the blue plate, from which he will take it and eat it off the floor. ***Arthur Bridges***

Cats have nine lives, which makes them ideal for experimentation. ***Jimmy Carr***

The cat in Number 70 will be writing next. ***Brendan Behan after hearing his brother had penned his memoirs***

A cat is a crossword puzzle with no clues. ***Mac O'Brien***

Cats are the fascists of the animal world. ***Brian Behan***

When the Irishman heard that curiosity killed the cat, he said, "What was he curious about?" ***Dave Allen***

Cats can hear a fridge door opening in the next parish. They'll sit on the edge of the table while you're eating and completely ignore your plate. They'll look the other way and convince you that nothing is further from their minds than the food which is in front of you. Yet without appearing to move an inch they will edge nearer and nearer to your plate. Turn your back for one second and your food is gone. *Pat Ingoldsby*

Cats only jump into your lap to check if you're cold enough to eat. *Anne Enright*

Cats are the only creatures on four legs that have perfected the art of training human beings. They can get you to the stage where you leap out of a warm bed at 4.30 a.m. because you hear a meow outside the front door. *Pat Ingoldsby*

To err is human, to purr, feline. *Robert O'Byrne*

There will always be some situations in life, like running over a neighbour's cat, that are socially awkward. *Graham Norton*

A writer without a cat risks taking himself too seriously. *Garrison Reed*

Its tail was a plume of such significance it almost wore the cat. *Hugh Leonard*

Cats won't chase after sticks and bring them back. They'll look at you with pity and amusement a couple of times, then wander away in search of higher intelligence. *Pat Ingoldsby*

# THE CELTIC TIGER

*The above term was allegedly coined by David McWilliams to describe the economic boom Ireland enjoyed from the late 1990s to 2007.*

The Celtic Tiger has become a mangy cat. *Vincent Browne*

When I first came to Ireland in 1990 everyone had a 1976 Ford Fiesta. Then the Celtic Tiger kicked in and they all disappeared overnight. *Des Bishop*

The Celtic Tiger turned Dublin into Disneyland with super-pubs. *Joe O'Connor*

All I remember from the Celtic Tiger is mortgages and round-abouts. *Colm Toibin*

Now that the Celtic Tiger has padded away into the foothills of extinction, we need a new national animal to symbolize the malaise we're in. Possible candidates might include the Housing Bubble Bunny, the Repossession Teddy Bear, the Negative Equity Leprechaun, the Rip-Off Ireland Rhino and the Bank of Ireland Security Lapse Banshee. *Joe O'Connor*

The Celtic Tiger isn't just dead; it's decomposing. *Pat Rabbitte*

# CENSORSHIP

I've set up my own Censorship Board and I hereby censor all censors. *Brendan Behan*

Shortly before she died, my mother told me that she had one great regret in life: that her son never had a proper job. *Former Irish film censor Sheamus Smith*

Sometimes the certificate given to a film depends on the state of the censor's piles when he's watching it. *Frank Hall*

The time seems far off now when villains invariably bit the dust and the scarlet woman atoned handsomely for her sins by intercepting the bullet intended for the hero, when the Hays Office made lovers keep one foot on the floor and when one unblinking look from Rita Hayworth was more carnal than any of today's full frontals. *Hugh Leonard*

I know nothing about films but I know the Ten Commandments. *James Montgomery, Ireland's film censor from 1924 to 1940*

If you weren't a censored writer when I was young in Ireland you probably weren't any bloody good. *Ben Kiely*

# CHARACTER

Deep down I'm quite superficial. *Charles Haughey*

To be a Dublin "character" you need to be able to stink to high heaven, cadge pints, curse in at least one language, throw a punch without either connecting or spilling your drink, worry horses, wear chains, claim to be a poet/writer/painter, and play an invisible kettle drum while farting the National Anthem. *David Kenny*

He is a character. Only people who haven't to earn their living can afford to be characters. *Terence de Vere White*

Characters aren't created by writers. They pre-exist and have to be found. *Elizabeth Bowen*

# CHARITY

Mother fucking Teresa. *Eamon Dunphy's reaction after Niall Quinn donated the proceeds of his testimonial match to charity*.

I read that Britney Spears gave away more than $300,000 to charities last year. Well done, but you'd think with all that money to spare, she'd get herself a decent haircut. *Eamonn Holmes*

Irish priests are still very much involved with charities in the developing world but it's a sign of the shifting power that, these days, Ireland's highest profile missionaries to Africa are Bob Geldof and Bono. *Frank McNally*

I once asked Frank Sinatra's confessor why he was doing so much work for charity. "Fire insurance," he replied. *Colm T. Wilkinson*

Charity begins at home, and generally dies from lack of outdoor exercise. *Bob Geldof*

I find the name of the charity Children in Need a bit superfluous. When was the last time you saw a child who wasn't in need? I've yet to hear one go, "Actually that's enough raspberry tart for me, I'm just going to clean the car." *Dylan Moran*

The slogan I've found most effective for charity work is simple: "Give us the fucking money." *Bob Geldof*

# CHAT-UP LINES

I went to a Muslim speed-dating evening. Everyone kept saying, "Nice eyes." *Sean Hughes*

Pardon me, darlin', but I'm writin' a phone book. Can I have yer number? *Traditional Irish chat-up line*

He told me he thought he'd seen my face somewhere before. I told him it was always on these shoulders. *Katy French*

What are you doing after the orgy? *Vincent Hanley*

She said she'd heard Latin lovers were the best endowed but I told her the truth of the matter was that it was the Irish and the Red Indians. "So what's your name?" she asked. "Tonto O'Shaughnessy," I informed her. *Des Sheehy*

Nice legs. What time do they open? *T-shirt slogan spotted by Peter Quinn*

Won't you come into the garden? I should like my roses to see you. *R. B. Sheridan to a female acquaintance*

I've got a big farm, I'd like to marry the one in the middle. Are you interested? *Fan letter sent to the pop group Sheeba*

There are many places I would like to go with you. Bed is most of them. *Pat Ingoldsby*

I asked her if she'd go out with me. "Not if you were the last man on the planet," she said. "I suppose a blowjob is out of the question?" I enquired. *Dave Harmon*

The favoured chat-up line of old men having had senior moments is, "Do I come here often?" **Terry Wogan**

I want you to have my children. Take them. I can't stand the little fuckers. **Sean Hughes**

# CHICK LIT

Chick lit is junk food for the brain. **Paul Howard**

The chick litters complain that their work isn't taken seriously by the literary establishment because they're women. Sorry, girls. It's because it's rubbish. **Eamonn Sweeney**

If you're a reader of popular women's novels you know the score. A woman who is beautiful, clever and sexy gets the man all her pals wanted and then her best friend sleeps with him or she gets breast cancer or her baby falls out of a tree. One way or the other, her husband can't stick her any more and leaves. At the same time her father gets Alzheimer's, her house burns down and her brother totals her sports car. At this point, all the women in her life she wasn't that pleasant to before her misfortunes start to arrive in battalions and rally round, bringing her scones, herbal teas, scented oils and sympathy. **Terry Prone**

Accusing a chick lit author of plagiarizing is a bit like accusing a size zero model of starvation dieting. **Liam Fay**

# CHILDHOOD

Since childhood is a time when you prepare to be grown-ups, I think it makes a lot of sense to completely traumatize your children. Get 'em ready for the real world. **George Carlin**

I didn't have an unhappy childhood but I was an unhappy child. **John Connolly**

I looked like a baked bean until I was thirteen. **Bono**

Worse than the ordinary miserable childhood is the miserable Irish childhood, and worse yet is the miserable Irish Catholic childhood. **Frank McCourt**

I had a rough childhood. I was breastfed by my father. **James McKeon**

When I was a child we watched many football games on the radio. **Con Houlihan**

As far as literary inspiration goes, a happy childhood isn't worth a fuck. **Frank McCourt**

# CHILDREN

Children are becoming very precocious nowadays. A boy in kindergarten said to his friend, "There's a condom behind the radiator," and the friend replied, "What's a radiator?" **Big O**

I have no children, luckily for them. **Samuel Beckett**

Children are like farts. People quite like their own. **Graham Norton**

Babysitters tell me a good way to keep a child quiet is to let him suck on a bottle of glue. **Hal Roach**

Kids aren't easy but there has to be some penalty for sex. **Bill Maher**

I'd like to have three children – one of each. **Katy French**

When you're dealing with a child, keep all your wits about you. Then sit on the floor. **Austin O'Malley**

There is no end to the violations committed on children by children, quietly talking alone. **Elizabeth Bowen**

Marie Stopes was an unplanned child. **Nell McCafferty**

"It is my view," proclaimed Farrell, "that if a child can be prevented from dying in its first year, it will have a better chance of living into its second." *Tony Butler*

I have an eight-year-old child and he's a bit deranged because he's been living with me for eight years. *Jason Byrne*

Children are just midget drunks. They greet you in the morning by kneeing you in the face and talking gibberish. *Dylan Moran*

Murphy was an atheist who married a Jehovah's Witness. Now they have children who knock at your door for no apparent reason. *Noel V. Ginnity*

You can tell a child is growing up when he stops asking where he came from and refuses to say where he's going. *Jason O'Donoghue*

My grandchildren are so wonderful I should have had them first. *Liz Kavanagh*

For anyone who has children and doesn't know it, there's a crèche on the first floor. *Message spotted in shopping centre*

With children it's a thin line between "I love ya" and "I'll fuckin' kill ya". *Brendan O'Carroll*

Children are bathed on a Saturday night for the same reason sheep are branded once a year — so you can gather them for counting and be reasonably sure of knowing your own the next time you see them. *John D. Sheridan*

When your kid is about fifteen or sixteen, someone takes them away and replaces them with a lookalike that's an absolute swine. When the kid is about twenty or twenty-one, they do another swap and you get your own child back. *Maire Geoghegan-Quinn*

# CHOICES

Someone said to me the other day, "Shall we eat or will we have a McDonald's?" **Dave Allen**

If I was given a choice between world peace and a Prada handbag, I'd dither. I am not proud of this. **Marian Keyes**

Women are funny. Last Christmas my wife gave me two neckties. I got up on Christmas morning, put one of them on, went downstairs, showed it to her, and the first thing she said was, "And just what was wrong with the other one?" **Dave Allen**

I'm not an outdoorsy type. If I was offered the choice between white-water rafting and being savaged by a rabid dog, I'd be likely to tick the box marked "Dog". **Marian Keyes**

I usually play golf with a friend of mine who's a priest. Last Sunday he couldn't make up his mind whether to go to church or to the golf course so he tossed a coin. The reason he was late was because he had to toss it seventeen times. **Dave O'Gorman**

A pretty girl said to a pensioner, "Let's go upstairs and make love." He replied, "I can't do both." **Big O**

A pessimist is one who when he has the choice of two evils, chooses both. **Oscar Wilde**

The American tourist arrived in the Irish hotel looking for a room. "Do you want one with a bath or a shower?" the hotelier enquired. "What's the difference?" he asked. "Well, you step into a shower," the hotelier explained. **Noel V. Ginnity**

I once told my dentist I'd prefer to have a baby than have a tooth out. He said, "You better make up your mind before I adjust the chair." **Maureen Potter**

# CHRISTMAS

An important Christmas ritual is putting up the tree. Like most rituals, it makes no sense. *David Slattery*

Every year people in Ireland ask one another "How did you get over Christmas?" as if it was the flu. *Clare Boylan*

Mulled wine. Check. Dodgy hangover cures. Check. Action Man for the crib to replace the missing baby Jesus. Check. *Colette Fitzpatrick*

Christmas, I have decided, is a doddle, a piece of cake in more than the comestible sense. It's those twelve bloody days afterwards that have one looking like a gangrenous elk, and displaying the *joie de vivre* of a pole-squatter with haemorrhoids. *Hugh Leonard*

It's customarily said that Christmas is done "for the kids". Considering how awful Christmas is and how little our society likes children, this must be true. *P. J. O'Rourke*

Happy stupid Christmas, everyone. Most of you will have bought all your gifts weeks ago. A few admirable souls will, however, be hoping that the garage is still open this afternoon. *Donald Clarke on Christmas Eve, 2011*

Things were so bad in our house one Christmas that when I asked Santa for a yo-yo, all I got was a piece of string. My father told me it was a yo. *Brendan O'Carroll*

Christmas Day is the feast of St Loneliness. *Paul Durcan*

My father asked me what I wanted for Christmas one year when I was a child. "Something to wear and something to play with," I said. He got me a pair of trousers with the pockets cut out. *Brendan O'Carroll*

Cancel Christmas — they found the body. *Graffiti*

Announcing you don't want to drink at Christmas in Ireland is akin to mentioning to the lads on the rugby team that you've just realized you're gay. *Sean Moncrieff*

The Irish Christmas Day has the highest incidence of coronary failure of any day of the year; Stephen's Day has the highest incidence of domestic violence, and January sees a peak in post-festivity suicides. Killing a family member or killing yourself are all traditional practices during the Irish Christmas. Very few tourists come to Ireland for Christmas Day to stay with Irish families, which is surprising and must be because they don't realize what they're missing. *David Slattery*

We could have a new hit single this Christmas: "I Saw NAMA Kissing Santa Claus". *Joan Burton on Ireland's National Asset Management Agency*

There are some people who want to throw their arms round you simply because it's Christmas and there are other people who want to strangle you simply because it's Christmas. *Robert Lynd*

Why do people run around like headless chickens in the run-up to Christmas? Do they not know it's coming? Have they not got calendars? *Maeve Binchy*

Anybody buying "Do They Know It's Christmas" can be assured that the pound they pay will literally go into someone's mouth. *Bob Geldof on the famous Live Aid song*

There are many types of uncle that pop in on Christmas Day. Most are drunk because, as they put it themselves, it's great when your children are old enough to drive. *Pat Fitzpatrick*

I propose we get all the designated drivers drunk on Christmas Day and put all the alcoholics on cold turkey. *Gerry Ryan*

Christmas is the one time of the year when people remember what really matters in life. Such as getting presents, getting squiffy and getting stuffed full of rich, unhealthy food. Plus you always have the perfect excuse to go shopping. *Eilis O'Hanlon*

With all the commercialism about, sometimes we forget the real meaning of Christmas — Bing Crosby's birthday. *Pat O'Brien*

It was towards the end of a four-day binge and I was alone in the house, paranoia-driven, trying to finish off my remaining bottle of vodka. I was down to my underpants and my main source of sustenance was baked beans. I remember looking out through my glass-frosted door and crying because I could see snow. I thought: How could my family leave me like this at Christmas? Then I realized it was August. *Ian MacPherson*

Christmas is a time of the year when you get drunk and buy presents for people you can't stand. *Brendan O'Carroll*

The best gift parents can give their children at Christmas is a hard kick in the pants. *Emer O'Kelly*

For children, Christmas starts at Halloween and goes on till about the middle of April. *John Moriarty*

# THE CHURCH

The Catholic Church has a new policy on child abusers: three strikes and you're a cardinal. *Sean Hughes*

Churches are spinning up all over the place and the Catholic Church is becoming very competitive as a result. This season they've apparently changed the ingredients of the Eucharist. It is now called "I Can't Believe It's Not Jesus". *Maeve Higgins*

There are so many shotgun weddings in Dublin they've nicknamed my local church "Winchester Cathedral". *Dusty Young*

The Church in people is more important than people in churches. *Shane Lynch*

The advent of tights was greeted with relief by religious people because they were so much less inflammatory than stockings and suspenders. An old Dublin lady once approached Edna O'Brien in church and said, without preamble, "Did you know that every time a young woman crosses her legs in church, the Virgin Mary blushes?" *John Walsh*

The Church knows a lot about angels, but fuck all about fairies. *Homosexual politician David Norris*

The Church is great on the rights of the unborn but not so good on the rights of the born. *Amanda Brunker*

I have nothing against the Church as long as they leave the drink alone. *Brendan Behan*

Keep Your Rosaries Off Our Ovaries. *Placard by abortion adherents in Ireland in 1997 when the Church campaigned against it*

The Christian Brothers are the paramilitary wing of the Catholic Church. *Eamonn Holmes*

The propagation of bingo is the ultimate role of the Catholic Church in Ireland. *John B. Keane*

The Catholic Church pre-dated psychoanalysis by two thousand years with the sacrament of confession. You go into a darkened room and tell a complete stranger your innermost thoughts and fears and, *voilà*, the priest gives you absolution. And for free. *Gabriel Byrne*

Have you heard about the New Wave Church in California? It has Three Commandments and Seven Suggestions. *Tom O'Dwyer*

Among the best traitors Ireland ever had, Mother Church ranks at the very top. *Bernadette McAliskey*

# CIGARETTES

A cigarette is the perfect type of pleasure. It is exquisite and it leaves one unsatisfied. What more can one want? *Oscar Wilde*

Smoking herbal cigarettes is like standing near a bonfire that won't light while trying to suck up the fumes through a straw. *Ruth Burke-Kennedy*

The three best things in life are a drink before and a cigarette after. *Adrian Lawlor*

I read in a book that cigarettes were bad for you so I had to give up reading. *Noel Purcell*

# CINEMAS

A Dublin cinema attendant was once asked what business was like. "To tell you the truth," he said, "when the place isn't half full it's half empty." *Doug Anderson*

The name of my local cinema when I was a kid was the Star. If you spelled it backwards you got "Rats", which about summed it up. *Patrick Bergin*

# CITIES

Singapore is a city up its own arse. Can't shout on the street, can't chew gum, can't open the back window of your car ... can't understand why anyone would want to go there. *Hector O'hEochagáin*

To take an active part in the artistic life of any small city is as cuddlesome a thing as to immerse oneself in a hip-bath of piranha fish. *John Ryan*

In Amsterdam, if it's fun then it's probably legal. *Hector O'hEochagáin*

If God wanted to give the world an enema he'd have stuck the tube in Beirut. *Hugh Leonard*

Limerick is the city of piety and shiety. *Brendan Behan*

Rome was a cheerful city where Catholicism, Communism and Hedonism were an accommodating trinity for the morally frail, unlike Limerick where the rains and the sermons brought gloom and despair to the quivering victims of Jansenist tyranny. *Malachy McCourt*

Newcastle: Funny accents, don't wear coats. Liverpool: Funny accents, sentimental. Manchester: Like to hang around independent record stores in parka jackets. Birmingham: Probably Asian or a lapdancer. *Dara O'Briain*

Ireland has three main cities: Dublin, Cork and Boston. *Richard O'Connor*

Rome reminds me of a man who lives by exhibiting to travellers his grandmother's corpse. *James Joyce*

Toronto will be a fine city when it's finished. *Brendan Behan*

Hong Kong is just Manchester with slanted eyes. *Peter O'Toole*

According to legend, Rome was founded by a character called Romulus who killed his brother Remus. If it was the other way round, Rome would be Reme, but a cappuccino near the Spanish Steps would still cost £10, and the waiter would still make a pass at your wife. *Pat Fitzpatrick*

Chiba is a concrete city. Unbroken, charmless concrete. The place has been reclaimed from the sea, and if the sea had any decency at all it would claim it back. *Tom Humphries*

New York is a place where you're not likely to get a bite from a wild goat. *Brendan Behan*

I told the taxi driver on the way to Helsinki that I was there for five days to shoot a TV show about the place. He said that was about four days too long. *Hector O'hEochagáin*

I had a really good time in New York, but it smells like a giant urinal. *Jared Harris*

Lenin said communism was socialism with electricity. New York is Paris with the English language. *Brendan Behan*

# CLASS

Work is the curse of the drinking classes. **Brendan Behan**

Extraordinary thing about the lower classes in England – they are always losing their relations. They are extremely fortunate in that respect. **Oscar Wilde**

Don't try to keep up with the Joneses. Drag them down to your level; it's cheaper. **Sean Kilbride**

I'm from the working class but there's now a class even lower than that. It's called the "We can't be bothered working" class. **Noel Gallagher**

There are only two classes of good society in England: the equestrian classes and the neurotic classes. **George Bernard Shaw**

Sadie Frost has more ass than class. **Ian O'Doherty**

They would have been working class, but there was no work. **Roddy Doyle**

The poor are there to scare the shit out of the middle class. **George Carlin**

What is middle-class morality? Just an excuse for never giving me anything. **George Bernard Shaw**

Mrs Danaher was buying a dog from farmer Clancy. She said, "I want one of which I can be proud. Does that one have a good pedigree?" The farmer said, "Madam, if that dog could talk, he wouldn't speak to either of us." **Hal Roach**

The Americans have no class structure. The British have nothing *but* a class structure. The Irish have a class structure but nobody has discovered what it is. **Terry Eagleton**

People keep comparing me to Cary Grant, but that's not me. I'm an Irish peasant, for God's sake. **Pierce Brosnan**

If you tell an Irish person you're travelling first class they'll go, "Bastard." You might be forgiven if you say you didn't pay for it. **Colin Murphy**

Working-class people get their ears pierced even before the umbilical cord is cut. **Ed Byrne**

# CLASSICAL MUSIC

By the time Beethoven died, he was so deaf he thought he was an artist. **Pat McCormick**

There are some sacrifices which should not be demanded twice of any man, and one of them is listening to Brahms' Requiem. **George Bernard Shaw**

Brahms' wantonness isn't vicious. It's that of a great baby rather tirelessly addicted to dressing himself up as Handel or Beethoven and making a prolonged and intolerable noise. **George Bernard Shaw**

I like Wagner's music better than anybody's. It is so loud that one can talk the whole time without people hearing what one says. **Oscar Wilde**

# CLOCKS

She told her husband she'd set the alarm clock for six. He said, "Why? There's only two of us." **Spike Milligan**

I once made love from 11.55 to 1.03. I think that was the night the clocks went forward. **Brendan O'Carroll**

Sinead O'Connor is like a stopped clock. She's right twice a day. **Liam Fay**

One can repair a noisy electric clock by turning it upside down for several hours and allowing the oil to circulate more evenly. I'm wondering if this would prove efficacious in the case of some vociferous drunks of my acquaintance. **Hugh Leonard**

Emmet was boasting about the new clock he'd bought. 'It goes eight days without winding." "And how long does it go if you wind it?" asked Orla. *Duncan Crosbie*

# CLOTHING

To most people a savage nation is one that doesn't wear uncomfortable clothes. *Finley Peter Dunne*

"I've got a bad stomach."
　"Well keep your coat on and no one will notice."
*Seamus O'Leary*

Even though I have the fashion sense of a scarecrow I don't think words like "Gwen Stefani" and "Best Dressed Female" should be used in the same sentence, as *Harpers & Queen* did recently. As her pictures show, Gwen's main looks range from porn queen to brothel keeper to "I got dressed in the pitch dark". *Moira Hannon*

Gay Byrne showed up at RTE one day wearing a loud purple and orange jumper that looked like a nuclear incident. Another night he proudly sported a mauve tie that had tiny coloured dots all over it, as though thousands of insects had chosen its surface upon which to commit hara-kiri. *Ferdia MacAnna*

In my mother's day if you set foot outside the door with a matching handbag and shoes you were an automatic contender for a Best Dressed list. *Martina Devlin*

That's a beautiful dress you're almost wearing. *Stephen Boyd to Brigitte Bardot on the set of* Shalako

Last night my girlfriend was wearing a dress so tight I could hardly breathe. *Sean Kilroy*

He said he'd give me the two jackets free if I bought one of them. *Caller to* Liveline *radio show*

Dress simply. If you wear a dinner jacket don't wear anything else on it. Like lunch. *Terry Prone*

If you're unsure whether your clothing is suitable for wear on a golf course, ask yourself if it combines the minimum imaginable taste with the maximum possible discomfort. *Michael Ryan*

It's not easy being a man. I had to get dressed today. And there are also other pressures. *Dylan Moran*

Remember when you fit into something at dawn to take account of the lattes and edibles you may consume throughout the day which could result in your strangling on your waistband by nightfall. *Terry Prone*

Larry Gogan: "What type of person would wear a tutu?" Contestant: "A bishop!"
**Exchange on Gogan's Just-a-Minute Quiz**

Don't let men pull the wool over your eyes. Keep your jumper on instead. *Monica Barnes*

We were so poor I had to be dressed in my father's hand-me-downs. The trousers were so big I had to open the fly to blow my nose. *Shaun Connors*

The thing about Anna is that she can be acutely perceptive but she's not great on practical things. Like remembering to get dressed before leaving the house. *Marian Keyes*

I bought a gorgeous frock yesterday. It would have fitted me perfectly if I could only have got into it. *Maureen Potter*

My BMW jacket has now taken on mythic proportions and weighs about half what I do. There are days I expect to unzip a pocket and find Lord Lucan riding Shergar. *Philip Nolan*

When Bill Clinton played golf he wore jogging shoes and his shirt was hanging out over painter's pants. Golf needs him like it needs a case of ringworm. *Rick Reilly*

When a masochist comes home from a bar, does he say, "Excuse me a moment, I'm going to slip into something uncomfortable"? *George Carlin*

I passed a woman with a T-shirt saying "Mongoloid Porn Inferno". I thought: That sounds like a busy evening. *Dylan Moran*

# COFFEE

Why do people who only drink tea say to their friends, "Let's meet for coffee"? *Jackie Fitzgerald*

I've stopped drinking coffee in the morning because it keeps me awake all day. *Jimmy O'Dea*

Only Irish coffee provides in a single glass all four essential food groups: alcohol, caffeine, sugar and fat. *Alex Levine*

I always got a pain in my eye when I drank coffee. Then one day I discovered the reason: I forgot to take the spoon out. *Kevin Gildea*

# COLOURS

Their uniforms were all different, chiefly green. *Sir Boyle Roche*

If a woman wears white on her wedding day as a sign of purity, why does a man wear black? *Justin Morahan*

What's orange and looks good on hippies? Fire. *Damian Clarke*

Only his varicose veins save him from being completely colourless. *Hal Roach*

I won't believe in colour TV until I see it in black and white. *Joe Linnane*

# COMEDY

Comedy acting isn't taken seriously enough. *Chris O'Dowd*

Half an idea and the panic of dying — that's how you write stand-up. *Dara O'Briain*

The best compliment I can give anything comical is that it's also stupid. *Graham Linehan*

The comedy I do isn't for the faint-hearted. And the faint-hearted should also avoid salt. *Jimmy Carr*

We don't try to make jokes in Ulster. We say serious things in a way that makes them appear funny when you see how serious they are. *Lynn Doyle*

I bring sudoku for something to do during the applause breaks. *Mary Bourke*

I'd be nervous if I wasn't nervous before a show. *John Colleary*

Jesus loves the Irish, which proves he has a great sense of humour. *Seamus O'Leary*

Lenny Henry, depending on your point of view, is either hilarious or someone who last said something amusing some time in 1987. *Bernice Harrison*

Not a shred of evidence exists in favour of the idea that life is serious. *Brendan Gill*

Nothing is funnier than unhappiness. *Samuel Beckett*

Farce is tragedy without trousers. Shoot a man in the stomach and it's drama. Shoot him in the backside and it's comedy. *Peter O'Toole*

Every comic is a manic depressive. *Rosaleen Linehan*

The reason Irish jokes are so simple is so English people can understand them. *Niall Toibin*

I did a stand-up gig in a prison once. Captive audience. *P. J. Gallagher*

My unhappiest moments as a stand-up comedian have been in hotel rooms pulling myself sideways before shows from nerves. Tears and semen aren't a good combination. *Tommy Tiernan*

# COMMUNISM

When I told my mother I was a Trotskyite she said, "What's that? It sounds like a horse." *Brian Behan*

Soviet Russia failed because it tried to tell the doctor he was no more important than the bin-man. *Gerry Ryan*

I have no time for champagne socialists. Half of them wouldn't know the difference between communism and rheumatism. *Brendan Behan*

Communism bothers me. They have nothing and they want to share it with us. *Hal Roach*

Becoming a communist is still one of the best ways of meeting middle-class women so it can't all be bad. *Brian Behan*

The Irish Labour Party — smoked salmon socialists and mohair Marxists. *Sean Kilroy*

Liberation theology established a toehold in Ireland in 1968. The Pray-In was born. This was the brainchild of a band of ecumenists who were quickly tagged Catholic Marxists, but the antics they provoked didn't recall Karl so much as Groucho. *Damien Corless*

I was in Montpellier at a meeting of the Communist Party. I couldn't afford to buy *Das Kapital*. If they were real communists they would have given it to me. *J. G. Farrell*

I'm a communist by day and a Catholic as soon as it gets dark. *Brendan Behan*

# COMPARISONS

Dealing with Bertie Ahern is like playing handball against a haystack. *Joe Higgins*

Introducing Georgia Salpa to Calum Best was like picking a beautiful rose and throwing it into a pile of shit. *Naomi McElroy*

Have you been watching *The X Factor*? Louis Walsh looks like a cross between the Crazy Frog and an extra from *Last of the Summer Wine*. And he claps like someone trying to catch a fart. *Katherine Lynch*

Sarah Palin has a lot in common with Osama bin Laden. They both support banning gay marriage, bringing God into the classroom, and increasing access to guns. *Abie Philbin Bowman*

Jim Furyk's swing is like an octopus falling out of a tree, or a man trying to kill a snake in a telephone booth. *David Feherty*

He's been breaking Olympic records like ninepins. *Des Lynam*

Ronnie Drew has a voice like a bulldog with a hangover. *Time*

I see Bertie Ahern is now advising the Chinese on their economy. After what he did to ours, that's a bit like Josef Fritzl giving advice on childcare. *Keith Farnan*

Paul Weller is like Victor Meldrew with a suntan. *Noel Gallagher*

Would ye look at the legs on her! Jaysus, they're like spaghetti on drugs. *Paul Ryan*

He looks like a dwarf that fell into a vat of pubic hair. *Boy George on Prince*

I'm a housepainter like Hitler. The only difference is that *Mein Kampf* never ran on the West End like *The Hostage* did. *Brendan Behan*

In ancient Egypt when the pharaohs died, forceps were inserted through their nostrils to pull their brains down from their skulls. I feel roughly the same sensation when I watch golf. *Kevin Myers*

Alex Higgins liked to compare himself to George Best but he was really more like Sid Vicious. **Simon Barnes**

Pierce Brosnan is an exceptionally handsome man but he always reminds me of the models in men's knitwear catalogues. **Paul Haggart**

George Moore's stories impressed me as being on the whole like gruel spooned up off a dirty floor. **Jane Barlow**

Life with Charlie Haughey was like Alice on a night out with Kafka in Wonderland. **P. J. Mara**

Elton John performing a duet with Eminem at the MTV awards is like me singing with Pol Pot. Elton said that Eminem was one of the most important artists of our time. That's like comparing the Sugababes to Aretha Franklin. **Boy George**

Shaw writes like a Pakistani who learned English when he was twelve in order to become a chartered accountant. **John Osborne on George Bernard Shaw**

My wife's snoring sounds like a cat drowning in porridge. **Ed Byrne**

He was about as graceful as a duck on roller skates. **John O'Byrne**

Her mouth was like a garment whose elastic had perished. **Clare Boylan**

I am becoming like the Irish Census: broken down by age, sex and religion. **Séan Mac Réamoinn**

# COMPENSATIONS

A friend's marriage broke up in Ikea. But she managed to pick up some mugs, and a small reading lamp. **Fiona Looney**

The only good thing to come out of tonight is that I got Robbie Keane's jersey. **Northern Ireland winger Niall McGinn after Ireland beat their northern neighbours 5–0 in the Carling Nations Cup in 2011**

My parents accepted me living in sin without a murmur. I think secretly they thought it would ensure that I ate properly. *Kevin Branagh*

By her seemingly effortless ability to be wrong about nearly everything, Andrea Dworkin is an essential guide to the culture and values of our time. *Declan Lynch*

I'm looking for compensation for psychological stress caused by the Barbra Streisand concert. I could hear her singing. *Shane Horgan*

The mechanic said to the car owner: "I couldn't repair your brakes so I made the horn louder." *Ted Bonner*

The only good thing I can say about Maggie Thatcher is that some good music came out of her time in office. *Christy Moore*

As far as I'm concerned, the benefit of being a black Irishman is that I pull more chicks. *Phil Lynott*

I Slept With Colin Farrell And All I Got Was This Lousy T-Shirt. *Shirt slogan spotted in Grafton Street*

What it lacks in excitement it makes up for in its complete lack of excitement. *Dara O'Briain*

A doctor was explaining to an Irishman how nature automatically adjusts to compensate for some physical disabilities. "For example," said the doctor, "if a man is blind, he often develops a keen sense of touch. If he is deaf, he develops his other senses." "I know exactly what you mean," said the Irishman. "I've noticed that if a man has one short leg, then the other leg is always a bit longer." *Nick Harris*

Beckham can't kick with his left foot. He doesn't score any goals. He can't head a ball and he can't tackle. Apart from that he's all right. *George Best*

# COMPROMISE

Swearing is a compromise between fighting and running away. *Finley Peter Dunne*

I was recently offered a TV advertisement by the Irish Tourist Board. I said, "I'll only do it if it presents the Irish in a realistic light. None of this blarney crap." They said, "It's £6,000 English money and you'll be finished by noon." I said, "I'll do it if I can keep the leprechaun suit." *Ian MacPherson*

Compromise is when you both agree she's right. *Ian O'Doherty*

I just saw "Sold Out" on a placard outside a Bob Dylan concert. Wasn't that in 1966 when he went electric? *Hugh Kenny*

I only agreed to appear in a Harry Potter film because my children threatened to disown me if I didn't. *Richard Harris*

It's not who you know, it's who you yes. *James McKeon*

John McCormack wanted to be Pope Pius, Legs Diamond and God, eventually settling for the latter. *Declan Lynch*

# CONFESSIONS

My intentions with women were never honourable. *Eddie Irvine*

I've had poetry readings of two people. *Nuala Ní Dhomhnaill*

Bless me Father, it's a minute since my last confession. *Frank McCourt*

I always keep my psychological baggage sort of half packed. *Liam Neeson*

I'm extremely suggestible. If I hear of anyone else being unwell, I start to develop their symptoms. Which is fine when it's an upset stomach or labour pains, but more of a challenge when it's a twisted testicle. *Marian Keyes*

My idea of recycling is using a beer can as an ashtray. *Richard Harris*

Confession is a rare and wonderful opportunity to be able to go in and talk dirty to a stranger. *Dermot Morgan*

# CONFRONTATION

When I see mothers in supermarkets trying to reason with three-year-olds I want to scream. You can't reason with a three-year-old. You just say, "Put that back, Jason, or I'll break your neck." *Twink*

Where would the Irish be without someone to be Irish at? *Elizabeth Bowen*

I give Herself the odd wallop with a baseball bat. She likes it. It shows I care. She gets me back with the frying pan when I'm dozing in the armchair. That's love. *Richard O'Connor*

Curious hospitality at a Co. Waterford pub when the barman not only took two swigs from a customer's pint but also hit him across the face. Michael Walsh had been tenpence short of the price of a pint so the pub owner decided to deduct what he estimated to be tenpence worth by drinking some of it. When one of Walsh's friends called him an ignorant fucker he gave Walsh two rattles across the face and pushed him off a radiator. **Waterford News & Star**

I'm used to the custard pies. I've even learned to like the taste of them. *Bono*

A defendant in a Wexford court once declared, "I've had seven sons and I've never raised my hand to any of them except in self-defence." *Sean Desmond*

# CONFUSION

I always thought backgammon was a side of bacon. *Spike Milligan*

Ever since Italia '90, every Irishman learned four words of Italian: "Olé, olé, olé, olé". Except they were Spanish. *Niall Toibin*

Moya O'Doherty to London policeman: "When is the next Mass?"
Policeman: "This is the Houses of Parliament."

I'll give that fella credit for one thing — he always pays cash. *Paul Ryan*

"Where were ye when I met ye on the bridge, Mick?"
    "I didn't notice ye as ye passed. Then when I looked around ye'd gone."
*Mr O'S*

Anyone who isn't confused in Northern Ireland doesn't really understand the problem. *John Hume*

I nearly went elsewhere but if I went there I wouldn't be here. *Brian Lenihan*

A heavy breather rang my wife but he didn't know she had asthma. After a few minutes he said, "Did I ring you or did you ring me?" *Frank Carson*

I never swung on a rope with fucking Tarzan. *Maureen O'Hara to a fan who confused her with Maureen O'Sullivan*

Who helps Brooklyn Beckham with his homework? *Michael Cullen*

Mary was a maniokleptic. She used to walk into shops and leave things. *Foggy Spellman*

You're never sure if the ball is going to bounce up or down. *Frank Stapleton*

If there's no God, who made Bono? *Chris Kelleher*

My last girlfriend used to fake an orgasm and pick fault with me at the same time. She went "Ooh!" and then said, "You're not even touching the sides." *Ed Byrne*

# CONSPIRACY THEORIES

No one knows exactly when conspiracy theories came into being but most historians now agree that the moon landings were faked by a secret trinity of JFK, Princess Diana and Elvis so that Marilyn Monroe could be blamed for 9/11. *Kevin McAleer*

Give Vietnam back to the Irish! *Jack MacGowran*

The anti-Bush people are boring because they're always trying to tell you stuff that will make you dislike him even more than you do, which is impossible. They get angry when you tell them you've heard their stories before so then they start making shit up: "Do you know how many people were executed in Texas last year? Fifty-one million. Guess how many of these were young black single mothers? Fifty-eight million. He pushed the button himself." *Dylan Moran*

JR shot John Lennon. *Sean Kilroy*

# CONTRACEPTIVES

Irish grandmothers go on the pill if they don't want any more grandchildren. *Denis O'Dea*

An Irish condom company once agonized about its packaging formats before deciding to present its wares in fours, eights and twelves. The fours were for junior civil servants: Monday, Tuesday, Wednesday, Thursday, and then home to the Mammy in the country for the weekend. The eights were for young urban professionals: Monday, Tuesday, Wednesday,

Thursday, Friday, Saturday and twice on Sunday. The twelves, on the other hand, were for married couples. January, February, March . . . **Tom Doorley**

Wearing a condom means having it off while you're having it on. **Frank Connolly**

I haven't the faintest idea why the Church should promote the strangulation of seed by the rhythm method rather than bouncing it against a piece of rubber. **Peter O'Toole**

My mother's idea of contraception was to prop a sewing machine against the bedroom door. **Sharon Corr**

Did you hear about the new Vatican birth control pills? You take one a night and they give you a headache. **Dave Allen**

Learn from your parents' mistakes. Use birth control. **Spike Milligan**

Guidelines for condoms are stupid. They say, "Slip it on to your member." I didn't know you had to be a member. I thought anyone could use them. **Brendan O'Carroll**

I wouldn't like to leave contraception on the long finger too long. **Jack Lynch**

Every one of the hierarchy should put a condom at the end of his crozier. They wouldn't make as much noise that way. **Padraig Standún**

Using condoms to stop the AIDS virus is ill conceived. **Dr Joseph McCarroll**

Dear Liam, contraception is an evil which has beset mankind for as far back as history records. Those who try to frighten people with demographic arguments should know that the whole population of the world could fit into the wee county of Louth. **Letter to Liam Cosgrove, Ireland's Taoiseach in 1973**

Buy me and stop one. **Message on contraceptive machine**

Italy is a country as devoted to the condom as Holy Communion. **Pól O'Conghaile**

I was amazed to find a condom vending machine in Connolly Station, particularly in view of Iarnrod Eireann's well-earned reputation of always pulling out in time. **Letter to Irish Independent** *on Ireland's railways system*

Priests use altarboys for contraception. **Dave Allen**

Over 155 million contraceptives have been imported into Ireland in recent years. Either a lot of people are using them or some fellow out there is making an awful animal of himself. **Fine Gael TD Bernard Durkan**

# CONTRADICTIONS

My only responsibility is to be irresponsible. **Bono**

I can't change the past. All we're trying to do is clean up the past. **Bertie Ahern**

The term "Irish Secret Service" is as big a contradiction as "British Intelligence". **David Norris**

The term Great Britain is an oxymoron. **Ardal O'Hanlon**

# CONUNDRUMS

We have a giraffe, we have a horse. But where's the horse with the long neck? **Bono**

Do you ever notice it's sick people who end up in hospitals? **Fr Dougal from Father Ted**

Environmentalists tell us every day that rainforests the size of Wales are destroyed. Why is it never Wales? **Jimmy Carr**

Why are a fat chance and a slim chance the same thing? **Cecil Sheridan**

There are three imponderables that dog us all: Who made the world? Would you have the price of a pint? Can I stay at your place tonight? *Christy Moore*

Why should we do anything for posterity? What's posterity ever done for us? *Sir Boyle Roche*

If there were no husbands, who would look after our mistresses? *George Moore*

Why do we never hear about lapsed Protestants? *Jack MacGowran*

Do engine drivers, I wonder, eternally wish they were boys? *Flann O'Brien*

Why is it that people in tubes get so agitated when I train my binoculars on them? *Michael Redmond*

If Betty Ford felt like a drink and knew she shouldn't, what clinic would she have gone to? *Liam Tuohy*

Do chickens get people pox? *Maureen Potter*

What is mind? No matter. What is matter? Never mind. *George Berkeley*

Why does Superglue not stick to the tube? *Dusty Young*

Why isn't the whole plane made out of the stuff they make the black box out of? *Joe Cuddy*

If we aren't supposed to eat animals, why are they made of meat? *Danny Cummins*

How do snorers not wake themselves up? *Ed Byrne*

If the Virgin Mary was assumed bodily into heaven, where does she go to the toilet? *Anne Enright*

Do Parisians play Scrabble with French letters? *Michael Cullen*

If Helen Keller had psychic ability, could you say she had a *fourth* sense? *George Carlin*

A man from Tourmakeady was asked if it was true that the Irish always answered one question with another. "Who told you that?" he said. *Mick Lally*

# COOKING

Her cooking verged on the poisonous. I have known no other woman who could make fried eggs taste like perished rubber. *Hugh Leonard*

I'm not much of a cook. I sometimes boil an egg in a teapot. *Patrick Kavanagh*

If I fry an egg, at the end of the enterprise the kitchen is going to look like a deranged bison that's been doing salsa dancing on every surface. *Terry Prone*

Ireland's main contribution to cosmopolitan cooking is deep fried lard, in which they dip more or less everything except their toenails — and even that's not certain. *Terry Eagleton*

Wanted: Cooker for woman with brown enamel sides. *Ad in trade magazine*

# CORRUPTION

You can't buy Irish politicians. All you can do is rent them. *Gene Kerrigan*

We should be careful not to be smug about the past. Substituting bankers for bishops and credit cards for rosary beads doesn't mean that authoritarian abuses have stopped. We've just swapped cassocks for pinstripes. *Eddie Holt*

Irishmen are against corruption, unless it's a Democrat. *Henry Spalding*

Sufficient unto the day is the evil thereof. *Vincent Dowling*

I'm not a bourgeois decadent yet but I'm saving up for it. *Brendan Behan*

The harp should be replaced by the fiddle as Ireland's national emblem. *Brendan McGahon speaking of social welfare fraud*

Hotel rooms conduce to corruption. The first thing you think when you enter one is, "What's the first thing I'm going to steal?" *Dylan Moran*

# COUNTRIES

I'm starting a campaign to have Finland removed as a country. We don't need it. *George Carlin*

In France, nobody under eighty wears a beret. Even then I'm sure it's only worn by one of those little old actors employed by the government to walk up and down the streets of deserted towns with a baguette under their arm to give the illusion that there are actually people living there. *Terry Wogan*

Jersey is like Tijuana with an excellent Neighbourhood Watch scheme. *Dara O'Briain*

I once asked my father what he thought of New Zealand. He said it looked as if everyone went away for the weekend. *Phelim Drew, son of Ronnie*

Switzerland has produced nothing but theologians and waiters. *Oscar Wilde*

The beaches in Spain are brilliant. They're all near the sea. *Foggy Spellman*

Three million tourists visit San Marino annually, mostly for three hours because that is all the time that is required. *Paul Kilduff*

# COWARDICE

The most distinctive characteristic of the successful politician is selective cowardice. *Richard Harris*

He asked me if I was a man or a mouse. I said, "A man. My wife is afraid of mice." *Danny Cummins*

I'm much more interested in cowards than heroes. *Frank McGuinness*

For karate they gave me a yellow belt. *James McKeon*

I'm a hero with coward's legs. *Spike Milligan*

Hatred is the coward's revenge for being intimidated. *George Bernard Shaw*

My father-in-law asked me if I made love to his daughter like a man on the wedding night or a mouse on the night after. "I did it like a rat," I told him, "on the night before." *Brendan O'Carroll*

# COWS

Paddy's cow took ill and he was inconsolable as he sat beside it in a field, surrounded by his family. "Is she dead?" his son asked him, choking back the tears. "Arrah no," said Paddy, "but d'ye know what it is, she recognizes no one." *Eamon Kelly*

The best way to pass a cow on the road when cycling is to keep behind it. *R. J. Macready*

Pupil: "My father put a sick cow in a hole and shot him."
Paddy Crosbie: "Did he shoot him in the hole?"
Pupil: "No, he shot him in the head."
*Exchange on* **The School Around the Corner**

Who first discovered how to milk a cow? And what in the name of God was he doing at the time? *Pat Ingoldsby*

Farmers aren't really people but we need them to kill cows. *Foggy Spellman*

The reason Irish cream costs so much more than milk is because it's much more expensive to train cows to sit on small bottles. *Bob Monkhouse*

A rich farmer with an ugly daughter can always make her pretty with cows. *Sean Desmond*

I asked a pupil to name four things that contained milk. He said, "Butter, cheese, and two cows." *Bryan McMahon*

# CREATIVE MATHEMATICS

Ireland will give 99 per cent — everything they've got. *Mark Lawrenson*

If Ireland finish with a draw in winning the game, that would be fine. *Jack Charlton*

I once spent a month in Roscommon one weekend. *Arthur Murphy*

If hindsight was foresight we'd all have 50:50 vision. *Bertie Ahern*

We need twenty points from our last four games. *Mark Lawrenson on Oxford United in 1988*

The last time we played England we beat them one-all. *Jim Sheridan on Ireland's "moral" victory over England in 1994*

This is the one in which Carl Lewis goes for the hat-trick of four gold medals. *Terry Wogan*

I'm writing an Irish trilogy. It has four books in it. *Brendan O'Carroll*

One drink is too many for me and a thousand not enough. *Brendan Behan*

If it wasn't for half the people in the world, the other half would be all of them. *Kevin McAleer*

I take an odd drink. One is odd, two is even, three is odd . . . *Sean Kilroy*

In married life three is company and two is none. *Oscar Wilde*

Colin Montgomery couldn't count his balls and get the same answer twice. *David Feherty*

# CRICKET

A lot of people think cricket is deadly boring. What they need is something exciting to watch. Like a little bit being cut off the end of the bat every time the batsman fails to score a run. *Pat Ingoldsby*

It even eclipses playing in the back garden with my son Niall. *Kevin O'Brien after Ireland beat England in the World Cup in 2011*

The reason Sam Beckett was such a miserable old bastard was because he wanted to play cricket for Ireland when he was a kid, and Ireland had, like, the worst cricket team in the world. *Shane MacGowan*

# CRIME

The parish priest came to our school when I was seven and he asked us what we wanted to be when we grew up. I said, "A bandit." *Con Houlihan*

Why do they put photos of criminals up in post offices? Are we supposed to write to them? *Michael Cullen*

You know the crime rate is out of control in Ireland when you can't send kids out on an Easter Egg hunt without dressing them up for *The Hurt Locker*. **Des Ekin**

If crime went down 100 per cent, it would still be fifty times higher than it should be. **John Bowman**

A French writer has paid the English a very well-deserved compliment. He says they have never committed a useless crime. **Patrick Pearse**

I'm not from the working class. I'm from the criminal class. **Peter O'Toole**

The last recorded crime in Liechtenstein was in 1956 when someone working in a government taxation department took a paper clip home from the office without permission. **Paul Kilduff**

Obviously crime pays. What criminal would be stupid enough to go to prison for nothing? **Richard Crowley**

We're told the streets of Dublin aren't safe any more. Really? I think the streets are very safe indeed. I have a few problems with the people that are on them though. **Joe Carmody**

Such is the prevalence of crime in Northern Ireland, it's now known as "Sicily without the sun". **Tony Thompson**

The government should nationalize crime. That way it wouldn't pay. **Kevin Marron**

There's not much crime on the streets of Dublin these days. They make house calls instead. **Hal Roach**

My brother is a criminal lawyer. Aren't they all? **Seamus O'Leary**

# CURES

Use Moses' cure for constipation: take two tablets and go up the mountain. **Larry McCabe**

The best cure for a hangover is to stay drunk. *Ronnie Drew*

My granny had cures for diseases that didn't even exist. *Tom O'Connor*

The best cure for seasickness is to sit under a tree. *Spike Milligan*

There's no cure for alcoholism except to stay in touch with sober alcoholics. *Brendan O'Brien*

"Will he live, doctor?" asked his anxious wife. "I'm afraid not," he answered, "but you'll have the satisfaction of knowing he died cured." *Tony Butler*

Why do we wait until a pig is dead to cure it? *Danny Cummins*

My greatest ambition is to find the ultimate cure for a hangover. *Terry Keane*

# CUSTOMS

I have nothing to declare but my genius. *Oscar Wilde at Customs after coming off a ferry*

I have nothing to declare but my penis. *Brendan Behan in similar circumstances*

Mary and Josephine go to England for a few days. Mary buys a skunk and wants to bring it back to Dublin but Josephine warns her they'll never let it through Customs. As they get to the airport Josephine asks Mary what she's going to do with it. Mary says, "Put it down my knickers." "What about the smell?" asks Josephine. Mary says, "If it dies, it dies." *Bono*

# CYNICISM

It's not that the Irish are cynical. It's rather that they have a wonderful lack of respect for everything and everybody. **Brendan Behan**

Evelyn Waugh was a misanthrope, but could be excused because he never got over having been christened with a girl's name. If a man called Evelyn is reading this he will probably hit me with his hockey stick. **Hugh Leonard**

Ireland has contributed nothing but a whine to the literature of Europe. **James Joyce**

There are two types of people in this world — those who wish Jeremy Clarkson a long, lingering death and those who would simply get the job done quickly. **Ian O'Doherty**

Years ago, if you were getting near to finding out how the government was on the fiddle you were called a Red. Now they've got a new word: Cynic. Well I'm a cynic and fucking proud of it. **Ronnie Drew**

When a true genius appears in the world you may know him by his sign: the dunces are all in confederacy against him. **Jonathan Swift**

Poor old Bob Geldof. Little did he know when he wrote his autobiography *Is That It?* that the title would be so prescient. **Brendan O'Connor**

# THE DÁIL

*The Dáil is the Irish seat of government.*

The Dáil has a valuable therapeutic function insofar as it keeps a number of potentially dangerous men off the public streets. **Donal Foley**

"About half of them." *Sean Lemass after being asked by a visiting journalist how many people worked in the Dáil.*

A resident shrink for the Dáil mightn't be such a bad idea. *Brendan McGahon*

The Dáil is the only place in Ireland where the Civil War is still going on. *John B. Keane*

Mystery surrounds the incident where a man had to be restrained by ushers as he tried to get into the Dáil. But why should we be surprised? He obviously heard that people in there get 100,000 euros a year for sitting on their arses. *Pat Flanagan*

# DANCING

The secret of doing the waltz properly is to behave as if your partner has BO. *Gloria Hunniford*

The priest at my school used to follow us to dances. He'd come between me and the girl I was dancing with and say "You have to keep this far apart" as he indicated his ruler. Presumably he was imagining my penis to be the same size. I always thought he was an incredible optimist. *Dave Allen*

Michael Flatley reminds me of someone with a spud stuck up his arse who's trying to squeeze it out without using his hands. *David Feherty*

A Florida court has ruled that exotic dancers must cover one-third of their buttocks. If only they could pass the same law for the cable guy we'd be in great shape. *Conan O'Brien*

When Ginger Rogers danced with Fred Astaire, it was the only time in movies when you looked at the man, not the woman. *Gene Kelly*

Only one part of the body must not move during an Irish dance — the bowels. *Jack McHale*

Irish people don't dance. They just stand in the same place and eventually start jumping up and down as if they hated the floor. *Keith Farnan*

The reason dogs aren't good dancers is because they have two left feet. *Val Doonican*

Riverdance created the idea that the Irish have become a sexy people. We're not. We're still the pot-bellied ugly bastards we always were. *Roddy Doyle*

I know one way to make my children scatter instantly. Get up and dance. *Terry Wogan*

He asked me if he could have the last dance. I told him he'd already had it. *Clare Boylan*

Dancing always seems to me to be superfluous. I'm ridiculous enough without it. *Oliver St John Gogarty*

Dancing is the perpendicular expression of a horizontal desire. *George Bernard Shaw*

A Kerry family of eleven invented the Charleston. They had only one toilet. *Laura Stack*

# DATING

Dates are only for the police. *Brendan Behan*

I indulge in serial monogamy. That's when you go out with one other person and they dump you. *Graham Norton*

The fellas today start off where the fellas of my time finished. *Eileen Reid*

Oisin has pulled this Aussie bird called Shona. If I called her a dog I'd have the ISPCA on my case for cruelty to animals. *Ross O'Carroll-Kelly*

John Wayne Bobbitt is now dating a bulimic. It's a perfect match. She can't keep anything down and he can't keep anything up. *Eilis O'Hanlon*

Dating a single father of three is never going to be a picnic, but nor does it need to be the opening twenty minutes of *Saving Private Ryan* with facepaints. ***Graham Norton***

For three years everything was going great between me and my girlfriend, but then she just upped and left me for a guy who wouldn't hit her. ***Jim Norton***

I don't have a girlfriend at the moment. I'm engaged to Inter Milan. ***Robbie Keane in 2000***

Girls are dynamite. If you don't believe that, try dropping one. ***Cecil Barror***

He told the therapist all five of his brothers were gay. The therapist asked him if anyone in his family dated women. "Yeah," he said, "me sisters!" ***Donal Creedon***

You're finished with nineteen-year-old girls the moment you bring the word "cholesterol" into a conversation. ***Dara O'Briain***

She who hesitates is won. ***Oscar Wilde***

Oh, the platonic bridges we've burned in the name of not going home alone. ***Róisín Ingle***

My sister went out with the captain of the chess team in high school. My parents loved him. They figured that any guy who took two hours to make a move was OK with them. ***Brian Kiley***

Courtship in Ireland is the period during which a girl decides whether or not she can do any better. ***Sean Desmond***

I have almost done with harridans, and shall soon become old enough to fall in love with girls of fourteen. ***Jonathan Swift***

When I reached the age of going out with men I was chaste because I was unchased. ***Terry Prone***

Bridget and Sean had been walking out for all of nineteen years. It was time they did something, so one passionate night Bridget says to Sean, "Sean my love, do you think 'tis time we got married?" "Arrah, 'tis to be sure, Bridget," Sean replied, "but who'd have us now?" ***Owen Kelly***

My ideal Valentine's date would be Marlon Brando over a candlelit dinner. **Colin Farrell**

Jeremy O'Hagan was carrying a torch for Fiona McManus but he wanted to see her before he spent money on a blind date. **Peter Cagney**

I joined a dating agency and went out on a load of dates that didn't work out. I went back to the woman who ran the agency and said, "Have you not got somebody on your books who doesn't care about how I look and has a nice big pair of tits?" She checked her computer and said, "Actually we have, but unfortunately it's you." **Karl Spain**

# DEATH

People die here but they're not permitted to grow old. **Hugh Leonard on the Dublin suburb of Dalkey**

Kim Jong-Il? Kim Jong-Dead. **Declan Lynch**

A great Irishman has passed away. God grant that many as great will follow him. **Obituary of Baron Dowse in The Times**

I plan to live to a ripe old age. In fact I'm planning to be the first person not to die. **Shane MacGowan**

If you're going to die, it is important to die of the right thing. No one in Ireland wants to die from cancer. Anything else will do. **David Slattery**

Fr Ted: "Someone I know is dying."
Fr Dougal: "Is it serious?"
**Father Ted**

I once heard a rumour that I died but it turned out to be someone else, much to my relief. **Eamon Kelly**

You haven't lived until you've died in Dublin. **Eamonn Mac Thomáis**

My grandad died in his rocking chair. I was five. I didn't know it would keel over when I climbed on the back. *Michael Redmond*

Even death is unreliable. Instead of zero it may be some ghastly hallucination, such as the square root of minus one. *Samuel Beckett*

I think about death all the time. I can't help it. I'm Irish. *Jack Nicholson*

In Ireland, radio is local to the nth degree. The most popular programmes are the death notices. Marriages and births come a poor second. *Terry Wogan*

My grandmother made dying her life's work. *Hugh Leonard*

I intend to die in bed at 110 writing poetry, sipping Guinness and serenading a woman. *Richard Harris*

"D'ye know what it is, Janey," he said, "there are people dyin' now that never died before." *Eamon Kelly*

Uncle Joe drank a bottle of varnish and died. He had a bad end but a lovely finish. *Frank Carson*

Dying penniless is usually regarded as a bad thing. As far as I'm concerned it's bloody good timing. *Cyril Cusack*

# DEDICATION

No alcoholic is more dedicated to his cause than an Irish one. It's almost like a religion. No less than total commitment will do or you're not accepted into the club. *Brendan Kennelly*

I played Bob Dylan's "Highway 61 Revisited" until the batteries ran out. I don't really know it yet. How could I? I've only been listening to it for twenty-two years. *Roddy Doyle*

Frank Duff was the head of the Legion of Mary, a religious organization dedicated to inanity and the making of tea. *Anne Enright*

In 1982 an airliner prepared for an emergency landing after it suddenly developed violent vibrations. Eventually the cause was traced to a super-keen jogger who'd locked himself in the toilet so he could do an hour's running on the spot. **Des Lynam**

Not many people ask for the latest Exchequer figures when dealing with respiratory failure, but he did. **Mark Fitzgerald on his father Garret, Ireland's former Taoiseach, who died in 2011**

# DEFINITIONS

Being drunk is feeling sophisticated without being able to pronounce it. **Niall Toibin**

Rock and roll is the sound of grown men throwing tantrums. **Bono**

An Irish gentleman may be defined as someone who'll hold the door open while his wife is taking the bins out. **Donal McCann**

An adult is just a tall child holding a beer. **Dylan Moran**

Golf is the cocaine of the correct, the rock-and-roll of the elderly. **Niall Toibin**

P. G. Wodehouse is English literature's performing flea. **Sean O'Casey**

A teenager is just an old person with sixty years deducted. **Pat Ingoldsby**

Ireland is a village in Trieste with Joyce, Devon with Sean O'Casey, Paris with Sam Beckett, Wilde in Reading Gaol – and an elderly degenerate proselytizing umbilical lasso known as the Archbishop of Dublin. **Brendan Behan**

Homosexuality is nature's attempt to get rid of the soft boys by sterilizing them. **F. Scott Fitzgerald**

An Irish ruffian is a man who would sharpen a knife on his father's tombstone to cut his mother's throat. **Blarney** *magazine*

"Mortgage" comes from the Latin word meaning "death". **Keith Farnan**

Home Rule is the art of minding your own business well. Unionism is the art of minding someone else's business badly. **Tom Kettle**

Foreplay, in Ireland, is the technical term for taking your socks off. **Joe O'Connor**

Golf is a game in which a ball one and a half inches in diameter is placed on a ball eight thousand miles in diameter, the object being to hit the small ball but not the larger one. **John Cunningham**

Habit is the ballast that chains a dog to his vomit. **Samuel Beckett**

A literary movement is five or six people who live in the same town and hate each other. **George Russell**

Mahatma Gandhi was a super-callused fragile mystic hexed by halitosis. **Stewart Flanagan**

Satire is a kind of glass wherein beholders generally discover everybody's face but their own. **Jonathan Swift**

A perfectionist is one who takes great pains – and then gives them to everyone else. **Pat Spillane**

# DELUSIONS

Lennox Robinson was often the worse for sherry. He once queued patiently for two hours for the Bing Crosby film *Going My Way* at the Capitol Cinema while under the impression he was waiting for the Dalkey tram. **Hugh Leonard**

In LA, people think that if they get wealthy and successful enough they won't die. **Gabriel Byrne**

To write is impossible but not yet impossible enough. That's how I cod myself these days. *Samuel Beckett*

Monk Gibbon saw Yeats as an unsavoury and all-powerful building contractor in the Bronx. *Conor Cruise O'Brien*

They say I slept with seven Miss Worlds. That's untrue. It was only four. I didn't turn up for the other three. *George Best*

# DENIAL

Ireland is now in danger of moving from Celtic Tiger to Celtic Ostrich. *David McWilliams*

# DEPENDENCY

I was so mean to my old boyfriend. He went to Co-dependents Anonymous and I used to page him there. *Mary O'Halloran*

Bob Dylan may soon have to rely on a Zimmerman frame. *Michael Cullen*

Nothing tarnishes the sheen of chemical co-dependency more than the mundane business of everyday life. Bills, grocery shopping, bills, house-cleaning, bills, the toilet seat being up, bills, his dodgy friends, bills, your friends that he doesn't like. And did I mention bills? *Anne Marie Scanlon*

# DEPRESSION

Nothing is more depressing than not having a reason for being depressed. *Tom Galvin*

They've now approved a Prozac-type drug for dogs who are depressed. This is good because it's hard for dogs to get therapy. They're never allowed on the couch. **Colin Quinn**

Seamus: "The best way to cure depression is to soap your arse and slide backwards down a rainbow."
Patrick: "I know. I tried it once but I got impaled on a leprechaun."
**Internet joke**

When people go to the doctor suffering from depression they give them anti-depressants. One of the side-effects is impotence. This makes you even more depressed. So they give you more anti-depressants. By this stage you're impotent and totally celibate as well as depressed. The only job that's open for you now is Pope. **Dave Allen**

Depression is so bad in Ireland at the moment, I hear the Samaritans are going ex-directory. **Maureen Potter**

Tom Cruise says there's no such thing as depression, that you can get better with physical exercise. Maybe he's right. Beating the shit out of Tom Cruise would be physical all right, and it would cheer me up. **David Feherty**

# DEPRIVATION

Due to government cutbacks, the light at the end of the tunnel has been cut off. **Ed Byrne**

Having guzzled his way through the day at Stansted and slurped his fill of wine on the flight, there were some difficult moments for Shane MacGowan on the touchdown at Dublin. He had to walk all the way from his airplane seat to the arrivals area without a drink. **Liam Fay**

I went on a diet once for two weeks but all I lost was a fortnight. **Derek Davis**

She is chaste who was never asked the question. *William Congreve*

I gave up smoking for Lent once. It was the longest half-hour of my life. *Brendan O'Connor*

# THE DEVIL

I am between the devil and the Holy See. My task is to prevent the Californication of Ireland. *Former Irish film censor James Montgomery*

A priest says to a man on his deathbed, "My son, do you renounce the devil and all his teachings?" The dying man replies, "With all respect, Father, this is really not the time to be making enemies." *Dave Allen*

May you be in heaven half an hour before the devil knows you're dead. *Old Irish blessing*

My mother used to be in the bridge club. Now people point at her in the supermarket and go, "There she is, that's the woman who spawned the devil child. She's had the devil inside her." My poor, poor mother. *Graham Norton*

I'll have a drink with the devil occasionally but I'm not moving in with him. I have too much respect for him to fuck with him. *Bono*

Did you hear about the man who couldn't keep up the payments to his exorcist? He was repossessed. *Noel V. Ginnity*

I made a bargain with the devil. I'd be famous and he'd get to fuck my sister. *George Carlin*

# DIETS

She'd been dieting very seriously and died of shortness of breath. *Tony Butler*

The second day of a diet is easier than the first because by then you're off it. *Jackie Gleason*

Doctor: "How is your husband doing with the diet I gave him?"
Wife: "Wonderful. He disappeared last week."
*Laura Stack*

I'm living proof that dieting makes you fat. *Marian Keyes*

Posh Spice stopped eating in the delivery room after her first child arrived and hasn't started again since. The mother of three claims seaweed wraps helped her regain her figure, but that sounds too much like food for me. *Róisín Gorman*

I've written a diet book. It's called *Put That Down, Fatty. Jimmy Carr*

My wife went on a fish diet. She didn't lose any weight and now she won't eat anything else but worms. *Gene Fitzpatrick*

I settled down to address my weight problem. One guy said that injections of the urine of pregnant women had worked wonders for a friend of his. There was the "Dr This" diet and the "Dr That" diet. There was the California diet, the Miami diet and the Westchester diet. I didn't know if I was going to lose weight or take a tour of the country. *Malachy McCourt*

I'm on a diet. That means I just eat two cream buns with my tea now instead of four. *Gerry Ryan*

I'm so neurotic I worry I'm going to lose weight when I go on a diet. *Grace Malloy*

I've been on the Slimfast plan. For breakfast you have a shake. For lunch you have a shake. For dinner you kill anyone with food on their plate. *Rosie O'Donnell*

# DIRECTIONS

She asked me if I could direct her to the Balbriggan stud. "My dear," I informed her, "I *am* the Balbriggan stud." *Brendan O'Carroll*

Never ask an English person for directions. They're too polite to tell you if they don't know the way and will send you somewhere else instead — usually Wales. *Joe O'Connor*

American tourist to Reilly: "Where's the nearest toilet?"
Reilly: "Anywhere between here and Athlone."
*Frank Hall*

I asked a man for directions once when I was in Wicklow. "Do you see that road?" he said. "Well, don't take that." *Ray McAnally*

A short cut is the longest distance between two points. *Murphy's Law*

Many a man that couldn't direct you to the drugstore on the corner when he was thirty will get a respectful hearing when age has further impaired his mind. *Finley Peter Dunne*

The tourist asked the Irishman how far it was to the hotel. "It's about a fifteen-minute walk," he told him, "if you run like hell." *Peter Hornby*

A couple of American tourists in Dublin ask a local person, "Excuse me, is that Christchurch over there?" The Dubliner says, "Well as far as I know they're *all* his." *Peter Quinn*

The likelihood of getting lost in Ireland is directly proportional to the number of times the direction-giver says, "You can't miss it." *Hal Roach*

The nearest hotel is over five miles in one direction and practically twelve in the opposite one. *Patrick Myler*

# DISEASES

When Ronald Reagan got Alzheimer's disease, how could they tell? *George Carlin*

Wouldn't you rather die of VD than old age? *Eithne Tynan*

Irish Alzheimer's means you forget everything but the grudges. *Ulick O'Connor*

For the older Irish man or woman who forgoes the more traditional choice of heart attack or massive stroke, there is still the option of Type 2 Diabetes, which is currently the rage. Back when we were all too poor to live to be old, only the elite could afford diabetes. Now it's within practically every Irish person's reach. *David Slattery*

Celibacy is now being quoted by some doctors as a disease. I am waiting for some senators to propose a law against it. *Fr Denis Faul in 1971*

I don't see alcoholism as a disease. You can walk away from the bottle. You can't walk away from cancer. You can't even walk away from dandruff. *Frank McCourt*

I like going to doctors so they can investigate me for diseases I don't have. *Tommy Tiernan*

Ireland is a fatal disease from which it is the plain duty of every Irishman to disassociate himself. *George Moore*

Does your epileptic fit or would you have to take it in a bit at the sides? *Jason Byrne*

I'd hate to be an alcoholic with Alzheimer's. Imagine pouring a drink and then forgetting where you put it. *Ronnie Drew*

# DISILLUSIONMENT

I lost my faith in rock stars in 1971 when I discovered The Grateful Dead took out life insurance. **Paddy Woodworth**

I'm so discouraged, sometimes I wish Noah built the *Titanic*. **Jimeoin**

I wish I was what I used to be when I wished I was what I am. **Tom Finlay**

After ten years of saving the whale we decided to forget the whale and concentrate on the bank account. **Larry Mullen on U2 in 1992**

# DIVORCE

Divorces are made in heaven. **Oscar Wilde**

You only have to mumble a few words in church to get married, and a few words in your sleep to get divorced. **Hal Roach**

A judge at an Irish divorce case gave his summing-up speech: "The Court awards your wife £50 a week." "That's very decent of you, Your Honour," Paddy shot up, "Sure maybe I'll even throw in a few bob myself." **Sean McCann**

I'm pretty sure my wife would divorce me if she could find some way of doing it that wouldn't make me happy. **Joe Cuddy**

I heard of a couple aged ninety and ninety-one respectively who were seeking a divorce. Asked by reporters on the steps of the courthouse why they'd waited so long they replied, "We were waiting for the children to die." **Joe O'Connor**

I've lost forty pounds since Christmas — 150 if you include the wife. **David Feherty after his divorce**

When I got divorced I went through the various stages of grieving: anger, denial, dancing round my settlement cheque . . . *Maura Kennedy*

My aunt always said divorce was worse than murder. *Edna O'Brien*

# DOCTORS

I wonder why you can always read a doctor's bill but never his prescription. *Finley Peter Dunne*

There is something splendidly Irish and reassuringly idiotic in staying away from the doctor because of illness. *Owen Kelly*

The Irish are fixated on drink. If an Irishman goes to a doctor with arthritis and he gets a prescription for some pills, his first question is, "Can I drink with these?" *Ardal O'Hanlon*

I went to the doctor and he told me I was suffering from hypochondria. "Not that as *well*," I said. *Jimmy O'Dea*

A man went to a doctor. The doctor said, "I can find nothing wrong with you. It must be the drink." "It's all right," the man said, "I'll come back when you're sober." *Shaun Connors*

Paddy: "Doctor, doctor, I'm haemorrhaging."
Doctor: "Where are you bleedin' from?"
Paddy: "Dublin."
*Bal Moane*

Doctors are all Puritans. *Samuel Beckett*

In the new Ireland we can't afford doctors – only spin doctors. *Pat Flanagan*

Men just won't go to the doctor. Even if their leg falls off they say, "Ah, I'm grand. I never really used it anyway." *Marian Keyes*

It is important not to have any tests when you go to the doctor because he may find something wrong with you. *David Slattery*

The doctor said to his patient, "I have some good news and some bad news. The good news is that you have twenty-four hours to live." The patient says, "What's the bad news?" The doctor says, "I should have told you yesterday." *Frank Carson*

I said to the doctor, "How do I stand?" He said, "It puzzles me as well." *Din Joe*

An epileptic had a fit in my apartment. The paramedics asked me what kind of a fit it was. I told them I hadn't much to compare it with but as a layman I'd give it about seven out of ten. *Sean Hughes*

Notice in Dublin doctor's waiting room: "Will patients please not exchange symptoms as it confuses the doctor". *Kevin Murtie*

I hate doctors. They'll do anything, anything, to keep you coming to them. They'll sell their souls. What's worse, they'll sell yours. And you'll never know it till one day you'll find yourself in hell. *Eugene O'Neill*

Doctors who play golf have one advantage over the rest of us. Nobody can read their scorecards. *Foggy Spellman*

Receptionists in doctors' surgeries are there to protect the doctor. "I'd like to see the doctor please." "Why?" "Well I was hoping he'd help me change the tyres of the bloody car!" *Dave Allen*

Last week I told my doctor my right arm ached whenever I lifted it. He replied, "Stop lifting it then." *Hugh Leonard*

The doctors say I'm an interesting case and generally patronize my belly. To think I used once to write plays. Now I'm just a bunch of interesting bowels. *John Millington Synge*

A man went to the doctor with a strawberry growing out of his head. The doctor said, "I'll give you some cream for that." *Marty Whelan*

# DOGS

If you want to keep your dog in line, walk him past the fur shop a couple of times a week. *George Carlin*

The real test for a dogfood salesman is whether he'll eat his product for his customers. *Albert Reynolds*

Did you hear about the dog who went to the flea circus? He stole the show. *Jack Cruise*

My dog's been eating garlic. His bark is worse than his bite. *Paul Malone*

My new dog Madge is a small terrier but on occasion she emits a smell like low tide in an industrial town in Eastern Europe. *Graham Norton*

Our dog Jack was anti-clerical. *Hugh Leonard*

A man put an ad in the *Cork Examiner* for a lost dog. When it came time to pay the bill he refused. "That dog came back on his own," he insisted. *Niall Toibin*

My dog is half Labrador, half pit bull. She bites off my leg and then brings it back to me. *Frank Carson*

Every dog has its day but only a dog with a broken tail has a weak end. *Seamus O'Leary*

Why is it that when the doorbell rings, the dog always thinks it's for him? *Noel V. Ginnity*

There's one difference between a poodle and a Rottweiler peeing on your shoe. You let the Rottweiler finish. *Joe Cuddy*

Seamus: "My dog's a mathematical genius."
Liam: "How can you tell?"
Seamus: "Every time I ask him what five minus three minus two is, he says nothing."
*Duncan Crosbie*

I've named my dogs Rolex and Timex. They're watchdogs.
*Pat Spillane*

Children know too much nowadays. My daughter saw two dogs having sex one day and asked me what was happening. I told her one dog had sore paws and the other one was giving him a lift home. She said, "Isn't it always the way? You try to do a favour for someone and end up getting fucked." *Brendan O'Carroll*

# DOMESTICITY

A friend of mine told me how to avoid doing jobs for the wife. "Put a red sock in with the washing when it's time for all whites," he advised, "she'll never ask you again." *Chris Barry*

You can't help feeling that if the Eamon de Valera generation had stayed home and changed the occasional nappy, Ireland might have been better off. *Joe O'Connor*

Hillary Clinton said that while Bill was testifying in the Paula Jones case, she was doing some household chores. Little things like sewing the President's pants to his shirts. *Conan O'Brien*

What is a teapot? *John Millington Synge*

Q. How can you tell if your wife is dead?
A. The sex is the same but the dishes are higher in the sink. *Brendan Grace*

One should not look to poets for handy hints. W. B. Yeats had trouble walking properly, let alone boiling an egg without cracking it. *Craig Brown*

I bought a non-stick frying pan a week ago but I can't get the label off. *Noel V. Ginnity*

The thing that irritates me most in life is burnt toast. It ruins my day if I get it for breakfast. Occasionally my cook has a domestic problem and I think she takes it out on my toast. *Micheál MacLiammóir*

I'm not much good around the house. When something malfunctions I tell my wife, "Get a man. Don't disturb me. I'm in my room listening to show tunes. Don't try to get in. I've blocked the door with Turkish Delights." **Dylan Moran**

I hate domesticity. You clean, you dust, you iron . . . and then six months later you have to do it all over again. **Rosaleen Linehan**

My wife said, "I'm sick of these four walls." So I knocked one of them down. **Joe Cuddy**

The last time I washed dishes was in the mid-seventies. **The Edge**

A man went to the doctor. He said, "Get up on the couch." The man said, "Why?" The doctor said, "I want to sweep the floor." **Marty Whelan**

# DRAMA

Drama for me is about not getting on. **Chris O'Dowd**

Most dramas have beginnings, middles and ends, but soap operas just have middles. **Wesley Burrowes**

I was in the school Nativity play as a child. I was supposed to play the donkey but that was boring so I put on my Batman costume instead. I wanted to save the day so I gave Mary an epidural. I even gave myself a line: "Push when you're ready, Mrs Christ." **Gearóid Farrelly**

The trouble with dramatists today is that they try to make life out of drama instead of drama out of life. **Sean O'Casey**

Irish drama rules O'Casey. **Graffiti**

# DRAMA CRITICS

Drama critics are there to show gay actors what it's like to have a wife. *Hugh Leonard*

Like all good drama critics, we retired to the pub across the road. *Eric Cross*

A drama critic is a man who leaves no turn unstoned. *George Bernard Shaw*

Drama critics stone the cast first. *Lennox Robinson*

# DREAMS

I had a dream last night that I was in bed with Marti Pellow. It was my first Wet Wet Wet dream. *Carol Tobin*

The Old Irish Dream was of Catholicism, nationalism, community, chastity, the Brits, the six counties, the Irish language, the famine, the underdog, getting a good job in the bank and the glamour of Grace Kelly. The New Irish Dream can best be summed up by "I want the biggest fridge, the best holiday, the newest car, the loudest sound system, the healthiest food, the best yoga posture, the most holistic world-view, the most talked-about wedding and the best sex with as many partners, in as many positions, as possible". *David McWilliams*

I used to dream about taking the ball round the keeper, stopping it on the line and then getting down on my hands and knees and heading it into the net. *George Best*

Hens dream. You can hear this for yourself if you eavesdrop. *Con Houlihan*

Life is perhaps most wisely regarded as a bad dream between two awakenings. *Eugene O'Neill*

Dreams work strangely. One minute you're in Casablanca with Cindy Crawford, the next you're in Castlepollard with Michael Crawford. *Joe O'Connor*

In dream language a large brown bear with a Bible on its head, shouting obscenities from a boat, means fear of intimacy with an Austrian, while a strong desire to kick the backside of someone who has deliberately stubbed out a cigarette in your mouth remains the universal symbol of either drowning slowly in a bath of organic brown rice or losing your car keys, depending on the cigarette. *Kevin McAleer*

The following conversation was overheard in Phoenix Park. "Do you dream of me, Michael?" "Ah Kate, my darlin', I can't sleep for dreamin' of ye." *Sean Desmond*

# DRINK AND DRINKING

There's only one thing to be said in favour of drink. It's caused many a lady to be loved that otherwise might have died single. *Finley Peter Dunne*

Drinking releases the inhibitions. And, hopefully, the bra strap. *Richard Harris*

I wasn't feeling myself so I went to the doctor. He told me to take a glass of hot milk after a bath. That was three weeks ago. I'm still drinking the hot bath. *Letter quoted by Jimmy Cricket*

I'm not a steady drinker. My hand shakes too much. *Josef Locke*

Drinking removes warts and pimples. Not from me but people I'm looking at. *Jackie Gleason*

Tobacco and alcohol warnings are too general. They should be more to the point: "People who smoke will eventually cough up small brown pieces of lung." And, "Warning: Alcohol will turn you into the same arsehole your father was!" *George Carlin*

Drinking in Ireland involves standing at the bar for long periods of time, followed by carrying back to the table (in one go) five pints, eight shorts with accompanying mixers, two large bottles of cider with accompanying glasses of ice, and three glasses of wine, one white and two red. You can hold the six packets of Tayto between your teeth. *David Slattery*

Mrs Doyle (with teapot): "What would you say to a cup, Father?" Fr Jack: "Feck off, cup!"
**Father Ted**

The Irish are the greatest tea drinkers in the world, with the result that home visits always turn into long tea-drinking sessions. Tea is a diuretic so remember to pick up your dirty underwear from the bathroom floor before the guests arrive. *Tadhg Hayes*

My father worried more about me ending up in a retail job in Burberry's than he did about me being an alcoholic. *Des Bishop*

The French drink for cuisine, the Irish for lining. *Michael Mee*

It is still common to see people running around the streets in a panic on Good Friday, gasping for an illegal drink, despite their own stockpiles at home. Everyone knows that a legal drink is not the same thing. Because the pub is supposed to be closed, being locked in produces a special social bond amongst the customers not available during normal opening hours. *David Slattery*

The only times I drink are when I'm thirsty and when I amn't. *Shane MacGowan*

When I think of the hardship involved in only having seven hours to drink on a Sunday my soul shudders. *Kevin O'Higgins inaugurating a Liquor Bill in the Irish Parliament in 1927*

I have a drink problem. I don't have enough money to pay for it. *Foggy Spellman*

Maloney tried desperately to give up the booze but in the end the demon drink conquered him. All he could do was keep getting his knees soled and heeled. *Peter Cagney*

Kevin is terrified of running out of drink at Christmas. He doesn't care how many people call around to his house as long as he has enough gargle to kill each and every one of them. Industry experts predict that by early December every year he is in a position to manipulate the Irish market in Carlsberg. **Pat Fitzpatrick**

Customer 1: "I was out for a few drinks last night and I woke up sneezing this morning."
Customer 2: "That's what you get for drinking out of a damp glass."
**Short Back and Sides**

You know you've had too much to drink when you go to bed with Liz Hurley and wake up with Red Hurley. **Bal Moane; Red Hurley is a — male! — Irish cabaret singer**

One in four Irish people never touch a drink, which makes the statistical achievements of the rest of them all the more impressive. **Frank McNally**

Scobie McCann was the first young fella I ever saw drunk. It was the day after his mother's wedding. **Brendan O'Carroll**

I used to have forty-six-inch hips before I started drinking low-fat milk. Now I have forty-six-inch knees. **Hal Roach**

Did you hear about the Irish vampire? He only drinks Bloody Marys. **Din Joe**

Drink is the curse of Ireland. If it isn't whiskey it's porter and if it isn't porter it's tea. Tea is the worst of the lot. The tea drunkards of Ireland. **St John Ervine**

Ben Kiely confided to me that one afternoon between O'Connell Street and the White Horse bar, a distance of less than seventy-five yards, no less than fourteen people invited him to have a drink. **Bill Kelly**

I didn't turn to drink. It seemed to turn to me. **Brendan Behan**

One tequila, two tequila, three tequila, *floor*. **Phil Lynott**

I drink like a fish. The only difference is we drink different stuff. **Brendan Behan**

Better belly burst than liquor be lost. **Jonathan Swift**

I was so drunk last night, the only way I could find out what I did was by trawling through my pub receipts. They went "Whiskey, whiskey, whiskey" and then "Whiskey and white wine". Christ, I thought, I pulled. So where is she? Then I checked some more. "Whiskey, whiskey, double whiskey . . . kebab". *Keith Farnan*

What does an alky do when his shit is bouncing off the walls? He phones another alky and they talk about fucking booze. *Lee Dunne*

I could sail the *QE2* to the Falklands on all the liquor I drank. *Richard Harris*

Murphy went to a pub that was offering "All you can drink for £10". "Give me £20 worth of that," he said. *Joe Cuddy*

There's only one thing worse than drinking. Thirst. *Mick Lally*

I would like to have drinking hours altered so that public houses will be permitted to open only between two and five in the morning. This means that if you are a drinking man you'll have to be in earnest about it. *Flann O'Brien*

If you drink enough wine you'll say things like, "Let's go potholing in Croatia. I think I know someone who'll drive us. Me." *Dylan Moran*

I hate the stereotyping of the Irish as a nation of drunks. I actually know two people who don't drink. Admittedly they're recovering alcoholics. *Ian Coppinger*

Not standing your round is a mortal sin in my family. There's always great competition to out-give and out-convivialize all the others. Hand-to-hand combat almost breaks out as people try to be the first to get to the bar. *Marian Keyes*

You never forget your first drink. That maiden sip was a rite of passage as psychologically important to the business of growing up as realizing that your parents were still "at it" occasionally, despite being older than dinosaurs, or that Timmy wasn't really sent off to live on a farm with the other dogs, he was actually put to sleep as a radical solution to some minor incontinence issues. *Eilis O'Hanlon*

# DRIVING

Always use hand signals when you're driving your car. The index and forefinger usually get the best results. *Brendan O'Connor*

I say, old son, you're doing very well, but should you be trying to change gear with the handbrake? *Hugh Griffith to Peter O'Toole during a holiday in the west of Ireland*

When you're doing your driving test for the forty-fourth time you don't give a shit any more. The examiner said to me, "I thought I told you to turn right there." I said, "You did, but I'm going to Wales instead to visit my sister. I told her I'd have a friend with me." *Michael Redmond*

The cardinal rule for driving in Ireland is: when in doubt, accelerate. *David Monaghan*

If you make a left turn from a right-hand lane you're probably just careless, and not at all what the driver behind called you. *Hal Roach*

"Now is when the dangerous part of your journey begins," the Southwest Airlines pilot says, "Please be careful driving home." *Terry Prone*

When my mother-in-law is driving the car and holds out her hand you can be sure of three things: she's going to turn left, right or just stop. *Des MacHale*

The potholes in Monaghan are so big, if motorists drive in a straight line the Gardai think they're drunk. *Michael Cullen*

The main curse of life is that when you're learning golf you hit nothing and when you're learning motoring you hit everything. **Dublin Opinion**

Then there was the Kerry girl who won all the top prizes for rock-and-roll. She drove a tractor with a loose seat every day to the creamery. *Laura Stack*

Detour – Drive Sideways. *Sign spotted in Co. Kilkenny*

As a rule I am so bored by driving I find it reviving to be frightened. *Edith Somerville*

Driving is a barbarous Irish custom, at least in the capital. Not having been to war for ages, the Irish have taken instead to massacring each other on the highways. *Terry Eagleton*

Have a drive in one of our cars and you'll never walk again. *Sign in garage*

It's safe to cross the streets in Switzerland. When I step within ten feet of a zebra crossing, irrespective of whether I intend to use it or not, all cars within a five-mile radius grind to a screeching halt. *Paul Kilduff*

There are drivers out there who would drive up to the second floor of Brown Thomas and park their cars in the Menswear section. *Ciaran Cuffe*

I filled the car with petrol, which cost only the proceeds from the sale of my firstborn, and drove into the centre of town. *Joe O'Connor*

# DROWNING

A hotel manager on the Costa del Sol told me he kept a lifeguard on duty all night because he was sick of coming down to the pool in the morning and fishing drunk Finns out of it, only very occasionally alive. *Philip Nolan*

When Tiger Woods' nine-iron slipped from his caddy's fingers and fell into the lake at the seventh green, one could be forgiven for imagining that it had drowned itself in despair. *Joe Hanratty on Woods' poor show during the 2006 Ryder Cup*

I nearly drowned once. Not all the sins of my past life flashed in front of me, just as many as could find their way in the queue. *Brendan Behan*

I tried to drown myself once but it didn't work. The goldfish wouldn't move over. *Jimmy Cricket*

Two Irish Feared Lost At Sea. *Alleged Irish newspaper reaction to the sinking of the* **Titanic**

When Myles na gCopaleen was in bed in hospital once, some fella brought him in a naggin of gin and a baby tonic. He filled Myles' glass with the entire contents of the gin, adding about a thimbleful of tonic. "Almighty God," Myles gasped, "are you trying to drown it entirely?" *Patrick Kavanagh*

The poor man drowned in a vat of whiskey. It took him three hours. It would have been faster but he came out a few times to relieve himself. *Eamonn Mac Thomáis*

If John Major was drowning, his whole life would pass in front of him and he wouldn't be in it. *Dave Allen*

The cruising trip was so much fun I had to sink my yacht to make the guests go home. *F. Scott Fitzgerald*

You've got to exchange the populations of Holland and Ireland. Then the Dutch will turn Ireland into a beautiful garden and the Irish will forget to mend the dykes and all will be drowned. *Otto von Bismarck*

# DRUGS

I don't need drugs. I'm crazy enough without them. *Louis Walsh*

I once overdosed on amphetamines. I was rushed to hospital and made to do the night shift. *Sean Hughes*

They're selling crack in my neighbourhood. Finally. *Kevin Brennan*

The best way to smuggle drugs these days is to stuff them up a dog's arse. The airport officials will think the sniffer dogs are just getting frisky. *Ardal O'Hanlon*

I don't do drugs. If I want a rush I just stand up when I'm not expecting to. *Dylan Moran*

Drugs turned me into a nice guy. **Des Bishop**

More and more people in Ireland are snorting cocaine now. It's as plain as the nose on your face. **Donal O'Dea**

When cocaine wants to get high, it sniffs Charlie Sheen. **Des Ekin**

I think my wife is on drugs. I came home unexpectedly the other day and the phone rang. When I picked it up she said, "Is the dope still there?" **Gene Fitzpatrick**

Every time you read about some famous person overdosing on drugs they're always really talented, like Janis Joplin or Jimi Hendrix or John Belushi. The people you *want* to overdose never would. Motley Crue would never overdose. Or New Kids on the Block. **Denis Leary**

Condoms are useless because they burst. And your stomach just can't cope with the sudden impact of two kilos of cocaine. **Ardal O'Hanlon**

I hate people who take drugs. Like the police. **Dusty Young**

I gave up cocaine when I realized I was spending a hundred quid for a gram of Ajax and a piece of nostril hair. **Ian O'Doherty**

Of course drugs were fun. That's what's so stupid about anti-drug campaigns. They don't admit that. **Anjelica Huston**

I did drugs for eighteen years but never got bad enough to say the Kaiser Chiefs were brilliant. **Noel Gallagher**

The suggestion that our kindly government, having bled the honest citizen dry with all manner of taxes on all manner of pretexts, may reward reformed drug addicts with free food vouchers brought a letter from one of my listeners who asked if his seventy-five-year-old mother could become a drug addict, please? Although never having taken an illegal substance in her life, she would be willing to give it a go if she could then give up, have a urine test once a week and thereby receive food vouchers to supplement her pension and help towards paying her council tax. **Terry Wogan**

Drug addicts should have their own Olympics. It's perfect. They're already in tracksuits. **David McSavage**

I refuse unequivocally to ever have anything to do with drugs. Again. *Keith Farnan*

# DRUNKENNESS

Did you ever get so drunk you thought you were in a karaoke bar whereas you were just watching a subtitled movie? *Sean Hughes*

I know your father was a great man, but he was never as drunk as my father. *John B. Keane*

You know when you walk into the kitchen and forget what you went in for? Being stoned is like that all the time. *Robbie Bonham*

An Irishman is never drunk as long as he can hold on to a blade of grass and not fall off the face of the earth. *Joan Larson Kelly*

I quite enjoyed the days when one went for a beer at one's local bar in Paris and woke up in Corsica. *Peter O'Toole*

I'm not an alcoholic, I'm a drunkard. That means you don't have to go to all those meetings. *Jackie Gleason*

Having sex while drunk is like trying to squeeze a marshmallow into a piggybank. *Tommy Tiernan*

I've never attempted to give up drink because, to be honest, I'm a much nicer person when I'm slightly drunk. *Fiona Looney*

After eight years of relentless chatter three nights a week at peak time, all *Wogan* will ever be remembered for will be George Best drunk as a skunk. *Terry Wogan on his TV show*

I always know my capacity for drink. I just get drunk before I reach it. *Barney McKenna*

My uncle staggered in the other night, loaded. His wife said, "Where have you been?" He said, "I bought something for the house." She said, "What did you buy for the house?" He said, "A round of drinks." *Jimmy Joyce*

I can get drunk on the smell of a printer's ink. *Bryan McMahon*

In the unlikely event that you need to describe your level of intoxication, the following classifications may be useful: well-oiled, pissed, rightly pissed, pissed as a coot, flootered, maggoty, airlocked, legless, langered, bolloxed, paralytic, on the floor. *Tadhg Hayes*

I once met an Irish surfer. These are two words that don't seem to belong together. I asked him how he did it. "Drunk," he replied. *Frank Gannon*

The only difference between an Irish wedding and an Irish wake is one less drunk. *Nick Harris*

The first time I got drunk was 1991. I know this because after a naggin of brandy I thought I was a fighter pilot who sang the U2 hit single "One" while simultaneously bombarding the urban sprawl below with the remnants of a snack box from Enzo's takeaway. *Brian O'Connell*

They tell me I had a good Christmas. *Alex Higgins*

When you're really drunk you can't even remember the *beginning* of a joke, never mind the end of one. *Dara O'Briain*

I don't like ATM machines. You're standing there drunk at one in the morning and they ask you things like, "Are you happy with your mortgage?" Christ, I don't even know if I'm happy with my sausage roll. *Dylan Moran*

# DUBLIN

Dublin is as ever, only more so. You ask for a fish and they give you a piece of bog oak. *Samuel Beckett in 1935*

Dublin Airport is an A&E ward for slightly healthier people. *David McWilliams*

The Nativity story was originally supposed to be set in Dublin but they couldn't find three wise men — or a virgin. *Des MacHale*

In Dublin you're worse off if you've written books than if you're illiterate. *Patrick Kavanagh*

As a born and bred Dubliner, with a lifelong unsentimental but deep affection for the place, I have in the past couple of years come to thoroughly dislike this clogged, short-tempered, loud, greedy, mean-minded, overpriced kip of a city. *Gene Kerrigan*

Dublin is a warm pool full of smiling crocodiles. *Patrick Kavanagh*

How do you cross Dublin without passing a pub? Go into all of them. *James Joyce*

If you don't drink or snort coke or sleep with Colin Farrell, there's nothing to do in Dublin. *Sinead O'Connor*

I love Dublin because it brings you down to earth. I was walking across Fitzwilliam Square when a man shouted at me from across the street, "I saw ya in the *Courier* and ye were fuckin' brutal." *Gabriel Byrne*

Dublin, though a place much worse than London, is not as bad as Iceland. *Dr Samuel Johnson*

Shay Given must be the only Irish international who didn't know where Dublin was. **The Manchester Evening News** *on the Irish keeper after Dion Dublin stole in behind him to score a goal in a soccer match*

City of experts and gawkers, crutches and cardboard cups, dead writers and spittle. *Pat Ingoldsby*

Dublin is like a young girl with too much make-up on. *Glen Hansard*

I disagree with Glen Hansard. I see Dublin over-pleased with itself for pissing outside a door, and then suddenly left scratching it when everyone has gone. *Una Mullally*

He told me he was from LA. I said I was from D. *Michael Redmond*

# EATING

I was a master of Chopsticks from a young age — unfortunately the wrong sort. *Aidan Cooney*

There's a brief window in most people's existence when sweets are not about life or death, they are more important than that. *Róisín Ingle*

The last man in the world whose opinion I would take on what to eat would be a doctor. It is far safer to consult a waiter, and not a bit more expensive. *Robert Lynd*

Ever since he became a star across the Atlantic, Ricky Gervais became a fitness fanatic. Americans don't like watching larger lads on the telly as they sit on the couch eating a Super Deluxe Mega Massive Burger with extra lard and complimentary twenty-inch Meat Murder Pizza, all washed down with an Ultra Extreme Super Large Diet Coke. *Pat Fitzpatrick*

You know you're getting older when the first thing you do after you've finished eating is look for a place to lie down. *Jack Cruise*

Never eat in a restaurant where you see a cockroach bench-pressing a burrito. *Pat McCormick*

It was a bold man who first swallowed an oyster. *Jonathan Swift*

Eat British beef. You won't get better. *Dusty Young*

I'm a light eater. As soon as it's light, I eat. *Derek Davis*

One can safely eat minestrone off the streets in Switzerland. *James Joyce*

The next time you go out for dinner, have a look around the table. If everyone is on your payroll, the chances are you've become a prick. *Bono*

Everything I eat has been proved by some doctor or other to be poison. *George Bernard Shaw*

My self-prepared dinners are in two courses. The first is served at 6.30 and the second — two Alka Seltzers — at 3.30 a.m. *Hugh Leonard*

Paddy and Mick were having their sandwiches in a pub. "You're not allowed to eat your own food in here," the barman told them. So they swapped sandwiches. *Gene Fitzpatrick*

# ECCENTRICITY

My granny never got out of bed except to go to funerals. *Brendan Behan*

Mary Monckton once stole a pet hedgehog but when it turned cranky she swapped it for a sponge cake. *Michael Nugent*

He's so tidy, every time he has a bath he washes the soap. *Jack Cruise*

If you present my father with a statement such as "Grass is green", he's quite likely to reply, "Ah yes, but what do you *mean* by green?" *Emma Donoghue*

I have heard of a man who had a mind to sell his house and therefore carried a piece of brick in his pocket which he showed as a pattern to encourage purchasers. *Jonathan Swift*

I'm Irish. We think sideways. *Spike Milligan*

Russell Brand's a big posh Essex boy who's got into Hare Krishna. "But Noel, darling," he said to me, "do you not believe in a higher existence?" I said, "Not dressed in a sheet banging a tambourine, you big jessie." *Noel Gallagher*

I can't go to work unless the bed is made. *Gerry Ryan*

Brendan Behan bought The Bailey bar by accident in 1955, having gone to the auction to procure an electric toaster. *John Ryan*

A Ballyshannon man was fined a total of £40 after appearing on charges involving an allegedly out-of-date tax disc on his vehicle. Gerry Harrison was requested by guards to hand over his disc when stopped near the town but proceeded to eat it instead. Asked why he had done so, he at first said he was hungry but later said the disc was not a disc at all but an air freshener cover on which there was displayed a scantily clad young lady. **Donegal Democrat**

A friend of mine might be accounted an eccentric since he takes his wife everywhere he goes. However, since he offers the plausible excuse that this is due to his having lost the key to the boot of his car and that he cannot therefore extricate her, he may more properly be regarded as a victim of circumstances. *Hugh Leonard*

Anna and Shane lived a free-spirited existence. They were the type who'd pop out for ten minutes to buy a Kit-Kat and the next time you'd hear from them they'd be in Istanbul, working in a tannery. *Marian Keyes*

# EDITING

Anyone who can improve a sentence of mine by the placing of a comma is looked upon as my dearest friend. *George Moore*

They also serve who only punctuate. *Brian Moore*

An editor once berated me for using the word "lugubrious" twice in a novel — once on page 12 and again on page 204. When I told John McGahern this story he said, "You shouldn't even have used it once." *John Banville*

I was working on the proofs of one of my poems all morning and took out a comma. In the afternoon I put it back in again. *Oscar Wilde*

# EDUCATION

I was educated in a school for emotionally disturbed teachers. *Frank McCourt*

There's nobody as daft as an educated man once you get him off the subject he was educated in. *Owen Kelly*

After completing my course in Foundation Maths, I find I still can't count my change. *Maeve Higgins*

The people of Northern Ireland have access to the best education system in the British Isles and use it skilfully to turn out maniacs and a disproportionate number of dazed zealots. *Gerry Anderson*

"Mary," complained the mistress to her new maid from the country, "I can write my name on the dust on the piano." "Oh Mam, isn't it wonderful to have the education," marvelled Mary. *Doug Anderson*

Education isn't everything. For a start, it isn't an elephant. *Spike Milligan*

My father wasn't very well educated. The first time he saw Brussels sprouts he said, "Who made a balls of the cabbage?" *Big O*

Never again will I be required to spell "onomatopoeia". Never again will I wish Shakespeare had given up halfway through *Hamlet* and let Claudius fall down a flight of stairs. *Carin Hunt after completing her secondary education*

Without any formal education that I am aware of, a bar of soap regularly outthinks me in the bath. *Pat Ingoldsby*

Attending an all-girls school had its advantages. For one thing, you didn't have to worry about how you looked in the mornings. *Dana*

# EGGS

I see eggs are going up again. God help the chickens. **Maureen Potter**

It was so windy last week our hen laid the same egg three times. **Des MacHale**

My wife asked me recently to make love to her at six a.m. on the kitchen floor. "Why?" I asked. "Because I want to time an egg," she replied. **Brendan Grace**

I asked this girl how she liked her eggs in the morning. "Unfertilized," she replied. **Milo O'Shea**

"Missus, are them eggs fresh?"
   "I only laid the counter, luv."
**Paul Ryan**

I knew a shopkeeper once who said his eggs were so fresh, the hens hadn't even missed them. **Eamonn Kelly**

# EGO

I was born to be rich and Rabelaisian and to wallow in mistresses and Napoleon brandy. I was not born to spend my days on cabbage and potatoes and to perish of TB or pneumonia in a smelly little dungeon in the concrete wilds of south-west Kimmage. **Christy Brown**

An alcoholic is an egomaniac with an inferiority complex. **Eugene O'Neill**

How could I have got a big head in Boyzone? I spent most of my time worrying someone would find out I couldn't sing. **Keith Duffy**

As God once said, and I think rightly . . . **Charlie Haughey**

Ian Paisley came home one night sopping wet. "My God," said his wife, "you're drenched." "How many times", he fumed, "have I told you to call me Ian when we're alone?" **Myler McGrath**

What do you get when you cross PMS with ESP? A bitch who knows everything. **Joe Lynch**

I knew I was God the day I started praying and realized I was talking to myself. **Peter O'Toole**

Mrs Patrick Campbell has an ego like a raging tooth. **W. B. Yeats**

Q. How many members of U2 does it take to change a lightbulb?
A. Just one. Bono holds the bulb and the world revolves around him.
**Q magazine**

If T. E. Lawrence hid in a quarry he'd put flags all around it. **George Bernard Shaw**

Whistler has always spelt art with a capital "I". **Oscar Wilde**

I've decided to buy Manchester City football club. I'm going to walk in and say, "You fuck off, you fuck off, you fuck off. And you — make me a cup of tea." **Noel Gallagher**

Everyone's entitled to my opinion. **Micheál MacLiammóir**

# ELECTIONS

My electioneering style? I kiss the mothers and shake hands with the babies. **Joe Costello**

I don't think I'll move to China. Over there they have elections every morning before bleakfast. **Niall O'Connor**

Q. What election is signified by white smoke?
A. An Indian chief.
**Exchange on Larry Gogan's Just-a-Minute Quiz**

Election counts are like being at your own post-mortem — without an anaesthetic. *Ruairí Quinn*

If you can fool all of the people some of the time, that's enough to get elected. *Garret Fitzgerald*

One watches the British election campaign with all the tenderness of a battered wife looking at her wedding photos. *Ann Marie Hourihane*

It's time we took the bull by the horns and elected a nice young heifer. *Willie Carey*

The Fermanagh by-election isn't about the IRA hunger strikes. It's about bread and butter issues. *Eamonn Malley*

England has elected a fat Andy Warhol as Mayor. *Dara O'Briain on Boris Johnson*

A politician thinks of the next election, a statesman of the one after that. *W. B. O'Carolan*

That gives a swing of over 20 per cent against the incumbent. Of course he's not the incumbent any more. Unfortunately he's dead. *David Hanly*

# ELECTRICITY

Touching These Wires Means Instant Death. Anyone Found Doing So Will Be Prosecuted. *Notice at electric station*

I bought my wife a chair for her birthday but unfortunately I can't get her to plug it in. *Bal Moane*

An Irish farmer came into money and was able to afford to have electricity in his house for the first time. "It's brilliant," he told a friend. "I just turn on the light and then I have no problem at all finding the matches for my candles." *Bryan MacMahon*

Tim: "My mammy had an argument with the electric company."
Conor: "Who won?"

Tim: "It was a tie. We don't get any electricity and they don't get any money."
**Hal Roach**

If you touch an electric wire on purpose, does it still count as a shock? **Mark Doherty**

# ELUSIVENESS

"Alex Higgins departed for heaven around midday on July 31, 2010. Months later, still no sign. Getting anxious, Peter."
**Twitter message**

There are three great philosophical questions we have to face: What is life? What is art? And, most importantly, where the fuck is Barney McKenna? **Ronnie Drew on his Dubliners colleague**

# EMBARRASSMENT

The worst moment of my life was walking into a roomful of people in AA and imagining them thinking, "What the fuck is he doing here?" **Gabriel Byrne**

Do you think it's possible to recover your sexual dignity if you're just about to get into bed with your lover and she notices a piece of wayward toilet paper sticking out of your bottom? **Michael Redmond**

A man once bought a packet of condoms in a shop because he was too embarrassed to buy my autobiography. **Terry Wogan**

The worst heckle I ever got at a book reading was when a child put up his hand and said, "Does this get good soon?"
**David O'Doherty**

The most embarrassing moment of my life was when Jack Charlton farted in front of Albert Reynolds and blamed me. *Andy Townsend*

I had an embarrassing experience eating spaghetti. I hiccuped and lassoed two people at the next table. *Jimmy Cricket*

My most embarrassing drunken experience was when I found myself being removed from a riverbank in Galway by friendly policemen after I had talked to some local swans and tried to copy their swimming techniques. *Pat Kinevane*

The most embarrassing moment of my life was when a caller told me on live radio that I had a voice like honey dripping on nipples. *Brenda Power*

You feel like watching his matches from behind the sofa. *Andy Townsend on Fernando Torres after a poor goal-scoring period with Chelsea in 2011*

The most embarrassing moment of my life was being in hospital and handing a bedpan to my neighbour. Admittedly she was a nurse. *Jason Byrne*

# EMIGRATION

This is the first time in my life that Irish people say to me, "Don't go to England, it's full of terrorists. Stay in Ireland instead." We have no terrorists at all now. They've all become playwrights. *Dara O'Briain*

I heard a charity appeal on the radio the other day that said it only takes ten euros a week to support a child in Africa. I'm thinking of moving my whole family out there. *Patrick Donovan*

I've been living in England for a while now and I've noticed there's one thing over there that we don't have in Ireland. Birmingham. *Michael Redmond*

To me, the definition of an emigrant is someone who has nothing to go home to, and lacks the wherewithal to go. The new variety, who can jack it in and piss off home, are expatriates. *Niall Toibin*

Alcohol for the Irish is emigration of the soul. *John Waters*

I've been in England for over sixteen years. The other day a man said to me, "Do you go home often?" I said, "Yeah, every night." *Owen O'Neill*

I came to America because I heard the streets were paved with gold. When I got there I found out three things. First, they weren't paved with gold. Second, they weren't paved. And third, I had to pave them. *Sean McKiernan*

Jonathan Swift was something of a rarity among famous Irish writers in that he actually lived and wrote in Ireland. *Evan McHugh*

I left Ireland an embittered exile. It was the done thing. *Ian MacPherson*

One of the reasons I left Ireland was to get away from singing priests. *Terry Wogan*

I was the only immigrant to Ireland when I first came here in 1992. There was even a special sign for me when I arrived at Shannon Airport. It said, "Wrong Way". *Des Bishop*

An Englishman was questioned at length by Australian immigration officials at Sydney Airport. In answer to the question "Do you have a criminal record?" he replied, "I didn't think that was necessary any more." *Paul Kilduff*

Last night I chaired an event where people tried to find out who was the greatest Dubliner of all time. An entrepreneur made a spirited case for Sean O'Casey, who loved Dublin so much he emigrated to Torquay. *Trevor White*

Where's the lovely Sally O'Brien and the way she might look at you? Apparently she's long gone and replaced by Miroslava from the Czech Republic, who works in a call centre. *Michael Parsons*

The reason I left Ireland was because I didn't want to have to pray in Gaelic. *Arthur Shields*

# ENEMIES

Love your enemies just in case your friends turn out to be a heap of bastards. *Karl Spain*

There's a famous New York producer who shall be nameless called David Richenthal who I'm pleased to say is an enemy of mine. *Michael Colgan*

"Our enemies," cried the politician, "will be deaf to our pleas for justice so long as we remain silent." *Tony Butler*

Survival is the best revenge on one's enemies. *Vincent Browne*

If you're seriously bent on becoming a real Dublin writer, it's important to make an enemy as soon as you can or nobody will take you seriously. *David Kenny*

If you sit long enough by the river, you'll see the bodies of your enemies floating by. *Brian Moore*

Money can't buy you friends, just a better class of enemy. *Spike Milligan*

# THE ENGLISH

The English like to invade countries but they get upset if they're followed home. *Tommy Tiernan*

The Englishman has all the qualities of a poker except its occasional warmth. *Daniel O'Connell*

You can go sauntering along for a certain period telling the English some interesting things about themselves, and then all at once it feels as if you've stepped on the prongs of a rake. *Patrick Campbell*

Ireland was the first oppressed nation to tweak the lion's tail and boot its eructating arse out, thereby leading the way for

India, Africa, Palestine and all the Arab nations to arise and rid themselves of the plague of chinless wonders who were sent out from England to make a bollocks of running their countries. *Malachy McCourt*

The English are a very literal people — they think you mean exactly what you say. *Olivia O'Leary*

The British beatitudes are beer, beef, business, bibles, bull-dogs, battleships, buggery and bishops. *James Joyce*

Liam never liked the English. In this he was helped, he said, by the fact that the English did not like themselves. *Anne Enright*

The people of England are never so happy as when you tell them they're ruined. *Arthur Murphy*

A good Nationalist should look upon slugs in the garden in much the same way as she looks on the English in Ireland. *Constance Markiewicz*

The Englishman does everything on principle: he fights you on patriotic principles; he robs you on business principles; he enslaves you on imperial principles. *George Bernard Shaw*

The English will believe anything as long as it's not the truth. *Edith Somerville*

The English can handle defeat very well but they can't handle victory. It brings out the snarl factor. *Colm Toibin*

When I was working in Britain I remember being struck by the importance given to things military. In the office at BBC's *Newsnight*, people became as excited as children at the prospect of a military story. "Let's drag in a few brass hats tonight, what?" burbled one happy presenter. There was a reverence shown to the security forces that we in Ireland once showed to the Church. *Olivia O'Leary*

# EPIDURALS

After I gave birth for the first time a friend of mine asked me what I had. I said, "An epidural." **Deirdre O'Kane**

The last time I had a baby I got an anaesthetic for the birth. Next time I'm having one for the conception as well. **Gráinne Deegan**

# EPIGRAMS

The lust shall be first. **Anna Murphy**

Why should I not fiddle while Byrne roams? **Flann O'Brien**

The trouble with mixing business and pleasure is that pleasure usually gets priority. **Dave Allen**

There's always one more son of a bitch than you counted on. **Sean Kilroy**

The chance of a slice of bread falling butter side down is directly proportional to the cost of the carpet. **Murphy's Law**

If it wasn't for Venetian blinds it would be curtains for all of us. **Monica Sheridan**

Distance may make the heart grow fonder but gossip makes the ears grow sharper. **Graham Norton**

What was it Burns said about the best-laid plans ganging aft aglae? A great artist but an appalling typist. **Ian MacPherson**

Never change nappies in midstream. **Colette Fitzpatrick**

There's no fool like a young fool. **Anna Nolan**

Teething rings are a baby's right to chews. **Monica Sheridan**

Opportunity only knocks once. If there's a second one, it's probably a Jehovah's Witness. **John O'Connor**

The darkest hour is just before the pawn. *Brendan Behan*

One thing doesn't always lead to another. Ask any addict. *Karl McDermott*

No man is an island, except when he's in the bath. *Kevin McAleer*

Marry in haste and repeat at leisure. *Cyril Cusack*

Beggars can't be boozers. *John B. Keane*

# EPITAPHS

On my gravestone I'd like them to put, "He didn't know what he was doing". *Terry Wogan*

A fairly typical tombstone in an Irish cemetery goes: "This gravestone is erected in memory of Seamus O'Driscoll, who was accidentally stabbed to death as a token of abiding affection by his loving wife". *Jack Cruise*

I want my epitaph to be what I once read on my dry-cleaning receipt: "It distresses us to return work that is not perfect". *Peter O'Toole*

I'd like my epitaph to be, "She finally got laid at last". *Yvonne Costelloe*

I told you I was ill. *Spike Milligan's suggested epitaph*

I often think a good inscription on an actor's headstone would be, "And just when he was getting the hang of it". *Donal McCann*

I want it to say more on my tombstone than: "He dated Julia Roberts and Barbra Streisand". *Liam Neeson*

"Dark and brooding". That'll be written on my headstone. For the next movie I make I'm going to dye my hair blond and wear a silly Buster Keaton smile. *Gabriel Byrne*

I only want two words on my grave: "Fuck you". *Shane MacGowan*

# EUPHEMISMS

What you take for lying in an Irishman is only his attempt to put a herbaceous border on stark reality. *Oliver St John Gogarty*

"'Tis a grand day for the time of year that's in it" justifies praising even the worst winter's day for the eternal Irish optimist. *Tadhg Hayes*

An Irishman will always soften bad news so that a major coronary is no more than a "bad turn" and a near-hurricane that leaves thousands homeless is "good drying weather". *Hugh Leonard*

I blew a cylinder head gasket. *George Hamilton after getting a heart scare in 2011*

When someone in Ireland says "Her legs aren't the best part of her" they usually mean they look like tree trunks. *Mary Mannion*

There are three stages of older life: Adulthood, Middle Age and "You're looking extremely well". *Jack Lynch*

I was walking in Central Park with a friend of mine and he stepped in some dogshit. He said, "Shit, I've just stood in some dog's doo-doo." The Americans now use "shit" for everything except shit. *Dave Allen*

A Hunt Ball is just a fancy way of saying "Piss-Up". *Anne Marie Scanlon*

My mother used to call farts "whispers". She told me not to worry about them. It was just my bottom "whispering". I felt fine about this until one day my granny asked me if she could whisper something in my ear. *Dave Allen*

A shithole in Ireland is referred to as "a disadvantaged area". *Des Bishop*

The most popular way of dying in Ireland is "peacefully". "Peacefully" covers deaths involving screaming that you don't want to go, clinging desperately to the bed-end shouting that you're still alive as they drag you towards the morgue, throwing yourself through the hospital window to end the agony, begging for drugs to numb the pain, and running two miles down the street in a flapping dressing-gown desperately seeking help from passing strangers who ignore you. *David Slattery*

Irish people have a favourite euphemism for death. The standard expression of sympathy at a funeral, delivered while shaking hands with the bereaved, is "I'm sorry for your troubles". This is said whether the deceased has died of natural causes aged 103, or was the victim of a drive-by shooting in a drugs feud. *Frank McNally*

My mother is gone to a better place – Grimsby. I believe "gone to a better place" is a euphemism for death. So is Grimsby. *Ian MacPherson*

Midlanders in Ireland are often described as "phlegmatic". Which is another word for thick. *Niall Toibin*

# EUROVISION

Johnny Logan won the Eurovision three times for Ireland. Once might be deemed unfortunate. Twice is just carelessness. Three times and you'd better quit while you're behind. *Declan Lynch*

Commenting on the Eurovision Song Contest sometimes makes you lose the will to live. *Marty Whelan*

The way Eurovision is going, the only way Ireland can ever win again is if we enter a chimpanzee and some nuns. *Dave Fanning*

# EXAGGERATION

We need to have a sense of proportion about things. I have great difficulty in regarding any public performance by Frank Sinatra as "The Ultimate Event". If he parted the Red Sea while singing "Songs for Swinging Lovers" we might be getting somewhere near it. *Pat Ingoldsby*

At the time of writing I've used some 9,855 nappies on three bottoms. *Fiona Looney*

I hail from the Lynches of Sligo. I went there and looked up the phone book but there are nine million Lynches in Sligo. *Jack Nicholson*

I've told you hundreds of times before — stop exaggerating. *Eamonn Andrews*

# EXAMS

My mother had high standards for me. When I did the Inter Cert I was criticized for "nearly not" getting an Honour. *Vincent Browne*

I once got 3 per cent in a maths exam for getting the teacher's name right. Passing it in the Inter Cert years later was probably due to a clerical error. *Tom Doorley*

O'Reilly got minus one in his exam. He spelt his name wrong. *Seamus O'Leary*

# EXERCISE

I often take exercise. Why, only yesterday I had breakfast in bed. *Oscar Wilde*

I was brought up in a place called Glenageary, a suburb of south Dublin where the only exercise anyone ever got was adultery, lawnmowing and going to the shops to buy cheap potent drink in the middle of the day. *Joe O'Connor*

The only exercise I get these days is walking behind the coffins of my dead friends who exercised. *Peter O'Toole*

My doctor told me to exercise. He said walking would get me into shape. "I already have a shape," I told him. "It's round." *Brendan Grace*

Success in a work-out for me means not falling off the machine. *Dara O'Briain*

I find thinking about exercise quite strenuous. *Malachy McCourt*

Biting my fingernails is the only exercise I get these days. *Marian Keyes*

# EXHIBITIONISTS

There was a flasher in Fitzwilliam Street today. The guards are looking for a man with black curly hair and . . . black curly hair. **In Dublin**

Hey Billy, your flies are open. Careful now or your brains will get cold. *Paul Ryan*

Murphy was in his eighties but every evening he dropped his trousers in front of people. He was regularly up in court. When the judge asked him if he had anything to say, the reply was always the same. "Well, judge, I was going to retire but I'd like to stick it out for six more months." *James McKeon*

# EXPECTATIONS

Well I didn't get as much as I expected, but then I didn't expect I would. *Brendan O'Connor*

You can safely appeal to the UN in the comfortable certainty that it will let you down. *Conor Cruise O'Brien*

When I first came to Dublin I thought every poet had a spare wife. *Patrick Kavanagh*

I once heard of an Irish transport official who left the railway gate ajar because he was "half expecting" a train. *T. P. McKenna*

# EXPLANATIONS

The reason I didn't take the corners against Russia in 1974 was because I was on the subs bench. *Johnny Giles*

Since 1983, more than thirty people have been killed in Post Office shootings. You know why? Because the price of stamps keeps changing. *George Carlin*

The reason I got married is because I hate men. *Dolores O'Riordan*

If they can't explain they'll have some explaining to do. *Pat Kenny*

The reason one sock always goes missing in the wash is because it goes to the sock goblin who lives in the tumble drier. *Aoibhinn Ní Shúilleabháinn*

The reason we forged our own music in U2 was because we couldn't play other people's very well. *Bono*

The reason Joseph and Mary took Jesus to Bethlehem with them was because it was hard to get a babysitter even in those days. *Des MacHale*

When I was playing against Dennis Wise once, he grabbed my tit. When I got changed I had five finger marks around the nipple, like a love bite. That took some explaining to the missus. *Jason McAteer*

It's far easier to explain to a three-year-old how babies are made than to explain the process whereby bread and sugar appears on the table. *Dervla Murphy*

We still get letters about "kicks" in snooker. There's no explanation. It's a little piece of dirt on the cue ball. *Dennis Taylor*

Why aren't the Kerry team allowed to own a dog? Because they can't hold on to a lead. *Pat Spillane*

It took me thirty-four takes to nail just one line in *Minority Report* but I had a good explanation. It was the morning after my birthday. *Colin Farrell*

A tourist guide was showing an American around Kerry. "This is the highest mountain in Ireland," he told him, pointing at Carrantuohill. "The one beside it looks bigger," said the American. "That's only because Carrantuohill was built in a hollow," the guide explained. *Niall Toibin*

# EXPLETIVES

Is there a more anodyne, watery-cup-of-tea piss word in the entire vernacular than "feck"? Dara O'Briain says "feck" and then winks at you like some gigantic school prefect, eager to let you know he's a bit naughty, but not naughty enough to utter to the headmaster the whole-hearted, bile-flecked "fuck" her merits. "Feck" is swear-lite, the curse to bring you home to Daddy. Saying it but, you know, not saying it. "Feck" is Ronan Keating. *Brian O'Connor*

How can I write the way Irishmen talk without using the F word? After all, that effer Lawrence got away with it. *Brendan Behan*

Daniel O'Donnell wouldn't say shit if his mouth was full of it. **Conor Tiernan**

Fuck, no. **Bob Geldof after being asked if he thought swearing in public was a bad example for his children**

Fr Ted: "Have you any idea why the date July 19 should be important to me?"
Fr Dougal: "No, you big bollox."
Fr Ted: "Don't say you've been reading those Roddy Doyle books again."
**Father Ted**

They say rather than cursing the darkness one should light a candle. They don't mention anything about cursing a lack of candles. *George Carlin*

I swore I'd give up cursing. *Barry Fitzgerald*

The reason I curse so much is because I don't like speaking English. I should be speaking Irish, which is a much more fluid language. "Fuck" is the chisel I use to break that barrier. *Tommy Tiernan*

My books were taken off the school curriculum because the Minister for Education decided they weren't literary. That's utter drivel. The decision to use the word "fuck" is a literary one. *Roddy Doyle*

I'm a window cleaner. I'm more a motherfucking window cleaner than some motherfucking motherfuckers. *Van Morrison*

I never heard him cursing and I don't believe he was ever drunk in his life. Sure he's not like a Christian at all! *Sean O'Casey*

Before I became a comedian I used to be a folk singer. Every time an audience heard me they'd go, "Oh folk." *Sil Fox*

My old man used to swear by Irish coffee as a remedy for

rheumatism. And the more he had of it, the more he swore.
**Donal O'Dea**

People are disappointed when I don't swear on stage. **Bob Geldof**

# EXTREMES

There are only two kinds of people who are absolutely fascinating: those who know absolutely everything and those who know absolutely nothing. **Oscar Wilde**

Some people say there's a God and some say there isn't. The truth probably lies somewhere in between. **W. B. Yeats**

We find ourselves in an Ireland characterized by pester-power for grown-ups, where no SUV is big enough, no model new enough, no orgasm climactic enough. No child is too young for highlights, no bum too fat for hipsters and no singer too tone-deaf to be a star. You just have to believe the hype and live the dream. **David McWilliams**

I arranged my wedding day for 29 December, which meant that the previous six months' hard-won weight loss was annihilated in a matter of minutes on Christmas Eve when I interfaced with a wheelie-bin-size of Roses. **Marian Keyes**

Extremist Catholics and extremist Protestants should get together to get rid of ecumenism. **Liam Desmond**

In August 2003 we saw a great day for Kerry sport when Gillian O'Sullivan won a silver medal in the European Championships. Then that same afternoon we saw Kerry implode against Tyrone in the All-Ireland semi-final. It was like winning the Lotto and then finding out you had only twenty-four hours to live. **Pat Spillane**

# EYES

My grandmother's eyebrows were so bushy, if you looked close enough you could see Skippy running through them. *Katherine Lynch*

You'll never guess who I bumped into in Specsavers yesterday. Everybody. *Dennis Taylor*

When you go forth to find a wife, leave your eyes at home but take both ears with you. *Sean Gaffney*

I used to hate it when my grandad came over to visit. It wasn't just because he was blind, but I'd always been told I had his eyes. *Michael Redmond*

I could never get to grips with the old housewives tale, "You can tell a Catholic because their eyes are too close together." *Gloria Hunniford*

A woman looks into the mirror and says disgustedly, "I feel fat and horrible. Say something nice to me." The husband replies, "Your eyesight's twenty-twenty." *Frank Carson*

I rang the optician. He's useless. He couldn't see me. *Jimmy Cricket*

My uncle was rejected as a lollipop man because he had only one eye. I was livid. The bastards could have put him on a one-way street. *Frank Carson*

One thing my mother could never say to me was "Your eyes are bigger than your belly". *An overweight Brendan Grace*

Bridget: "I've broken my glasses. Will I have to be examined all over again?"
Dr O'Kane: "No, Bridget, just your eyes."
*Peter Cagney*

I used to know a priest who had stained-glass lenses in his spectacles. *Jimmy Cricket*

My wife always closes her eyes when we make love. She hates to see me enjoying myself. *Brendan Grace*

Someone gave George Bush an iPod. He said, "Where can I get one for the other eye?" *Craig Ferguson*

I need my shades for when I'm being insincere. *Bono*

# FACEBOOK

Facebook is like having a butler for your emails. *Dara O'Briain*

I like writing things on Facebook like, "Last night I woke up naked behind a skip. It wasn't Rohypnol. I'm just a whore." *Mary Bourke*

I've never really understood the concept behind Facebook. You have 233 friends and you're sitting in a room alone. It's a bit like giving an online burger to a famine victim in Ethiopia. *John Colleary*

# FACES

Nick Nolte has a face that looks like a truck ran over it. *Neil Jordan*

Broderick Crawford's face resembled an aerial view of the Ozarks. *Hugh Leonard*

Isadora Duncan's face looked as if it had been made of sugar and someone had licked it. *George Bernard Shaw*

Robert Sheehan's cheeks look like they were sculpted by the molten tears of a fallen angel. *Naomi McElroy*

If Lon Chaney is the man of a thousand faces, Charlton Heston is Chaney minus 999 of them. *Hugh Leonard*

Peter O'Toole has a face not so much lived in as infested. **Paul Taylor**

He has one of those characteristic British faces that once seen are never remembered. **Oscar Wilde**

My entire face is asymmetrical. In photographs, when I'm frozen in place, I look like something Picasso painted in his Cubist period. **Marian Keyes**

I have a face like a five-mile stretch of bad country road. **Richard Harris**

Celine Dion walked into a bar. "Why the long face?" asked the barman. **Seamus Donleavy**

Thelma Ritter had a face that wasn't only lived in; it was virtually a tenement. **Hugh Leonard**

A man's face is his autobiography. A woman's is a work of fiction. **Oscar Wilde**

Rowan Atkinson has a face like a gerbil with lockjaw. **Terry Wogan**

# FAILURE

I couldn't throw a ball as a child. That sort of marked you out to be a priest if you came from an Irish Catholic family. **John McGivern**

Go on failing. Only next time try to fail better. **Samuel Beckett**

The Irish love failure. In their folklore success is inexcusable but the fumbled ball, the lost promotion, the one drink too many are to them the stuff of romance. They turn the winner's laurels into a salad for the loser to eat, adding clichés for seasoning. **Hugh Leonard**

I've done so much degenerating I'm beginning to liquefy. **Gerry Ryan**

This year I've hit more balls than Sir Elton John's chin and still missed sixteen cuts in a row. *David Feherty*

He's completely unspoiled by failure. *Frank Carson*

*Rattle and Hum* is perceived as one of U2's failures. We sold twelve million copies of the record. That kind of failure I can live with. *Paul McGuinness*

Fail to prepare, prepare to fail. *Roy Keane*

It's unfair to call me a failed Third Division footballer. What I am is a failed Second Division footballer. *Eamon Dunphy*

# FAIRYTALES

"Mammy, why do fairytales always start with the words 'Once upon a time'?"
   "Not all of them do, darling. Some begin with 'After I'm elected...'"
*Jack Cruise*

Once upon a time there were three bears. Now look how many there are. *Luke Kelly*

I come from an Irish family in Brooklyn. A few stockbrokers, a smattering of intellectuals and 40 per cent of the New York police force. My uncle the cop used to read me bedtime stories: "Humpty Dumpty sat on the wall, Humpty Dumpty fell – or was pushed – from the wall. The perpetrator has not been apprehended. Three male Hispanics were seen leaving the area." *Colin Quinn*

# FAITH

I first began to have doubts about my faith when, at twelve years of age, I saw the local parish priest install a lightning conductor on our church. *Ed Byrne*

If God wanted us to believe in him, he'd exist. *George Brent*

You're better off believing in God than not doing so. If you believe and He's not there you'll never know it but if you don't and you arrive at the Pearly Gates He's liable to say, "You're not welcome here. You're an atheist." *Ben Dunne*

I have friends who tell me they've lost their faith but they still bless themselves and beat their breasts any time they pass a church or an ambulance. It's like a kind of Morse code born of fear. *Des Bishop*

One way of describing the collapse of spiritual values in Ireland would be to say that the people didn't so much stop believing in God as that they came to believe God no longer believed in them. *John Waters*

I don't profess any belief in an orthodox sense. It seems to me that the mystery of life is too great, too wide, too deep, to do more than wonder at. Anything further would be, as far as I'm concerned, an impertinence. *John Huston*

I'm not a lapsed Catholic but rather a collapsed one. *Brendan Gill*

Raising the issue of faith in public dialogue today is a bit like inviting the first wife to the second wedding. *Sean Mullan*

I tried to be an atheist but I didn't have the faith. *Colin Farrell*

# FAME

A lot of young women today say they want to be writers when what they really mean is they want to get published. They want the fame but not the hard work. They want to be on *The Late Late Show*. They give me a big fat pain in the arse. *Marian Keyes*

At the height of my fame I couldn't take the dog for a walk during rush hour because motorists would be so busy honking at me that they'd run up each other's backsides. *George Best*

Fame is a comic distinction shared by Roy Rogers' horse and Miss Watermelon of 1955. *Flannery O'Connor*

Although I love what I do with a passion, there are times when I wish I was Johnny from up the road. *Daniel O'Donnell*

Behind every famous man is a woman who says there's a woman behind every famous man. *Hal Roach*

I may not be known outside Ireland but I'm world famous in Dublin. *Butch Moore*

My main claim to fame is my uncanny resemblance to a garden gnome. *Dermot Whelan*

Fame won't bring you happiness but it can get you a good table in a restaurant. *Gerry Ryan*

I am, to my almost certain knowledge, the only undisputed genius of the MacFiach line. Great Uncle Alisdair found fame of sorts as drag artiste Sweet Alis MacFiach while my distant cousins Joel and Ethan Clooney received an Academy Award nomination for Best Short Film by Identical Twins. *Ian MacPherson*

I'm so unfamous I've never even heard of me. *Mary Bourke*

Fame is as much of a trap as a joy. You can't suddenly step off the merry-go-round and say, "I'm going to become a clothes designer." *Chris de Burgh*

Those whom God hates he makes famous. Then He gives them an Equity card. *Donal McCann*

With nine bathrooms, an indoor swimming pool and eleven toilet bowls, I finally have a pot to piss in. *J. P. Donleavy*

One night at the bar in Folk City, Bob Dylan said to me, "Hey man, my records are *sellin'*. I'm goin' to be as big as the Clancy Brothers!" *Liam Clancy*

I've come a long way from boiling water in a billycan in a plumber's shed in Dublin. *Gabriel Byrne*

There's no such thing as fame in Ireland because everyone knows everyone. There aren't six degrees of separation between people, only one. They say things like, "He's not famous. Sure my girlfriend fucked his brother." *Des Bishop*

The whole "being spotted" thing is fine. It's like, "Yeah? Picture? Fine." Smiley face. Then I'm back buying cereal in Sainsbury's. *Robert Sheehan*

Fame is failure disguised as money. *Brendan Behan*

Fame hasn't changed my life. My neighbour Angela is still hanging over the back wall asking for the kid's ball back. *Mary Byrne after her X Factor experience*

I'm famous because I know Bono. *Adam Clayton*

A lot of people come up to me in bars just to tell me they don't know who I am. How busy their lives must be. *Ed Byrne*

Celebrity is more important than talent. British kids will remember Ken Russell not for directing *Women in Love* or *Tommy*, but as the geriatric bloke who walked out of *Celebrity Big Brother* after Jade Goody shouted at him because he wouldn't stop snoring. *Philip Nolan*

# FAMILIES

It was reported today that Osama bin Laden had fifty brothers and sisters, which absolutely shocked me. I had no idea he was Catholic. *Conan O'Brien*

I'm the eldest of eight children and there's one thing which always gives me true hope for the future: we've managed to spend all of Christmas Day together without any single one of us being actually stabbed. *Joe O'Connor*

He was a good family man. Everywhere he went he started a new family. *Liam O'Reilly*

Asked by a magistrate why he stole 757 sweaters, 733 men's shirts, 460 dresses, 403 jackets, 83 pairs of socks and 286 pairs of children's trousers, worth in all about £14,000, the defendant replied, "I have a large family." *Sorcha Kelly*

The typical west of Ireland family consists of father, mother, twelve children and resident Dutch anthropologist. *Flann O'Brien*

I have certainly known more men destroyed by the desire to have a wife and child and to keep them in comfort than I have seen destroyed by drink and harlots. *W. B. Yeats*

The other day my mother told me I was adopted. It came as a bit of a shock to me — despite the fact that the rest of my family are all Chinese. *Sean Hughes*

If you have a big family in Ireland you're either a good Catholic or a bad Protestant. *Daniel O'Donnell*

I've been in the media game all my life. It's not too different from being in a family of bakers. *Bob Geldof*

If you cannot get rid of the family skeleton, you may as well make it dance. *George Bernard Shaw*

The general rule at Irish family gatherings is that you should only discuss topics in which you have no real interest. *David Slattery*

There were only three occasions in life when you'd find our whole family together: family wedding, family funeral, or if I brought home a bag of chips. *Ardal O'Hanlon*

# FAMINES

Experts have discovered there was no potato famine in Ireland. We just forgot where we'd planted them. *Dylan Moran*

The next thing the revisionists will be telling us is that all the people who died in the Famine were suffering from anorexia nervosa. *P. J. O'Mara*

No wonder Bob Geldof is so interested in famine. He's been dining out on *I Don't Like Mondays* for over twenty years. **Russell Brand**

In the opening lecture, visiting historian Professor H. Doody developed his thesis that the Great Famine coincided with an almighty surplus of chocolate biscuits. **Ian MacPherson**

Famine might come back, so fill your boots. **Pat Fitzpatrick**

You couldn't have a famine in Ireland now. People would just eat out. **Kevin McAleer**

Alfred Hitchcock: "One look at you, Mr Shaw, and I know there's famine in Ireland."
George Bernard Shaw: "One look at you, Mr Hitchcock, and I know who caused it."
**Attributed exchange between the two legends**

Irish people eat like their lives depended on it — perhaps because they once did. **Ray McAnally**

Irish people were at their happiest during the Famine. Conversations went like this: "How are you doing, Sean?" "Arrah, not too bad. Let's eat some nettles." **Des Bishop**

Nobody should have died during the Famine. The potato failed but there was lots of cabbage. The Irish refused to eat it. "It has a depressing smell," they said, "a bit like the inside of a psychiatric hospital." **Tommy Tiernan**

# FAMOUS LAST WORDS

Merciful Jesus, what have I done to you? **Phil Lynott to his mother**

Dear Elise, seek younger friends. I am extinct. **George Bernard Shaw**

Is there one who understands me? **James Joyce**

There were no last words. His wife was with him to the end. **Spike Milligan**

Dennis Hopper's dying wish was to have his family around him. He might have been better off with some more oxygen. **Michael Cullen**

My wallpaper and I are fighting a duel to the death. One or other of us has got to go. **Oscar Wilde, who is also credited with the farewell line "I am dying, as I have lived, beyond my means"**

Thank you, sister, and may you be the mother of a bishop! **Brendan Behan**

I have no intention of uttering my last words on the stage. Room service and a couple of depraved young women will do me quite nicely for an exit. **Peter O'Toole**

Born in a hotel room and now, goddamit, dying in a hotel room. **Eugene O'Neill**

I find I am but a bad anatomist. **Wolfe Tone after cutting his throat in prison in a botched suicide attempt — he didn't die immediately**

Now will someone give me a cigar? **John Ford**

# FANS

A fan is someone who, if you've made an idiot of yourself on the pitch, doesn't think you've done a permanent job. **Jack Lynch**

When they first installed all-seater stadiums, everyone predicted the fans wouldn't stand for it. **George Best**

One of the perils of attending sports events is having to put up with obnoxious, loudmouth opposition fans. But you can usually deal with that. What's worse is having to put up with obnoxious loudmouth fans of the team you're supporting. **Frank McNally**

Getting my first fan mail was really exciting until someone told me Rin Tin Tin used to get six thousand letters a week. And he was a dog. **Gabriel Byrne**

I'm a big fan of Samuel Beckett, except he wrote beautifully and I write about poo. **Mark Doherty**

The Irish soccer fans always enjoyed celebrating more when they lost than when they won. **Eamon Dunphy**

I knew the face of Irish soccer had changed the day my coalman started talking about Gelsenkirchen. **Nell McCafferty**

I am a real fan. On soccer afternoons my waistband dips provocatively at the back, revealing just the right amount of buttock cleavage. **Tom Humphries**

I'm terribly sorry if I cannot answer all my fan letters personally but if I did that I'd be my secretary and my secretary would have to do the acting. **Peter O'Toole**

# FARMERS

What's got eight legs, three hands and two wings? A farmer on a horse holding a chicken. **Big O**

I was born in London to a couple of publicans who came to Ireland when I was six and then made the predictable progression from pub-owning to turkey farming. **Sharon Horgan**

Paddy Smith announced recently that ostrich farming had begun in England. He wondered if it might take on here in Ireland. I was surprised he hadn't noticed we've been growing our own for years — particularly politicians. **Dick Walsh**

I remember family evenings around the fire, my father fretting about the coming harvest and my mother trying to console him because he was a chartered accountant and he didn't have to worry about that sort of thing. **Michael Redmond**

A gentleman farmer is a man who gets his scarecrows measured for new suits every four months. **J. P. Donleavy**

The farmers of Ireland are living from hand to mouth like the birds of the air. **Sir Boyle Roche**

What's the definition of an Irish farmer? A man out standing in his own field. **Des MacHale**

"Mick's farm is in an awful state," mourned Patrick. "It's completely overgrown with undergrowth." **Tony Butler**

Farmers are the only people who can lose money every year, live well, educate their children, and die rich. **Hal Roach**

# FARTING

My worst vice is farting in the bath. **Dave Allen**

In my radio show I can go as low as the lowest common denominator. I once asked a guest if they could fart the National Anthem. **Gerry Ryan**

I asked the players who wanted to take a penalty. There was an awful smell coming from some of them. **Mick McCarthy**

The silent farts are the worst of all. I call them SBDs: silent but deadly. It's a form of letting off without letting on. **Jason Byrne**

Breaking bread with another human being is such a basic pleasure, but if it's pitta bread with beans, then the only things that will be broken are teeth and wind. **Graham Norton**

Football managers get sacked for farting in the wrong direction these days. **Joe Kinnear**

I was so tense I could hear the bees farting. **Mick O'Loughlin**

Beckett once wrote a play called *Breath* that consisted of about twenty seconds of silence followed by a huge breath. I'm thinking of doing a similar one called *Fart*. **Brian Behan**

In Ireland, rather than a gerontocracy, we're living in a fartocracy. A rough definition of a fartocracy is a country run by old farts pushing sixty who have no intention of relinquishing their power. *Will Hanafin*

In the last ten minutes of the match I was breathing out of my arse. *Former Ireland International footballer Clinton Morrison*

# FASHION

Irish women wouldn't know fashion if it tottered up to them on ten-inch heels. *Paul Costelloe*

She told me forties fashions were back so I went out and got her a gas-mask. *James McKeon*

A specialist in women's fashion once said of me, "When you see Nell at a press conference you don't know whether to give her a hand-out or a penny." She was referring to the fact that I am the worst-dressed journalist, if not female, in Dublin. *Nell McCafferty*

Fashions, after all, are only induced epidemics. *George Bernard Shaw*

Fashion is a form of ugliness so intolerable we have to alter it every six months. *Oscar Wilde*

There's nothing as unfashionable as yesterday's fashion. *John McGahern*

Women are wearing their dresses so short these days they'll soon have four cheeks to powder all at once. *Dave Allen*

I was up in Camden market and I saw this guy who wasn't wearing a leather jacket and I thought: *Poser. Sean Hughes*

# FATALISM

How many Irish people does it take to change a lightbulb? None. They're happier sitting there in the dark. *Arthur Mathews*

# FATHERS

I became a father last Saturday. My immediate future will doubtless be a never-ending series of clean-ups, nappy changes and conversations about the colour of babies' bowel movements. *Olaf Tyaransen*

My dad is very cool. In fact he's cold. He's dead. *Graham Norton*

Somebody told me I should tell my dad I love him before he dies, but what happens if I do and he lives for another twenty years? I don't think either of us could stand the embarrassment of that. I'd have to kill him. *Ardal O'Hanlon*

My father never let the facts get in the way of a good story. *Ben Kiely*

As far as Irish law is concerned, the status of a separated father is somewhat akin to a visitor from Mars. *Bob Geldof*

I have the typical Irish relationship with my parents. I love them but I don't particularly like them. *Sean Hughes*

My father took the Dublin position on me: "My son the big eejit". *Bono*

We're not the men our fathers were. A good job, in a way. If we were we would be terribly old. *Flann O'Brien*

# FAVOURITES

My favourite word is floccinaucinihilipilification. *Brush Sheils*

People often ask me what my favourite drink is and I always give the same answer. The next one. *George Best*

I have only two favourite books — my eyes and my ears. *Sean O'Casey*

My favourite U2 song? We haven't written it yet. *Bono*

Vinnie Jones' favourite group is Take That. *Michael Cullen*

# FEARS

The people of Ireland used to be afraid of parish priests. Now they're afraid of newspaper editors. *Michael D. Higgins*

I'm very, very afraid of dogs, even nice dogs. Most dog owners simply insist I haven't met the right dog yet. *Marian Keyes*

I live in terror of not being misunderstood. *Oscar Wilde*

We were all mortally afraid of Credo, as we called him behind his back. He moved and spoke majestically, never referring to himself as a priest but as "a priest of God", as if his ordination had been in the nature of a personal appointment by divine warrant. *Hugh Leonard*

The three main things to beware of in life are the hoof of a horse, the horn of a bull and the smile of an Englishman. *Seamus McManus*

What has kept U2 together? Fear of our manager. *Bono*

They say there's nothing to fear but fear itself. That, of course, is complete rubbish. The correct phrasing should be "You have nothing to fear but scary things". *Ian O'Doherty*

Some of my best work has been fuelled by the fear that it might turn out to be my worst. *Róisín Ingle*

My wife and I are getting closer every day. We have to — we're afraid of the kids. *Gay Byrne*

The greatest fear I ever felt was the time I found myself surrounded by six angry Serbs. But hey, that's the price you pay if you want your car washed in London these days. *Sean Hughes*

Madonna said she was scared of her stalker and saw him everywhere she went. Which is kind of how I feel about Madonna. *Conan O'Brien*

If there is one British thing the Irish have always learned to fear, and with good reason, it is British diplomacy. *Sean O'Faolain*

# FEET

Last year I had a foot operation. This year I'm going to play it by ear. *John Aldridge*

Benny Coulter has his left foot in the right place. *Colm O'Rourke*

Mick McCarthy will have to replace Tony Cascarino because he's quickly running out of legs. *Mark Lawrenson*

Kilbane's head is better than his feet. If only he had three heads, one at the end of each leg. *Eamon Dunphy*

Most players would give their right arm for Jason Wilcox's left foot. *Mark Lawrenson*

*My Left Foot* went to my head. *Brian Friel after that movie's success*

Where the dropping of bricks is concerned, I can say with hand on heart that I have never in my life put my foot in it. It has always been both feet or nothing. *Hugh Leonard*

If you fall off that wall and break your legs, don't come running to me. *Biddie McGrath*

When you're having sex you put your face in places you wouldn't normally even put your feet. *Tommy Tiernan*

Samson died from fallen arches. *Paddy Cole*

You know, Bridie, standing up all day is great for me piles. *Paul Ryan*

There's nothing keeps the feet warm like an empty petrol tin full of hot water. *Patrick Myler*

I've got difficult feet. Lengthways they're size ten and sideways size twelve. *Patrick Campbell*

I went to the doctor with a pain in my left foot. "It's age," he said. "Then why do I not have a pain in the right one as well?" I asked. "They were born on the same day." *Joe Cuddy*

People slag me off about my right foot but without it I couldn't use my left one. *Former Mayo footballer John Morley*

# FEMINISM

The last thing I wanted to be called was a feminist. Feminists were shrill, hairy-legged harridans who couldn't get a boyfriend. Did you know you can be a feminist and (a) wear pink, (b) have sex with men, and (c) enjoy a good laugh? *Marian Keyes*

Feminism is the result of a few ignorant and literal-minded women letting the cat out of the bag about which is the superior sex. *P. J. O'Rourke*

I was never sure who post-feminists were but when I looked around I saw that we went to the gym a lot, we bought plenty of shoes, and most of us still had crappy, badly paid jobs. But apparently it was our fault now, not the system's. *Marian Keyes*

No man is as anti-feminist as a really feminine woman. *Frank O'Connor*

Rock the system, not the cradle. *Mary Robinson's message to women when she was elected President of Ireland in 1990*

# FIANNA FÁIL

*Fianna Fáil was Ireland's former leading political party*

Fianna Fáil has about as much credibility on the economy as Osama bin Laden had on peace movements. *Pat Rabbitte in 2011*

There are lies, damn lies, and Fianna Fáil party political broadcasts. *Barry Desmond*

Fianna Fáil seems to me to be still redolent of top hats, motorcades, museums and the odd distant wave from a passing limousine. *John Bruton*

Your average Fianna Fáil politician is likely to say something like "We must tighten our belts for the lean times ahead" before unbuckling his own one and ravishing your sister. *David Kenny*

Fianna Fáil is a populist movement of the centre-left or centre-right, depending on wind conditions. *Frank McNally*

Fianna Fáil has a great chance of winning the next election, but only if they change the rules and turn it into a raffle. *Michael Cullen*

For God's sake don't legalize abortion in Ireland for you're killing not alone a baby but the future voters of Fianna Fáil. *Pauline Davey*

I suspect what people wanted was just to get rid of Fianna Fáil. They would have voted for anybody short of Saddam Hussein. *Michael Taft on Fine Gael's defeat of Fianna Fáil in Ireland's 2011 general election*

If Bono ever decided to throw in the rock thing, he would have a huge future in Fianna Fáil. *Bertie Ahern*

# FIGHTING

A man was treated in a Belfast hospital tonight for a broken nose, a fractured jaw and a black eye. He received the injuries when fighting for his girlfriend's honour. But it appeared she wanted to keep it. *Peter Cagney*

Where would an Irishman be without a prayer in a fight? *Pat O'Brien*

Fighting for peace is like fucking for chastity. *Brendan O'Carroll*

There's a story that an Irishman came upon a fight involving a dozen or more bods and politely asked, "Is this a private fight or can anyone join in?" *Malachy McCourt*

As an Australian I was brought up in an Anglo-Irish country. Part of the weirdness of our personality is that inside every Aussie there's an Irishman fighting an Englishman. *Phillip Royce*

An Irishman is never at peace unless he's fighting. *Brendan Behan*

Public brawling is never a good idea unless you're a drunken rock star with serious drug issues, in which case it's obligatory. *Anne Marie Scanlon*

Ireland is a peaceful country and we'll fight anyone who says otherwise. *Richard O'Connor*

# FILMS AND FILM-MAKING

It's actually in my contract: "Must get naked and have intense sex scenes." *Michael Fassbender*

Annoyingly, Clint Eastwood's new biopic of J. Edgar Hoover does not feature Leonardo DiCaprio prancing around in a pink frock. **Donald Clarke**

My favourite film is clingfilm with ham sandwiches. **Katherine Lynch**

*Moby Dick* was the most difficult picture I ever made. I lost so many battles during it I even began to suspect that my assistant director was plotting against me. Then I realized that it was only God. **John Huston**

One of the reasons Western films never took off in Ireland was because of names. Somehow, "Don't shoot Seán, Séamus!" doesn't do it for me. **Noel V. Ginnity**

John Huston was a charming crocodile. **Neil Sinyard**

Do you remember when we went to *The Ten Commandments*? Before it started, this couple behind us had broken five of them. **Jimmy Cricket in a letter to his mother**

My film career is unexceptional. I was in *About Adam* but got edited out due to the fact that I was an extra in unimportant scenes. Well, *scene*. Other than that you can see my arm in the Lyric FM ad with *The Shawshank Redemption* theme. **Karl Spain**

I hear they're making a new version of the Moses story. I believe it looks good in the rushes. **T. P. McKenna**

No matter what you write in America, there's always talk of The Movie. You could write the Manhattan telephone directory and they'd say, "So when is The Movie?" **Frank McCourt**

I don't know how God managed. I'm having a terrible time. **John Huston on directing The Bible**

The port is jammed with yachts, some the size of the Holyhead ferry, and many are leased by hustlers touting films that will never be made. One has to make a distinction between the real phoneys and the fake phoneys. **Hugh Leonard on the Cannes Film Festival**

The most difficult things to portray in a movie are sex and prayer. **Patrick Bergin**

No one can begrudge Robert Downey Jr his spectacular comeback in recent years. Except those who sat through *Iron Man 2, Due Date* and *The Soloist*. **Paul Byrne**

It costs more to make a bad film than a good one. **John Huston**

Watching *Lawrence of Arabia* recently I kept thinking things like, "Weren't we shooting that bit when Omar Sharif got the clap?" **Peter O'Toole**

A lot of movies now are what I call McMovies. They're thought up by marketing people for a target audience and they deal with a very limited range of subjects. It's like they've come to the end of the road. The monster is eating his own tail now and it will keep eating until it annihilates itself. **Gabriel Byrne**

Movie-making is fickle. One minute you're hot, the next you're making movies in Mexico about snakes or giant cockroaches taking over the planet and telling people at some dingy bar that you used to be somebody once. **Colin Farrell**

The budget for *Season of the Witch* was huge. We shot in the Alps. I thought they were going to move them. **Robert Sheehan**

Film is a humiliating medium. You can't fool a 70 mm lens. It's terrifying what it picks up. You can see what time someone hobbled to bed. You can see the germs having a party in his eyeballs. **Peter O'Toole**

Your face is up there 125 feet by 70 feet so you better take this shit seriously. **Pierce Brosnan**

All screenplays should be betrayed when they're turned into films. That's what directors are for. **John Banville**

# FILM REVIEWS

She does most of her acting with her teeth. **John Kelly on Jennifer Connelly in A Beautiful Mind**

I can watch *The Getaway* any time. There's an intensely violent pump-action shotgun scene which is worth watching for itself alone. And it shows you how to beat up your wife. **Shane MacGowan**

Keira Knightley's performance consists of mumbles interspersed with that characteristic gape-mouthed smile of astonishment. Unusually for the star of *Avatar* and *Terminator Salvation*, Sam Worthington gets through whole paragraphs of dialogue without flinging a robot from a skyscraper. **Donald Clarke on Last Night**

If Peter O'Toole had been any prettier in *Lawrence of Arabia* it would have to have been called *Florence of Arabia*. **Noel Coward**

*Tomb Raider* makes *Indiana Jones* look like *Citizen Kane*. A batch of eight scriptwriters worked on it. Presumably they had names like Bubbles and Cheetah and were paid with ripe, juicy bananas. **Joe O'Shea**

*Two Weeks' Notice* is as flat as the line on a broken heart monitor. Hugh Grant and Sandra Bullock have all the finesse of a child's crayon scrawl. I've seen more chemistry between two parked cars. **Pat Stacy**

*Forrest Gump* is a shit movie, partly because Tom Hanks is in it. **Donal Ruane**

Farrell's bleached-blond hair and thick Dublin accent made him come across not as a Macedonian king but rather an assistant manager at a fast food joint. **Paul Byrne on Colin Farrell in Alexander**

*The Princess Diaries* is a light comedy entirely free of gross humour. You could bring your granny to it – if you didn't like your granny. **Donald Clarke**

*Alexander* stank like a dead fish in a rubbish bin behind a glue factory. **Eamonn Sweeney**

It should have been called *The Bridges of Menopause County*. **Brush Sheils on The Bridges of Madison County**

# FILM STARS

There are two kinds of people in this world — those who adore Sandra Bullock and those who should be exterminated. *Ian O'Doherty*

Whatever it was that Pierce Brosnan never had, he still hasn't got it. *Phil Carroll*

Maureen O'Hara always looked as if butter wouldn't melt in her mouth — or anywhere else. *Elsa Lanchester*

Quentin Tarantino has the vocal modulation of a railway station announcer, the expressive power of a fence post and the charisma of a week-old head of lettuce. *Fintan O'Toole*

I remember my brother saying once, "I'd like to marry Elizabeth Taylor." My father said, "Don't worry, son, your turn will come." *Spike Milligan*

The best way to deal with stars is to talk to them about things they don't know. Try to give them an inferiority complex. If the actress is beautiful, screw her. If she isn't, present her with a valuable painting she will not understand. If they insist on being boring, kick their asses or twist their noses. That's about all there is to it. *John Huston*

I told my girlfriend she reminded me of a film star. Lassie. *Brendan O'Carroll*

Keanu Reeves is going to play Superman in a new movie. The villains don't use kryptonite to stop him. They just use big words. *Conan O'Brien*

Charlton Heston made a big comeback in *Planet of the Apes*. He's now beginning to act like one. *Tim Pat Coogan on Heston's bleatings about gun control*

Jennifer Lopez has as much star power as a broken lightbulb. *Philip Molloy*

Michael Caine is an over-fat, flatulent, sixty-two-year-old windbag. *Richard Harris*

# FISH

I went into a pet shop and asked them if they had *Rambo II*. "Don't be ridiculous," the assistant told me, "this is a pet shop." "OK," I said, "give me *A Fish Called Wanda* instead." **Brendan O'Carroll**

Nine out of ten shark attacks take place in water. Of the 10 per cent that take place out of it, the most common scenarios are on the decks of fishing boats, people falling out of bed during shark-based dreams, and stuffed sharks falling from their mountings and crushing people in museums. **David O'Doherty**

I prefer catching mice to fishing. At least then I can sit down and watch the telly instead of standing in a wet field somewhere worried about getting pneumonia, or being raped by hillbillies. **Ardal O'Hanlon**

I've eaten so much fish recently, my stomach goes in and out with the tide. **Jimmy Cricket**

Fishing is a jerk at one end of a line waiting for a jerk at the other end. **Dusty Young**

# FLOWERS

I bought him some flowers to tell him I loved him but they didn't say a word. **Kate O'Brien**

Garage flowers should only be purchased when going to visit someone in a coma, and even then you'd better pray that they don't wake up. **Graham Norton**

When a man brings his wife flowers for no reason, there's a reason. **Molly McGee**

A woman saw her husband coming home with flowers. She said to her friend, "That's me on me back for a week now with me legs open." Her friend said, "Why? Have you no vases?" *Brendan O'Carroll*

# FLYING

If the Air Corps had a frequent flyer programme, government ministers could probably get to the moon and back on their accumulated points. *John Bruton*

I'm a nervous flier so I take Valium before I go on a plane. I still think I'm going to die but I don't give a shit. I'm more worried about the fact that I'll miss the end of the in-flight movie. *P. J. Gallagher*

Michael Jackson was afraid of flying – but then again Michael Jackson was afraid of everything except Disneyland. *Terry Prone*

Murphy walked into a tourist office to book a seat on a plane. "Where would you like to sit?" the lady behind the desk asked him. "Inside," he told her. *Joe Cuddy*

Naomi Campbell takes enough transatlantic flights to have a hole in the ozone named after her. *Aingeala Flannery*

"Were you away at all this year, Mary?"
   "Oh yeah, we went to Tenerife."
   "Where's that?"
   "Jaysus I don't know, luv, we flew."
*Paul Ryan*

The pilot on a plane told his passengers, "I have some bad news and some good news. The bad news is we've been hijacked. The good news is that he wants to go to Disneyland." *Dusty Young*

There's nothing better than flying on a new airline and arriving in a new city. Well, nothing apart from mutually climactic orgasmic sex, or a large-size Mars bar all to oneself. *Paul Kilduff*

If God meant us to be airborne he wouldn't have invented the ground. *Eilis O'Hanlon*

Laws of Air Travel:
1. Your departure gate will always be the furthest from the terminal, regardless of number.
2. The plane will not shake until the meal is served.
3. The amount of turbulence will be in direct proportion to the heat of your coffee.
4. The person next to you will either be a white knuckler or will have need for the little white bag.
5. When you finally get to the lavatory, the "Return to Your Seat" sign will go on.
*Hal Roach*

The last time I was on a plane a sign came up saying "In the event of an emergency, do not panic". What are we expected to do — the crossword? It's like, "We're going to crash. What's eleven across?" *Brendan O'Carroll*

The pilot performed a perfect landing through the fog by sight alone. But a hundred or so items of underwear will never be the same again. *Hugh Leonard*

# FOOD

I can never trust a person who doesn't love food. It's a sign of meanness of spirit. *Joe O'Connor*

If only they'd talk about turnips. *James Joyce to Samuel Beckett when listening to a group of pseudo-intellectuals discussing literature*

One man's meat is another man's *poisson*. *Flann O'Brien*

Give up the mad maple syrup, Beyoncé. I want to see you eating pizza like the rest of us. And wearing big knickers to hold your stomach in afterwards. *Martina Devlin*

I'm quite convinced that in about ten or twenty years' time when you buy food it will have a message on it saying: "Warning. Food is Dangerous to Your Health". *Dave Allen*

A lad from the local deli told me they had a new range of cheese in stock from Jerusalem: Cheeses of Nazareth. *Peter Quinn*

Broccoli, green beans and asparagus can only be enjoyed by nerds, nuns and people with bowel disorders. *Dan Buckley*

It's a terrible world where your child says to you, "Daddy, is this organic?" I grew up with Angel Delight. That was the main course. *Dylan Moran*

The humble cornflake is sometimes maligned. Someone once told me there's more nutrition and fibre in the cardboard box than the cereal. *Paul Kilduff*

One of the old reliable canards about the English was that they were uninterested in food. It was never clear whether this was because English food was terrible or whether English food was terrible because the English weren't interested in it. *Dara O'Briain*

My chewing gum is chewed. *Edward of Jedward*

Once in Cork city a beaming waitress set in front of me a plate awash with watery beans and peas, potatoes with the consistency of a bar of Lifebuoy soap and a steak which not only resembled a mummified hand from the crypt of St Michan's but actually moved as I stared at it. *Hugh Leonard*

Irish parents assume you'll realize they love you because they feed you every day. The Irish way to say "I love you" is "Get the stew into you now, good man". *Des Bishop*

Don't serve a starter for Christmas dinner because it is too difficult to manage a main course, dessert and secret drinking on top of one. *David Slattery*

Ronnie Whelan says he hates graffiti. In fact he hates all Italian food. *Michael Cullen*

I'm not against using preservatives in food. What I'm against is any loaf of bread that has a life expectancy greater than my own. *Hal Roach*

A stewardess on Aer Lingus asks a passenger if he'd like lunch. "What's on the menu?" he asks. "Well, there's chicken, beef, salmon or duck." "What's the duck like?" "It's like a chicken but it swims." *Terry Wogan*

Fr Ted: "Dougal, you can't sit around here watching TV all day. Chewing gum for the eyes."
Fr Dougal: "Ah no thanks, Ted. I've got these crisps here."
**Father Ted**

# FOOLS

If anyone is described as an old fool, you may rest assured that he was a young fool as well. *J. P. Mahaffy*

The wise are polite all the world over but only fools are polite at home. *Oliver Goldsmith*

Though marriage makes man and wife one flesh, it leaves them still two fools. *William Congreve*

# FOOTBALL

You have to put your shoes in Daniel Levy's shoes. *Mickey Quinn*

Listening to a modem starting up for ten minutes through a loud hailer would be soothing compared to having to endure one of Steve Staunton's press conferences. People have been known to get tinnitus of the eyes from reading his newspaper interviews. *David Kenny*

I have a suggestion for Roman Abramovich. Use your money to buy all the best players in the world for Chelsea. Then buy all the other teams in England and the rest of Europe. And make sure they only have shite players. You'll win everything.

Then hopefully you'll shag off back to the arse-end of Russia or wherever it is you're from. *Paddy Murray*

Our group has been called the Group of Death. I prefer to think of it as the Group of Debt. *George Hamilton on Ireland's pairing with recession-hit Italy and Spain in the draw for the 2012 European Championship*

I came to Ireland about six weeks after you beat Romania in the World Cup – and about eight weeks before you stopped celebrating. *Des Bishop*

David Beckham is the Anna Kournikova of football. How can someone who doesn't use his left foot, who doesn't know how to head the ball, doesn't tackle and doesn't score many goals be considered a great player? *George Best*

Ray Treacy got fifty-six caps for Ireland, and thirty of those were for his singing. *Eamon Dunphy*

It's difficult to play well against poor opposition but San Marino tried their best. *Colman O'Neill on Ireland's narrow victory over San Marino in the European Championship qualifying match in 2007*

If the Estonians played any deeper they'd have been in another country. *Mark Lawrenson*

I've got a love–hate relationship with soccer officials. They love me and I hate them. *Liam Tuohy*

If bullshit was electricity, the modern football industry would be a power station. *Brian O'Connor*

If we win I'm taking the whole squad to Portugal for four days of sunshine and golf. If we lose, they'll be in for extra training and then off to a caravan site in Bangor. *Joe Kinnear before a tussle with Everton in 1998; Bangor got the vote*

Football is all very well as a game for rough girls but it is hardly suitable for delicate boys. *Oscar Wilde*

After the joy of hammering a burst ball against a wall, the only surprises left for my son now are sex and Elvis. *Roddy Doyle*

In the Dark Ages BC (Before Charlton) when we were crap, tickets for home games were as abundant on the streets of Dublin as nightclub vouchers midweek. *Conor O'Callaghan*

Stephen Ireland is a riddle inside a mystery wrapped up in an enigma. *Garry Doyle on the troubled star who refused to play for his country*

There's a word you don't hear around footballers' dressing rooms any more: mortgage. *Niall Quinn*

When I pick a team I don't pick the eleven best, I pick the best eleven. *Brian Kerr*

Terry Venables brought England to within a penalty shoot-out of the final of Euro '96 with a team that contained a complete headcase, an alcoholic, a drug-user, a wife-beater, a juvenile delinquent and a man with a variety of personality disorders. And that was just Gazza. *Dion Fanning*

The FA Cup Final is a great occasion, but only until ten minutes to three o'clock. That's when the players come on and ruin the whole thing. *Danny Blanchflower*

It was a no-win game for us, though I suppose we can win by winning. *Gary Doherty*

Emile Heskey was played out of position in South Africa – by about six thousand miles. *Michael Cullen*

A good defeat is a good result for Liechtenstein. *Paul Kilduff*

You know what I like about you, Gary? Very little. *Martin O'Neill to Gary Lineker*

My big hope for the future of football is that it will remain as the focal point of the community, that Crystal Palace will qualify for Europe ... and that one day a British commentator will manage to pronounce Paul McGrath's name properly. *Sean Hughes*

Sunderland is run a bit like Ireland. We drink a lot and run around like nutters. *Jason McAteer*

The nearest we get to a Latin influence is when the lads go down to the local restaurant on Friday at lunchtime. *Martin O'Neill on Leicester*

It was grand playing for Nottingham Forest. Brian Clough just told me to get out, get the ball and pass it to his son Nigel. *Roy Keane*

When I played with Barnsley it was a smalltown club with a chip on its shoulder. Later I went to Millwall, a club with a chip on both shoulders. *Mick McCarthy*

A chap was once trying to get me to play for his club in America. "We'll pay you $20,000 this year," he said, "and $30,000 next year." "OK," I replied, "I'll sign next year so." *George Best*

You know the movie *Speed* where the Los Angeles police officer finds himself on a bus rigged with a bomb? And it's going to explode if the bus goes any slower than 50 mph? That was me when I arrived at Aston Villa. *Paul McGrath*

At Arsenal, if there was a hole in your sock you weren't allowed to wear it. *Niall Quinn*

Paddy stopped following Manchester United because he said it was a waste of good toilet rolls. *Peter Cagney*

For Wimbledon to compete in the Premiership with our finances is like going into a nuclear war with bows and arrows. *Joe Kinnear*

"Why is Manchester United always on telly, Daddy?" asks my five-year-old curiously. "Are they like *Coronation Street*?" *Tom Humphries*

I'm what you'd call ethnically Catholic. Don't believe in God, still hate Rangers. *Dara O'Briain*

There are Manchester City fans who will tell you they're the real representation of Manchester, not Manchester United. The argument held more water when the blue club wasn't spending money like a Kennedy in a Boston brothel. *Brian O'Connor*

There's only one club in Europe that you can leave Manchester United for – Barcelona or Real Madrid. **John Aldridge**

It's a Renaissance. Or, put more simply, some you win, some you lose. **Des Lynam**

If England get a point it will be a point gained as opposed to two points lost. **Mark Lawrenson**

The centre-backs are playing like they've only played twice together before, and that's because they have. **Sean O'Driscoll**

He caught that with the outside of his instep. **George Hamilton**

Your subject is the Football World Cup. It's not just Football and it's not just the World Cup. It's the Football World Cup. **Henry Kelly in a quiz show**

It's a tale of two systems, and both are exactly the same. **Mark Lawrenson**

Chesterfield 1, Chester 1. Another score draw in the local derby. **Des Lynam**

Jack Charlton isn't always right but he's never wrong. **Johnny Giles**

The decisions decided a lot of things but I'll leave other people to decide. **David O'Leary**

They've got to retreat ten metres, or ten yards in old money. **Tom Tyrell**

The longer the game went on, you got the feeling that neither side really wanted to lose. **Mark Lawrenson**

If we'd taken our chances we'd have won – at least. **David O'Leary**

They've just had a huge chunk of slice. **Paul Walsh**

Giggs did everything there but score or pass. **Tom Tyrell**

Last week's match was a case of cat and dog. **John Aldridge**

That was six of a dozen and one of the other. **Andy Townsend**

I hope Joey Barton goes on to have a fabulet season. **Chris Hughton**

Lee must attempt to keep Cech the Czech in check. *Jimmy Magee*

If I don't get the contract I want I won't sign it, but that's not a threat. *Roy Keane*

I find the growing intervention of the footballing authorities into football a rather worrying trend. *Kenny Cunningham*

It's *déjà vu* all over again. *George Hamilton*

What that situation really needed was a little eyebrows. *George Hamilton*

He hasn't made any saves you wouldn't have expected him not to make. *Liam Brady*

These managers all know their onions and cut their cloth accordingly. *Mark Lawrenson*

The Spanish manager is pulling his captain off. *George Hamilton*

To describe his players as pawns on a chessboard would be unfair – to chess. A better comparison would be to draughts. *Roy Keane on Jack Charlton's managership of the Irish football team*

I've seen big men hide in corridors to avoid him. *Martin O'Neill on Brian Clough*

The players will say the manager has been underlined. *Ronnie Whelan*

Ever since I was appointed manager of Sunderland I've been walking around the place looking like I've got a coat hanger in my mouth. *Mick McCarthy*

Anyone who's thinking of applying for the job of Scotland manager in the next eight or nine years should go and get themselves checked out by about fifteen psychiatrists. *Martin O'Neill*

Great managers have to be ugly and swear a lot. *George Best*

I had no interest in going straight into football management after my playing career ended. My plan was to chill out for a few years and spend time with my family but they got fed up with me. My wife dropped me off at the stadium. *Roy Keane*

There's only one certainty in football: managers get sacked. *Brian Kerr*

I asked the manager for a ball to train with. He told me they never used a ball at Barnsley. The theory was that if we didn't see it all week we'd be hungry for it on Saturday. I told him that, come Saturday, I probably wouldn't recognize it. *Danny Blanchflower*

Players win matches but managers lose them. *Liam Harnan*

Most chairmen go through nine managers. When I was at St Patrick's Athletic I went through nine chairmen. *Brian Kerr*

The managerial vacancy at the club remains vacant. *Fran Fields*

I managed so many youngsters at Millwall, I had to burp and wind them after every game. *Mick McCarthy*

Barring a personality transplant, Roy Keane's only job at Old Trafford will be as a player. *George Best*

I'm not saying he's going to field a weakened team. It just won't be as strong. *Mark Lawrenson*

# FOREIGNERS

I'm dreading the day they employ a foreigner in my local chemist. I visualize a scene where I go in for Xanax and come out with Durex. *Richard O'Connor*

Maybe the recession is a racist conspiracy, the government's plan to get rid of all the foreigners. *Karl Spain*

The Germans have historically done two things well — Christmas and surrendering. *Philip Nolan*

# FORGIVENESS

Forgive your enemies but remember their names. *Robert Kennedy*

England has forgiven us magnanimously for all the injuries she inflicted on us long ago. *Oliver St John Gogarty*

Let me say before I die that I forgive nobody. *Samuel Beckett*

The Irish forgive their great men only when they're safely buried. *Charles Stewart Parnell*

The Irish forgave Gaddafi for all his war crimes because he was once photographed holding a hurley stick. *John Colleary*

Always forgive your enemies. Nothing annoys them so much. *Oscar Wilde*

# FRIENDS

It's in our thirties that we want friendship. By the forties we realize that won't save us any more than love did. *F. Scott Fitzgerald*

Real pain for your sham friends. Champagne for your real friends. *Francis Bacon*

A friend is someone who lets you help. *Bono*

A man cannot be too careful in his choice of enemies. *Oscar Wilde*

George Bernard Shaw hadn't an enemy in the world but none of his friends liked him. *Oscar Wilde*

The Bible tells us to forgive our enemies. It doesn't say anything about our friends. *Peter O'Toole*

It's worth remembering, any time you get the urge to be reckless on Facebook in the belief that your friends would never do you down, that Benjamin Franklin once opined that three people can keep a secret — if two of them are dead. **Terry Prone**

# FUNERALS

I'd like a Joycean funeral with florid black horses going through the streets of Dublin. And please, would the ladies wear some pretty hats? **Mary Kenny**

A stooped old man stood deep in thought watching the funeral procession pass by. I whispered to him, "Who died?" He said, "The man in the coffin." **Seamus Flynn**

If I were asked what I thought would be the national sport of Ireland's future I would say without hesitation — funerals. **Alan Bestic**

I used to gatecrash funerals for the free booze. One day a woman found me out and asked me to leave. "With an attitude like that," I said to her, "I don't know how you ever make any friends." **Michael Redmond**

Funerals are Ireland's most frequent and important carnivals. **John McGahern**

The funeral has the added attraction over other gatherings in that it is totally spontaneous. **Tadhg Hayes**

Funerals beat weddings hands down for the Irish for one very important reason: you don't have to buy a present for the host. **Cathal O'Shannon**

The West's a wake. **Flann O'Brien**

I have a sense of humour that would cause me to nearly break out laughing at a funeral — providing it wasn't my own. **Brendan Behan**

It is bad manners to begin courting a widow before she comes home from the funeral. *Seamus McManus*

A man died on his holiday in Spain and the corpse was flown home. At the funeral someone said, "Isn't he a lovely corpse? That fortnight must have done him the world of good." *Shaun Connors*

Given the unlikely option of attending a funeral or a sex orgy, the dyed-in-the-wool Celt will always opt for the funeral. *John B. Keane*

We do funerals really well in Ireland because we know the value of not being embarrassed about braying with laughter about something when there's a corpse right beside you. *Mary McEvoy*

My mother only commented on my clothes once. She said, "Nell, will you get a frock for my funeral?" *Nell McCafferty*

Franco's funeral. *Brendan Behan, after being asked what he would like to see on a visit to Spain*

Peter O'Toole looks like he's going around just to save funeral expenses. *John Huston*

I once heard of an Irishman who said he'd die happy if he could only live to see his own funeral. *George Brent*

You can always get a good funeral in Ireland but it's not a good country to live in. *John Broderick*

There'll be few at the funeral if you die in harvest time. *Sean Desmond*

Funerals in Ireland are so jolly they should be called funferalls. *James Joyce*

I don't like funerals. In fact I may not even go to my own one. *Brian Behan*

# THE FUTURE

Everyone reaches the future at the rate of sixty minutes an hour whatever he does, whoever he is. **C. S. Lewis**

My concern about Ireland's future could be put into the navel of a flea and still leave room for a bishop's humility. **Hugh Leonard**

I don't believe in fortune tellers. I never saw a newspaper headline yet that said "Psychic Wins Lotto". **Chris Barry**

I once knew a girl who overdosed on the morning-after pill. She got propelled into the future. **Kevin Gildea**

# GAELIC FOOTBALL

They shot the wrong Michael Collins. **Ollie Murphy, unhappy with a referee who bore the same name as the Irish martyr after Donegal beat Meath in a 2003 football match**

I don't write tragedies. **John B. Keane, after being asked if he would write a play on Páidí O'Sé's time as manager of Kerry**

I'm not happy with our tackling, lads. We're hurting them but they keep getting up. **John B. Keane, attempting to rouse the Kerry football team**

We were out-tacticalled on the night. **Laois manager Justy McNulty in 2011 after a defeat**

If Offaly ever win the National League again it will be the greatest accident since the *Titanic*. **Paul O'Kelly**

If I ever insinuate that I'm returning to county management I will tell my wife to have me shot straight away. **Ger Loughnane**

If anything goes wrong anywhere it seems to be my fault. Next thing I'll be blamed for the Famine. **Kildare manager Kieran McGeeney after a defeat in 2011**

What have Sinn Féin and Tyrone got in common? Sinn Féin have a better chance of seeing an All-Ireland. *Colm O'Rourke*

I love football. I just don't like it. *John Maughan*

Q. What's the difference between a dead dog on the road and a dead Meath fan?
A. There are skid marks in front of the dog.
*Pat Spillane*

There are really only two football teams in Ireland: Dublin and Anywhere But Dublin. *David Slattery*

The best excuse I ever got from a player who was late for training was the one who told me the wheel fell off his mobile home. *Eugene McGee*

In rugby you kick the ball. In soccer you kick the man if you cannot kick the ball. In Gaelic you kick the ball if you cannot kick the man. *Sean McCann*

The first half was even. The second half was even worse. *Pat Spillane*

The poet Patrick Kavanagh was also a footballer. Let me rephrase that. He played in goal for Monaghan, which may be a different thing entirely. *Niall Toibin*

Gaelic football, riddled by dowdiness, is populated now by small, tremulous pygmies who snipe at each other by means of blowdart innuendo. *Tom Humphries*

Q. Why do the Dublin footballers ride ladies' bicycles?
A. They have difficulty getting their balls over the bar.
*Pat Spillane*

# THE GAELIC LANGUAGE

The Irish are working hard to restore Gaelic. If they're not careful they'll learn to speak it and then they'll be sorry. *Stephen Leacock*

The main reason I love the Irish language is because it reminds me of puking. *Denny O'Reilly*

Forty years ago, in the dark days of literary censorship, Ronnie Drew came up with a good idea. He suggested that all the masterpieces of literature then banned by the censors should be translated into Irish and sold to the public in cheap, government-subsidized editions. "This," he wickedly pronounced, "would provide the Irish people with the greatest possible incentive to learn their own language." *Declan Kiberd*

Louis XVI asked Count Mahoney if he understood Italian. Mahoney replied that he did as long as it was spoken in Irish. *Sean McCann*

More people speak Chinese to each other in Northern Ireland than Irish. *Unionist MP David Taylor, rubbishing the suggestion that the primarily Protestant university of Queen's in Belfast should have Gaelic signs erected on the premises*

The Irish language adds under-soil heating to the sometimes frozen pitch surface of English. *Frank McNally*

The Gaelic expression for a black man is "fear gorm", which actually means "blue man". I grew up believing blacks were like the Smurfs. *Keith Farnan*

It is worth remembering that if Irish were to die completely, the standard of English here would sink to a level probably as low as that obtaining in England, and it would stop there only because it could go no lower. *Flann O'Brien*

My old teacher used to say we'd all be speaking German if Hitler had won the war. Not if they taught it the way they teach Irish here. *Pat Flanagan*

# GAMBLING

If God didn't mean us to gamble He'd never have invented marriage. **Paul Malone**

The betting man is enviable for only one thing: he knows what to talk about to barbers. **Robert Lynd**

I used to think Gamblers Anonymous was when you got a friend to put the bet on for you. **Sean Hughes**

I once ate a tin of dogfood for a bet. I lost the bet because I bet that I *wouldn't* eat it. **Michael Redmond**

Cigarettes and alcohol can only kill you but gambling can make you poor. **Declan Lynch**

I bet I can make you give up gambling. **Anthony Bluett**

# GAY MARRIAGE

Gay marriage will never work. It's difficult enough when you have even *one* man in a marriage. **Graham Norton**

I believe in gay marriage. Why shouldn't they have to suffer like the rest of us? **Mary Kenny**

I'm not really in favour of lesbian weddings. It would mean *both* parties turning up late. **Tom O'Dwyer**

# GEOGRAPHY

Irish geography is unusual in that the mountains are ringed round the coast rather than stacked in the middle. This is thought to be a way of trying to stop the natives from emigrating. **Terry Eagleton**

Anyone who believes the way to a man's heart is through his stomach flunked geography. *Robert Byrne*

# GOALS

This is the last and final goal from the Turks. *Damien Richardson*

Our twenty-first goal was offside. *Brian Kerr after his Under-18 side demolished a UN team 22–0 in Cyprus*

More football later, but first let's see the goals from the Scottish Cup Final. *Des Lynam*

If you don't want to know the score in the other game, look away now. Actually it's one-all. *Broadcaster Bill O'Herlihy*

It's 1–1, and if there are no more goals it'll be a draw. *Tommy Smyth*

It was the sort of goal to make your hair stand on your shoulders. *Niall Quinn*

The best thing for them to do is to stay at 0–0 until they score a goal. *Martin O'Neill*

I was at Maine Road when City lost 4–0 to Wimbledon. They could have been two up after five minutes and if they had, the result might have been different. *Jim Beglin*

A goal is going to divide the match in many ways. *David O'Leary*

There's no telling what the score will be if this one goes in. *George Hamilton*

All strikers go through what they call a glut when they don't score goals. *Mark Lawrenson*

When I said they'd scored two goals what I meant, of course, was they only scored one. *George Hamilton*

The secret of football is to equalize before the opposition scores. *Danny Blanchflower*

To be a great game, one of the teams has to score first. *Mark Lawrenson*

There's an old saying in football that he who scores next when it's 3–1 can influence the outcome of a game. *Tom Tyrell*

Reporter: "Do you think you'll score today, George?"
George Best: "No, I've got a game."

Southampton have beaten Brighton by three goals to one. That's a repeat of last year's result when Southampton won 5–1. *Des Lynam*

Shay Given almost single-handedly won the match for Newcastle, although obviously he didn't score the goals. *George Hamilton on the Newcastle keeper*

For some men at least, in the match between football and sex, football will always scrape home on goal difference. *Joe O'Connor*

Interviewer: "Ian Wright said scoring a goal was better than having sex with his wife. Would you agree?"
Keith O'Neill: "I don't know. I never shagged his missus."

Neil Lennon wasn't sent off for scoring a goal, and that's what annoys me. *Martin O'Neill*

Even though I'm Irish, my children will be brought up as English kids. I will love my English child even if he scores the winning goal for England against Ireland in Croke Park. *Dara O'Briain*

In an Irish five-a-side, even if the score is 10–1, it's always "Next goal wins". *Des Bishop*

Ireland thrashed San Marino 2–1 with the decisive winner coming in the ninety-fifth minute. *Paul Kilduff*

It was no problem. I used to play Gaelic. *Former Northern Ireland keeper Pat Jennings after scoring a famous goal from a kick-out*

The score is two-all in favour of Rovers. *Philip Greene*

# GOD

Frank Sinatra is living proof that God is a Catholic. *Bono*

I called the Scientology office but just got their voicemail. I wonder if God has voicemail. *Paul Flood*

God has to be rescued from religion. *Sinead O'Connor*

The Greeks said God was always doing geometry. Modern physicists say he's playing roulette. *Iris Murdoch*

Why do we always assume God is a man? Maybe God is a woman. Maybe God is black. Maybe God is a black woman. Maybe He's dead. Maybe He's a dead black woman. *Dave Allen*

I sometimes think that God, in creating man, overestimated his ability. *Oscar Wilde*

God has to be a woman. If he was male he would have put testicles on the inside. *James McKeon*

It is sad. One half of the world does not believe in God and the other half does not believe in me. *Oscar Wilde*

God made the world in six days and rested on the seventh. The eighth he set aside for answering complaints. *Maureen Potter*

God can be a bastard sometimes. He doesn't mind you saying that. *Sinead O'Connor*

I used to think of God as a kind of celestial Jeremy Beadle. *Marian Keyes*

God's best trick was managing not to exist and also fuck my life up at the same time. *Sean Hughes*

I don't believe there's a God who says, "If you drink, do drugs and swear and rob houses you're not sitting on my cloud." *Noel Gallagher*

God was satisfied with his work. That is fatal. *Samuel Beckett*

I prefer to think God isn't dead, just drunk. *John Huston*

God plus one is a majority. *Michael D. Higgins*

Ignore God and he might just go away. *Donald Clarke*

# GOLF

Colin Montgomerie hit a three-wood 300 yards down the left side of the fairway. If he'd rented a car, filled the tank full of rocket fuel and brought along an Ordnance Survey map of the West Midlands he couldn't have sent it any further. *Lawrence Donegan*

I wish it had bitten me a little lower down. *David Feherty, whose arm swelled up to twice its normal size after being bitten by a snake at Wentworth*

A typical round of golf: one minute you're bleeding, the next you're haemorrhaging, the next you're painting the Mona Lisa. *Mac O'Grady*

Golf was invented specifically to allow Irish males to buy other Irish males presents without attracting any embarrassing suspicion about the motive involved. An Irish male can buy anyone a box of golf balls or a putter. If stuck, you can buy golf balls for your entire family and friends. If they don't play golf, you can suggest they should take it up for the New Year. *David Slattery*

When you play from a rough lie your buttocks are clamped as you pray that the recipient of the venomous swipe doesn't fly out like a wounded snipe across the green into the same crap. *David Feherty*

Darren Clarke has been partnered with Sergio Garcia, Lee Janzen and himself. *Con Murphy*

"What's your score?" the country club interviewer asked the new club member. "Not so good," replied the golfer. "It's sixty-nine." "Hey, that's not bad. In fact it's very good." "I'm

glad you think so. I'm hoping to do better on the next hole."
**Hal Roach**

My father used to say golf just fucked up a good walk. **Keith Duffy**

It is now not generally believed that golf originated in Scotland. No Scotsman would invent a game in which it was possible to lose a ball. **Des MacHale**

The Ryder Cup is like a golf version of the Eucharistic Congress. For the less zealous, it's more like an Electric Picnic for the sensible shoes generation. **Miriam Lord**

Seve Ballesteros spent so much time in the woods, he carried an axe as one of his clubs. **David Feherty**

Bobby Locke even hooked his putts. **Christy O'Connor**

It was as if I'd placed a garlic tiara on the head of Dracula's granny. **Lawrence Donegan after waving his marshal's armband at a woman during the Ryder Cup**

Golf is the only game in the world in which a precise knowledge of the rules can earn you a reputation for bad sportsmanship. **Patrick Campbell**

Switzerland may be the world's biggest public golf course. **Paul Kilduff**

I'm the big brash fella who gives the ball a massive wallop and doesn't give a fiddler's toss where it ends up. **Ronan Rafferty**

To acquire a media pass for the Ryder Cup I only had to submit my family tree, some old diaries, my blood group and inside leg measurement. **Lise Hand**

At the second tee I'm told if I go right I'll end up in the trees. I go right. There follows the most scary woodland scene since *The Blair Witch Project*. **Liam Mackey**

Good news: ten golfers a year are hit by lightning. **George Carlin**

The fervent hordes progress with unshakable faith from the altar of the first tee to the shrine of the green. Yea, though they walk through the valley of the squelching muck they shall feel no distress, for Tiger is with them. *Miriam Lord during Tiger Woods' dominance of the game*

Running water meets leafy shade on a golf course and on the last day of summer you wouldn't want to be anywhere else. That is until you top your drive, scuff another couple of shots, hit the solitary tree in the middle of the fairway and three-putt on the green. *Liam Mackey*

Colin Montgomerie looks like a bulldog licking pee off a nettle. *David Feherty*

Hopeless golfer to caddy: "I'd move heaven and earth to break ninety."
Caddy: "Try heaven. You've moved enough earth already!"
*Terry Wogan*

There's no place for a caddy or his player to hide on the pro tour. If the cannibals don't get you, the quicksand will. *John O'Reilly*

The first thing to understand about caddying is that it's not brain surgery. It's much more complicated than that. *Lawrence Donegan*

A caddy is a small boy employed at a liberal stipend to lose balls for others and find them for himself. *Hal Roach*

My caddy found my ball in the bushes after an hour. I told him it looked very old. "It's a long time since we started, sir," he replied. *Frank Carson*

Asking Jack Nicklaus to redesign Augusta was like asking Andy Warhol to repaint the Sistine Chapel. *David Feherty*

Spain's Guadiana course has more out of bounds than Alcatraz. *Christy O'Connor Jr*

I thought I'd encountered every hazard but on this course you have to take into account the curvature of the earth. *David Feherty on the Crooked Stick course during the 1991 PGA Championship*

As for the event held annually at Augusta — what's so great about flowerbeds and misogyny? *Lawrence Donegan*

Mark Brooks could finish his swing under a coffee table. **David Feherty**

Prince Andrew's swing is about as reliable as my microphone lead. **Eamonn Holmes**

If David Feherty hadn't been a golfer he would probably have been a wringer-outer for a one-armed window-cleaner. **Myles Dungan**

Eamonn Darcy has a golf swing like an octopus falling out of a tree. **David Feherty**

I swing like a toilet door on a prawn trawler. **David Feherty**

My backswing off the first tee put him in mind of an elderly lady of dubious morals trying to struggle out of a dress too tight around the shoulders. **Patrick Campbell**

# GRAFFITI

In 1986 a notice in the maternity unit of the Belfast city hospital warned the staff: "The first five minutes of life are the most dangerous". Underneath someone wrote: "The last five are pretty dicey too". **Allen Foster**

I once saw a fantastic thing written on a wall in Dublin. It said, "God is dead. Nietzsche." Written underneath was "Nietzsche is dead. God." **Bono**

Oedipus – ring your mother. **Graffiti from toilet door of University College Dublin**

I was in France once and I saw a sign saying: "Please do not pluck the leaves". Someone had written below it: "The wind cannot read". **Con Houlihan**

Explosive expert required: willing to travel unexpectedly. **Graffiti at army depot**

If you're tired of sin, come in. **Notice on church door. Someone added underneath: "If not, see Biddy round the back after Mass!"**

Smoking cures cancer. **Graffiti in Dublin pub toilet**

# GRAVEYARDS

I like Italian graves. They look so much more lived in. *Elizabeth Bowen*

Kilbarrack is the healthiest graveyard in Dublin because it's near the sea. *Brendan Behan*

"Before I'd allow myself to be buried in a Protestant cemetery," sniffed Sister Theresa, "I'd rather be dead." *Henry Spalding*

I live near a graveyard which has a sign that says: "Do not use the footpath to the crematorium. It is for patrons only." *Dave Allen*

Teacher: "Why was President de Valera buried in Glasnevin?"
Pupil: "Because he was dead, sir."
*Mary Feehan*

Glasnevin Cemetery is the dead centre of Dublin. *Alice Glenn*

Personally I have no bone to pick with graveyards. *Samuel Beckett*

Never make a task a pleasure, as the man said when he dug his wife's grave only three feet deep. *Seamus McManus*

Dublin in 1948 was like a graveyard with lights. *Lee Dunne*

I met my love in a graveyard,
I did her before we were wed.
I laid her on top of the tombstone —
We did it to cheer up the dead.
*Doggerel attributed to Brendan Behan*

# GREETINGS

A merry Christmas to you all. Or as the late Humphrey Bogart observed when he took up geometry, "Here's looking at Euclid." *Hugh Leonard*

For me, Sophia Loren is the most beautiful woman in the world. Even when she said hello to you, you melted. *Stephen Boyd*

In most countries when you say hello to people they say hello back. In Ireland they say "Fuck off". But it really means the same thing. "Fuck off" is a term of endearment here. *David McSavage*

Hello, I'm the devil. *Alex Higgins to Stephen Hendry after coming back to snooker from a ban for bringing the game into disrepute*

I wish you all a dull Christmas. Could wish you nothing better: I feel so sorry for December. *Polly Devlin*

Cork people have a way of saying hello that makes it sound like an accusation. *Dylan Moran*

The phrase "How are you?" isn't a question in Ireland; it's a greeting. If you treat it as a question and reply to it, people will start running the other way. *Maeve Binchy*

If you watch Irish people in their natural habitat they will commonly greet one another with an insult. This is really a sign of affection. A compliment in Ireland is treated with the utmost suspicion because it is always associated with an ulterior motive. *Des Bishop*

Before I start attacking him, let me wish the Minister for Finance well. *Arthur Morgan*

When I arrived at Richard Harris's door once I was greeted by his wife with the words, "Hello Malachy, when are you leaving?" *Malachy McCourt*

The phrase "Have a nice day" sounds more like a threat to an Irish person than a good wish. He thinks: Fuck off, I'll have whatever kind of day I fucking like. *Tommy Tiernan*

The existential conundrum "Oh, it's yourself" is a common form of address for the Irish. It deftly avoids any possible social death from mislaying a name. **Dara O'Briain**

There was a time Irish people used to make up their own expressions. Now we copy them from American soaps. I even hate "Hi" as a greeting. What ever happened to "Howiye"? **Ronnie Drew**

One of my standard responses to "How are you?" is "If I was any better, God would be jealous." **Malachy McCourt**

A woman greeted me recently with the words, "God bless you, I believe you've just turned seventy-five. You don't look a day over seventy-four." **Brendan Kennelly**

I don't like greetings. After you say hello to someone you think: What will I say next? "Would you like a pineapple?" **Dylan Moran**

Good evening ... Well, that was my new material. Nice to have it out of the way. **Ian MacPherson**

# GROSSNESS

Why do I not like Marlon Brando? Because I don't enjoy actors who seek to commune with their armpits. **Greer Garson**

One day when Brendan Behan was not all that much advanced in alcoholicity, he felt the need to expose his genitals to a pub half-full of indifferent boozers. It was a depressing illustration of what Paul Valéry meant when he wrote: "When one no longer knows what to do in order to astonish, one offers one's pudenda to the public gaze." **John Ryan**

If Chris Rea joined up with Dire Straits, they could call themselves Diarrhoea. **Eanna Brophy**

I'm not saying the pub I drink in is rough but they have a pig on the counter for an air freshener. **Sil Fox**

I don't agree with people who say their wife is their best friend. If you were scratching your private parts while watching a football match on TV your best friend wouldn't nag you. Your wife would. *Jason Byrne*

Watching Steve Davis play snooker is like watching your stools float. *Alex Higgins*

I guess I was a bad boy growing up. Besides shitting in my pants, I would also shit in other people's pants. *George Carlin*

TV shows get more gross as the years go on. Take *The Fear Factor*, for instance, where someone had to eat a kangaroo's anus. That gets a bit tedious after a while. I have a better idea: make them eat a kangaroo's anus while it's still attached to the kangaroo. *Simon O'Keeffe*

Today's singers are too bland. Janis Joplin used to come out in clothes woven from her own vomit. *Dylan Moran*

Riley was arrested for gross indecency. His defence was that he'd only done it 143 times. *Peter Cagney*

I've never understood the expression "Death before dishonour". That's a big price. I'm OK with a lot of dishonour. I'd happily fellate a Smurf to avoid death. *Dylan Moran*

I have been assured by a very knowing American of my acquaintance in London that a young healthy child well nursed is, at a year old, almost delicious, nourishing and wholesome food, whether stewed, roasted, baked or boiled, and make no doubt that it will equally serve in a *fricasse* or a ragout. *Jonathan Swift*

If anybody is thinking of moving in with their boyfriend or girlfriend, don't. Get them to move in with you instead. You're in a much better position that way. So if she comes in and says, "You left a dirty plate in the sink," you can say, "Yes, but I've stopped shitting in the bed." *Ed Byrne*

# GUILT

Most of the things I've done are my own fault so I can't really feel guilty about them. *George Best*

I've got a Protestant mentality and a Catholic work ethic, which means I can sit on my arse all day and not feel guilty about it. *Bernadine Corrigan*

Verdict of an Irish jury: "We find the man who stole the mare not guilty." *Sean McCann*

I was flushed with Catholic guilt until I was nineteen and a half. What stopped it was an experience with a German student on top of the Sugar Loaf mountain on a wet Sunday afternoon one October. *Christy Moore*

Catholic guilt is what makes sex fun. If you're not feeling guilty about it, what's the point of doing it? Sex for Catholics is always so much better. *John Connolly*

The thriller is the cardinal literary form of our time. All the twentieth century wants to know is one thing: who's guilty? *Brigid Brophy*

In a Dublin court today an Irishman pleaded guilty to being inebriated behind the wheel of a vehicle. He said he left a party early because he'd been too drunk to sing. *Sean Dunne*

Damien Boyd, appearing before District Justice Bob O'hUadaigh on a petty larceny charge, was asked, "How do you plead, guilty or not guilty?" "I don't know," he replied, "I haven't heard the evidence yet." *Bernard Neary*

# GUINNESS

Some people boast about being in the *Guinness Book of Records*. I'm famous for being in the Record Book of Guinnesses. *Richard Harris*

The reason there are more piano players than violinists in Ireland is because it's too hard to balance a pint of Guinness on a violin. *Leo Moran*

An Irish cocktail has been defined as a pint of Guinness with a potato in it. *Henry Kelly*

An Irish queer is a man who'd walk across twelve bottles of Guinness to get to a naked woman. *Lee Dunne*

Had a tour of Americans in the other day and was handing out a few pints of Guinness. One of the Americans was watching and came up to the bar and said, "That looks real good. I'll have to try a pint of your Guinness now that I'm here in Ireland. But can I get one without the cream? I'm lactose intolerant." *Barman quoted by Peter Quinn*

He was a bottle-fed infant. He could have been breastfed but he preferred Guinness. *Peter Cagney*

Q. During what month do the Irish drink the least Guinness?
A. February.
*Ray MacAnally*

An Irishman is essentially a mechanism for converting Guinness into urine. *Niall Toibin*

# GYNAECOLOGISTS

The best working environment for a gynaecologist is a womb with a view. *Fran Dempsey*

Gynaecologists enter houses by putting their hands through the letterbox. *Des Hackett*

If it's wet, dry it. If it's dry, wet it. Congratulations, you are now a gynaecologist. *Patrick Murray*

Gynaecologist Seeks Suitable Opening. *Ad in* **Cork Examiner**

# HAIR

Even when Micheál MacLiammóir took to writing autobiographies in later life, they were generally about as reliable as his hairpieces. *Sheridan Morley*

I'm not that fussy about my hair. Having said that, it does take me at least eight hours to get it just right. This is called sleep. *Sean Hughes*

God is cruel because he's not just satisfied with making men go bald. That would be too easy. What he does is pull the hair out of their heads through the nose and ears. *Fergal O'Byrne*

I sent my son to Bobby Charlton's School of Excellence. He came back bald. *George Best*

Talk about being shrewd. I know a fellow who gave his wife six different wigs. No matter what colour hair she finds on his collar now, he's covered. *Hal Roach*

Fussiness? We had to reshoot the whole first ten days of *Hello Again* because Shelly Long thought her hair was wrong. *Gabriel Byrne*

Customer in barber shop: "How's my hair looking there?"
Barber: "You have alopecia. Have you seen a doctor about it?"
Customer: "Yeah, I got a prescription for it. He says it's caused by stress."
Barber: "That's right. Have you had anything unusually stressful going on recently?"
Customer: "Yeah. I'm a bit stressed about losing my feckin' hair!"
**Short Back and Sides**

My girlfriend has a red head. No hair, just a red head. **Sean Kilroy**

Tony Blair is just Margaret Thatcher with bad hair. **Boy George**

I went to the barber to get my hair cut. "You're going bald," he told me. "Well you'd better get a move on then," I said. **Gene Fitzpatrick**

Micheál MacLiammóir wore a bald wig over his actual one to show he wasn't bald. Which begs the question: why did he wear one at all? **Niall Toibin**

# *HAMLET*

Are the commentators on *Hamlet* mad or only pretending to be? **Oscar Wilde**

*Hamlet* is a terrific play but there are too many quotations in it. **Hugh Leonard**

It's only a matter of time before an actor is chosen for the role of Hamlet by the size of his penis. **Micheál MacLiammóir**

To pee or not to pee, that is the question. **Clodagh Sheehy**

# HANGING

No more hanging? What's this country coming to? **Patrick McCabe**

There's no satisfaction in hanging a man who does not object to it. **George Bernard Shaw**

The army works like this: if a man dies when you hang him, keep doing it until he gets used to it. **Spike Milligan**

The garter has hanged more men than the halter. *Dennis O'Keeffe*

Once they abolish hanging in this country they'll have to hang twice as many. *Sir Boyle Roche*

# HANGOVERS

Brendan was the type of man to complain that his hangover was due to a bad pint he got ... probably the twenty-seventh. *Brian Behan on his brother*

You can write with a hangover. That's why so many writers are alcoholics. *Neil Jordan*

Kingsley Amis once recommended sex as a cure for a hangover. This makes sense, because if I thought Kingsley Amis was going to make love to me I'd certainly avoid getting drunk. *Joe O'Connor*

The best cure for a hangover is to find a good book and go to bed with it. Better still, find a woman who will read it to you. *David Feherty*

The best cure for a hangover is to stay drunk. *Donal McCann*

I hit a shot into the trees once when I was suffering from a hangover. There was method in my madness. I had a man in there with a flask of coffee and a hair of the dog. *Former golf professional Christy O'Connor*

I once saw a man taking alternate sips of Scotch and Alka Seltzer, thereby acquiring and curing a hangover simultaneously. *Hugh Leonard*

In Ireland we measure how good a time we had by how we feel the next morning. "How did you get on last night?" "Fantastic. I can't see." *Dylan Moran*

I hardly ever suffered from morning sickness when I was pregnant because I was so used to hangovers. *Caitlin Thomas*

I know I've got Irish blood because I wake up every day with a hangover. *Noel Gallagher*

# HAPPINESS

Anybody who's happy should see a doctor. It's not achievable in this world. *Donal McCann*

The Irish people won't be happy until everyone has more money than everyone else. *John B. Keane*

Only a fool would write out of happiness. *John McGahern*

I never touch alcohol when I'm happy, but it's a well-known fact that Irish men are never happy. *Richard Harris*

Most international studies of human happiness show that the average Irish person derives 63 per cent of his or her sense of well-being from watching England lose football matches. *Declan Lynch*

Van Morrison looks as if he'd be much happier working in a sewer. *Fiona Looney*

I have a very happy relationship with my wife. I try to see her as much as I can. *Brendan Grace*

Happiness is no laughing matter. *Richard Whately*

Happiness for an Irishman is being married to a nymphomaniac who owns a racecourse above a pub and turns into a pizza after sex. *Michael Dwyer*

Happiness makes the Irish feel sad. *David McSavage*

Larry Gogan: "Complete the phrase, 'As happy as . . .'. I'll give you a clue. Think of me."
Contestant: "A pig in shite."
*Exchange on Gogan's Just-a-Minute Quiz*

# HEADACHES

She'd give a headache to an effin' aspirin. *Brendan Behan*

Henry VIII wanted to have sex with his wife so she could give him a son but she told him she had a headache. "I've got something that will cure that," he said. *T. P. McKenna*

*In vino headachitas.* *Vincent Dowling*

The ideal sexual experience in Ireland is simultaneous headaches. *Stephen Boyd*

Women refuse sex because of headaches. Men use it to get rid of them. *Dylan Moran*

# HEALTH

I lost my health drinking to other people's. *Brendan Behan*

Dying can damage your health. Every coffin contains a Government Health Warning. *Spike Milligan*

Any sort of check-up frightens me. I always expect them, after consulting their charts, to say, "It's not looking good, Mr Hughes. In fact, according to my notes, you're dead." *Sean Hughes*

The doctor gave my father six months to live. When he couldn't pay the bill he gave him another six. *Dusty Young*

Very few nations are as obsessed with their own unhealthiness as the British. If they cured cancer in the morning, the papers would lead with "Heart Disease on the Rise". *Dara O'Briain*

There are some things I like to get off my chest occasionally. Like phlegm. *Frank Hall*

Modern man has not lost faith. He has just transferred it to the medical profession. *George Bernard Shaw*

A health addict is someone who eats health food so he won't ruin his health and have to eat health food. **Hal Roach**

It is impossible to have health in Dublin. Of any kind. **Samuel Beckett**

# HEARING

My wife says I never listen to her. At least I *think* that's what she says. **Joe Lynch**

My granny wore a hearing aid that she kept at low because whenever she turned it up it whistled, and every dog in Dublin rushed to her side. **Terry Wogan**

She talks so loud you'd be hoarse listening to her. **Eamonn Mac Thomáis**

Eleven of the residents in the old folks home have AIDS. The other thirty-one can hear all right. **Frank Carson**

My eyes aren't what they used to be. They used to be my ears. **Spike Milligan**

Mrs O'Toole had twenty-six children because she was a bit deaf. Every night when she went to bed her husband said, "Will we go to sleep or what?" And she said, "What?" **Shaun Connors**

Lady with deaf aid wishes to meet man with contact lenses. **Classified ad in In Dublin**

# HEAT

Occasionally Ireland has three consecutive days when the sun shines. We call that a heatwave. We walk around semi-naked and complain about the awful heat. The rest of the time we wear overcoats and moan about the cold. **Richard O'Connor**

If you see an Irishman with a tan, it's rust. *Dave Allen*

With all the heat at the World Cup, it was very hot. *Robbie Keane*

We've just had a heatwave. It lasted all day Tuesday. *Richard O'Connor*

My skin is so ginger, I get sunburn opening the fridge. *Colin Murphy*

His car was so old it had a heated windscreen at the back to keep your hands warm while you're pushing it. *Ted Bonner*

# HEAVEN

If you go to heaven without being naturally qualified for it you will not enjoy yourself there. *George Bernard Shaw*

My concept of heaven is everyone walking round in chocolate Rice Krispies slippers. My concept of hell is everyone walking round in chocolate Rice Krispies slippers, melting. *Jason Byrne*

I've never understood the concept of heaven. If it's invisible, why did God put a wall and a gate around it? *Dave Allen*

Well you're up there now with Our Lord, Stalin and Bob Marley, and my parents. Let me take this opportunity to say hello to them. Hello Mammy and Daddy. I hope they're looking after you up there. *Fr Dougal administering the Last Rites to Fr Jack — after a fashion — in* **Father Ted**

I want to die when I'm ninety with a mountain of pillows behind me and sixty priests and forty nuns praying fervently that I'll go to heaven. *Brendan Behan*

"Daddy, will Fr Ted get to heaven?
   "Of course, dear."
   "But how?"
   "Because he's not a real priest."
*Internet joke*

The heaven religion promised wasn't the one we wanted. Heaven was having chips when and as often as you wanted them. Ditto for ice cream. Heaven was having an annual to read any time of the year. Heaven was a Chuck Connors *Rifleman* rifle. **Gene Kerrigan**

My concept of heaven is having the remote control all to myself. **Brenda Power**

One of the consolations of heaven, if we ever find ourselves there, will be that there will be no writers in it. **John McGahern**

If God has any sense of humour, I'm the only one who's going to be in heaven. **Dave Allen**

My idea of heaven is moving from one smoke-filled room to another. **Peter O'Toole**

I want to go to heaven, but if Jeffrey Archer is there I'd prefer to go to Lewisham. **Spike Milligan**

I found it necessary at a very early age to try and imagine heaven. I also tried to list the contents of God's pockets. My father was somewhat taken aback when I suggested a box of matches, on the basis that "Hell might go out". **Tom Doorley**

# HEIGHT

People tell me I look a lot taller on TV. That always surprises me because my TV is only a foot high. **Andrew Maxwell**

I went to a jockeys' convention once. It was the only time in my life when I was the tallest man in the room. **Brendan O'Carroll**

I'm told I'm the same height as Napoleon but that's not very cheering. **Graham Norton**

Bobby Collins was so small we used to say he was the only player in the league who had turn-ups on his shorts. **George Best**

The tall blonde told the attendant in the shop that she wanted a pair of flat shoes. "To wear with what?" he enquired. "My small, rich boyfriend," she explained. *Angela O'Connor*

I was never overweight, just under-tall. The correct height for my weight at the moment is seven feet ten and a half inches. *Brendan Grace*

I'm so small, my first job was a lumberjack in a mushroom factory. I later went on to become a podiatrist for Dolly Parton but quit because I don't like working in the dark. *Noel V. Ginnity*

Sophie Dahl told me an interesting thing about a "spinner". Baffled, I asked her what it was. She said it was a girl who was so small she could sit on top of a man during sex and do a 360-degree turn. I was impressed. *Jason O'Callaghan*

An Irishman who was four foot six inches tall offered his services to a circus. He claimed he was the tallest dwarf in the world. *Peter Hornby*

I am not very tall. As they say in Westmeath, I should have sued the council for building the road too close to my arse. *Mary McEvoy*

Michael Owen isn't the tallest of lads but his height makes up for that. *Mark Lawrenson*

I'd marry a midget just for the handicapped parking. *Kathleen Madigan*

# HELICOPTERS

The thing about helicopters is that they don't want to fly. They'd much rather crash. *Gerry Ryan*

It's pretty easy to recognize a Kerryman on an oil-rig. He's the one throwing breadcrumbs at the helicopters. *Des MacHale*

# HELL

Hell hath no fury like a woman's corns. *Notice in chiropodist's waiting room*

When I was a boy, hell was a terrible place. But in today's hell a snowball would last a long time. *John B. Keane*

My wife converted me to religion. I never believed in hell till I married her. *Joe Lynch*

I wouldn't like to go to heaven and be surrounded by all these goodie-goodies. Hell, on the other hand, would be full of the most interesting people. If God really wants to punish me, He'll send me to heaven when I die. *Dave Allen*

I know that when I die, hell won't do. I'll be forced to spend my days navigating a multi-storey car park while getting a root canal by a dentist in three-quarter-length tracksuit bottoms. *Jackie Kavanagh*

That's what hell must be like — small chat to the babbling of Lethe about the good old days when we wished we were dead. *Samuel Beckett*

If priests were allowed to marry they'd know what hell was really like. *Patsy McGarry*

Hell is any Jack Nicklaus-designed golf course. *David Feherty*

What if God is a woman? Not only am I going to hell but I'll never know why. *Josef Locke*

I'd much prefer to be in hell with my Guinness than up in heaven with my Harp. *Ferdia MacAnna*

I would prefer heaven for climate but hell for society as all my friends are Protestants. *Fr Sean Healy*

If there's music in hell, it'll be the bagpipes. *Joe Tomelty*

# HEREDITY

The Flynns couldn't have children, explained Murphy, because sterility was hereditary on both sides of the family. *Tony Butler*

Insanity Is hereditary. You get it from your children. *T. P. McKenna*

I come from a long line of sales people on my mother's side so I have no problem ringing the doorbell and asking people to let me in. Until I show them the Tupperware. *Bono*

# HIPPIES

A masturbating hippie is a self-raising flower. *Donal Tiernan*

It's easy to recognize an Irish hippie. He's the one wearing the psychedelic donkey jacket and the flared wellingtons. *Sean Hughes*

The Phoenix Park was a sea of colour. That weekend they were holding a hippie convention. I saw a sign saying "Keep On the Grass". *James McKeon*

Why did the lifeguard not save the hippie? Because he was too far out, man. *Philip O'Farrell*

You can always recognize an Irish Catholic hippie – he gives up pot for Lent. *Sean Kilroy*

# HISTORY

In Precambrian Ireland we expected trains to break down. We expected coffee to taste like diesel oil. We expected pop music to be performed by decrepit wedding singers wearing sideburns the size and shape of Scandinavia. *Donald Clarke*

Irish history is confusing. Nobody can agree what happened so we just ignore it, except to have parades from time to time. *Richard O'Connor*

History is a nightmare from which I am trying to awake. *James Joyce*

Aunt: "How did John get on in his history exam?"
Kerry mother: "Bad, but it wasn't his fault. He was asked questions about things which happened before he was born." *Mary Feehan*

We're now approaching Belfast Airport. Please fasten your seatbelts, extinguish your cigarettes, and put your watches back three hundred years. *Niall Toibin*

# ADOLF HITLER

Where did Hitler get the idea for the goosestep? His mother must have brought him to Irish dancing classes as a child. *Tommy Tiernan*

Sex always has consequences. When Hitler's mother spread her legs that night, she effectively cancelled out the spreading of fifteen to twenty million other pairs of legs. *George Carlin*

More lampshades were broken in Britain by golf clubs than by Hitler's bombers. *Val Doonican*

Larry Gogan: "What was Hitler's first name?"
Contestant: "Heil."
*Exchange on Gogan's* **Just-a-Minute Quiz**

It's foolish to think Hitler's first name was Heil. Everybody knows it was Herr. *Hugh Leonard*

A Sinn Féin president in a government of Northern Ireland? That's like Hitler in a synagogue. *David Trimble*

Hitler had an Irish relative called Patrick who was a waiter in the Shelbourne Hotel. When the war ended, obviously he couldn't keep the name. He changed it to Damien Hitler. *Tommy Tiernan*

# HOLIDAYS

I'm just back from my holidays and I'm as brown as Halle Berry. *Deirdre O'Kane*

I knew this man and his doctor gave him two weeks to live. The man said, "Could I have the last week in June and the first week in July?" *Paul Malone*

The first-time holidayers are the worst. No matter where they go they always come back expressing a wish to live there. To me the pure joy of holidays is returning home, checking your phone messages, opening your post and disposing of the milk you forgot to throw out. *Sean Hughes*

Last year I brought my wife around the world on a holiday. She said she enjoyed it but next year she wants to go somewhere else. *Jack Cruise*

The man who said "You can't take it with you" never saw my family pack for a holiday. *Hal Roach*

I'm back for another holiday. *Brian Keenan after returning to Beirut in 2007 — he had once been a hostage there for five years*

A holiday is the time of year when you load up the car with half a ton of luggage, the wife and six kids, grandmother and grandfather, two dogs and the budgie, and then tell the neighbours you're going to get away from it all. **Hal Roach**

It's odd how some people can go away for a week, yet it takes them at least two to tell you all about it. **Sean Hughes**

A perpetual holiday is a good working definition of hell. **George Bernard Shaw**

People go on holidays to get away from it all, and then open their bags to find they've brought it all with them. **Maureen Potter**

Women have two choices for their holidays. They can go to the mountains and see the scenery, or go to the beach and *be* it. **Paul Malone**

I remember a holiday in Cyprus where I kept ringing reception to re-stock the fridge with alcohol. I thought I was being very clever and that nobody would notice, until the end of the week when we went to pay our bill and the mini-bar tab came to £1,300. **Paul McGrath**

My dad is Irish and my mum is Iranian, which meant we spent most of our family holidays in Customs. **Patrick Monahan**

# HOLLYWOOD

Hollywood is the sun-kissed Pompeii. **Pat O'Brien**

Hollywood is full of what we in Dublin call gobshites. **Pat O'Connor**

Dublin was a great preparation for Hollywood. It can be a very bitchy, back-stabbing, gossipy backwater. **Gabriel Byrne**

If you've got a ponytail, a nice Armani suit and the gift of the gab, you can make it in Hollywood. **Liam Neeson**

Clara Bow is alleged to have laid everything in Hollywood but the linoleum. **Dan O'Herlihy**

In Hollywood, nothing fails like success. *Colm Meaney*

Hollywood isn't all glamour. The most exciting thing about my last week there was a mailman bringing me an ironing board cover. *Angela Lansbury*

Hollywood is a quagmire crawling with Judas Iscariots, eagerly waiting to crucify me on high. *Brendan Behan*

I don't want to be that arsehole sitting in the pub and someone turns round and says, "See him there at the end of the bar? He could have made a fortune but after he went to Hollywood he pissed it all up against a wall." *Jonathan Rhys-Meyers*

People talk to me about the refinement and sophistication of James Bond. The reality is that he'd be deaf by now, with emphysema and fucking arthritis as well. *Pierce Brosnan*

Hollywood buys a good story about a bad girl and changes it to a bad story about a good girl. *Richard Harris*

Hollywood aristocrats are people who can trace their ancestry right back to their parents. *Stephen Boyd*

In Hollywood you have to be a bit mad to stay sane. *Peter O'Toole*

Hollywood promises are printed on snowflakes. *Pat O'Brien*

The old joke that changing agents is like changing deck chairs on the *Titanic* is as accurate as the day it was coined. There's another ancient saw about agents, to wit: "You can take all the sincerity in Hollywood, fit it into a flea's bellybutton, and still have room left over for six caraway seeds and an agent's heart." *Malachy McCourt*

I watched Liam Neeson's career take off and I thought "Jesus, great". Then I saw Gabriel Byrne take off, and then Stephen Rea, and then Patrick Bergin. And I thought: "Jesus Christ, I was out here before the lot of them, doing fucking *Remington Steele*." *Pierce Brosnan*

The true objective of the Hollywood Don Juan is not so much the lady's bedroom as a story in the gossip columns. *Philip Dunne*

# HOME

Home is where the hurt is. *Kitty Holland*

Give me a home where the buffaloes roam and I'll show you a houseful of dirt. *Marty Allen*

In most Irish homes there's a terrifying picture which appears to represent a doleful hippie ripping his chest open. It represents the Sacred Heart of Jesus. Frequently it is accompanied by the black-and-white image of a hairy-nosed gaffer, his hand wrapped in bloody bandages. This is Padre Pio. Richard Gere is also popular. *Sean Kelly*

I come from a broken home. I broke it. *Colin Murphy*

I was born at home because I wanted to be near my mother. *Joe Duffy*

# HOMOSEXUALITY

It's better to give than to receive — as I discovered in prison. *Ian Coppinger*

There isn't a well groomed man in Ireland who isn't gay. They're all rugged, like the landscape. I wouldn't know whether to fuck them or frame them. *Deirdre O'Kane*

I hate the term "gay". Why can't they just call us queers? *Micheál MacLiammóir*

It was Adam and Eve in the Garden of Eden, not Adam and Steve. *David Quinn*

You can get gay anything now — gay tea, gay coffee, gay lager. The last one is like straight lager except it goes down easier. *Graham Norton*

It is crucial that straight people have gay friends nowadays.

If you don't have a gay friend, get one as soon as you can. That way, you can pepper sentences with "My gay friend" references, which is very "now". *Pat Fitzpatrick*

In 1850 homosexuality was punishable by death. In 1900 it only merited a jail sentence. In 1960 it was made legal. I'm getting out before it becomes compulsory. *Sean Kilroy*

I'm Not Gay But My Boyfriend Is. *T-shirt slogan*

A politician was asked what we should do about the Homosexual Bill. He said, "I think we should pay it." *Brendan Courtney*

I used to get a lot of taunts about being gay. One man said he'd like to come round to my house and stick a submachine gun up my arse and pull the trigger. Then he thought for a moment and said, "Only you might enjoy it." *David Norris*

The Greeks gave us the Olympics, philosophy and homosexuality. If you lost a race you were buggered, but at least you knew why. *Keith Farnan*

I went into a toilet and there was a sign saying "Beware of Homosexuals". When I came out there was another one saying the same thing. Then I saw a sign attached to the skirting board. I bent down to read it. It said, "You have been warned twice". *Frank Carson*

Have you heard about the rear admiral's vice? It was the vice admiral's rear. *Tim McGarry*

Did you hear about the two Irish gays? Michael Fitzmaurice and Maurice Fitzmichael. *Tom O'Hara*

Sean: "My mother made me a homosexual."
Seamus: "If I gave her a ball of wool would she make me one too?" *Sean Gaffney*

"Paddy," asked the barmaid, "what are those two bulges in the front of your trousers?" "Ah," said Paddy, "they're hand grenades. The next time that queer O'Flaherty comes feeling my balls, I'll blow his bloody fingers off." *Mr O'S*

Why are so many Irishmen gay? Have you seen the women? *Seamus O'Leary*

Oscar Wilde was an Irishman who invented modern queerness. Micheál MacLiammóir was a queer who invented his Irishness. *Adrian Frazier*

Heterosexuals who hate homosexuals should stop having them. *Michael Cullen*

Two, four, six, eight/How do you know St Patrick's straight? *Chant coined by the Irish Lesbian and Gay Organization in 1993 after being banned from participating in the St Patrick's Day Parade in New York that year*

You can be Irish in New York and you can be gay, but you can't be both. *Ann Maguire, spokesperson for ILGO, on the same theme*

# HONEYMOONS

Steve Staunton's honeymoon as manager of Ireland lasted about as long as one of Britney Spears' marriages. *Kevin Palmer*

The honeymoon is over when the wife barks at you and the dog hands you your slippers. *Paddy Reilly*

Did you hear about the Irish newlyweds who sat up all night on their honeymoon waiting for their sexual relations to arrive? *Mr O'S*

It was on my honeymoon I started writing the album called *War*. Go figure. *Bono*

# HORSES

I was born on the seventh day of the week, seventh day of the month, seventh month of the year, seventh year of the century. I was the seventh child of a seventh child and I have seven brothers. On my twenty-seventh birthday at a race meeting I looked at a race-card to pick a winner in the seventh race. The horse numbered seven was called Seventh Heaven, with a handicap of seven stone. The odds were seven to one. I put seven shillings on this horse. It finished seventh. *Anthony Clancy*

A horse show is a lot of horses showing their arses to a lot of horse's arses showing their horses. *Denis Leary*

If Caligula could make a consul of his horse, why should anybody be surprised if a politician makes an ass of himself? *John B. Keane*

I backed a horse at twenty to one. It came in at a quarter to four. *Donal McCann*

When I was a teacher, one of my pupils described a zebra as "a horse with Venetian blinds". *Bryan McMahon*

I tried horse-race gambling once but gave up when the horse I backed fell early on. I know this happens all the time but this particular race was run on a flat course. Afterwards I stuck to the poker machines, which I still have fond memories of, regardless of losing my money each time. I can remember it as if it was yesterday. In fact it *was* yesterday. *Sean Hughes*

He should have played one of the horses. *Donald Clarke on Robert Taylor's performance in* **Knights of the Round Table**

Greg Norman reminds me of the movies. Every time you think he's going to get the girl and ride off into the sunset, his horse breaks a leg. *Rick Reilly*

It has been said that Ireland is to horse-racing what Brazil is to soccer. If you think this is a slight exaggeration you're probably right. The Brazilians are not that good. *Frank McNally*

One of the worst things that can happen in life is to win a bet on a horse at an early age. *Danny McGoorty*

Two kinds of people in Ireland own horses: posh people and people who are on the dole and live in caravans with ten other family members. *Ed Byrne*

First Man: "Did you put a few bob on the horse I told you to?"
Second Man: "I did."
First Man: "And?"
Second Man: "He stood up to shit and he's shitting still!"
*Edna O'Brien*

# HOSPITALS

"Well whaddya know," the newly arrived angel said to St Peter as he was handed a harp, "the doctors were right for a change. They said I'd be out of hospital in a week." *Henry Spalding*

Fr Dougal: "Fr Stone has been in there a long time. Do you think he's dead?"
Fr Ted: "They're probably doing tests."
Fr Dougal: "What sort of tests — general knowledge?"
Fr Ted: "No, no. Medical tests."
Fr Dougal: "Sure what would he know about that, Ted."
**Father Ted**

Notwithstanding the attention of Dr O'Donnell, the patient is making rapid progress. *Patrick Myler*

A hospital should have its recovery room adjoining the cashier's office. *Francis Walsh*

The best way to tell if an Irish person is recuperating in hospital is when he starts to blow the foam off his medicine. *Brendan O'Carroll*

# HOUSES

In 1968 I lived in a house in Rathmines where the bedsits were subdivided so small it eventually caused a nuclear explosion. *Kevin McAleer*

The big thing in every house when I was growing up was the kitchen. We always called it the back-kitchen no matter where it was located. Then we got notions about ourselves and extended it so now it became the "back" back-kitchen. After that we put on another extension so it became the "back-back" back-kitchen. But the original part was still called the back-kitchen. Even if it was at the front of the house. *Jon Kenny*

In England, one's house is one's home. In Ireland, one's house is one's house. Once it has been perfected it can become a home, but not before perfection has been achieved, and perfection is always a roll of wallpaper away. *David Slattery*

Did you hear Fred West's house is up for sale? What a horrible place that would be to live. Gloucester. *Graham Norton*

There's always a wonderful selection of confectionery available at my parents' house. Unlike most houses, though, this isn't in addition to the usual foodstuffs. It's instead of them. *Marian Keyes*

The reason I didn't run for President of Ireland was because I didn't want to move to a smaller house. *Bono*

When you live in a madhouse it is wise to become a lunatic yourself. *Philip Dunne*

# HUMILITY

Humility is my best quality. *John Huston*

I'm a genius. I'm just too humble to say so. *Michael O'Leary*

Irish people can't take compliments. Tell them they look great and they'll say, "How could I? Wasn't I just kicked in the head by a bullock?" *Deirdre O'Kane*

# HUNGER

I'm so hungry I'd eat the back door buttered. *Tadhg Hayes*

I spent a few impoverished years in Paris, but one can starve very well on French bread. *James Stephens*

I used to hear people saying that God never creates a mouth without sending something to fill it. Maybe, but it seems to me he sometimes sends the food to the wrong address. *Patrick Kavanagh*

The colourful Irish phrase for being hungry is "I'd ate [eat] the arse off a farmer through a tennis racquet". *Mary Kenny*

My dietician recommended all sorts of ways of getting used to hunger, such as not thinking about food, drinking lots of water, and going to bed early. But I find that rolling around on the floor and crying hysterically for several hours at a time helps too. *Joe O'Connor*

# HURLING

Getting a one-on-one chat with Osama bin Laden would have been less trouble than face time with a Galway hurler. *Tom Humphries*

Hurling and sex are the only two things you can enjoy without being good at them. *Jimmy Deane*

I love Cork so much that if I caught one of their hurlers in bed with my missus, I'd tiptoe downstairs and make him a cup of tea. *Joe Lynch*

It's like trying to climb Mount Everest when you've been practising on Carrantuohill. ***Donal O'Grady on moving from Division 2 to the Munster Senior Hurling Championship***

I'm always suspicious of games where you're the only ones that play it. ***Jack Charlton on Ireland's "ownership" of the game***

No, but I had to explain it to the people of Wicklow when I got back. ***Wicklow native Dara O'Briain to interviewer Des Cahill after Cahill had asked him if he had to explain the rules of hurling to the British after he left Ireland***

Hurling and Gaelic football are played among the diaspora in Britain and America but marketing the sports to a broader constituency is a problem, especially in the US, where "hurling" is something you do when you have a violent stomach upset. ***Frank McNally***

There's a lot of politics in hurling. I don't think Henry Kissinger would have lasted a week on the Munster Council. ***Ger Loughnane***

# HUSBANDS

The supportive husband cooks and cleans and plays with the kids but still manages to work late, attend conferences, play golf, and take career-enhancing overseas trips. He also asks out loud where his socks are. ***Terry Prone***

I'm ready to find my ex-wife a suitable new husband so I can stop paying her alimony. But Ivan the Terrible is dead, isn't he? ***Peter O'Toole***

Woman 1: "I don't know what to make of my husband."
Woman 2: "How about mincemeat?"
***Seamus O'Leary***

A dog of a husband isn't just for Christmas, he's for life. ***Graham Norton***

When her third husband died, her hair turned quite gold from grief. ***Oscar Wilde***

# HYGIENE

My grandmother took a bath every year whether she needed one or not. *Brendan Behan*

The time-honoured way to decide whether intimate garments are in need of laundering is to throw them against the bedroom wall and see if they stick. If that happens, scrape them off the wall, go into the bathroom and wait for the offending articles to walk in after you. *Joe O'Connor*

The first apartment I ever stayed in was so dirty you had to wipe your feet on the way out instead of on the way in. *Gabriel Byrne*

In an Irish kitchen, cleanliness is next to impossible. *Robert O'Byrne*

I belong to a generation that saw washing its hair once a week in the bath as the height of personal hygiene. *Joe O'Connor*

Her swarthiness owed as much to a grudge against soap and water as to pigmentation. *Hugh Leonard*

If you go long enough without a bath, even the fleas and lice will leave you alone. *Sean Kilroy*

People used to have a bath once a week in Ireland. Now we shower several times a day, pretending to be Protestants. *Ian Coppinger*

# IDENTITY

John Lennon thought he was God. I just think I'm John Lennon. *Noel Gallagher*

I was talking to my nan about Ant and Dec. She didn't know which one Dec was. I said, "Do you know which one Ant is?" She said, "Yes." *Jimmy Carr*

Ronan Keating thinks he's Elton John but he's actually Cliff Richard. *Louis Walsh*

I drink therefore I am. I'm drunk therefore I was. *Seamus O'Leary*

During my book tour for *A Monk Swimming* I was told by hundreds of people how much they loved my brother's book, *Angela's Ashes*. That's when I got the idea of telling people my next book would be called *I Read Your Brother's Book*. Indeed, I was blamed for not actually being my brother. I now pledge to all those naysayers that some day I will write *Angela's Ashes* and change my name to Frank. *Malachy McCourt*

I am therefore I think. Is that putting Descartes before de horse? *Paddy Masterson*

I'm not a writer with a drinking problem. I'm a drinker with a writing problem. *Brendan Behan*

I was in a bookshop in Ireland recently and a guy came up to me and said, "Are you who you think you are?" *Paul Merton*

I like Dolly Parton but I couldn't class her as a friend. She's too busy being Dolly Parton all the time. I'd find that very exhausting. *Graham Norton*

An Englishman, an Irishman and a Scotsman were sitting at a bar. The Englishman said, "I went into my daughter's room today and found a half-empty bottle of vodka. I didn't even know she drank." The Scotsman said, "I went into my daughter's room and found a half-empty pack of cigarettes. I didn't even know she smoked." The Irishman said, "That's nothing. I went into my daughter's room today and found a half-empty box of condoms. I didn't even know she was a boy!" *Nick Harris*

I used to be. *Donal McCann, after being asked by a reporter if he was Donal McCann*

I always liked the idea of playing with ambiguity when I was on stage. People went: Is it a bird? Is it a plane? No, it's Boy George. *Boy George*

I think I'm more me on stage than I am most places. I don't know if there's any one person that is me. Like The Edge says sometimes, I'm a nice bunch of guys. **Bono**

The main character in Kafka's *The Metamorphosis* wakes up one morning to find he's a slug, which will be a sensation familiar to anyone who's drunk Budvar for fifty cents a pint in the Czech capital. More terrifying than waking up as a slug, though, is to wake up in a foreign city after a night of cheap booze and find that you're still yourself. The same self that did those goosesteps in the Old Town Square in front of angry riot police, and said to a girl afterwards that she reminded you of a poledancer back home. **Pat Fitzpatrick**

Once I was like, "Look, John, that's you on TV." Then I realized it was me. **Edward from Jedward**

Ryanair have a proud history of stopping passengers. In 2003 they refused boarding to "It Girl" Tara Palmer Tomkinson because she didn't have a passport. She forgot "It". Apparently she retorted, "Do you know who I am?" She was lucky not to suffer the fate of a US passenger who once shrieked the same riposte to a check-in agent, who used a public address system to speak to the entire departures terminal: "We have a passenger here who does not know who he is. If anyone can help him find his identity please step forward to this counter." **Paul Kilduff**

The investigation took a dramatic turn when we shaved off his beard and discovered it wasn't him at all. **Pat Ingoldsby**

I was on the street. This guy came up to me and said, "I thought you were someone else." I said, "I am." **Colm O'Regan**

# IDOLS

They'd praise my balls if I hung them high enough. **Brendan Behan**

When I was a young girl I fell madly in love with Marlon Brando. I knew all the lines of *On the Waterfront* almost off by heart. I read up about his life and I wasn't happy with some of the women he was dating in Hollywood. Every week I wrote him a letter telling him he should come home to me in Dublin and I'd mind him. I used to get letters back saying "Thank you for being a member of Marlon Brando's fan club", usually accompanied by a photo of him looking moody on a motorcycle, from *The Wild One*. I kept thinking, They don't understand: I don't want to be a member of his fan club, I want to be his *wife*. *Maeve Binchy*

Michael Collins could have buried his grandmother in concrete and people would still have sympathized with him. *Neil Jordan*

# IGNORANCE

He knows nothing and thinks he knows everything. That clearly points to a political career. *George Bernard Shaw*

My mother used to say, "Joe is too dumb to quit anything he starts." *Joseph McCarthy*

If I say that he's extremely stupid, I don't mean that in any derogatory sense. *Barry Fitzgerald*

Dublin is a city with a very dense population. *Dusty Young*

Ask me who's shagging who and I'm a Grade-A student, but ask me who's in charge of the country's finances and I couldn't pick them out of a line-up. *Amanda Brunker*

How long did it take you to become so ignorant? *James Young*

She's so dumb she'll buy anything marked "Down". Last week she brought home two dresses and an escalator. *Hal Roach*

I'm not very well read. I used to think Fellatio was a character in Shakespeare. *Vincent Hanley*

When you're from Kerry and you're as ignorant as us, you have to be fierce clever. *Dick Spring*

Ignorance is like a delicate exotic fruit; touch it and the bloom is gone. *Oscar Wilde*

Paddy: "I'm not a complete idiot."
Mick: "Why? What bit is missing?"
**Dusty Young**

Ignoranse is bliss. **Brian Carmody**

# ILLNESS

Nothing trivial, I hope. **J. P. Mahaffy, upon hearing of the illness of a rival**

"Would you mind if I played through?" the golfer enquired of the others on the fairway. "My wife has just been diagnosed with a serious illness and I have to play the last few holes in a rush." **Joe Linnane**

I was feeling as sick as the proverbial donkey. **Mick McCarthy**

I had to leave my job as road-sweeper due to illness and fatigue. My boss got sick and tired of me. **Jimmy Cricket**

I'm trying to recover from a bout of influenza at the moment so feel only in the mood for prayer and cursing. **Sean O'Casey**

I am often asked to give advice to young writers, but advice is unimportant. They're sick. Writing is an incurable illness. **Hugh Leonard**

# IMAGE

The media has always portrayed me as Mr Perfect, the boring boy next door. I don't make good copy for them. There are no sex and drug scandals. I'm not drying out in some famous clinic. I don't sleep in an oxygen tent. **Daniel O'Donnell**

There have been three big phases of my celebrity. With The Boomtown Rats it was Bob the Gob. With the Live Aid thing it was Bob the God. Then it settled down to a general omnipresence. **Bob Geldof**

I had the image of being a moody boor just because I concentrated hard. **Christy O'Connor**

Ireland doesn't do subtlety. If it's got a big logo and is instantly identifiable as "designer" from the top of the 46A bus, we want it. **Melanie Morris**

People's images of me range from vilification to sanctification. Both piss me off. **Bob Geldof**

I've been described as a writer's writer. This means that both writers and readers hate you. Writers because they're threatened, and readers because they feel you're not for them. God forbid that I should write to be read by writers. **John Banville**

My children see me as the baby of the house, not the other way round. **Richard Harris**

Dara O'Briain is a smug tuberous lump whose success in Britain is grounded entirely on his bovine, slurring, supersized Paddy persona. **Gwen Halley**

There's no mystique around me. The only thing that's around me is a microphone. **Van Morrison**

I often talk to English kids about Ireland. At a recent talk I asked them to put up their hands and tell me something they knew about Ireland. "You drink," one kid said. Another said, "You smell." And then came the most damning of all: "You're poor." **Keith Farnan**

Aldous Huxley was a stupid person's idea of a clever person. **Elizabeth Bowen**

Colin Farrell is regarded as something of a hellraiser in Los Angeles, but in that town anybody still awake after tea-time can gain such a reputation. **Donald Clarke**

# IMITATION

My only talent at school was copying. I was asked to write a poem once so I decided to steal one from a collection. I was seven. I picked "Easter 1916" by William Butler Yeats after first checking the class list to make sure he wasn't that new guy with the monocle and cape. *Tommy Tiernan*

Elvis Costello kidnaps clichés and makes them his own. *Roddy Doyle*

Isn't it great the way Europe has been copying Ireland? Take the smoking ban – we kicked the puffers out on to the streets years ago and it's been followed by a string of other countries. Then we taxed the plastic bag. Again, the others latched on to it. Imitation is the best form of flattery. I can just see the rest of Europe dying to get its hands on our gangland violence, traffic jams, A&E queues, amazing cancer screening system, and our vomit-strewn streets. *Pat Flanagan*

I got all Bob Dylan's records and a guitar and learned the words off by heart, but the guitar was too big for me so I bought a harmonica instead and played it through my nose. *James McKeon*

He was not merely a chip off the old block but the old block itself. *Edmund Burke*

# INACCURACY

He kicked wide of the goal with great precision. *Des Lynam*

My golfing partner couldn't hit a tiled floor with a bellyful of puke. *David Feherty*

Italy had more misses in that match than Henry VIII. *Bill O'Herlihy*

If Lee Harvey Oswald had been a Dublin forward, JFK would still be alive and kicking. *RTE commentator on a Gaelic football match*

In Germany you don't mention the war. In Kildare you don't mention the wides. *Damien Lawlor*

Raoul Moat was the only Englishman to get three shots on target during the World Cup. *Michael Cullen, after Moat had gone on a killing spree in the summer of 2010*

I didn't think he'd miss it again on the action replay. *Sil Fox*

A Shi'ite effort. *David Feherty on a poor shot he played in the Dubai Classic*

# INCOMPETENCE

I was undoubtedly the worst library assistant in the history of Dublin City Council. Perhaps there was a previous recalcitrant claimant to this title, but if so, they bricked him up alive in a cavity wall behind the Non-Fiction section. *Dermot Bolger*

I tried to play like Jack Nicklaus but ended up more like Jacques Tati. *David Feherty after a poor golfing display*

I wouldn't know how to open a bank account. I wouldn't know how to go about getting a postal order. I wouldn't know how to send a registered letter. The one time I went to a Post Office I ended up at the wrong counter. I'm the product of a very long childhood. *George Best*

Edgington tying a bootlace could end up with a broken arm. *Spike Milligan*

If the fourth official had done his job it wouldn't have happened, but I don't want to blame anyone. *John Aldridge*

That bitch couldn't act her way out of a brick shithouse. *John Ford on Maureen O'Hara*

# INFERIORITY

The Irish have such a national inferiority complex that when someone pays us a compliment we take it as an insult. *Michael Noonan*

A Kerry footballer with an inferiority complex is one who thinks he's just as good as everyone else. *John B. Keane*

The Ireland I left was a charming country with an inferiority complex. The one I go back to visit now has a superiority complex, which is slightly less endearing. *Terry Wogan*

# INFIDELITY

Sir Christopher Dilkes' bed was so large, he was alleged to be able to keep his wife in one part of it and his mistress in the other, neither being aware the other was there. *Tony O'Reilly*

I have no time for infidelity — as I was telling the wife's sister in bed the other night. *Conal Gallen*

Many a wife thinks her husband is the world's greatest lover: she just can't catch him at it. *Hal Roach*

I wouldn't trust my husband with a young woman for five minutes, and he's been dead for twenty-five years. *Kathleen Behan*

Mary Stavin is the only woman to whom I was faithful. Almost. *George Best*

Is adultery a sin only adults can commit? *John Banville*

Having it away with a backing singer while his wife stayed home looking after their three young children may have been the one noteworthy thing that this dripping milksop of an artist has done since he first started churning out music so suffocatingly bland that it makes The Carpenters look hardcore by comparison. *Eilis O'Hanlon on Ronan Keating*

A woman I know had seven husbands, including three of her own. *Noel Purcell*

One can always recognize women who trust their husbands. They look so thoroughly unhappy. *Oscar Wilde*

What do Iris Robinson and Ikea have in common? One dodgy screw and the whole cabinet falls apart. *Quip quoted to Peter Quinn after the wife of Northern Ireland First Minister, Peter Robinson, had an extra-marital fling in 2010*

Why do men cheat? Because they can. *Peadar de Búrca*

What are the three words you don't want to hear when you're making love? "Darling, I'm home." *Frank Carson*

Infidelity, or "cheating" as they now call it, is on the rise. There's an old joke about Moses coming down the mountain with his tablets of stone. "The good news," he beams, "is that I got them down to ten. The bad news — adultery's still in." *Mary Kenny*

# INFLUENCES

It was Mussolini who inspired me to go into comedy. *Brendan O'Carroll*

I think I got my rebellious streak from my father. He used to hurl abuse at people and then ask them for money. But then he left the priesthood. *Sean Hughes*

People seem to think that Jack Charlton and myself were influenced by one another. Untrue. I was an arrogant bastard long before I got involved with him. *Mick McCarthy*

My father had a profound influence on me. He was a lunatic. *Spike Milligan*

# INJURY

Ian Snodin and I have both been out injured. He's put on weight and I've lost it, and vice versa. *Ronnie Whelan*

I wasn't long in training before I tore a stomach muscle. Which was a real pain in the arse. *Mick McCarthy*

That's the first time I've ever seen anyone limping off with a sore finger. *Gene Morgan*

The only time I ever heard anyone talking about hamstrings as a football player was when they were hanging out of butchers' shops. *Mick Byrne*

Paul McGrath limps on water. *Tom Humphries*

Achilles tendons are a pain in the butt. *David O'Leary*

I'm suffering from repetitive strain injury. It comes from my golf. I keep going "Putt, putt, putt". *Val Doonican*

Isn't it funny how all newspaper stories about Irish social events seem to begin with "Among the injured were ..." *Peter Hornby*

Jamie Carragher looks like he has cramp in both groins. *Andy Townsend*

He's got a knock on the shin there, just above the knee. *Frank Stapleton*

The groin's a little sore but after the semi-final I put it to the back of my head. *Michael Hughes*

Book-signing is different from what it used to be. Everybody has a mobile phone now, with a camera. Last time, I got repetitive strain injury from all the signing. This time I'm sure it will be lockjaw as well from all the smiling. *Terry Wogan*

# INSOMNIA

Insomnia is a terrible problem but it's not worth losing any sleep over. *Frank Kelly*

I prefer nightmares to insomnia. *Samuel Beckett*

Back at the hotel I can't get to sleep. It sounds like the room next door is occupied by two sumo wrestlers with Tourette's Syndrome working their way slowly through the Reader's Digest Guide to Sado-Masochism and Bondage. *Joe O'Connor*

I didn't sleep. I never do when I'm over-happy, over-unhappy, or in bed with a strange man. *Edna O'Brien*

# INSULTS

You would vomit a better face. *James Joyce*

May his pigs never grunt. May his dogs never hunt. May his hens never lay. May his ass never bray. May a four year old bug build its nest in his lug. *Nell Flaherty*

You're as thick as manure and only half as useful. *Cathy Shivnan*

Your head would look better if you wore it closer to your face. *John O'Dwyer*

If anyone ever offered you a penny for your thoughts, that would be inflation. *Cormac McCarthy*

You shouldn't put more fire in the script. Vice versa. *John Huston to a screenwriter*

Could you tell me what's on your mind — if you'll excuse the exaggeration? *Aidan Grennell*

Lord Carson's spiritual life has been exaggerated by a chronic attack of mental gallstones. *Oliver St John Gogarty*

As an outsider, what do you think of the human race? *Maureen Potter to a heckler during one of her shows*

What do you use for contraception — your personality? *Ditto stand-up comedian Ed Byrne*

Colin Montgomerie is a few fries short of a happy meal. His mind goes on vacation and leaves his mouth in charge. *David Feherty*

I thought you were a person of sincerity and reason, but I find you are just a typically abusive Trotskyite shit. *Tomás MacGiolla in a letter to George Galloway*

His love bites were self-inflicted. *Hugh Leonard*

It was hard not to admire her intelligence, her iron will, her confidence and her control. But all in all I thought she was a bit of a wanker. *Dave Fanning after an interview with Madonna*

# INTELLIGENCE

I first became aware of the great intelligence of dolphins when I was in swimming and they kept ganging up on me and dunking my head under the water. *Sean Hughes*

In my whole life I have only met three and a half girls as intelligent as the men I've met. *J. G. Farrell*

When the judge called Mike an idiot he agreed. After all, he was no fool. *Des MacHale*

If you want to seem wise, just think of something stupid and don't say it. *Owen Kelly*

An oxymoron is when two contradictory concepts are juxtaposed. As in "footballing brain". *Patrick Murray*

# INTERRUPTIONS

I haven't spoken to my wife for twenty years. I don't like to interrupt. **Bal Moane**

Did I just interrupt you? And if not, why? **Vincent Browne to Richard Boyd Barret on Tonight with Vincent Browne**

Please don't talk while I'm interrupting. **Ulick O'Connor**

# INTERVIEWS

According to *In Dublin* magazine, Neil Jordan once used the expression "Y'know" 125 times in a twenty-five-minute interview. **Philip Molloy**

This is the forty-sixth interview I've done about wanting privacy. **Glenda Gilson**

Doing interviews is a bit like going to a psychiatrist. **Enya**

No murder victims were interviewed during our research. **Today FM**

The daftest question I've ever been asked by an interviewer is, "If you could be a biscuit, what biscuit would you be?" **Ronan Keating**

Robert de Niro spoke eight words to me when I tried to interview him about his film *Analyse This*. Coming from him, that's practically a novel. **Dave Fanning**

Colin Farrell's TV interviews have more beeps than the M50 at rush hour. **Anita Mullan**

My worst experience is being asked in interviews what an album is about, and having no fucking idea. **Larry Mullen of U2**

# INTIMIDATION

I never spoke to John Banville without feeling like a janitor's son approaching the headmaster at a public school. *Fergal Keane*

Even dead Irish poets posed some sort of threat to Paddy Kavanagh. *Anthony Cronin*

You see him coming at you, menacing as a shark's fin above the water's surface on a crowded beach. He has that vein on his temple that looks as though he's got a worm crawling under his skin. And his eyes ... the heat off them could give you third-degree burns. *Tom Humphries on Roy Keane*

Being a rock star is like having a sex change. People stare at you, follow you down the street shouting comments, and touch you up. I now know what it must feel like to be a woman. *Bono*

If I saw Charlie Haughey buried at midnight at a crossroads with a stake driven through his heart I should continue to wear a clove of garlic round my neck just in case. *Conor Cruise O'Brien*

Gene Mauch's stare can put you on the disabled list. *Tim McCarver*

Michael Caine compares himself to Gene Hackman. This is foolish. Hackman is an intimidating and dangerous actor. Mr Caine is about as dangerous as Laurel and Hardy, or indeed both, and as intimidating as Shirley Temple. *Richard Harris*

# INVENTIONS

We should be eternally grateful to the person who invented the idiot box on the envelope that tells you where to place the stamp. *Karen O'Byrne*

According to popular sporting legend, the noble art of hurdling was invented at Exeter College in 1850. Some well-to-do students had hired local horses for an impromptu point-to-point event but found the horses so hopeless at jumping they decided to dismount and jump the fences themselves. *Des Lynam*

I can forgive Alfred Nobel for inventing dynamite, but only a fiend in human form could have invented the Nobel Prize. *George Bernard Shaw*

Then there was the Dublin man who invented a waterproof teabag. *Kevin Murtie*

It was the Irish who invented the lavatory, but then the English came along and ruined it all by putting a hole in it. *Godfrey Quigley*

Alexander Graham Bell invented the phone. That was fine. But then he went and invented another one. *Dave Allen*

I once knew a man who thought Freddie Mercury invented the thermometer. *Paul Malone*

Demand for an Irish digital watch has broken all records. It's a new type of watch. When you press the button, a little red arrow appears pointing to the nearest pub. *Peter Cagney*

# INVITATIONS

I must decline your invitation owing to a subsequent engagement. *Oscar Wilde*

There's nothing I hate more than not being invited to parties I wouldn't be seen dead at. **Christina Moriarty**

Frank Harris is invited to all the great houses of England ... once. **Oscar Wilde**

# IQ

Pop stars usually have the intelligence quotient of a piece of toast. **Joe O'Connor**

Most soccer players have an intelligence rating so poor that if they dropped a point on the IQ scale you'd have to water them. **Richard O'Connor**

Paul Gascoigne wore a number 10 jersey. I thought that was his position but it turned out it was his IQ. **George Best**

The IQ level of at least half of the contestants on *Blankety Blank* makes *Fawlty Towers* seem by comparison as funny as hypothermia. **Hugh Leonard**

Did you hear about the Kerryman who moved to Cork and lowered the average IQ of both counties? **Vincent Dowling**

# IRELAND AND THE IRISH

What is it about Irish immigrants and panelling? We had panelling in the ceiling and on the floor. My mother even had a dress made out of panelling. It's like they got off the boat at Ellis Island and "Forget about the Freedom of Speech thing. All we want is panelling." **Denis Leary**

The people at *Lonely Planet* have just published the latest edition of their guide to Ireland. You know how these things usually go. The decent burghers of, say, Navan will become red-faced at the suggestion that their town is a swampy, banjo-picking backwater. Officials will pretend to fits of the vapours upon reading that the Blarney Stone might be nothing more than a cheesy tourist trap. Some hotel that serves beetles with its porridge contacts the lawyers. *Donald Clarke*

You're not a proper member of an Irish club until you're barred. *Michael Davitt*

Ireland deserves to be dragged into a bush and fucked. *Sinead O'Connor*

The land of saints and scholars has become a land of limousines and lapdance parlours. *Frank McNally*

The Irish have the thickest ankles in the world, and the best complexions. *John Berryman*

Ireland's chief contribution to humanity is freckles. *Ardal O'Hanlon*

The Irish bottle up their grievances rather than deal with them. And when they have enough saved up, they either go mad or write a book. *Frank McNally*

Irish people are Italians who can't dress, Jamaicans who can't dance. *Bono*

Someone once said that Eamon de Valera was the Spanish onion in the Irish stew, but today's main ingredients consist of Brussels sprouts, sauerkraut and a good dash of bitter lemon to round it off. *Paddy O'Brien*

In Ireland there's a precedent for everything except common sense. *Ben Kiely*

The Irish could be accused of being emotionally stunted because we give the impression we have only a few emotions. The two most frequently used are friendliness and complaining. *David Slattery*

The main way Irish people meet is by getting drunk and having sex with strangers. *Tommy Tiernan*

An Englishman thinks seated; a Frenchman standing; an American pacing; an Irishman afterwards. *Austin O'Malley*

Ireland is the old sow that eats her farrow. *James Joyce*

The main thing you need to know about the Irish is that we only enjoy something when we feel we're not entitled to it. *Fintan O'Toole*

Ireland was a nineteenth-century country up until about 1970. *John McGahern*

The trouble with the Irish is that to your face they're all behind you but behind your back they're at your throat. *Donal McCann*

We Irish don't invade countries. We infest them. *Tommy Tiernan*

In Ireland the inevitable never happens and the unexpected constantly occurs. *J. P. Mahaffy*

Ireland is a country three hundred miles long and a hundred miles thick. *Niall Toibin*

Irishness is not primarily a question of birth or blood or language. It is the condition of being involved in the Irish situation – and usually of being mauled by it. *Conor Cruise O'Brien*

Ireland is a small but insuppressible island half an hour nearer the sunset than Great Britain. *Thomas Kettle*

The reason Ireland's emblem is a harp is because the country is run by pulling strings. *Maureen Potter*

Ireland used to be eight people without teeth fighting over a bag of crisps in Grogan's pub. Then we got rich and it cost 400,000 euros to live in a tree. *Dylan Moran*

While they may be descended from the Celts, a fearless people whose warriors were known to run naked into battle, most modern-day Irish people would think twice before running naked into the bathroom. *Frank McNally*

Being Irish means driving a German car to an American-themed pub for a Belgian beer, then grabbing an Indian curry on the way home before sitting on Swedish furniture to watch British programmes on Japanese TVs. *Internet joke*

# IRELAND AND THE IRISH
# – BY THE ENGLISH

"You disapprove of the Swedes?"
  "Yes sir."
  "Why?"
  "Their heads are too square, sir."
  "And you disapprove of the Irish?"
  "Yes sir."
  "Why?"
  "Because they are Irish, sir."
  *P. G. Wodehouse*

The Irish ignore anything they cannot drink or punch. *James Boswell*

There was a time every girl in the Emerald Isle had orange hair and a face the colour of straw. Now it's the other way round. *Jeremy Clarkson*

We have always found the Irish a bit odd. They refuse to be English. *Winston Churchill*

The Irish are very emotional. My mother cries during beer commercials. *Barry McCaffrey*

The Provisional IRA have admitted responsibility for the Irish entry in the Eurovision Song Contest this year. **Not the Nine O'Clock News**

The Irish are a very moral race. Booze and brawling are their only vices. *John Braine*

The Irish don't want anyone to wish them well. They want everyone to wish their enemies ill instead. *Harold Nicolson*

The Irish don't know what they want and they won't be happy till they get it. *Bob Monkhouse*

Gladstone spent his declining years trying to guess the answer to the Irish Question. Unfortunately, whenever he was getting warm, the Irish changed the question. *W. C. Sellar*

# IRONY

An author at the Frankfurt Book Fair is basically an inconvenience. *Joe O'Connor*

The most famous Irish short story, *The Dead*, is famous for, among other things, not being very short. *Frank McNally*

It was a big moment for me being on Conan O'Brien's show but my cable was turned off at the time because I didn't pay the bill so I couldn't afford to watch it. *Chris O'Dowd*

When people agree with me I always feel that I must be wrong. *Oscar Wilde*

The first time I cursed on TV, my father rang me and said, "Wash your fucking mouth out." The irony of Irish fatherhood. *Tommy Tiernan*

All real drinkers hate the taste of it. *Eugene O'Neill*

Sheila Wingfield is known more for being neglected than for anything else. *Alan O'Riordan*

Writing about being disconnected made me connected. *Marian Keyes*

There's something ironic about a member of the Corrs opposing the dumping of toxic waste. *Brendan O'Connor on Jim Corr's campaign to have the Sellafield nuclear plant closed down*

Sometimes a fireman will go to great lengths to save a raccoon that's stuck in a drainpipe, and then go out on the weekend and kill several of them for amusement. *George Carlin*

Cecil Day-Lewis said the enemy of good art was the pram in the hall. But guess what was in *his* pram? Daniel Day-Lewis. *Dominic West*

Nothing does more to activate Christian divisions than talk about Christian unity. *Conor Cruise O'Brien*

Isn't there something ironic about saying you bought a condom in a shop called Virgin Megastore? *Brendan O'Carroll*

An Irishman who was living in the States told me he didn't want to go back to Ireland because there were too many immigrants there now. *Des Bishop*

When you drop the soap in the bath, it goes to the last place you go groping for it. This is intuitive. *Pat Ingoldsby*

# ITALY AND ITALIANS

Italy turns up at the World Cup in Armani suits looking the dog's bollox. The Irish team arrives in green blazers and dodgy brogues. *Phil Babb*

It seems you can only play in the English Premiership these days if you're Italian. *Brian Kerr in 1998*

I've dated lots of Italian girls and I'd hate to generalize about them. But they're all mad. *Ian O'Doherty*

I'm glad I wasn't born in Italy. I can't speak a word of Italian. *Jack Cruise*

People do not stay in Brindisi except to die. *John Broderick*

And then there was the Irishman who went to Pisa and thought the tower was straight. *Rosaleen Linehan*

# JAZZ

I would define jazz as sound having an epileptic fit. *Tommy Tiernan*

I hate jazz. What's wrong with having a rhythm? I want something I can tap my foot to without sounding as if I'm trying to send a message in Morse code. *Marian Keyes*

You never know what to expect with stand-up comedy. I played a gig in Milan once to an audience who thought they were going to be eating pizza and listening to a jazz quartet. *Jason Byrne*

# JESUITS

A humble Jesuit would be like a dog without a tail, or a woman without a pair of knickers. *Flann O'Brien*

I have nothing against Jesuits but I wouldn't want my daughter to marry one. *Patrick Murray*

I have a Jesuitical streak in me but it was injected backwards. *James Joyce*

I blame my irregular heartbeat on being forcefed a diet of irregular verbs in five dead languages. It came as no surprise in later years to learn that not only is there no Father Christmas and no God, but the entire third conjugation of neuter nouns in Latin was invented by sadistic Jesuits in 1955. *Kevin McAleer*

# JESUS CHRIST

We know Jesus was Irish because he lived at home till he was thirty, he went into the building trade for a while, most of his friends were blokes, he liked boozing it up at weddings, he thought his mother was a virgin, and she thought he was God. *Damien Fitzpatrick*

Two guys came knocking at my door once and said, "We want to talk to you about Jesus." I said, "What's he done now?" *Kevin McAleer*

Jesus was a Palestinian freedom fighter. *Gerry Ryan*

If Jesus Christ was on earth today you'd probably find him in a gay bar in San Francisco working with people suffering from AIDS. *Bono*

When I was a kid I thought Jesus spoke with a rural Irish accent. I thought he looked like Jon Bon Jovi when in reality he probably looked more like Yasser Arafat. *Joe O'Connor*

Jesus must have been fit. He cleared the temple. *Sil Fox*

Is Jesus the same as God? *Nora Barnacle*

St Patrick said the leaves of the shamrock represented the Blessed Trinity: the Father, the Son and the Holy Spirit. That's why four-leaf clovers are so lucky. You get an extra Jesus. *Stephen Colbert*

Jesus is coming. Everyone look busy. *Spike Milligan*

The Irish people hate each other in the name of Jesus Christ. *Bernadette McAliskey*

If Jesus came down from the cross and married my wife, he'd have been back up there in five minutes hammering the nails into himself. *Brendan Behan*

I have a theory that Jesus suffered from bi-polar depression. He never cracked a joke in thirty-three years. No wonder he spent his time thinking about the next life. *Patrick Farrell*

# JEWS

Ireland has the honour of being the only country in the world which never persecuted the Jews — because she never let them in. *James Joyce*

The Jewish Mafia is called Kosher Nostra. *Paul Byrne*

I'm not a full Jew, just Jew-ish. *Amy Huberman*

A lot of people are giving out about the film *The Passion of the Christ*, saying it's anti-Semitic because it makes out that the Jews killed Christ. Well it wasn't the Mexicans. *Dylan Moran*

What would you get if you crossed an Irishman with a Jew? A lepracohen. *Colm O'Hara*

I'm half Jewish and half Irish. One half of me wants to get drunk and the other half doesn't want to pay. *Dusty Young*

I was raised half Jewish and half Catholic. When I'd go to confession I'd say, "Bless me Father — and you know my attorney, Mr Cohen?" *Bill Maher*

A Catholic and a Jew had an argument about religion. Finally the Jew said, "OK, let's agree to differ. You worship God in your way and I'll worship Him in His." *Hugh Leonard*

I know a man who thought the Gaza Strip was a Jewish night-club. *Big O*

# JOBS

I was fired from my job in a diner after someone asked me what marinated mushrooms were and I said, "They're mushrooms that grow by the sea." *Deirdre O'Kane*

The best job I ever had was driving a forklift in a Guinness factory. *Liam Neeson*

I once worked in a rubber factory in Acton where the noise and smell together left you feeling you'd been raped by the Brigade of Guards. *Lee Dunne*

The best way to get your husband to do something is to suggest he's too old for the job. *Mary Keane, wife of John B.*

Letter from a Dublin firm: "We beg to inform you that all vacancies are full". *Sean McCann*

My brother has an unusual job. He finds things before people lose them. *Conor Tiernan*

Dave is bitter after being forced to go and live in Australia because there were no jobs here for people with a Masters in Greek and Roman civilization. And now he's back to tell us all that Ireland is a backward dump with rubbish weather. And, by the way, you're all ugly. *Pat Fitzpatrick*

I don't regard what I do as a job. Delivering coal – now *that's* a job. *Comedian Brendan O'Carroll*

A proper job is one in which you hope to remain for at least forty years. During these years you may become an elected politician, complete a prison sentence or be forced to emigrate. But with a proper job there will always be a desk for you when you are eventually thrown out of office, released early from jail or allowed to return from exile. Your eventual retirement will not be marked by any change in effort. You will simply no longer be required to turn up at the office. *David Slattery*

To me a job is an invasion of privacy. *Danny McGoorty*

Jesus said, "Come forth, Lazarus." But he came fifth and lost the job. *James Joyce*

I once saw a reference written by a man for a job applicant he didn't like. It read simply, "I have known this applicant for twenty years. He does not smoke." *Owen Kelly*

Suitable job for an Irish politician: taking blind greyhounds out to piss. *Sean Kilroy*

Murphy asked an employer for a job. The employer said, "I don't even have enough work for the people I already have." Murphy said, "Don't worry, I won't do much." *Joe Cuddy*

I got a job in a hardware shop. This fellow came in and said, "I want some nails." I said, "How long do you want them?" He said, "I want to keep them." *Jimmy Cricket*

The easiest job in the world must be the weather forecaster in southern Spain: "Er, tomorrow is going to be hot." *Paul Kilduff*

A man went for a job on a building site. The foreman said, "Can you make tea?" He said yes. "Can you drive a forklift?" The man scratched his head. "How big are the teapots?" *Shaun Connors*

# JOURNALISM AND JOURNALISTS

Journalists usually sport thick-lensed glasses, wear six pairs of ropey sandals, kiss holy medals, carry secret membership cards of the Communist Party, and are homosexuals. Most of them are communistoids without the guts of real red-blooded communists or Roman Catholics without the effrontery of a Pope Pius XII. Sometimes they're a mixture of the two: spineless, brainless mongoloids — but as maliciously perilous as vipers. *Ian Paisley*

Columnists are ultimately disposable, even bio-degradable. Our priceless prose ends up lining the bottom of a cat litter tray, or tossed into a recycling bin — which at least is good for the environment. *Pat Stacey*

Mick McCarthy breaks into a rash if he's within thirty yards of an NUJ card. *Tom Humphries on the former Republic of Ireland manager's attitude to members of the National Union of Journalists*

During my time at the *Mirror* I worked under John Kearns and Neil Leslie. Both of them taught me a great deal about tabloid newspapers, like how to use the word "spine-chilling" frequently. *Jason Callaghan*

There is much to be said in favour of modern journalism. By giving us the opinions of the uneducated, it keeps us in touch with the ignorance of the community. *Oscar Wilde*

Where journalists are concerned, there's no word so derogatively stinking that it sums up the congested stink of their constipation. *Caitlin Thomas*

I was flattered when asked to write seven hundred words for the *Guardian* as it gave me the opportunity to use my entire vocabulary. Twice. *Sean Hughes*

Who writes the *Irish Times* editorials? They read like they've been done by an old woman sitting in a bath with the water getting cold around her fanny. *Charlie Haughey*

When you write for a national paper, young people often ask you how they might go about "getting into journalism". There are as many ways to "get into journalism" as there are ways to fuck up your life in general, and the only one I wouldn't recommend is to win a place at one of our institutes of journalism. Otherwise you might be a very bright spark with Pulitzer potential who can write like an angel, and two years later you might emerge saying things like "I'm doing a bit of rusurch for Runan Collins at the mument" with a straight face. *Declan Lynch*

Investigative journalism consists of putting a well-known figure on a spit and getting the public to turn him. *George Bernard Shaw*

Van Morrison wouldn't authorize a journalist to write his shopping list. *Brenda Power*

I've met two varieties of journalist: those who displayed their "serious" credentials by dressing like the homeless and those who appeared to spend their entire lives attending functions at foreign embassies. *Marian Keyes*

Journalism is the only job that requires no specialized knowledge of any kind. *Patrick Campbell*

I hate journalists. There is nothing in them but tittering, jeering emptiness. *W. B. Yeats*

Keep taking the tabloids. *John Feeney*

# JUDGES

The judge was stern. "O'Driscoll," he rapped, "have you ever been up before me?" "I don't know," O'Driscoll replied. "What time do you get up at?" *Doug Anderson*

I didn't agree with Jeffrey Archer's sentence. Four years is fair enough for perjury but the judge might have added another four for writing those dreadful books. *Paddy Murray on Archer's 2001 conviction*

# JURIES

If you want to be let off jury service, the word now goes: turn up with neat hair and tidy clothes. *Mary Kenny*

A former boxing champion appeared before a judge and jury charged with receiving stolen property. As it was being sworn in, the judge asked him, "Do you want to challenge any members of the jury?" Pointing at one of them he replied, "I wouldn't mind going a few rounds with that twerp over there." *Bernard Neary*

"Tell the jury where you were on the night of the crime," asked the barrister. "I was nowhere at all," replied the witness. *Tony Butler*

We left the jury to drink themselves stupid, but they were stupid before they started. *Eric Cross*

The jury's decision was unanimous. They sent out for another barrel of Guinness. *Mido Cooligan*

A Cork man appeared in court on a serious charge. The judge asked him if he was represented by counsel. He replied, "No, Your Honour, but you'll be glad to hear I have some very good friends on the jury!" *Sean McCann*

You have been acquitted by a Limerick jury and you may now leave the court without any other stain on your character. *Richard Adams*

# ROY KEANE

You were a crap player and you're a crap manager. The only reason I have any dealings with you is that somehow you're manager of my country. And you're not even Irish. You English cunt, you can stick it up your bollox. *Keane's outburst to Mick McCarthy before the 2002 World Cup at the training ground in Saipan*

As he waded in with one expletive after another I asked myself, "Was this my captain? Was this the man who could serve Ireland as a role model for our children? The answer was no." *McCarthy in response*

Ireland's secret formula: find an island with a red light zone but no soccer pitch, go on binges and send your best player home. *The **Daily Mail** on Keane's subsequent expulsion from the squad by McCarthy. The newspaper was referring to Saipan's unsatisfactory training facilities*

He came, he saw, he went home. **I, Keano**

# KIDNAPPING

I don't know why Kate and Gerry McCann went to visit Pope Benedict about the kidnapping of their child. I know he's a Nazi but, come on, I can't see how he could have been involved. *Sean Hughes on the abduction of Madeleine McCann*

People often ask me why I didn't try to escape my captors after I was kidnapped. The answer is . . . it would have been difficult trying to avoid detection walking around Beirut in my underpants. *Brian Keenan*

# KISSING

"You know you're the first girl I've ever kissed," said the Irishman as he changed gear with his knees. *Vincent Dowling*

I once tried to French-kiss a girl in the Gaeltacht and my tongue got caught in her dental brace. *Joe O'Connor*

Japanese researchers are working on a remote kissing machine that will allow separated lovers to engage in simulated tonsil activity. According to one of the boffins, "Kisses are haptic communications on the mouth that can express deep emotion. If we mutually present the haptic sensation to each mouth we can convey the expression of emotion." Hmm. If that's how the Japanese describe kissing, perhaps their lack of interest in sex is a little more understandable. *Ann Sexton*

When I had my first French kiss I thought: This is terrible, it's just dental collision. *Gerry Ryan*

Only one arrest was made at the Belgium versus Ireland game in Brussels. It was an Irishman with a painted moustache who attempted to kiss a police horse. *Patrick Murray*

Girl: "Giz a kiss."
Bloke: "Let me swally me phlegm first."
*Overheard in Dublin*

Some men kiss and tell. George Moore tells but he doesn't kiss. *Sarah Purser*

What was the difference between Pope John Paul II and other men? Other men kissed women and walked on the ground. *Kevin Myers*

Her nostrils are so big, when you kiss her it's like driving into a two-car garage. *Hal Roach*

Then there was the Kerry woman whose mouth was so big it took two men to kiss her. *Laura Stack*

You can't kiss an Irish woman unexpectedly, only sooner than she thought you would. *Peter Cagney*

Kissing don't last. Cooking does. *Mary Banotti*

There's one foolproof way to find out if your friend is gay. He probably is if he closes his eyes when you kiss him. He probably isn't if he closes *your* eyes when you kiss him. *Noel V. Ginnity*

I've always been amused by the Blarney Stone. Only the Irish could persuade people to kiss something that Norman soldiers had urinated on. *Dave Allen*

Lord, I wonder what fool it was that ever invented kissing.
*Jonathan Swift*

This guy asked me if I'd kiss him under the mistletoe.
"Darling," I said, "I wouldn't kiss you under an anaesthetic."
*Deirdre O'Kane*

# KNICKERS

A woman threw her knickers at me when I was on stage one night doing my comedy act. When I was finished she asked for them back. "Normally I wouldn't need them," she explained, "but they're part of a set." *P. J. Gallagher*

Women have good knickers, bad knickers, sexy knickers, weekend knickers and work knickers. Us lads, we've just got jocks and jocks. *Ray D'Arcy*

To cover up the ticking of our body clocks, we're wearing soundproof knickers on stage tonight. *The Nualas*

The law is like a woman's knickers — full of dynamite and elastic. *John B. Keane*

A quick grope by the gate or in the back seat of a car was as far as I ever went in sexual terms in my youth. In those days I still believed you might get pregnant through your knickers.
*Gloria Hunniford*

The most famous piece of advice as to the preserving of schoolgirl modesty was that girls should not wear black patent leather shoes. In theory it enabled unusually hawk-eyed lechers to see the reflection of their knickers in the polished instep. *John Walsh*

When I fix toilets, I do such a good job you'd want to hold on to your knickers or they'll be sucked down the shore. *Plumber Bob Merrigan*

# KNIVES AND FORKS

Don't spoon in bed. It soon turns into knives and forks. *Jason Byrne*

If it was raining soup, the Irish would be out with forks. *Brendan Behan*

He's the only person I know who made his fortune with a knife and lost it with his fork. *Oliver St John Gogarty on a fellow surgeon who was bankrupted after being cited for infidelity in a divorce case*

My circumference was built with a knife and fork. *Derek Davis*

# LANGUAGE

It's widely believed that many Germans, realizing the difficulty of using their own language, have given up on it entirely and instead communicate with each other now via large brass bands. *Paul Kilduff*

Soft words butter no parsnips. *Sean O'Riada*

The language we use for transporting things from place to place is perverse. If it's freight sent by ship it's a cargo, and if it's freight sent by car then it's a shipment. *Dave Allen*

German sounds like tin foil being eaten by a typewriter as it's being kicked down the stairs. *Dylan Moran*

If ye heard the language of him. Jaysus, if me mother was alive she'd turn in her grave. *Paul Ryan*

Arnold Schwarzenegger was inspired to go into politics by George Bush, who proved you can be successful at it even if English is your second language. *Conan O'Brien*

English is the perfect language to sell pigs in. *Michael Hartnett*

Cleanliness is only next to Godliness in an Irish dictionary. *George Brent*

If you can't baffle them with brilliance, bamboozle them with bullshit. *Brush Sheils*

Brendan Behan was the only trilingual bisexual I ever met. *John Montague*

There's a language in China that only two people speak ... and they fell out! *Paddy Cole*

To put it very simply, if we de-leverage beyond the equilibrium point, we provide headroom for the new lending. *Michael Noonan not being very simple*

The days of good English has went. *Ray Houghton*

In the old days people in Ireland actually used sentences. Now a conversation is like, "Yeah. Right. I mean, like, *totally*." *Jon Kenny*

Sometimes I find the news on the radio very confusing. A golfer on the green uses his "patter". The actual stroke is called a "patt". Yet if the golfer's name happens to be Pat he's now called "Pet". "Pet played a good patt". The golf course in question can either be in "Dablin" or "Belfost". I think we should all go back to speaking in Irish. *Pat Ingoldsby*

Irish people say things like, "Are you reading that newspaper you're sitting on?" The preferred answer is: "No, I'm just doing the crossword with me arse!" *Brendan O'Carroll*

Irish people speak through a half-code of mysteries. "Will you have a cup of tea?" asks Person A, putting on the kettle. "No, I'm in a terrible hurry," says Person B, taking off their coat. "A half-cup then," says Person A. *Brendan Killeen*

The Irish no longer speak in a manner rooted to the soil. That's so yesterday. Instead we jabber in American. Everything is, like, so cool. Everybody is a guy. Only some know where it's at. When required, they step up to the plate. They cut to the chase to beat the band. Have a nice day is just around the corner. You get the picture? **Michael Clifford**

Finnish, sadly, often makes more sense when read backwards. **Paul Kilduff**

Why are children called dyslexic when they're more likely just thick? We use dyslexia as an excuse for practically everything nowadays. "Why were you unfaithful?" "I'm dyslexic. I didn't realize I was going to a whorehouse. I thought I was going to a *warehouse*." **Sean Hughes**

The Dutch all have perfect English since they accepted the fact that the rest of Europe doesn't fancy speaking as if it's rolling snot around the back of its throat. **Philip Nolan**

# LAUGHTER

Being a comedian has its perks but I've never yet laughed a woman into bed. **Tommy Tiernan**

T. S. Eliot wasn't far wrong when he said the main problem for the dramatist today was to keep his audience amused. While they were laughing their heads off you could be up to any bloody thing behind their backs. **Brendan Behan**

Nothing is as laughable as the things we cry at. **John B. Keane**

John Wayne thought John Ford was a lucky stiff with a minimum of talent who would kick his mother down the stairs if he thought it would get a laugh from the neighbours. **James Henaghan**

Laugh and the world laughs with you. Cry and they'll think you're drunk. **Jimmy Cricket**

Manslaughter is a terrible thing. Women's laughter is even worse. **Joe Lynch**

Would a laughing stock be a set of cattle with a sense of humour? *Jack Cruise*

Laugh and the world laughs with you. Slip on a banana skin and rupture your scrotum and it also does. *Vincent Dowling*

Could you laugh a bit quicker? I'm only here for three minutes. *Big O*

# THE LAW

He broke the law when he was born because his parents weren't married. *George Bernard Shaw*

Centuries ago an Irish scholar boasted that there had been no law-breaking in his region for several decades. He didn't mention that there was no law either. *Terry Eagleton*

An Irish alibi is proof that you were in two places at the same time. *Tony Butler*

The Irish legal system is weighted heavily in favour of the Church. As far as I know, it's still illegal to hit a nun. *Ian MacPherson*

Beneath every law lurks a lovely loophole. *Pat Shortt*

God is the most maligned person in history. He should sue for libel. Or she. Or it. *Sinead O'Connor*

How many witnesses do they need before Jehovah's trial starts? *Tom Shields*

In Britain they've passed a law prohibiting you from physically educating your children. I'm disappointed. I used to bound home from work looking forward to striking them. *Dylan Moran*

A layman may drink six pints of ale with his dinner but a monk may drink only three. This is so he will not be intoxicated when prayer-time arrives. *Ancient Brehon law*

An appeal is when one court is asked to show its contempt for another one. *Finley Peter Dunne*

# LAWYERS

You might as well employ a boa constrictor for a tape measure as go to a lawyer for legal advice. *Oliver St John Gogarty*

I've spent a number of unforgettable days of my life standing in corridors adjacent to courtrooms, surrounded by three or four lawyers, each of whom I was paying the equivalent of a month's salary to stand around telling me bad jokes. For considerably less than I was paying these jokers I could have flown Billy Connolly on a chartered Concorde to entertain me in my home. *John Waters*

A lawyer will do anything to win a case – even tell the truth. *Patrick Murray*

Everyone who ever said "Talk to my lawyer" put down the phone and thought to himself, "Oh shit." *Pete Ferguson*

Of all the cubs being suckled by the Celtic Tiger, by far the fattest, sleekest and best nurtured are the lawyers. *Pat Rabbitte*

# LAZINESS

I like to think I'm straddling the lines between consciousness and catatonia. *Dylan Moran*

You're not an agnostic, Paddy, you're just a fat slob who's too lazy to go to Mass. *Conor Cruise O'Brien*

My idea of exercise is striking a match for a cigarette. *Anne Marie Scanlon*

I write from my bed. So far it's worked out nicely. Especially since I've started turning myself regularly to avoid bedsores. **Marian Keyes**

Damien Duff has been known to suffer from Adhesive Mattress Syndrome. **Brian Kerr**

I'm not a fan of idleness. In fact when I see these old people whose life amounts to waking up in the morning with the thought of "Nearly time for bed" I say, let's legalize euthanasia. And let's not confine this to age either. Any person who spends more than eight hours on a couch watching television should also be given the big injection, unless of course they have the excuse of having a hangover — then it's perfectly understandable. **Sean Hughes**

Normally your adult Irish male cannot be roused to vacate the sofa unless the house is actually on fire. If he gets off his backside to wander down to the end of the garden he nearly sends a postcard saying "Wish you were here". **Joe O'Connor**

I'm not saying he was the laziest man in Ireland but he was the only person I knew who flushed bread down the toilet to feed the seagulls at the coast. **Terry Adlam**

I used to know a man who was so lazy he'd sit in front of the fire crying out, "Help — I'm burning!" **Brendan O'Carroll**

All I want to do is sit on my arse, fart and think of Dante. **Samuel Beckett**

# LEGS

I went back to the Isle of Man quite literally with my tail between my legs. **J. P. Donleavy**

This is Vincente Fernandez of Argentina. You'll notice that he walks with a slight limp. This is because he was born with one leg shorter than the other two. **Roddy Carr, commenting on the Irish Open Golf Championship**

Kevin Kilbane's head is better than his feet. If only he had three heads, one on the end of each leg. *Eamon Dunphy*

My knees are on their last legs. *Paul McGrath*

Donegal girls have been given a special dispensation by the Pope to wear the thickest part of their legs below the knees. *Sean Desmond*

# LEPRECHAUNS

A leprechaun without a pot of gold is like a rose without perfume, a bird without a wing or an inside without an outside. *James Stephens*

Ireland found the pot of gold but lost the leprechaun. *Brendan McGahon*

Flag-waving leprechauns. *Eamon Dunphy's view of delirious Irish soccer fans during the 2002 World Cup*

# LESBIANISM

I once got a terrific email from a bystander in the struggle of the sexes. She signed it "Mary Ellen, a sixty-year-old, one-kidneyed, unrepentant, aggressive, abrasive but cheerful, horseback-riding lesbian who found true love in the Southwest". *Maureen Dowd*

How do you recognize an Irish gay? He has a girlfriend who's a lesbian. *Sean Kilroy*

When I was a teenager back in the eighties, a school friend told me not to link her arm. "They'll think we're lezzers," she said. I'd never heard the word before so she enlightened me to this sexual abnormality suffered by a disgraceful minority. It sounded bad enough to be up there with afflictions such as leprosy, and on a moral par with large-scale drug-taking. I reckoned my best bet was to stick with the other species, the ones from Mars: men. **Mags Treanor**

A journalist once asked me if I had ever slept with a woman. I replied that I had been accused of being many things in my life, but never a lesbian. **Micheál MacLiammóir**

Ellen DeGeneres and Anne Heche are talking about having a baby. The reason they're worried is because if it's anything like Ellen it's going to take much longer than nine months to come out. **Conan O'Brien**

A child asked her mother, "What's a lesbian, Mammy?" Her mother said, "Ask your father when she comes home." **Noel V. Ginnity**

Back in Mum's day, choice of orientation meant using a compass instead of a map to find your way to Sodality meetings. A dyke was something vague in geography class, something Dutch boys put their fingers into. **Joe O'Connor**

# LESSONS

I'll learn you to speak proper. **John B. Keane**

I learned from a Sandra Bullock film that to be a responsible functioning adult capable of having healthy relationships with other adults, you must first be able to take care of a plant, and then an animal. Only at that point should you go for coffee or have triplets with someone. As things stand, I'm two cats and just under half a dog and a yucca away from there. Mind you, in a different Sandra Bullock film I learned that the best thing to do if you're stuck in a dead-end job is to pretend to be engaged to a man in a coma, so I just don't know what to believe. **Maeve Higgins**

Flying lessons: crash courses given. **Graffiti spotted in the toilet of Dublin Airport**

# LETTERS

I got a letter from my mother saying, "Since you left home your father has become a sex maniac. He tries to make love to me any chance he gets. Please excuse the wobbly writing." *Frank Carson*

I wonder if St Paul ever got any replies to all those letters he sent to the Corinthians? *Din Joe*

As I write this letter I have a pistol in one hand and a sword in the other. *Sir Boyle Roche*

I always get letters from people when I call Galway a town instead of a city, although I never do. *Broadcaster John Bowman*

Libel letters are the Oscars of journalism. *Róisín Ingle*

I don't think my wife likes me very much. When I had a heart attack, she wrote for an ambulance. *Frank Carson*

I miss abusive letters. Not that I ever read them. As the poet nearly said, "Full many a blower is born to be flushed unseen". *Hugh Leonard*

I've just arrived in England. On the boat over, the weather was dreadful. The sea was so rough a fellow fell overboard. He shouted out, "Drop me a line." I said, "What's your address?" *Jimmy Cricket*

I once got a letter from a woman compiling a book of letters, asking me if I had one I could contribute. When I wrote back to her to say I hadn't, she asked me if she could use that one. *Roddy Doyle*

# LIBRARIES

I had the wrong idea of working in a mobile library. I imagined it meant chain-smoking cigarettes and chatting up women when the van was quiet, or screaming abuse at children fighting over Enid Blyton, then retreating under the counter while the bodies were carried out. *Dermot Bolger*

When I lived in Ireland as a young man it was said that if two old ladies went round to a library and said a book was dirty, it was withdrawn pending investigation and possible banning. *Brian Moore*

A drunk man walks into a library and in a very loud voice says, "I want to order fish and chips." The librarian explains that he's in a library. The man apologizes, then whispers, "I want to order fish and chips." *Kevin Gildea*

One day during my time as a librarian a young man asked to see me. He wanted to complain about an indecent book. I asked him what was indecent about it and he said there was a dirty word in it. I asked where, and he promptly replied, "Page 164." I read the page and asked, "Which one?" He pointed to the word "navel". *Frank O'Connor*

The first thing to have in a library is a shelf. From time to time this can be decorated with literature, but the shelf is the main thing. *Finley Peter Dunne*

I was once knocked down by a mobile library. I was lying in the middle of the road screaming in agony and the driver gets out and says, "Shhhh!" *Jimmy Cricket*

Walking in a library door is like being raped by an army. *Eiléan Ní Chuilleanáin*

A circulating library in a town is an evergreen tree of diabolical knowledge. They who are so fond of handling the leaves will long for the fruit at last. *R. B. Sheridan*

# LICENCES

Did you hear about the guy who bought a black and white licence for his dog after getting one for his TV? He thought it would be cheaper. *Milo O'Shea*

There's a myth that all Italians are good-looking. Many of them are, but I've seen creatures dandering about the piazzas of Florence for whom you'd need a licence if you wanted to keep them in the house. *Joe O'Connor*

The reason a dog is a man's best friend is because a dog licence is cheaper than a marriage one. *Dusty Young*

# LIES

Bryan McFadden said of me, "You know the way in England you have Elton John, OBE? In Ireland it's Jason O'Callaghan OFP — Overweight Fat Prat." I guess if Elton is an OBE and I'm an OFP, Bryan must be an OBL — Outright Bloody Liar. *Jason O'Callaghan*

The most traumatic thing about my First Holy Communion was that I couldn't think of anything I'd done wrong. I was so desperate to do the right thing I made up a whole series of sins that I hadn't committed. Then came my first taste of Catholic guilt when I realized that by having no lies to tell I had actually told a lie by pretending that I had. *Ian Dempsey*

Last night I was lying in bed with the wife. I was lying to her and she was lying to me. *Brendan Grace*

When my brother told me God had built everything in the world I called him a dirty liar because I heard my father say only bricklayers could build houses, and I knew God wasn't a bricklayer. *Christy Brown*

The need to lie was already with John Ford while he slept peacefully in his mother's womb. *Maureen O'Hara*

I will never marry again, never. Being married means making excuses and I'm not a good liar. To lie you have to have a good memory, and I can't remember anything I've done for years. *Richard Harris*

It's untrue to say my dog can talk. If he says he can he's a bloomin' liar. *Jack Fennell*

Women are to blame for all the lying men do because they're continually asking questions. *Hal Roach*

The only thing we know for certain about sex is that everyone lies about it. *Bob Geldof*

Optimistic lies have such immense therapeutic value, any doctor who cannot tell them convincingly has mistaken his profession. *George Bernard Shaw*

You tend to lie a lot as an adult. It's part of your means of getting around. You know when you're late and you say, "I'm so sorry, the traffic was terrible. And there was a fire as well. And a small boy. I had to give him an eye operation and all I had was a spatula and a banana." *Dylan Moran*

# LIFE

Life is a mess. We don't remember being born, and death isn't an experience, so all we have is this chaotic middle bit, bristling with loose ends, in which nothing is ever properly finished or done with. *John Banville*

They say life is a gift. If so, could I have the receipt so I can go back and change mine? *Sinead Murphy*

The day after tomorrow is the third day of the rest of your life. *George Carlin*

I understand life isn't fair, but why couldn't it just once be unfair in my favour? *Christy Murphy*

Life is the ever dwindling period between abortion and euthanasia. *Patrick Murray*

My life has been a succession of failed attempts to recover from experiences I have never had. *Samuel Beckett*

Life is overrated. Two-thirds of it is "lie" and half of it is "if". *Denis Buckley*

I've got a wonderful life. I just don't particularly enjoy it. *Sean Hughes*

Life is a sexually transmitted disease. *Brian Moore*

Life begins when the foetus can exist apart from its mother. In this case, most Irish teenagers are legally dead. *Jeff O'Connell*

We must present life as vaudeville. It's a fucking joke, a sad sick joke. If there's a God up there he must be like Beckett. *Richard Harris*

Life is shit. The only things that get us through it are anticipation and afterthought. *Sean Hughes*

Life is a football game with everyone offside. *F. Scott Fitzgerald*

Life is perhaps most wisely regarded as a bad dream between two awakenings. *Eugene O'Neill*

Life is a bad playwright. *Hugh Leonard*

Life is simple for a man. When he's a child he has one finger up his nose and the other on his penis. Then he gets taller. *Dylan Moran*

# LIFE AND DEATH

They say my writing has made me immortal, but what good is immortality when you're dead? *George Moore*

It's about time people didn't have to worry about whether they're going to be burned to death before they wake up in the morning. *SDLP Assembly member Danny O'Connor in 2001*

What a paradise Ireland would be if it had as much affection and respect for the living as it has for the dead. *Micheál MacLiammóir*

He had been sentenced to death but saved his life by dying in jail. *Tony Butler*

A visitor to a little hamlet in Ireland commented, "What a quiet little place." The local constable said, " 'Tis quiet to be sure. We haven't buried a living soul in years." *Mr O'S*

He died in his sleep so he doesn't know he's dead yet. If he wakes up, the shock will kill him. *Biddie McGrath*

We have to have something that the dead can live with. *A Sinn Féin official in 1994*

Is there life before death? *Graffiti spotted by Seamus Heaney in a burned-out area of Belfast*

"If my wife was alive today," Paddy lamented, "she'd be a year dead." *Henry Kelly*

I wouldn't believe Charles Haughey was dead even if he told me so himself. *Hugh Leonard*

I wrote John Broderick's obituary when he was still alive. It's standard practice for newspapers to run a morgue full of ready-to-run obituaries because people tend not to inform the papers in advance that they're planning to pop their clogs. *Declan Lynch*

# LITERARY CRITICS

I never had any time for literary critics. I wouldn't pay too much attention to a fella who couldn't get a hard-on were he to start telling me how to go about getting laid. *Lee Dunne*

Have you ever seen a statue erected to a critic? *Daniel O'Donnell*

When Keats was my age he had been dead for eleven years. This clearly gave him an unfair advantage with the critics. *Joe O'Connor*

Dublin critics know everything about everything. You can't stand for five minutes sheltering from the rain without being told you made a bollocks of it. *Lee Dunne*

Critics should only criticize dead Russians. *Maeve Binchy*

The lot of critics is to be remembered for what they failed to understand. *George Moore*

Literature is the only art whose critics use the same medium as that used by the artist. How astonishing it would be if the actor's performance were to be criticized through the medium of acting. How many of the existing drama critics would remain in their job? *Micheál MacLiammóir*

Critics? I love every bone in their heads. *Eugene O'Neill*

I wrote *Finnegans Wake* to keep the litcrit brigade in sinecures for the rest of the century. *James Joyce*

Dylan hated intellectualizing his work. One time someone asked him to explain his poem *Ballad of the Long-Legged Bait* and he replied, "It's a description of a gigantic fuck." *Caitlin Thomas*

# LONDON

I like the Irish but I can't quite understand how the sentence "I'm from London" in a Dublin pub tends to be heard as "I am Oliver Cromwell". *Jo Brand*

I'm not British. I'm an Irish Londoner. *Dara O'Briain*

They say you play London twice in your life, once on the way up and once on the way down. It's nice to be back. *Ian MacPherson*

I wanted to play to the bright young Irish so I came to London. *Sean Hughes*

You may know a man for twenty years in London without finding out he hates you like poison. *George Bernard Shaw*

# LONELINESS

Corkmen are lonely even when they're at home. *Niall Toibin*

Loneliness is a crowded room. *Sinead O'Connor*

If you had a brain cell, it'd die of loneliness. *Tom O'Connor*

If it's a poor thing to be lonesome, it's worse maybe to go mixing with the fools of the earth. *John Millington Synge*

# LONGEVITY

Iron gates will last for ever. Afterwards they can be used for making horseshoes. *Sir Boyle Roche*

It has been scientifically proven that people who don't drink or smoke live longer. It serves them right. *Moss Keane*

Hearing of a friend who had a coffin made for himself, Paddy exclaimed, "That's a wonderful idea. It should last a lifetime." *Joan Larson Kelly*

In its current materialization, the Irish Christmas lasts at least twelve days, when we stay at home from work with enough food to see us through a limited nuclear conflict. *David Slattery*

And they said the marriage wouldn't last. Well, they left the church together, didn't they? *Milo O'Shea*

When George Moore was eighty he was asked how he'd managed to have such a long life. "I believe," said Moore, "it is due to the fact that I never smoked, drank or touched a girl — until I was ten years of age." *Tony Butler*

If you want to reach the age of eighty-five, get a stomach ulcer when you're twenty-five. You'll take such good care of yourself for fear of upsetting the ulcer, you'll outlast all around you. *Lynn Doyle*

Jack Nicholson and my daughter lived together for twelve years. That's longer than any of my marriages lasted. *John Huston*

I didn't know either of my parents but given my longevity they were probably deckhands on Noah's Ark. *Hugh Leonard*

Pessimists live longer than optimists. I'm always calm in a crisis, and one day it will be the death of me. *Terry Wogan*

Dickie Rock has been in the music business for approximately 142 years. *Ronan Collins*

# LOVE

My wife asked me if I'd still love her if I won the Lottery. "Yes," I said, "but I'd miss you terribly." *Joe Cuddy*

I was just thinking — love is fickle. And I'm in love at the moment. But I'm not any more. *Ardal O'Hanlon*

You say stupid things to the person you're in love with. Like, "Here's all my money." *Sean Hughes*

Love is just a word used by poltroons in polyester suits. *Dylan Moran*

Not only do I love her, I worship the ground her father struck oil on. *Gene Fitzpatrick*

She always told me she was crazy about Ireland, but it was me I wanted her to love! *Stuart Townsend on his former long-term partner Charlize Theron*

In Ireland you're allowed to say you love God, babies and horses that win, but anything else is a softness in the head. *Frank McCourt*

I loved Mick Jagger smearing words like soft butter across my face. **Bob Geldof**

I would have made love to a goat to know what love is. **Samuel Beckett**

To love oneself is the beginning of a lifelong romance. **Oscar Wilde**

One loves with one's toes and ears and tongue and fingers and eyelashes and stomach and knees and hair and bottom and teeth and . . . well, everything. **J. G. Farrell**

What I like about love is the tragedy of it all. If a relationship shows the slightest signs of not becoming tragic, I make it so. As soon as I meet a girl, even before we have our first date, I've already worked out how it will end. **Richard Harris**

Sure I love my brother. But not as much as I love Pot Noodle. **Noel Gallagher**

The most appealing thing about owning a dog is the loads of unconditional love that comes your way in return for giving them a tin of food once a day and cutting their toenails once a year. **Maeve Higgins**

I loved her so much I named my first ulcer after her. **Dusty Young**

George Bernard Shaw had a lengthy love affair with Ellen Terry without ever meeting her. Isn't that so peculiarly Irish? **Jeananne Crowley**

I told her I loved her so much I wouldn't give her toe for the world, and I'd be up to see her the following day if it wasn't raining. **Hugh Malone**

Love means never having to say you're sorry. Marriage means never having a chance to say anything. **Hal Roach**

Irishmen love everybody. You have been warned. **Brendan Courtney**

I know my mother loved me. When I was having a bath she'd throw in things for me to play with. Like the hairdryer. **Brendan O'Carroll**

This thing called love. There's none of it, you know. It's only fucking. **Samuel Beckett**

# LUCK

I've always been unlucky. One Christmas I got a packet of batteries and they weren't included. **Brendan Grace**

Sometimes you get a piece of toilet paper and you blow your nose with it. That piece of toilet paper probably considers itself lucky. **Jimeoin**

My luck is so bad, I went to a funeral last week and caught the wreath. **Foggy Spellman**

Everybody says "The luck of the Irish". No one says "The bad luck of the Irish", which seems a lot more appropriate. **Frank Gannon**

He deserved the free kick but was fortunate to get it. **Tommy Smyth**

My definition of bad luck: catching AIDS from a Quaker. **George Carlin**

British people sometimes have these misconceptions about Ireland. They use the phrase "The luck of the Irish". Whenever I hear that I think: Hang on — invasion, colonization, famine, mass emigration, sectarian strife. That's why I don't do the Lottery. **Kevin Hayes**

# MALAPROPISMS

The world is my lobster. **Keith O'Neill**

Somebody has been spreading allegations, and I think I know who the allegators are. **Drogheda Urban District Councillor**

My mother told me never to worry about sticks and bones.
**Bertie Ahern**

United go home having given one of the top Division Two sides a much more difficult day than most plaudits expected.
**Roddy Collins**

It's so cold today you'd need your terminal underwear on.
**Paul Ryan**

I didn't expect a standing ovulation. **Willie Bermingham**

It's slightly alarming the way Manchester United decapitated against Stuttgart. **Mark Lawrenson**

The crowd gave the players an arousing reception. **Packie Bonner**

We want to dehumanize the social welfare system. **Oliver Reynolds**

Don't upset the appletart. **Bertie Ahern**

My favourite Irish joke concerns the worker on the building site who's asked if he knows the difference between a joist and a girder. "Of course I do," he says. "Joist is the man who wrote *Ulysses*, and Girder wrote *Faust*." **Mary Kenny**

According to my son, trigonometry is having three wives at a time. **Shona Tubridy**

Juventus are waiting to re-modelize their stadium. **Trevor Welch**

# MALAPROPISMS IN CHILDREN'S ESSAYS

When a man has more than one wife he's called a pigamist.

In France even pheasants drink wine.

A virgin forest is where the hand of man has never set foot.

Flora and fauna were two Siamese twins.

The masculine of vixen is vicar.

Mary raped Jesus in swaddling clothes.

An Indian baby is called a caboose.

Insects is burned in churches.

The Vacuum is a large empty space where the Pope lives.

It was lovely being in Paris listening to all the pheasants singing the Mayonnaise.

# MARRIAGE

In 1972 I married for the fifth time. This was tantamount to putting my finger in the sea-snake's mouth. *John Huston*

The only proper basis for marriage is a mutual misunderstanding. *Oscar Wilde*

I married "The One". On a scale of one to ten. *Mary Bourke*

If you marry the wrong woman there's nothing like it — and if you marry the right woman there's nothing like it. *Sean Desmond*

If my wife really loved me she'd have married someone else. *Conal Gallen*

When the blind lead the blind they fall into a ditch. Or matrimony. *George Farquhar*

Marriage is a custom brought about by women who then proceed to live off men and destroy them completely, enveloping them in a destructive cocoon and then eating away at them like a poisonous fungus on a tree. *Richard Harris*

One doesn't have to get anywhere in a marriage. It's not a public conveyance. *Iris Murdoch*

Marriage is the process whereby a woman turns an old rake into a lawnmower. *Danny Cummins*

It was the perfect Irish marriage. She didn't want to, and he couldn't. *Mick Lally*

We're having our tenth anniversary this year. Sarah says it's called a tin one so I'm going to buy her something made of tin to celebrate it. **Ken Doherty**

The only thing I have against marriage is the hours are too long. **Joe Cuddy**

I'm married to a lovely lady called my wife. **Tommy Tiernan**

There was a glorious era in my life during which my contemporaries went one by one to the altar with the ecstatic insouciance of a Versailles under-chef heading for the guillotine. **Hugh Leonard**

The best thing about marriage is the fact that you don't have to plan the fucking wedding any more. **Ed Byrne**

Irish drinking society insists that unmarried couples give their friends a big day out. This is what marriage is about in Ireland now. **Pat Fitzpatrick**

My first marriage lasted five minutes. **Maureen O'Hara**

The real drawback of marriage is that it makes one unselfish. **Oscar Wilde**

Marriage is wonderful. It's my wife I can't stand. **Frank Carson**

I have never been a fan of that pre-marital ritual known as the hen party. I'd rather stick baby hedgehogs in my eyes than sit through an evening where a normally dignified friend agrees to suck beer through a straw that resembles a part of the male anatomy. **Róisín Ingle**

He married her to get rid of her. **Noel Purcell**

I'm eighteen years married and my wife and myself still hold hands. It's just as well because if we let go we'd probably fucking kill each other. **Brendan O'Carroll**

I got married in a pub. I suppose it sent out some kind of signal to my wife. **Ronnie Drew**

Peaches Geldof has decided to remarry at twenty-two. When I was twenty-two, the only thing I'd done twice was my Leaving Cert. **Anna Nolan**

I am not in favour of long engagements. They give people the opportunity of finding out each other's character before marriage, which I think is never advisable. *Oscar Wilde*

The first year he talks and she listens. The second year she talks and he listens. The third year they both talk and the neighbours listen. *Donald McGill*

I drew up a pre-nuptial arrangement with my wife. If we separated, the house was to be split 50-50. She'd get the outside and I'd get the inside. *Pat Redden*

My marriage to Patsy Kensit wasn't arranged, it was *deranged*. *Liam Gallagher*

# MARRIAGE PROPOSALS

The traditional Irish marriage proposal goes like this: "How would you like to be buried with my people?" *Noel Purcell*

Once a week is quite enough to propose to anyone. *Oscar Wilde*

I said to my girlfriend's father, "I'd like to marry your daughter." He said, "Have you seen her mother?" I said, "I have, but I'd still prefer to marry your daughter." *Foggy Spellman*

Honest Workman With Corkscrew Would Like To Hear From Widow With Inheritance. *Notice spotted in pub*

The reason I proposed to my girlfriend was because I got bored watching TV. Her father is worried I might divorce her for the same reason. *P. J. Gallagher*

I said no a few times after he asked me because I was enjoying being proposed to. For my previous marriages it was me who did the proposing. *Sinead O'Connor after she became engaged to Barry Herridge in 2011; the marriage only lasted a week*

An Irish marriage proposal: "You're *what*?" *Milo O'Shea*

# MARTYRS

Martyrdom is the only way a man can become famous without ability. *George Bernard Shaw*

Cathleen Anorexia encourages women to join a male death-cult which has a peculiarly masochistic martyrology. *Edna Longley*

# MASS

I have been a daily communicant for eighteen years on the promenade at Sandymount. *Paul Durcan*

When I heard Mass over the radio I didn't understand all the priest said, especially when he spoke in that funny language which father told me was called Latin. I often asked myself what made the priest say all his prayers in Latin. My brother Peter said it was because the saints only spoke Latin and God couldn't understand English. *Christy Brown*

Jesus himself wouldn't have been able to stick a Mass in Poland. *Tom Galvin*

My experience of Mass-houses has been exclusively confined to weddings and funerals for a long time now. A couple of years ago a memorial service for a colleague threatened to degenerate into farce as the assembled heathens attempted to figure out the complexities of sitting, kneeling and standing by furtively observing each other's movements. It was a bit like Groucho Marx's famous "mirror scene" in *Duck Soup*. *Declan Lynch*

Isn't it remarkable that all the worst crimes of republican violence have been committed immediately after Mass? *Ian Paisley*

I believe everything the Catholic Church teaches is true, but I let my wife go to Mass for me. *Brendan Behan*

When I was in Thailand I saw a woman put a candle out with her lady bits. Everyone else at the Mass was freaked out. *Neil Delamere*

Many people's main reason for going to Mass on Sundays is because it's where all the pretty girls congregate. *John McGahern*

The only time you will see Irish people praise the Lord with gusto is at midnight Mass on New Year's Eve where we prime ourselves with a few hot whiskeys before belting out "Joy to the World" as if it were "Olé Olé Olé" at the World Cup. *Pat Fitzpatrick*

You could fault the late Cardinal Lefebvre and his devotees on the grounds that they were clearly insane, but you have to award them full marks for their espousal of the Latin Mass. In the days when you didn't have a clue what the priest was saying you could ponder the mystery of your own ignorance and even say a few prayers. Now you just read a few lines off a sheet with all the fervour of Albert Reynolds reciting the minutes of a Longford County Council meeting. *Declan Lynch*

# MASTURBATION

The boy who showed me how to masturbate saw God while on drugs, and then became a monk. *Bob Geldof*

Jane Russell increased the masturbation rate in Dublin to the point where it went off the graph when I was young. *Lee Dunne*

Sex is like anything else. If you want it done right you have to do it yourself. *Donal Keaveny*

My chat-up line to Merle Oberon was: "I spent half of my youth jacking off to photographs of you." Then I went to bed with her and proved it. *Richard Harris*

I smoke weed and I masturbate. I don't do both at the same time. That gets tricky. *Sinead O'Connor*

Ireland is a nation of masturbators under priestly instruction. *Brian Moore*

One of my first sexual tingles was sliding down a bus stop. I slid down one in Malahide and thought, "That's lovely." So I did it again. I was into bus stops for months after that. I had a crush on one particular one outside the library. It was the most sexually fulfilling bus stop in Malahide. I found it very hard to get into women afterwards. You can't slide down a woman. *Pat Ingoldsby*

I've seen masturbation defined as pollution. If that's the case, Greenpeace needs to shut me down. *Des Bishop*

If you're a Catholic you're led to believe that masturbation is a mortal sin. So if you die without receiving confession you'll go straight to hell and eternal flames. Which is a bit of an incentive to stop wanking. But usually not enough. *Michael Redmond*

# MEMORY

I'll never forget my wedding night. And thanks to Rohypnol, my wife will never remember hers. *Ian O'Doherty*

I remember your name perfectly. I just can't think of your face. *Oscar Wilde*

Anyone who remembers the sixties wasn't there. *Des Hanafin*

I have been in journalism for more years than I care to forget. *Con Houlihan*

My father discovered a cure for amnesia but he forgot what it was. *Noel Purcell*

I don't remember making *Miami Vice*. At least that's my excuse to all the people who thought it was shite. *Colin Farrell*

Always tell the truth – it means you have less to remember. *Alice Glenn*

I wrote a song about Michael Collins once. I don't sing it because I can never remember anything I write. *Brendan Behan*

I can't remember the last time I had amnesia. *Sean Keating*

Go out in Dublin for an evening you'll never forget and it usually ends up as a night you can't remember. *Dusty Young*

You're supposed to be the Memory Man, aren't you? So could you tell me what fucking hotel I booked into tonight? *Drunken Irish fan who'd lost his way to football commentator Jimmy Magee during a World Cup qualifier Ireland played in a foreign city; Magee had always been noted for his encyclopedic recollection of data*

The reason they're called hummingbirds is because they've forgotten the words. *Eamon de Buitléir*

Bono is great at sorting out issues of world importance but he forgets the small things like where he is, and so on. *The Edge*

It only takes one drink to make me drunk. The problem is, I can't remember if it's the fifteenth one or the sixteenth. *Luke Kelly*

I always had a strange memory. I have "I know that face from somewhere" moments in the street, only to realize later it was my brother. *Richard O'Connor*

People say to me, "Ian, do you remember where you were when Kennedy died?" I was only eight at the time but I do. I was leaning out of the sixth-floor window of a hotel in Dallas. With a rifle. Funny how things like that stay with you. *Ian MacPherson*

I have no recollection of going to bed, which is always a worry, the more so in London with the frequency of murders – I wouldn't have an alibi. *Sean Hughes*

You know you're getting old when your wife tells you you're only interested in one thing ... and you can't remember what it is. *Joe Lynch*

I'm not saying Sil Fox is old, but he remembers the *first* of the Mohicans. *Noel V. Ginnity*

# MEN AND WOMEN

My ideal man would have the brains of Albert Camus, the appearance of Humphrey Bogart and the domestic habits of a coyboy. *Edna O'Brien*

The main difference between men and women is that men are hunters and women are bargain hunters. *Deirdre O'Kane*

Men are from Mars, women are from Venus, and farts are from Uranus. *Jason Byrne*

My boyfriend and I have all-bets-are-off Celebrity Romance lists. Orlando Bloom, Johnny Depp and Paul McCartney are at the top of mine. He has Julie Andrews and Pamela Ballantine on his – which is a bit scary, but at the same time oddly reassuring. *Róisín Ingle*

Who needs a man when you have undiagnosed chlamydia, nascent late-onset alcoholism, and a forty-year mortgage? *Martha Connolly*

John Wayne used to say I was the greatest guy he ever knew. *Maureen O'Hara*

At twelve I was six foot, stooped and with a massive nose and ears. When all you want to do is touch girls and it's the last thing they want, that's difficult for a hunchback. *Chris O'Dowd*

Inside every fat woman there's a thin woman trying to get out, and outside every thin woman there's a fat man trying to get in. *Séan Mac Réamoinn*

Calum Best is an arrogant octopus with no manners who persists in trying to grab my arse. *Katy French*

The majority of Irish men are bastards, and they're fuckin' useless in bed. *Mary Coughlan*

Men have the same degree of passion about women as women have about handbags. *Dylan Moran*

The whole man thing just fucks you up until you get it out of your system. *Sinead O'Connor*

Diamonds are a girl's best friend. A man's best friend is his dog. What chance have we all to get it on? *Deirdre O'Kane*

I refuse to consign the whole male sex to the nursery. I insist on believing that some men are my equals. *Brigid Brophy*

I only know one thing about women. It's that they're filthy. *Chris O'Dowd*

You can't win an argument with a woman. If you agree with her she'll say, "You're only saying that to annoy me." *Frank Hall*

Most women just want a kitchen and two kids, and bugger the man. Or rather *not* bugger him. *Brian Behan*

There are three kinds of men who can't understand women: young men, old men, and middle-aged men. *Joan Larson Kelly*

Irish women like the simple things in life. Like Irish men. *Mary Coughlan*

# MENTAL ILLNESS

Even in the nuthouse they were afraid to take me in, because I'm Sinead O'Connor. *Sinead O'Connor*

I don't think he's 1,000 per cent mentally. *Eamon Dunphy*

Two out of every one people in Ireland are schizophrenic. *Jimeoin*

If I could afford a nervous breakdown I'd give it away to someone more deserving. *John B. Keane*

I'm a nymphomaniac, hypochondriac, anorexic, suicidal, demonic, perverse, racist, psychotic sociopath with delusions of grandeur. *Susan O'Keeffe*

I wanted to know how babies were conceived. My mother told me. I thanked her very much. Wasn't it terribly sad my mother was going mad? *Maeve Binchy*

# MIRACLES

Ireland hasn't had an officially approved miracle since the Virgin Mary put in a frustratingly brief appearance in the small town of Knock in 1879. This is an embarrassingly long time for one of the most pious nations on earth. God ought to see to it immediately. *Terry Eagleton*

An Irish boy in a wheelchair went to the baths at Lourdes looking for a miracle but came out as unable to walk as he went in. His disappointment was brought to a rapid end by his mother, who roared, "You ungrateful little bastard! Look — there's a new set of tyres on the chair." *Philip Nolan*

# MIRRORS

The only time I come home happy from shopping is when I've inadvertently tried on things in shops with mirrors that lean forward and knock ten pounds off my silhouette. *Marian Keyes*

If your doctor warns you that you have to watch your drinking, find a bar with a mirror. *John Mooney*

A looking-glass does nothing for me but I have a face which reacts favourably to a glass with a drink in it. *John B. Keane*

I still think of myself as I was twenty-five years ago. Then I look in a mirror and see an old bastard and realize it's me. *Dave Allen*

A woman said to me, "Why don't you come up to my bedroom? I have a mirror on the ceiling." I said, "That's no good to me. I don't shave in bed." *Frank Carson*

The reason they put mirrors around the fruit in supermarkets is so you look at yourself in them and go, "Fuck it, I'm dying. I better eat some of this." They don't have mirrors beside the eclairs. *Dylan Moran*

# MISAPPREHENSIONS

Mrs Clarke: "My husband, now there was a man who really was afraid of Virginia Woolf."
Fr Ted: "Why? Was she following him or something?"
**Father Ted**

I used to think being bisexual meant you'd only had sex twice. *James O'Loghlin*

People think spies drive Lotus Esprit Turbos that convert to submarines when necessary. The reality of the situation is that they're to be found in white Camry station wagons with a baby seat in the back. *Dave Callan*

James Joyce liked to believe a woman was an animal who micturates once a day, defecates once a week, menstruates once a month and parturates once a year. *Edna O'Brien*

Barber: "Did you hear *Michael Collins* is being released this week?"
Customer: "I thought he was dead."
*Exchange quoted by Peter Quinn; the barber had been referring to the Neil Jordan movie*

Dubliners know everything. A real Dub will tell you that Gepetto invented the telescope, Galileo is a liqueur and Sir Walter Raleigh discovered the three-speed bike. *David Kenny*

When you're on the periphery it's not the periphery. It's the centre. *Mary Robinson*

When you're putting well at golf you're a good putter. When your opponent is putting well he *has* a good putter. **John D. Sheridan**

A man came out of the toilet once in my pub and said to me, "Would ye ever tell me why ye put the cigarette machine in the jacks." He'd been looking at the condom dispenser. **Jackie Healy-Rae**

# MISPRINTS

The peace talks in Northern Ireland were interrupted by the security farces. **Belfast Telegraph**

RTE Fiances To Be Probed. **Irish Press**

1951 witnessed the biggest census of copulation ever undertaken by the State. **Evening Herald**

After couples marry, they go into the vestry and sigh. **Belfast News Letter**

In many parts of County Sligo, hares are now practically unknown because of the unreasonable laughter to which they have been subjected in recent years. **Sligo Champion**

US To Give $50 To Indonesia. **Irish Times**

Widows made to order. Send us your specifications. **Connacht Tribune**

# MIXED METAPHORS

I don't think it helps people to start throwing white elephants and red herrings at each other. **Bertie Ahern**

Fabio Capello needs to nail his hammers to the mast. **Andy Townsend**

We're not prepared to stand idly by and be murdered in our beds by the IRA. *Ian Paisley*

He's not the sharpest sandwich in the picnic. *Tony Cascarino*

All along the untrodden paths of the future I can see the footprints of an unseen hand. *Sir Boyle Roche*

The midfield are like a chef trying to prise open a stubborn oyster to get at the fleshy meat inside. *George Hamilton*

He put all his eggs in one basket and pulled out a cracker. *Dennis Taylor*

These managers all know their onions and cut their cloth accordingly. *Mark Lawrenson*

It's just sour grapes and he should take it on the chin. *Neil Blaney*

The Dutch have tasted both sides of the coin now. *Andy Townsend*

If we haven't got the razor-edged salesmen on the coal face nobody's going to bring home the beef. *Albert Reynolds*

I smell a rat. I see him forming in the air and darkening the sky but I'll nip him in the bud. *Sir Boyle Roche*

Newcastle are finally going to end their London bogey. That would be a ghost — no, an albatross — off their backs. *Tom Tyrell*

# MOBILE PHONES

The first mobile phone I owned was the size of a small washing machine. *Joe Duffy*

They're now talking about selling mobile phones to three-year-olds. What would a three-year-old want with a mobile phone? To ring another three-year-old and say, "Can't talk, I'm in the buggy"? *Colin Murphy*

Mobile phones have gone too far. I've seen mothers phone their kids in the supermarket to find out which aisle they're in. "I'm at the freezer section. Are you over at the baked beans?" **Richard O'Connor**

Why do we call them mobile phones? The phone doesn't move by itself. Sometimes I wish it would. **Con Houlihan**

So Naomi Campbell has been ordered to clean floors for five days as punishment for throwing her mobile phone at an assistant. Well she's always been a dirty little scrubber. **City Slicker**

# MODELS

Claudia Schiffer seems to have forgotten she's a model. Glam frocks now only have her cheekbones to hang from. Recent attempts to open a jar of baby food caused a whole body fracture. **Roisin Gorman**

Was there ever a supermodel who didn't claim to have been an ugly duckling as a child? **Emily Houricane**

They say supermodels won't get out of bed for less than ten grand. Were you ever offered ten grand to *stay* in bed? **Pat Kenny to Dawn French**

If Pete Doherty wasn't shagging a supermodel, nobody outside of *NME* would give a shit about him. **Noel Gallagher**

For me, a supermodel is something you make with an Airfix kit. **Joe O'Connor**

# MONEY

If the Wright Brothers were alive today, Wilbur would have to fire Orville to reduce costs. **Herb Kelleher**

I rang the bank and asked how much money was in my current account. The man on the other end of the line wanted to know my mother's maiden name. "It's not a joint account," I told him. "I would have been too young to open one with her before she got married." *Kevin McAleer*

If golf wasn't my living I wouldn't play it if you paid me. *Christy O'Connor*

Money isn't everything. As long as you have your health you can always sell a kidney. *Michael Cullen*

Ireland's economic policies of the late forties and fifties were about as effective as a lifebelt made of lead. *Donal O'Dea*

If the milkman calls, the money is under the statue of Our Lord being attacked by the Romans. *Dermot Morgan to Frank Kelly in* **Father Ted**

Money can't buy you love, but it can get you some really good ginger biscuits. *Dylan Moran*

My father used to say to me, "Money isn't everything. It's just 99.9 per cent." *Gerry Ryan*

I have no money and therefore resolve to rail at all who have. *William Congreve*

In spite of the cost of living, it's still very popular. *Garret Fitzgerald*

Money is a bit like manure. It's no good unless you spread it around. *Ben Dunne*

Liechtenstein makes Switzerland look cheap. I'm stunned at the bill I receive after a modest dinner with one beer. Around these parts, one can either dine out or take out a mortgage. *Paul Kilduff*

A creditor of mine told me he was surprised he hadn't received any money from me in the last three weeks. I'm not, because I didn't send him any. *James Young*

These days I feel like a very large flamingo. No matter which way I look there's always a very large bill. *Joe O'Connor*

The typical Irishman likes to see himself as indifferent to material wealth. Ideally he would also like to be extremely rich. Then he'd have a better chance to show everybody how uninterested he is in money. *Frank McNally*

U2's The Edge asked me to give him a snooker lesson once. The figure of seven grand was mentioned for an hour's play. I wasn't sure if I had to pay him for the honour or if he was going to give it to me! *Ken Doherty*

I asked my wife what she'd like for her anniversary. "A divorce," she replied. I said, "I wasn't intending to spend that much." *Frank Carson*

I see Georgia Salpa has pulled out of the *Sleeping Beauty* panto. It seems she didn't want to work for Buttons. *Brendan O'Connor*

Ever since the IMU bail-out, every child in Ireland effectively owes the government 60,000 euros at birth. Believe me, there are babies inside their mother's wombs at this very moment going, "I'm not coming out!" *Keith Farnan*

# THE MOON

Two Irish astronauts landed on the moon. One of them got out to stretch his legs while the other fiddled around with the controls inside. A few minutes later, the latter heard a knock on the door. "Who's there?" he asked. *Jimmy O'Dea*

The reason there are no dogs on the moon is because there are no trees up there. *Dave Allen*

There's a foolish saying that such a one knows no more than the man in the moon. I tell you, the man in the moon knows more than all the men under the sun. Don't the moon see all the world? *George Farquhar*

My ambition is to have Neil Armstrong on a chat show and talk to him at length about everything I can think of except his trip to the moon. *Ardal O'Hanlon*

Teacher: "Which is more important to us, the moon or the sun?"
Pupil: "The moon, because it gives us light at night when we need it. The sun only gives it in the daytime when we don't."
**Hal Roach**

After I got sent to prison I was told I'd be there so long I wouldn't see freedom again until they were running day trips to the moon. **Gerry Conlon**

If a Cork astronaut went to the moon, his first words to NASA after looking round would be, "It's not Cork." **Tommy Tiernan**

Charlton Heston is so square he could drop out of a cubic moon. **Richard Harris**

Murphy had a pub on the moon but he closed it down. No atmosphere. **Big O**

It's now over forty years since the Americans ruined my life by landing on the moon. I'd gone for my early morning moon-walk with my dog Boris on the Sea of Tranquillity. I'd just sat down to read my stars in the *Sun* and eat a Milky Way when next thing I knew the Eagle has landed and I'm choking on grey dust from the turbulence and Boris is going crazy on the leash and howling at the earth. **Kevin McAleer**

# MOTHERS

Being a mother sometimes means doing things you don't like. While changing a nappy once, I ended up with poo in my mouth. Don't ask me how. **Fiona Looney**

Nature has designed it cleverly that women become instantly attached even to the most hideous baby imaginable. **Gerry Ryan**

Fr Dougal: "I don't know any women, Ted."
Fr Ted: "What about your mother?"
Fr Dougal: "She's not exactly what you'd call a woman."
**Father Ted**

My mother used to call me "Little bastard" when I was a baby. I was the youngest of eleven so she may well have forgotten my name. The other one sort of stuck. I've been trying to live down to it ever since. *Brendan O'Carroll*

Whatever else is unsure in this stinking dunghill of a world, a mother's love is not. *James Joyce*

It's not that I half knew my mother when I was young. I knew half of her — the lower half. *Flann O'Brien*

# MOTHERS-IN-LAW

I have a soft spot for my mother-in-law: the Bog of Allen. *Frankie Blowers*

After his wife died, Paddy was asked to sit beside his mother-in-law in the carriage on the way to the funeral. "I'll do it I suppose," he said grudgingly, "but 'twill spoil the day for me." *Eamon Kelly*

Mixed emotion is watching your mother-in-law drive over a cliff in your new Ferrari. *Brendan Grace*

My brother left his wife because of another woman. Her mother. *Dusty Young*

I have an attachment for my mother-in-law. It fits over her mouth. *Frank Kelly*

My mother-in-law reminds me of a Scud missile. You can see her coming but there's nothing you can do about it. *Joe Cuddy*

"Mr Corrigan, I'd like to have a day off to attend my mother-in-law's funeral."
   "So would I, Flynn, but she's a picture of health."
*Joan Larson Kelly*

The insurance money was so paltry, Mick often regrets the fact that his mother-in-law fell off the cliff. *Paddy Cole*

My mother-in-law is away on holiday but three times a week I have a woman come in and nag me. *Des MacHale*

An Irish lawyer was once asked what the penalty for bigamy was. "Two mothers-in-law," he replied. *Peter Hornby*

# MOTHER TERESA

Mother Teresa was the Frank Sinatra of the fundamentalist lyric. *Declan Lynch*

Mother Teresa was a wicked old crone. *Eamonn McCann*

# MOTIVATION

I hate men. That's why I got married. *Dolores O'Riordan*

I could not have gone through the awful wretched mess of life without having left a stain upon the silence. *Samuel Beckett on why he became a writer*

I don't drink because I have problems or I want to escape. I just love being drunk. *Richard Harris*

As a teenager I really only went to Mass to see ridey young fellas. *Fiona Looney*

Drinking provides a beautiful excuse to pursue the one activity that truly gives me pleasure: hooking up with fat hairy girls. *Timothy Walsh*

I knew an eighty-five-year-old man who married a girl of eighteen. He said he wanted someone to answer the rosary for him. *Eamon Kelly*

I eat to keep my mind off food. *Brendan Grace*

It's difficult to motivate football players if they earn forty grand a week, have mistresses everywhere, and three Mercs. *Joe Kinnear*

A woman in Irish Ferries was found to be earning the princely sum of one euro a week to be a beauty therapist. What kind of motivation is that? Can't you just see it? "You want a bikini wax? Here's some Velcro from my runners. Colonic irrigation? Let's see – here's a toilet brush, gets right under the rim!" *Neil Delamere*

There's a myth abroad in literary circles that you paint your masterpiece when you're starving in the gutter. That cliché is a crock of shit. When you're starving in the gutter what you're thinking about is where your next meal is coming from. *Dermot Bolger*

There was a time when people went into politics to get things done. Now most of them just want to plant their arses in a state car and shag everything else. *Charlie McCreevy*

At rock bottom, the urge to write may be the same as the urge that makes a baby squall for attention. *Deirdre Purcell*

I write in order to keep myself in liquor. *Brendan Behan*

When you get older you find yourself watching a lot of daytime TV. The main function of this is that it enables you to become bored and angry at the same time. *Dylan Moran*

A man from Carrick-on-Suir who admitted stealing £20 from a collection box in a public house explained to the local court that he'd committed the burglary because he couldn't sleep. **Midland Tribune**

I went into pop music because I wanted to get rich, get famous and get laid. *Bob Geldof*

I started writing plays because I felt I wasn't going to be able to. If you can, why bother? *Tom Murphy*

There are some movies I did to pay the rent. *Liam Neeson*

The priest asked O'Reilly why he drank. "Booze killed me mother," he said, "and booze killed me father. I'm drinking for revenge." *Peter Hornby*

# MULTI-TASKING

I'm not going to pretend I'm one of those marvellous people who sits on tons of committees and is running around visiting hospices and organizing fundraisers. Who hasn't got time to brush her hair because one of her seven foster children has stuffed a towel down the toilet and flooded the house. The fuel that keeps me in perpetual motion is stupid tittle-tattle, tidying cutlery drawers and queueing in Lidl for cheap yoga equipment. *Morag Prunty*

I can't multi-task. I once had an appointment with my dentist and my gynaecologist the same morning. I ended up lying in the wrong direction in the chair. Which was very upsetting for my dentist. *Sonya Kelly*

Victoria Beckham couldn't chew gum and fart at the same time, let alone write a book. *Liam Gallagher*

I wrote one of my books rocking a pram with one hand and typing with the other. *Anne Enright*

Some sports are worse than others. Rugby, for instance, is a fussy game which interferes with one's ability to write. During a cricket match, on the contrary, I almost finished a six-thousand-word essay while fielding third man. I would certainly have completed it if a member of the opposition hadn't unplugged my typewriter. *Ian MacPherson*

It's no coincidence that England's main contribution to world cuisine has been the sandwich — a food that allows you to eat with one hand while continuing your game with the other. *Dara O'Briain*

# SAMANTHA MUMBA

The press write a lot of silly things about Samantha Mumba. Should we call it Mumba Jumbo? *Michael Cullen*

With regard to my TV appearance with Samantha Mumba, the answer to your first question is, "No, I didn't." The answer to your second one is, "Yes, I did want to." *Des Bishop*

# MURDER

Killing your wife is a natural thing that could happen to the best of us. *Brendan Behan*

Murder is considered less immoral than fornication in literature. *George Moore*

When we want to read of the deeds that are done for love, whither do we turn? To the murder column. *George Bernard Shaw*

In-laws are hard work. Sorcha's old man has officially tried to kill me twice — once with his bare hands and once with a letter-opener he outbid Derek Quinlan for at a charity auction for I can't remember focking what. *Ross O'Carroll-Kelly*

My mother worshipped the ground I walked on. If I told her I'd just killed six people she'd say, "They deserved it, son." *Gerry Ryan*

When a man wants to murder a tiger he calls it sport. When a tiger wants to murder him he calls it ferocity. *George Bernard Shaw*

Yesterday Paddy made a real killing in the stock market. He shot his broker. *Peter Cagney*

I lost my temper with Montgomery Clift so many times on the set of *Freud*, at one point he asked me if I was going to kill him. I told him I was considering it. *John Huston*

Most karaoke bars in Manila have taken Frank Sinatra's "My Way" off their playlists because of the number of people who have been shot while giving their all at it. **Terry Wogan**

A man has only to murder a series of wives in a new way to become known to millions of people who have never heard of Homer. **Robert Lynd**

Could one enter a plea of justifiable homicide for decapitating oafs who come unbidden and sit beside one in pubs in the sacred hour between five and six p.m.? **Hugh Leonard**

Almost everyone who has committed a murder knows that the business has its tragic side. **Robert Lynd**

I've been married for eighteen years. You only get seven for murder. If I'd killed her when I thought about it first I'd have been out eleven years ago. **Brendan O'Carroll**

# MUSIC

When you spend your life in a family band, they sometimes forget you might have developed emotionally since you were six. **Andrea Corr**

My first record was a criminal one. **Katherine Lynch**

People say country music isn't about real feeling. It is. But the feeling is always self-pity. **Fintan O'Toole**

Once there was just Riverdance. Now there are a whole bunch of competing knock-offs. These stretch from lavish stage shows to three sisters jumping up and down in a pub in Kerry while getting their photo taken by American tourists saying things like, "I think they're laughing at us, Harry." **Pat Fitzpatrick**

The music business has all the sincerity of a whore's kiss. **Sinead O'Connor**

Louis Walsh has done more damage to Ireland's culture than Cromwell. **Cathal McCarthy**

A few years back, Daniel O'Donnell's manager insisted he be shifted from the mainstream charts to the middle-of-the-road ones to boost sales. Unfortunately it wasn't the middle of the road during rush hour. **Seconds Out**

The term rock 'n' roll comes from the gutter. It means fornicating in a car. **Outlook** *magazine*

I didn't have much classical voice training, apart from smoking a lot of cigarettes. **Ronnie Drew**

When I started broadcasting on Lyric FM on Sunday afternoons I thought the listenership would be five old ladies somewhere in a home for the bewildered, and three musical cocker spaniels. **Gay Byrne**

*The X Factor* isn't quite the ratings powerhouse it used to be, despite Louis Walsh's best efforts to blink the audience into submission. **Laura Slattery**

*The X Factor* is just karaoke with a big budget. **Katherine Lynch**

Leonard Cohen was born Leonard Nimoy in Toronto in 1934. He grew his ears long in the sixties in protest against the Vietnam War and withdrew to the Greek island of Vulcan. His first book of poetry, *I'm a Lumberjack*, remained in the Ontario Top Ten for fifty-seven years. **Kevin McAleer**

Barber: "I can't believe Michael Jackson is dead. It's like a hoax to promote the tour. Maybe he'll be resurrected in three days."
Customer: "Michael Jackson? Surely he's Charlie Chester."
Barber: "Well that was never proved. But he's brown bread now."
Customer: "Or white bread."
**Short Back and Sides**

What's the difference between the James Last orchestra and a bull? A bull has the horns out front and the arsehole at the back. **Damien Corless**

Billy Connolly tells us he was an abused child. I think it all goes back to that woeful banjo-playing. Put in his parents' place I'd probably have abused him too. **Bob Geldof**

In the old days the record business people used to say, "We're in it for the lowest common denominator." Now I feel we're way below that. **Van Morrison**

If Morrissey's a genius, what's he doing in a fucking pop group? **Shane MacGowan**

The only thing worse than a rock star is a rock star with a conscience. **Bono**

Musical talent today means looking good while lipsynching to a cover version. **Joe O'Shea**

We're like two scientific experiments after which you end up with the same result. **Jedward**

1978 was a really exciting time for U2. We'd just discovered F sharp minor so we had a fourth chord. We'd only had three up to then. **Bono**

Everyone with an accordion in Ireland in 1969 became a showband. **Brendan Bowyer**

One of the reasons Jedward endure is because they're Jedward. You're not going to find one of them expressing his individuality by making a jazz concept album based on James Joyce's *Dubliners*. **Shane Hegarty**

Westlife are a collection of tone-deaf, spud-faced chancers. **Hermione Eyre**

After I graduated from university in 1975 I knew what I wanted in an ideal world: gainful employment in the Irish music industry. This left me with one major hurdle to overcome: there was no such thing as the Irish music industry. **Dave Fanning**

Sometimes I think being in U2 is like being in one long meeting. Your own life is just a tea break between meetings. **Adam Clayton**

I'll be great when I'm finished. **Van Morrison**

The drain-gurgling rasp renders lyrics indecipherable. Even on harmonica he flirts with dissonance, shrill as an irate seagull. The "Tangled Up in Blue" chorus comes off like Scooby Doo on a mescaline bender. *Joe McNamee on Bob Dylan during a Cork gig in 2011*

If you want loyalty in the music business, buy a dog. *Louis Walsh*

That was played by the Lindsay String Quartet, or at least two-thirds of them. *Sean Rafferty*

Ronnie Drew's voice is so deep it makes Lee Marvin sound like a castrato. **Sunday Times**

George Michael was a Boyzone fan until he discovered it was a band and not somewhere backstage. *Michael Cullen*

Shortly after I joined The Dubliners, a row broke out in a pub with everyone telling everyone else to fuck off. The next day I got a phone call from Ronnie Drew. "Are you all right for Friday?" he said. I said, "But the group broke up last night." And he said, "Oh for fuck's sake, don't take any notice of that kind of thing. It happens every week." *John Sheahan*

I'd sooner lie upside down in a puddle with a pitchfork in my backside listening to Barry Manilow's B-sides than watch *X Factor*. They call that a talent show? It's enough to drive a five-year-old Mormon to cut-price Lidl lager. *Mick the Maverick*

# MUSLIMS

Irish people love Muslims. They've taken a lot of heat off us. In the old days we were the terrorists. Now we're the Riverdance people. *Andrew Maxwell*

At a Muslim strip show the punters shout, "Show us your face! Show us your face!" *Noel V. Ginnity*

I was talking to an Islamic man about the burka. He told me Western women wear them too. "No they don't," I said. "Yes they do," he said. "It's called Max Factor." *Peter Quinn*

The weather in Ireland reminds me of being in a Muslim country. Sometimes it's Sunni but mostly it's Shi'ite. *P. J. Gallagher*

I believe Muslim women should be allowed to wear the burka for one good reason: in summer they make me laugh. *Sean Hughes*

I had a long relationship with a young Muslim girl. Even today I wonder what she looked like. *Ian McPherson*

Did you hear about the Irish Muslim? He prays to Arrah. *Tommy Tiernan*

# NAMES

I'm a flute player, not a flautist. I don't have a flaut and I've never flauted. *James Galway*

My name is an anagram of Go Get Beers. *George Best*

FIFA stands for Forget Irish Football Altogether. *Mick McCarthy*

A man in a Dublin pub once told me I was a fool to have married Maradona. *Sean Penn, the ex-husband of Madonna*

My young son calls popcorn "cock porn". It can get a bit embarrassing when he's asking me to order it for him at the cinema. *Tommy Tiernan*

Robert de Niro named his son Raphael after the hotel in Rome where he was conceived. The boy must be grateful it wasn't the InterContinental. *Michael Cullen*

My sister's friend had a baby a couple of weeks ago. The child's grandmother asked her what name she was thinking of giving it. When she said "Marc with a C", the grandmother said, "Carc?" *Overheard in Dublin*

When I was thirteen I got really bad acne. I was called Pizza Face, Brunch and, more worryingly, Join the Dots. *Keith Duffy*

Wells Cargo was my stage name. *James McKeon*

"A man broke into a house and disturbed a married couple in bed. He put a gun to the woman's head and said, "What's your name?" "Elizabeth," she replied. The robber said, "I won't shoot you because my mother was called Elizabeth." He then turned to the man. "What's your name?" he asked. "Paddy Murphy," the man replied, "but my friends call me Elizabeth." *Noel V. Ginnity*

As kids we all had nicknames for each other. Mine were "poof" and "pansy" from as early as I can remember. I was the pink sheep of the family. *Boy George*

I've woken up with women whose names I don't remember. *Richard Harris*

I'm glad I didn't have to commentate on any of the matches played by the Danish national soccer team in the 1950s. There were sometimes six players in the side all called Nielsen: "The ball's with Nielsen. Passes to Nielsen. Over to Nielsen. He's got Nielsen and Nielsen up there with him in support. . ." *Des Lynam*

I once wrote a book under a pen name. Parker. *Tom O'Dwyer*

Part of the problem with Ireland is that everything is named after someone. In Dublin there's a railway station called Sydney Parade. For many years I thought Sydney Parade was one of the leaders in the 1916 Rising. *Joe O'Connor*

I'm the only man in the world whose first and second names are both synonyms for "penis". *Peter O'Toole*

Eoin Hand sounds like a synonym for masturbation. *Des Tuomey*

I think it was "Something-ov". *Ronnie Whelan on being asked who he swapped football jerseys with after a soccer game with Russia*

Che Guevara was of Irish descent. They only called him Che for a nickname. He was christened Seamus. *Short Back and Sides*

My grandson was named after the two Irish Popes: Bono and John Paul. **Brendan O'Carroll**

Then there was the woman who wanted to meet Mr Finis. She said he must be a great man because his name was at the end of most French books. **Laura Stack**

They've named a new soup after Daniel O'Donnell. Thick Country Vegetable. **Gene Fitzpatrick**

My husband is Jewish and I'm Irish Catholic. We've decided to raise our children Jewish but I got to pick the names: Mary Magdalene and Sean Patrick. **Jeannie McBride**

Sometimes I'm asked if Daniel O'Donnell is my real name. I always reply, "Would anyone make up a name like that?" **Daniel O'Donnell**

My name may be Lynott, but my attitude to life is, "Why not?" **Phil Lynott**

I don't like people naming their kids after soccer players. Why not name them after your favourite flower? "Have you met my son Convallaria Majalis Murphy?" **Richard O'Connor**

O'Neill refused to call his son Patrick because, as he said, "Every Tom, Dick and Harry is called Patrick these days." **Tony Butler**

What would you call a Kerryman hanging from a ceiling? Sean D'Olier. **Páidí O'Sé**

What would you call a Kerry bullet that came back? Rick O'Shea. **John B. Keane**

# NARCISSISM

The only thing Enrico Caruso grabbed when he was caught in the 1906 earthquake in San Francisco was a photograph of himself. **Malachy McCourt**

An actor can only have one great love – himself. **Peter O'Toole**

Nobody can be kinder than the narcissist when you react to life on his terms. *Elizabeth Bowen*

Some writers would make a drum out of the skin of their mother's arse, the better to sound their own praises. *Brian Behan*

I sometimes think I must be the only person in Britain who's featured on the front, centre and back pages of a daily newspaper — all on the same day. *George Best*

# NATIONALITY

A Frenchman is an Italian with a bad temper. *Dennis McEvoy*

When you're lying drunk at the airport, you're Irish. When you win an Oscar, you're British. *Brenda Fricker*

I don't see myself as Irish or American. I'm a New Yorker. *Frank McCourt*

I'm Irish and Dutch. Which means my idea of a good time is to get drunk and drive my car into a windmill. *Kris McGaha*

I hate these American politicians who pretend to be Irish to get the Irish vote. Ronald Reagan said he was Irish because his great-great-great-great-great-great-great-great-great-grandmother was a fossil underneath a stone in Galway Bay. *Ian MacPherson*

The man who was born American, lived a German and died a British traitor at the end became what he was all along — an Irishman from Connemara. *Ludovic Kennedy on Lord Haw-Haw*

I am not French. *Au contraire. Samuel Beckett*

The Belgians will play like their fellow Scandinavians, Denmark and Sweden. *Andy Townsend*

Austrians are like Germans with a sense of humour. *Mark Cagney*

"De Valera is the greatest Irishman since St Patrick," he said. "But St Patrick wasn't an Irishman," I protested. "Neither was Dev," he whispered triumphantly. *John B. Keane*

A true football fan is one who knows the nationality of every Republic of Ireland player. *Ken Bolam*

The Russians are the only government to live up to their expectations. They've promised nothing and that's exactly what they've given. *Bob Geldof*

I'm not Irish. If a man is born in a stable it doesn't make him a horse. *Duke of Wellington*

The critics have missed the most important thing about me and my work — the fact that I am Irish. *Eugene O'Neill*

A few years ago I was as Irish as shish kebab. *Former US senator George Mitchell on being "adopted" by the Irish after he helped broker the Good Friday Agreement which brought peace to Northern Ireland in 1999*

The English don't seem to realize Wayne Rooney is Irish. Well, (a) his name is Rooney, and (b) look at the fuckin' head on him. That isn't an international soccer star. That's a minor hurler from Offaly who got lucky. *Dara O'Briain*

My name is Barack O'Bama of the Moneygall O'Bamas. I've come home to find the apostrophe we lost somewhere along the way. *Barack Obama during his 2011 visit to Ireland*

Barack Obama can't have Irish roots. When he was in Offaly he went into a pub, had a pint of Guinness, and left shortly afterwards. A true Irishman would have stayed there for the day and been carried out at closing time. *Brendan O'Connor*

# NATURE

The sun shone, having no alternative, on the nothing new. *Samuel Beckett*

I have never seen snow. Snow doesn't like me. It melts before I come. *Jack B. Yeats*

God made the grass, the air and the rain. And the grass, the air and the rain made the Irish. And the Irish turned the grass, the air and the rain back into God. *Sean O'Faolain*

If you stop and smell the roses, sooner or later you'll inhale a bee. *Eamonn Mac Thomáis*

If a queen bee were crossed with a Friesian bull, would the land flow with milk and honey? *Oliver St John Gogarty*

Catholics look at a beautiful sunset and think: "I'm not allowed to enjoy that. Give me some mud." Sunsets are for Protestants. *Dylan Moran*

# NEEDS

All I need is a bed, a toilet, a chair and a drinks cabinet. *Shane MacGowan*

These days I need a rubdown to get down the stairs in the morning. *Niall Quinn*

What I'm looking for is a blessing that's not in disguise. *Kitty O'Neill*

What do women want? Not much. Pre-emptive empathy and telepathy, things like that. What do men want? Lingerie. *Dylan Moran*

# NEGATIVITY

The cup of Ireland's misery has been overflowing for centuries but is not yet full. *Sir Boyle Roche*

I reckon no man is thoroughly miserable unless he be condemned to live in Ireland. *Jonathan Swift*

A farmer approaching his hundredth birthday was interviewed by a local reporter. "I suppose you've seen a lot of changes in your life," said the reporter. The old man replied cheerfully, "Yes, and I've been *agin* them all." *Eric Cross*

I'm so pessimistic I'm even pessimistic about the pessimism of other pessimists. *Jack MacGowran*

Only in Ireland could a nation — America — be satirized for using a phrase like "Have a nice day." An Irish Barack Obama wouldn't say "Yes we can." He'd shake his head and go, "Maybe." *Des Bishop*

Yeats has reached the age where he won't take yes for an answer. *Oliver St John Gogarty*

If the word "no" was removed from the English language, Ian Paisley would be struck dumb. *John Hume*

I am troubled. I am dissatisfied. I am Irish. *Marianne Moore*

Was there ever a nation with such a spiteful face towards each other as ours? Our biggest industries are undertakers and glaziers. *Kathleen Behan*

San Marino play like men who expect to encounter visa problems if they approach the halfway line. *Tom Humphries on the beleaguered football team*

Ulster dyslexics say "On". *Geoff Hill*

# NEIGHBOURS

My two biggest problems at the moment are neighbours and haemorrhoids. *Spike Milligan*

If you could see yourself as your neighbours do, you'd probably move. *Mary Crosby*

The strange thing about our society is that we use holidays as an excuse to get away from the people we surround ourselves with, and yet we all holiday in the exact same places. This means you can row with the neighbours all over again, only this time in a more interesting climate. *Sean Hughes*

Do not love your neighbour as yourself. If you are on good terms with yourself it is an impertinence. *George Bernard Shaw*

There's nothing as consoling as finding that one's neighbours' problems are at least as great as one's own. *George Moore*

My Dalkey neighbours will always see me as a big noisy girl on a bicycle. *Maeve Binchy*

Jonathan Swift hated his neighbour as much as himself. *W. B. Yeats*

People use dogs to crap on their neighbours seeing as how they themselves would be arrested for the same conduct. *Brian Behan*

In my usual type of hotel the walls are so thin you can hear your next-door neighbour's inner doubts. *Joe O'Connor*

Any Dublin cinema provides ample evidence that it is an infinitely worse sin to take one's neighbour's wife than his life. *Hugh Leonard*

# NEW MEN

I'm a New Man. I can express my feelings. I am in touch with my feminine side, my inner child, my personal karma. I cry at films. I iron my socks. I hug trees so hard there's been a bit of talk in the neighbourhood. *Joe O'Connor*

I don't have any problem at all with changing a nappy and then going down to the pub and talking about football. I'm not a new man or an old man. I just happen to be a man. *Roddy Doyle*

Irish men only cry when they're trying to assemble Ikea furniture. *Michael Cullen*

Old men pretend to be new men to get new women to go to bed with them. *Katy French*

# NEWSPAPERS

Newspapers are unable to distinguish between a bicycle accident and the collapse of civilization. *George Bernard Shaw*

Cats know with absolute certainty which part of the newspaper you're trying to read. This is the only place in the whole house where they decide to sit. *Pat Ingoldsby*

The *Irish Times* — that last bastion of the semi-colon. *Con Houlihan*

I left the *Irish Press* to go into journalism. *Kevin Marron*

Newspapers are paid to get it wrong. *Emmett Corrigan*

A newspaper headline you'll never get to see: Police Warn Of Trouble From Golf Hooligans. *Robert O'Byrne*

# NEWSPAPER HEADLINES

Wife Died After Attempting To Commit Suicide

Girl Found With Detective In Her Boot

Mrs Reagan Better After Fall

Rape Man: I Thought She Was My Wife

Mounting Problems For Young Couples

Prisoners Escape After Execution

Enraged Bull Injures Farmer With Axe

Deaf Mute Gets New Hearing In Court

Milk Drinkers Are Turning To Powder

Drunk Gets Nine Months In Violin Case

20-Year-Old Friendship Ends At Altar

Lucky Man Sees Friends Die

Stiff Opposition Expected To Undertakers' Strike

Police Discover Crack In Australia

Dead Woman May Have Disturbed Burglar

Test Tube Babies Face Life Of Misconceptions

# NIAGARA FALLS

Niagara Falls is simply a vast amount of water going the wrong way and then falling over unnecessary rocks. *Oscar Wilde*

If I swam backwards up Niagara Falls, no doubt some journalist would preface the achievement by saying "Self-confessed homosexual swam backwards up Niagara Falls". *Self-confessed homosexual David Norris*

Niagara Falls is the second biggest disappointment of the average honeymoon. *Oscar Wilde*

# NICENESS

Everyone is too nice in Japan. No wonder Gary Lineker went there. *Noel Gallagher*

Deborah Kerr is nice. So are Greer Garson and Julie Andrews. In fact all the English actresses are damned nice. Except Hayley Mills — thank God. *John Huston*

A nice actor is almost a contradiction in terms. When it comes to looking for work, most of us would hang our mothers. *Niall Toibin*

# NORTHERN IRELAND

There's no real difference between Northern Ireland and the rest of the country. It's just six of one and twenty-six of the other. *Kevin McAleer*

Northern Ireland is like Beirut, only without the Christians. *Adrian Walsh*

Ulster Unionists aren't loyal to the Crown but to the half-crown. *John Hume*

They say the situation in Northern Ireland isn't half as bad as they say it is. *Dennis Taylor*

People in Northern Ireland write "Sod the Pope" on walls because it takes too long to write "Sod the Moderator of the Free Presbyterian Church". *Sean Kilroy*

In the late 1960s the British discovered Northern Ireland, later diagnosed as Ulcer. *Craig Brown*

You might as well discuss better terms for the annihilation of Jews with Hitler as discuss with Southern Ireland the way forward for the North. *Ian Paisley*

Ulster Unionists never miss an opportunity to miss an opportunity. *Conor Cruise O'Brien*

Free Northern Ireland. Just send six box tops and a large stamped addressed envelope. *Patrick Kielty*

Let's do away with the border and all become Germans. *Joe McCarthy*

I wouldn't be surprised to discover that there are people so happily innocent of politics that they believe Jack Charlton is the Anglo-Irish Agreement. *Con Houlihan*

I believe Hugh Grant is going to visit Northern Ireland. He should find a lot to identify with here. After all, his problems began with 69 too. *Patrick Kielty*

Pathetic, sectarian, mono-ethnic and mono-cultural. *David Trimble on the Republic of Ireland in 2002*

He must have stopped taking the tablets. *Peter Robinson on Trimble's outburst*

Now that we have peace in the North we should bring republicans into the mainstream. How about a republican newspaper with a Page Three girl. She'd have sweat all over her bikini because of the balaclava. *P. J. Gallagher*

# NOSES

I'm very popular in Israel because of my big nose. *Joe Dolan*

With a nose as big as mine, cocaine would be a very expensive habit. *Chris de Burgh*

If a writer says he doesn't read reviews of his work, his nose will grow longer and longer until eventually it falls off. *Hugh Leonard*

Shay Given has shaken off a broken nose to play today. ***Des Lynam***

It's written in rock 'n' roll that all you need is love. But you also need a great nose. ***Bono***

My wife snores. She had her nose broken a few times as a child. Obviously it didn't work because she still does it. ***Ed Byrne***

# NOTICES

**On a building site:** Nightwatchman Patrols This Area 24 Hours A Day

**In a factory:** Closing Down, Thanks To All Our Customers

**In a shop:** Ears Pierced While You Wait. Pay For Two And Get Another One Done Free

**In a car window:** Wife And Dog Lost. Reward For Dog

**In a garage:** Free Estimates At Almost No Cost

**In an office:** Passport For Sale: Owner Going Abroad

**In a chemist:** We Dispense With Accuracy

**In a café:** Open 24 Hours A Day, Longer At Weekends

**In a funeral parlour car park:** Positively No Exit From Here

**In a laundrette:** Leave Your Clothes Here And Go Out And Enjoy Yourself

**In a theatre:** Good Clean Entertainment Every Night Except Sunday

**In a travel agency:** Why Don't You Go Away?

**In a restaurant:** Lunch Served From 2.30 To Mid-October

**In a hotel:** If You Have Any Desires During The Night, Ring For The Chambermaid

**In a hospital:** The Psychiatry Department Is Round The Bend

**In a neglected shop:** Customers Wanted. Apply Within

**In a newspaper column:** Happy Home Wanted For Lovely Dog. Will Eat Anything — Loves Children.

Trespassers Will Be Used. *Notice spotted in Trinity College Genetics Department, Dublin*

Back In Ten Minutes — Sit! *Sign in vet's office*

No Credit Given To Cash Customers. *Notice in shop*

The Management Takes No Responsibility For Injuries Received In The Rush For The Bar At Closing Time. *Pub notice*

Wanted: Man To Wash Dishes And Two Waitresses. *Hotel notice*

Closed Tonight For Official Opening. *Notice outside community centre in Waterford*

Miracles We Can Handle Today. The Impossible Takes a Little Bit Longer. *Notice in TV repair shop*

Meeting At 7 p.m. Please Use The Large Double Doors. *Notice outside Overeaters Anonymous meeting in Dublin*

There Will Be No Last Train Tonight. *Notice in Irish railway station*

# NOVELS AND NOVELISTS

I'm sick and tired of novelists who write novels about novelists writing novels about novelists. *John Broderick*

When I asked my mother what she thought of my first novel she said, "How would I know what I thought of it? I was far too busy making sure I wasn't in it!" *Brian Moore*

A good way to write a novel is to go into a pub, sit down and listen. *Maeve Binchy*

It is the sexless novel that should be distinguished. The sex novel is now normal. *George Bernard Shaw*

I imagine I'll have about eleven readers. *James Joyce after completing* Ulysses

There's a very big difference between novels and poetry. You starve with one of them. *Dermot Bolger*

I come from a long line of unpublishable Tiernans who have novels in the closet. *Tommy Tiernan*

Encouraged by the money Marian Keyes and Cecilia Ahern make with chicklit, I'm writing a boylit novel. It's the story of Malcolm, a successful twenty-something who's having trouble finding a woman. All they want to do is drink Fat Frogs and flash their boobs while he likes to cry over nothing and sometimes go to fortune tellers. One night while drinking Chardonnay with his best friends Alan and The Hamster he cries for three hours and they can't make him stop. The End. *Pat Fitzpatrick*

The reader is the ultimate author of my novels. *John Banville*

Modern technology, which has put a man on the moon, cannot produce a novel typescript that doesn't look like a telephone directory. *Joe O'Connor*

# NUANCES

If I go into a pub in Belfast and say, "I am not Irish, I am a Belfast Protestant," I'll be told, "Right, Paddy, whatever turns you on." *Sam McAughtry*

The only trouble with Seamus O'Sullivan is that when he's not drunk he's sober. *W. B. Yeats*

Ray McAnally was the kind of actor that, if a director asked him to cry, he'd say, "Which eye?" *Liam Neeson*

Meredith is a prose Browning — and so is Browning. *Oscar Wilde*

In a butcher's shop in town, a girl asked for a pound of rashers. The butcher asked her what type. The girl replied, "The ones you fry." *Overheard in Dublin*

I'm not annoyed at you. I'm annoyed at the fact that you *thought* I was annoyed at you. *Sharon Whelan*

# NUDITY

You can always tell the best man at a nudist wedding – it's sticking out a mile. *Colm O'Regan*

Naked, I have a body designed for burial. *Spike Milligan*

I regret not being more scantily clad when I was younger. If I'd known I was going to get old and fat I'd have gone around stark bollock naked. *Sinead O'Connor*

# NUMBERS

It's just come out that Katie Melua miscounted. There aren't nine million bicycles in Bejing, only eight million, eight hundred thousand, three hundred and twenty-seven. *Dave Gorman*

Paul Scholes has four players in front of him – five if you count Pat Neville. *Darragh Moloney*

I pined for the lure of Bridie, perhaps the loveliest of the seventeen Gallagher sisters, her slightly crossed eyes and unfortunate ears notwithstanding. We were already linked amorously in the public mind through no act of my own. The parish priest had the tedious notion of joining both our families in stage wedlock for a production of the world's first Catholic musical, *Seventeen Brides for Seventeen Brothers*. *Ian MacPherson*

I can count on the fingers of one hand the ten games when we've caused our own downfall. *Joe Kinnear*

# NUNS

Make friends of both nuns and whores. And when you're talking to them, forget which is which. *Brendan Francis*

Nothing entertaining ever happened in the Ireland of long ago unless you were a sheep, a terrorist or a nun. *Joe O'Connor*

I found being a lesbian ex-nun who worked in a skateboard firm less strange than being a *Big Brother* contestant. *Anna Nolan, runner-up in the show in 2000*

Nuns wore such long habits when I was growing up, I thought they had no feet. I imagined them spinning around the convent on castors, or being moved by someone with a remote control. *Brendan Grace*

Aren't nuns great, Ted? You don't feel as nervous with them as you do with real women. *Fr Dougal in* **Father Ted**

Hearing nuns' confessions is like being stoned to death with popcorn. *Sean Kilroy*

I once considered becoming a nun simply for the outfits. *Julia Sweeney*

When I was young I wanted to be a nun but I prayed the vocation would go away because of the sex thing. *Sinead O'Connor*

# OBITUARIES

I read the Obituary column every morning. If I'm not in it, I get up. *Micheál MacLiammóir*

My father used to open the Obituary page of the newspaper and say, "Right, let's see who gave up smoking yesterday." *Tommy Tiernan*

No matter how dead you may feel, you're not dead in Ireland until your death notice appears in the *Irish Independent* newspaper. Even if you've witnessed a death first hand you should await the publication of the notice in the *Indo* before being absolutely certain. If you have hired an assassin to kill a rich relative you should not hand over the final instalment of the fee until you read in the *Indo* that your relative has died "unexpectedly". **David Slattery**

Why do people in Ireland always die in alphabetical order? **T. P. McKenna**

# OLD AGE

The first point to make about old age is that, whatever its disadvantages, it beats the alternative. **Terry Prone**

I'm a year younger than Mickey Mouse. **John Montague on his eightieth birthday in 2009**

What's the use of being old if you can't be dumb? **John O'Hara**

May you live to be one hundred years — with one extra year to repent. **Ancient Irish blessing**

These days I get a standing ovation for just standing. **Maureen Potter at seventy-one**

The years hang like old clothes, forgotten in the wardrobe of our minds. Did I wear that? Who was I then? **Brian Moore**

People keep telling me you get grumpy as you get older. I've been grumpy since I was ten. **Bob Geldof**

I've reached the age in life where I'm profoundly grateful when a girl says no to me. **Sean Kilroy**

Don't get old in Ireland. They'll put you on telly for your entertainment and then torture you with nostalgic songs. **Pat Fitzpatrick**

You know you're getting on in years when they knock down the ground where you've made your debut. *Pat Jennings*

It's a strange thing about the Moriartys. They never mind too much about dying but they hate growing old. *Joe O'Toole*

You know you're getting old when you open the fridge with a hammer in your hand. *Terry Wogan*

Jack Nicholson isn't sexy any more. In fact he wouldn't look out of place in a DIY store on a Thursday afternoon availing himself of the OAP's discount. *Ciara Dwyer*

The gods bestowed upon Max Beerbohm the gift of perpetual old age. *Oscar Wilde*

Private intimations of advancing age are one's own business, but when policemen begin stepping out of your way and the occasional grey-haired woman flashes you a lascivious wink, it is plainly time to reach for either the bottle of hair-dye or *The Lives of the Saints*. *Hugh Leonard*

The village doesn't have an oldest inhabitant. He died. *Tom Mathews*

When Fred Davis started playing snooker the Dead Sea was only sick. *Ken Doherty*

# ONE-MAN SHOWS

The last time I was in England I did a one-man show. I think he enjoyed it. *Dusty Young*

I love doing my one-person show. At least I give myself the cues properly. *Micheál MacLiammóir*

My main difficulty is that I can't act, I can't sing, I can't play the piano, I can't dance and I'm not a comedian. In terms of a one-man show this is . . . restricting. *Gay Byrne*

# ORGASMS

What's the difference between a Catholic wife and a Jewish one? A Catholic wife has real orgasms and fake jewellery. **Matthew Carey**

Academy Awards are like orgasms. Only a few of us know the feeling of having had multiple ones. **John Huston**

Genghis Khan is supposed to have died having sex. I suppose you could say he came and he went. **Michael Dwyer**

Neil Kinnock looks like a tortoise having an orgasm. **Patrick Murray**

Sex with my wife is just one more thing for her to moan about. **Big O**

Feminism has gone too far. It's now the men who are faking the orgasms. **Frank Tuohy**

Daytime TV. American chatshow hostess faking an orgasm because a C-list chef is making pavlova. **Pat Fitzpatrick**

I know my last girlfriend faked her orgasms. Because I asked her to. **Ed Byrne**

Q. How can you tell when a Northside Dublin girl has an orgasm?
A. She drops her chips.
**Peter Crosbie**

# OSCARS

Did you hear Meryl Streep giving her Oscar speech for *The Iron Lady*? She turned up dressed like a crumpled cigarette wrapper in a thunderstorm. **Mick the Maverick**

Why should I want to participate in Hollywood's Oscar bollox? It's fourteen hours to get there and fourteen hours back, plus two hours of fucking stupidity and kissing people's fucking cheeks. Fuck that. *Richard Harris*

After I won the Oscar for *My Left Foot* I bought a new house because the one I was living in had no mantelpiece and that's where I wanted to put it. *Brenda Fricker*

I didn't show up at the awards ceremony to collect any of my first three Oscars. The first time I went fishing. The second time there was a war on, and on the last occasion I was suddenly taken drunk. *John Ford*

Did you hear about the film star who called his baby Oscar because he thought it was his best performance of the year? *James Healy*

Will Martin Scorsese ever make a film bad enough to win an Oscar? *Declan Lynch*

This has the makings of a hell of a weekend in Dublin. *Daniel Day-Lewis, holding up the Oscar he won for* **My** Left Foot

# OUTER SPACE

The Great Wall of China is supposed to be the only man-made object on earth visible from space, but I'd say Venus Williams' nipples would give it a run for its money. *Eilis O'Hanlon*

The Irish space programme has run into a technical hitch. The astronaut keeps falling off the kite. *Peter Hornby*

An American tourist was boasting to Jack McCarthy about how the Americans had put a man on the moon. "That's nothing," said Jack. "The Irish are planning to put a man on the sun." "Don't be ridiculous," said the tourist. "He'd be burned to a cinder." "Oh we've thought of that," said Jack. "We're sending him up at night." *Duncan Crosbie*

# OWNERSHIP

My father always said, "Own the land you live on. Then you can piss on it without being arrested." *Richard Harris*

The drive-in bank was established so that the real owner of the car could get to see it once in a while. *Hal Roach*

I'm the proud owner of a Prince Charles teapot. It doesn't reign but it pours. *Abie Philbin Bowman*

Charlie Haughey wasn't happy to be just running Ireland; he wanted to own it. *Frank Cluskey*

There's no such thing as a cat owner. It's not possible to own an animal which imagines it's doing you a major favour by living in your house. *Pat Ingoldsby*

# PARANOIA

I once knew a man who spent half his life tying up his boot-laces under lamp-posts. He had an invincible belief that detectives followed him and he was never content until he had allowed whoever was behind him to get past. *Robert Lynd*

I'm a paranoid in reverse. I suspect people of plotting to make me happy. *Dave Allen*

One thing I've noticed is that people on ladders get very paranoid if complete strangers start climbing up behind them. *Michael Redmond*

My doctor told me I was paranoid. Well he didn't exactly say it, but I know that's what the bastard was thinking. *Tom Kenny*

I'm a paranoid dyslexic. I believe Marilyn Monroe was killed not by the CIA but the ICA — The Irish Countrywomen's Association. *Martin O'Keeffe*

# PARENTS AND PARENTHOOD

I always felt my mother was ashamed of me. She had shutters on the pram. Sometimes she picked me up in her arms and walked away after throwing me in the air. It was very embarrassing. I was nineteen at the time. *James McKeon*

"You know," said Paddy in a reflective mood, "the happiest parents are those without children." *Peter Cagney*

I wish either my father or my mother, or indeed both of them, as they were in duty both equally bound to it, had minded what they were about when they begot me. *Laurence Sterne*

The authoritarian Irish parent is world famous, as is his frequently neurotic child. *Noel Browne*

Mine wasn't the traditional Irish mother. In fact she was English. *Ian MacPherson*

Did you hear about the couple who were so liberal they tried to adopt a gay baby? *Graham Norton*

My mother was American but she was raised in the proper Irish way, by alcoholics. *Des Bishop*

There are no illegitimate children, only illegitimate parents. *Bernadette McAliskey*

Almost anyone can look after a baby. The demanding phase of parenthood begins when they *stop* being babies. *Mary Kenny*

Parents are people who practise the rhythm method of birth control. *Peter O'Toole*

Jesus must have been Irish because his father, Joseph Christ, wasn't at his crucifixion. It's so typical of an Irish father to miss out on his son's most golden moment. If Jesus told him he rose from the dead three days later he would probably have said, "I suppose you think you're great now, do ye? And your mother home alone for the whole weekend." *Tommy Tiernan*

It is now possible to have five parents: sperm donor, egg donor, surrogate mother who carries the foetus, and two adoptive parents. It renders the statement "He has his mother's eyes" rather meaningless. *George Carlin*

Gay Byrne: "How many children have you?"
John B. Keane: "Only four, but I'm making negotiations through the proper channels for the fifth."
*Exchange on* **The Late Late Show**

Trying to bring up children today is a bit like hanging on to an aircraft as it's taking off. *Gabriel Byrne*

When I'm trying to manage the kids at Christmas I can understand why some animals eat their young. *Brendan O'Carroll*

Becoming a father is like arriving in Osaka after a nine-month flight. Exotic, and also a bit disorienting. *Trevor White*

I was an ambitious minx after I got married. I left my children with all sorts of babysitters. Half of them could have been Myra Hindley. *Mary Kenny*

As the years go on, my parents seem to become smaller and smaller. I'm not worried about them dying any more, just disappearing. *Sean Hughes*

# PARKING

I've decided to stop driving drunk. I can never remember where I've parked the bloody car. *Dave Allen*

Thunder is God trying to parallel park. *Graham Norton*

Paddy claims his wife is the only person in the world who parks her car by ear. *Joe Kenny*

I find few things as heartbreaking as watching a woman trying to reverse a car into a space any smaller than Leitrim. *Kevin Myers*

If God intended us to fly he'd have organized more parking at Dublin Airport. *Big O*

A single yellow line on an Irish road means you can't park here at all. A double one means you can't park here at all at all. *Mick Lally*

# PARTIES

I didn't invite Britney Spears to my twenty-first birthday party because she didn't invite me to hers. *Tadhg O'Reilly*

The only time I feel fully relaxed at a party is when I'm in the bathroom. *Pat Ingoldsby*

There's a pecking order for celebrities at after-show parties. One time both Prince and Madonna circled a block in their limos for twenty minutes because neither of them wanted to be the first to arrive. *Boy George*

If anybody complains that they're feeling a bit drunk too early at your party, just show them Shane MacGowan and say, "That's what pissed is. How do you feel now?" They'll say, "Much better thanks. I'll have a triple vodka." *Pat Fitzpatrick*

Children's parties aren't what they used to be. What's happened to all those games we used to play, like running around torturing the weakest member of the group? *Dylan Moran*

Christy Brown partied so much after the publication of *Down All the Days* it should really have been called *Up All the Nights*. *Georgina Hambleton*

The reason Ireland won the Eurovision annually in the good old days was because every other country wanted to come and party next year in Europe's then hippest capital. *Paul Kilduff*

Ordinary parties are bad enough but the Christmas party is a vile scraping from between the gnarled toes of Satan. By

7.30 you are already tipsy. By 8.05 you are laughing for no apparent reason. By 8.15 you are reciting Monty Python sketches. By 9.10 you are having a vicious argument with your best friend about Bosnia, the North or Aston Villa. *Joe O'Connor*

The dying process begins the minute we're born but accelerates during dinner parties. *Carol Matthau*

A party was thrown in Hollywood for the wrap-up of the Marlon Brando film *A Countess from Hong Kong*. The film was such a flop, it was suggested they dump it and release the party instead. *Brian Behan*

The Christmas party never really gets going until someone photocopies their bum in the boss's office. *Katy French*

# DOLLY PARTON

"I'd like to bump off Dolly Parton."
  "You mean knock off."
  "I know what I mean!"
*Seamus O'Leary*

Pamela Anderson has just told her Hollywood agent she's refusing to do a film with Dolly Parton. Apparently the town isn't big enough for the four of them. *Paul Hamilton*

My luck is so bad, if Dolly Parton had triplets, I'd be the one on the bottle. *Frank Carson*

# PATIENCE

I'm a patient man. I once spent six months on a paragraph trying to get it right. I take my lead from Arnold Schoenberg. He was once informed that a violin concerto he wrote would require a soloist with six fingers to play it. He replied, "I can wait." *John Banville*

There's only one problem about instant gratification: it takes too long. *Owen O'Neill*

The way it is with life, you can't always wait for the green man to cross the road. *Ronnie Drew*

God give me patience, but make it fast. *Twink*

I'm dreadfully impatient, and sometimes I get impatient with myself about that. *Gay Byrne*

An unwatched pot boils immediately. *Mary O'Dowd*

I'm compulsive but also indecisive. I don't know what I want but I want it now. *Dylan Moran*

# PATRIOTISM

Dying for Ireland was always a greater virtue than living for it. *Noel Browne*

An author's first duty is to let his country down. *Brendan Behan*

Pat O'Donnell spent eight years fighting for his country. Then the owner retired and the pub was closed. *Peter Cagney*

There's a thin line between dying for Ireland and killing for it. *John Hume*

"I died for Ireland," shouted the excited speaker, "and what's more I'll do it again if necessary." *Tony Butler*

When I'm in England I drink a lot even when I don't want to. Otherwise I feel I'd be letting my country down. *Ardal O'Hanlon*

I've only been Irish since I moved to England. Back home there didn't seem much point. *Dermot Carmody*

I'm inclined to cast a bleak eye on anyone who tells me he's proud to be Irish. It is, after all, only by an accident of birth that he's not wearing a dhoti and a few scabs and assuring Mother Teresa that he wouldn't leave Calcutta for his weight in chapattis. *Hugh Leonard*

Patriotism is the virtue of the vicious. *Oscar Wilde*

Foxrock has no roads named after republican heroes. Dying for Ireland was always considered a terribly working-class idea here. *Ross O'Carroll-Kelly on the fashionable Dublin suburb*

# PEOPLE AND PLACES

Who wants to go to Gdansk? There isn't a lot there after you've seen the shipyard wall. *Michael O'Leary*

I told a man I was from Fermanagh. He said, "Is that near anywhere?" *Owen O'Neill*

Derry is a vibrant city, in many ways living up to its title as the Belfast of the North. *Ian MacPherson*

Larry Gogan: "Where's the Taj Mahal?"
Contestant: "Opposite the Dental Hospital."
*Exchange on Gogan's Just-a-Minute Quiz; the contestant was speaking of a restaurant in Dublin going by that name*

I enjoyed Sark, but going up and down all those cliffs gave me charwoman's ankles. *Louis MacNeice*

I come from Clones, where everyone looks like everyone else. *Barry McGuigan*

A Tyrone woman will never buy a rabbit without a head in case it turns out to be a cat. *Ben Kiely*

The Irish Midlands is often referred to as Darwin's Waiting Room. *Joe O'Connor*

We're now going to Wembley for live second-half commentary on the England–Scotland game – except that it's at Hampden Park. *Eamonn Andrews*

Navan is a cultureless fuckin' hole of a town – the only place in Europe that's spelt the same forwards as backwards. That says a lot about it. The knacker yard of palindromes. Suggest an Arts Festival and you'll get the answer, "What would we want with an Arts Festival – haven't we got a Shoppin' Centre." *Tommy Tiernan*

I came to Nantes two years ago and it's much the same today except that it's completely different. *Brian Moore*

The town I come from was so small, the local fire brigade was a ten-year-old bed-wetter. *Joe Cuddy*

Vaduz is so small that if you miss your bus stop, the next stop could be in another country. *Paul Kilduff*

Eamonn Keane once called a Garda a "Clare fucker". When he brought him to court, the judge said, "And to which portion of this appellation do you take offence?" *Niall Toibin*

People in Scotland abuse you in the hope that you'll abuse them back. If you don't they're disappointed. *Ed Byrne*

"See Naples and die," they say. Having driven in that city I understand what they mean. *Joe O'Connor*

The first time I saw a play of mine performed abroad was in that Bangkok of the western world, Oldham, Lancashire, where on a clear day one can see the fog. *Hugh Leonard*

Sweden is jaw-slackeningly dull. Staring at it for too long, drool drips from your chin like an old person plonked in a wheelchair in the conservatory of a nursing home, contemplating the world beyond. I would sooner invite Kathy Bates around with two blocks of wood and a lump hammer. *Philip Nolan*

The Jamaicans are just as laid-back as the Irish. On my first day there I spent three and a half hours waiting for my breakfast. Everything I asked for got the answer, "Yeah, man, soon come." The sex was also interminable. *Deirdre O'Kane*

# PERSISTENCE

Boozing with Brendan Behan called for the thirst of a camel, the stamina of an ox, the stomach of an ostrich and a neck like a jockey's bollox. *Bill Kelly*

Go on, go on, go on, go on, go on, go on, go on, go on, go on, go on, go on, go on, go on, go on, go on, go onnnnnnnnnnnnnnnn! *Mrs Doyle trying to persuade anyone one cares to mention to have a cup of tea on Craggy Island in* Father Ted

I can't go on, I must go on, I'll go on. *Samuel Beckett*

Once a woman has decided to knit a jersey, nothing short of paralysis will stop her. *John D. Sheridan*

# PHILANTHROPY

She's the sort of woman who lives for others. You can always tell the others by their hunted expression. *Cecil Day-Lewis*

There's nothing I wouldn't do for my wife and nothing she wouldn't do for me. We spend our life doing nothing for each other. *Brendan Grace*

In view of all the controversy about U2, may I relate my experiences with the band. After a brilliant gig at the LA Coliseum, myself and some friends waited for them in the car park. After about fifty minutes, all four band members arrived and started talking to us. They invited us back to their hotel. We had a delicious four-course meal and went for a swim in the luxury pool. Then Bono noticed I had a slight cough and offered to pay for a heart and lung transplant. My friend mentioned that her mother had an incurable illness so Larry and Adam stayed up all night working on a new antidote. Luckily it worked and her mother is now a big U2 fan. Then Bono gave us £10,000 each. Then, not to be outdone, The Edge promised to buy every one of us a luxury home in the Caribbean. *Sharon Dulux*

As a considerate spouse I believe in sharing everything with my present wife, and have carried this togetherness to the point where I have given her the cold I had last week. *Hugh Leonard*

# PHONES

One thing has always puzzled me about wrong numbers: they're never engaged. *Owen Kelly*

I'm out at the moment, but should you be the chairman of Barcelona, AC Milan or Real Madrid I'll get straight back to you. *Joe Kinnear's answerphone message*

They should have automatic buttons on phones that you can activate whenever you're about to ring your mother: "If you feel like having a looney conversation that's going to make you feel guilty for a week afterwards, press 1." *Mary Bourke*

The local phone box down the road was the centre of my social life growing up. We used to congregate there and spend a lot of time talking about ringing women who never answered. *Jon Kenny*

Delaney was asked if he talked to his wife while he was making love. "Only if there's a phone handy," he explained. *Shaun Connors*

I was recently approached by a pretty girl in Grafton Street who was collecting for Concern. They do it by standing order nowadays. She wanted my bank account details and my phone number. I said I would agree if she gave me hers. *Kevin Lynch*

Last night I got bored with making obscene phone calls so I decided, against my principles, to watch television. **Richard O'Connor**

If you want the telephone company to repair your phone in Ireland you don't ring them up because they won't reply. Instead you talk to that fellow with the cast in his left eye you keep bumping into in the supermarket who, someone has told you, is the brother of a woman who goes out with a clerk in Telecom Éireann. The phone will be repaired within the week. **Terry Eagleton**

I never hung up on a crossed line because the conversations, even though mostly nonsense, helped me with my dialogue. Otherwise my characters would just have blabbered on ad nauseam like myself. **Maeve Binchy**

Vodafone phones don't get married in my house because the reception would be terrible. **David O'Doherty**

Every night Shamus used to make love to his girlfriend over the telephone but the local council put an end to it yesterday. They evicted the couple because they wanted to repaint the kiosk. **Peter Cagney**

The best way to recognize an obscene phone caller from Ireland? The heavy belching. **Bernard Manning**

# PHOTOGRAPHS

I'm so short I'm the only person in the world whose feet are in his passport photograph. **Noel V. Ginnity**

If you look like your passport photo, you're too ill to travel. **Bill O'Herlihy**

Don't worry. That's just God taking your photograph. **Bono to Sophia Loren after she was frightened by lightning on a plane once**

People in other countries come up to you when you're

famous and drool over you. In Ireland they come up and say, "I think you're thick. Now will you pose for a photo of myself and the wife." *Jason Byrne*

Writing poetry is my way of taking photographs of myself. *Gabriel Byrne*

From the vantage point of the twenty-first century, old photos of showbands with their cheesy grins, crooked teeth and gorse-bush hair can resemble gargoyle identity parades, but to sixties Ireland these men were sex on legs. *Damien Corless*

I sent a picture of myself to the Lonely Hearts but they sent it straight back. They said, "We're not that lonely." *Jimmy Cricket*

Murphy kept a photograph of his mother-in-law above the fireplace. He said it kept the children away from the fire. *Hal Roach*

I wanted to stir some shit. *Sinead O'Connor on why she tore up a photograph of Pope John Paul II on television*

An Irishman brought a photograph of his son to be digitally enhanced. He said to the shop assistant, "He's wearing a hat in this photo and I'd like you to take it off." "That shouldn't be too much of a problem, sir," said the assistant. "We can touch it up for you. Tell me, on which side does your son part his hair?" "Come on now," said the Irishman, "you'll see that when you take his hat off." *Nick Harris*

# PIZZAS

I once went into a pizza parlour and was asked whether I wanted it sliced into four or eight slices. I told them four because I didn't think I could manage eight. *Jason McAteer*

My idea of perfection is a man who turns into a pizza after sex. *Deirdre Walsh*

# PLAYS AND PLAYWRIGHTS

Good acting covers a multitude of defects. It explains the success of Lady Gregory's plays. *Oliver St John Gogarty*

I think it's time there was an innovation to protect the actor from the vagaries of directors. Given a good play and a decent set, you could chain a blue-arsed baboon in the stalls and get what is known as a production. *Peter O'Toole*

Why have I never produced a play? Because I am too busy producing playwrights. *Stephen Behan, the father of Brendan*

The best line I ever wrote in a play was "Yeah". *Billy Roche*

Samuel Beckett's plays remind me of something Sir John Betjeman might do if you filled him up with Benzedrine and then force-fed him intravenously with Guinness. *Tom Davies*

There are thousands of ways of writing plays but only two kinds of play: bad and good. *Sean O'Casey*

*Waiting for Godot* is a play in which nothing happens. Twice. *Hugh Kenner*

When Picasso was asked when a painting was finished, he replied, "When the gentleman from the gallery comes to hang it." As a playwright I've discovered a play is finished when the gentlemen from the press come to hang the playwright. *Dermot Bolger*

If there is one thing I cannot do it is talk about my work, or explain it – except perhaps over the third bottle. *Samuel Beckett*

Playwrights only puts down what we says and then charges us to hear it. *Denis Murphy*

Sometimes I start writing a play about a guy climbing up a mountain and end up writing one about the guy who carried his gear. *Billy Roche*

This play will be repeated tomorrow night so that those who missed it before will have an opportunity of doing so again. *Sign outside a theatre in Dublin*

# POETS AND POETRY

All bad poetry springs from genuine feeling. *Oscar Wilde*

Poetry sections are usually put in the back of bookshops, like pornography. *Desmond Clarke*

Ever since Stephen Dedalus, poets have tended to look at themselves as if they were angels on loan from heaven instead of scruffy old bolloxes going around the place looking for a bit of inspiration. *Brendan Kennelly*

I once left Yeats to himself in my room. At lunchtime he told me he had done an excellent morning's work, having written four lines and then destroyed them. *John Drinkwater*

"Let us remember," the lecturer in English told his class, "that the greatest living poets are dead." *Tony Butler*

The only people who have trouble with poetry are the people who link it with "Literature". It's much more akin to mountain walking, or dancing with yourself at two a.m. *Theo Dorgan*

Reader: "Miss Moore, your poetry is very difficult to read." Marianne Moore: "It is very difficult to write."

Dylan Thomas wasn't a poet. He was just a Welsh alley cat screaming. *Kathleen Behan*

The reason people don't care much for poetry is that most poets don't care much for people. *Paul Muldoon*

Poetry is bad enough without it being long as well. *John B. Keane*

Quarrelsome poets are like ferrets fighting for the mastery of a septic tank. *Sean O'Brien*

Poetry is language in orbit. *Seamus Heaney*

Compassion and art don't mix. A fellow poet was castigated for watching an old lady being chased by a Rottweiler through a London park. She was eventually impaled on the perimeter railings as she tried to escape. He failed to intervene. If he had, however, how could he possibly have written "Lines Composed Upon Watching an Old Lady Being Chased by a Rottweiler and Impaled on the Railings at Finsbury Park"? *Ian MacPherson*

The inhabitants of Dublin know as much about poetry as my arse knows about snipe-shooting. *Patrick Kavanagh*

When the times don't rhyme, neither should poetry. *Desmond Egan*

Poets should never marry. *Maud Gonne McBride*

The best time to write an elegy is when you're feeling cheerful, and the best time to write a cheerful poem is when you're in the dumps. *Michael Longley*

Indifference to poetry is one of the most conspicuous characteristics of the human race. *Robert Lynd*

In the present climate, where poetry is less a fate and more a career choice, the level of conformity to the invisible pecking order and the smart-casual dress code makes a banker's convention, by comparison, seem a riot of anarchy. *Harry Clifton*

To be a published poet is not a sane person's aspiration. *Bernard O'Donoghue*

I'm not very well today. I can only write prose. *W. B. Yeats*

Teacher: "Could you tell me something about the great Kerry poets of the eighteenth century?"
Kerry girl: "They're all dead."
*Laura Stack*

# POLICEMEN

The police arrested O'Malley, who was drunk on battery acid, and O'Shalley, who thought he was a firework. They put them both in a cell overnight. In the morning they charged O'Malley and let O'Shalley off. *Terry Adlam*

Do you want a pint or a transfer? *Alleged comment by Charles Haughey to a policeman who caught him in a pub after hours*

Derry is the only football ground in Europe where the presence of the police would actually provoke a riot rather than prevent one. *Eamonn McCann*

I wanted to be a policeman but I was ruled out when they discovered my parents were married. *Brendan Behan*

Being an Englishwoman, she held the curious theory that the police exist for the protection of the public. *George Bermingham*

In the mid-nineteenth century the population of Ireland went from eight million to four million. Two million died and two million went off to become policemen in New York. *Bono*

There is something wrong with a work of art if it can be understood by a policeman. *Patrick Kavanagh*

Brahms is just like Tennyson: an extraordinary musician with the brains of a third-rate village policeman. *George Bernard Shaw*

Norman Mailer asked me if I had a police escort when I was in Dublin. "Yeah," I told him, "but I'm usually handcuffed to the bastards!" *Brendan Behan*

Paddy Murphy stood before the magistrate. "Who brought you here?" he asked. "Two policemen, sir." "Drunk, I suppose?" said the judge. "Yes sir," replied Paddy, "both of them." *Ernest Forbes*

Policeman: "Anything you say may be held against you."
Burglar: "Miss Ireland."
*Kevin Murtie*

If you slip the edge of your offside tyre over a continuous white line in an empty lane at four o'clock in the morning, a squad car immediately pops out of the long grass. *Patrick Campbell*

When St Patrick drove the snakes out of Ireland they all swam to New York and joined the police force. *Eugene O'Neill*

# POLITICAL CORRECTNESS

If we're to be politically correct, should Carmencita Hederman not be called Carpeoplecita Hederperson? *Tony O'Rourke*

The Women's Coalition wishes to be all things to all men. *Sammy Wilson*

Political correctness came early to Ireland. In the 1890s, when the campaign for women's suffrage was in its infancy, a Wexford shopkeeper put the following notice above his door: "Women, without distinction of sex, will be served". *Sean Desmond*

I don't believe certain groups deserve extra-special names. Crippled people are crippled, they're not differently abled. It's a perfectly honourable word. It's in the Bible: "Jesus healed the cripples". He didn't engage in rehabilitative strategies for the physically disadvantaged. *George Carlin*

A man in a wheelchair heckled me once. He said, "I notice you don't make fun of me like the rest of the people in the audience – are you afraid?" I said, "OK. You'll never make a stand-up comic." *David McSavage*

# POLITICIANS

Being a politician is like being a baseball manager. You have to be smart enough to understand the game and dumb enough to think it's important. *Eugene McCarthy*

Politicians, even in the 1940s, always loved a soundbite. Having won the war, they spoke of the need to win the peace. *Tom Doorley*

First God made morons, imbeciles and complete idiots. That was for practice. Then he made politicians. *Sean Kilroy*

Politicians are like nappies. They should be changed often. And usually for the same reason. *Pat Shortt*

An honest politician is one who, when bribed, stays bribed. *Daniel O'Connell*

Eamon de Valera always reminded me of a cross between a corpse and a cormorant. *Oliver St John Gogarty*

I could pick out some great politicians right now, but there are some who are lumps of inarticulate muttering dust who should be buried in bogs. *Brendan Kennelly*

I realized Bill Clinton was a laid-back president the night I was at a function in the White House and he said goodbye to me with the words, "I'm turning in early, Bertie, don't forget to close the door on your way out." *Bertie Ahern*

Bill Clinton always came across as a man who knew he was born to be President while George Bush had the gait of one who inherited the hand-me-down suit. *Shane Hegarty*

An Irish politician is a man who's never passed the oral-anal stage of development. In other words he's still talking through his arse. *Terry McGeehan*

If a politician says yes he means maybe. If he says maybe he means no. And if he says no he's no politician. If a lady says no she means maybe. If she says maybe she means yes. And if she says yes she's no lady. *Shane O'Reilly*

An Irish politician is a man of few words but he uses them often. *Eamon Nally*

Merlyn Rees wrestled with his conscience and the result was a draw. *Paddy Devlin*

The reason there are so few female politicians is that it takes too much time to put make-up on two faces. *Maureen Murphy*

Bush & Son: Family Butchers, 1988–2008. *T-shirt slogan spotted in Galway*

Dogs can be trained to avoid all sorts of things that are bad for them but politicians insist on flirting with the high moral ground even though they have a gut instinct that this is akin to a naked man running blindfolded through a sawmill. *Declan Lynch*

"Oh God, I've just been raped by a politician!"
"How do you know it was a politician?"
"I had to do all the work."
*Myler McGrath*

Charlie Haughey is a cross between Frank Sinatra and Mother Teresa. *Colin McClelland*

Babies have a civil right not to be kissed by every passing politician. *Joe Higgins*

David "Just Call Me Dave" Cameron has somehow managed the incredible knack of being nothing to all men. *Ian O'Doherty*

Mothers all want their sons to grow up to be President but they don't want them to become politicians in the process. *John F. Kennedy*

A politician who complains about the press is like a fishmonger giving out about a bad smell. *Charles Haughey*

A great leader is one who keeps the streets clean of litter. *W. B. O'Carolan*

Tony Blair says he would like to get involved more closely with environmental issues. Climate change: the last refuge of the failed politician. *Terry Wogan*

George Bush is depriving some village of an idiot. *Liam Thornton*

George Bush reminds every woman of her first husband. *Jane O'Reilly*

When I was growing up, Irish presidents were viewed as shadowy figures who, like the Russian heads of state, could quite conceivably die in office and nobody would notice for months. There was a sense that people were only parachuted into the job if they'd failed to get a better one, or because they owned more than one good suit. *Fiona Looney*

# POLITICS

We have two types of democracy in Ireland. Dublin democracy works by holding a referendum and then allowing the Government to judge the result. If the government thinks the result is wrong, the referendum is held again. *Paul O'Sullivan*

Choosing between Fianna Fáil, Fine Gael and Labour is akin to choosing between jumping from the thirteenth, fourteenth or fifteenth storey of a skyscraper. *Joe Duffy*

Our ancestors believed in magic, prayer, trickery, browbeating and bullying. I think it would be fair to sum that list up as "Irish politics". *Flann O'Brien*

In politics you never really believe anything until it's been denied at least once. *Ian Foster*

Politics is a virus for which there's no antibiotic. *Dick Burke*

I know the hat size of every one of my constituents. *Oliver J. Flanagan*

Bono's mouth is so full of American political cock I'm surprised he can still talk. *Sinead O'Connor*

Fine Gael's tax plans are like a set of ill-fitting dentures. *Michael McDowell*

I believe Sinn Féin are amalgamating with the Green Party. They're going to call themselves Guns 'n' Roses. *Conal Gallen*

I read in the paper that Bertie Ahern is going to 'buck' up the economy. There has to be a misprint there somewhere. *Maureen Potter*

A socialist is a Protestant variety of communist. *Conor Cruise O'Brien*

Bono wants to change the world by embracing it. I get angry and want to punch its lights out. We're the Laurel and Hardy of international politics. *Bob Geldof*

The main difference between a caucus and a cactus is that the pricks are on the outside of a cactus. *Ben Briscoe*

I was never much for politics. I used to think a socialist was a guy who enjoyed going out a bit. *George Best*

When Brian Cowen became Taoiseach, Ireland was on the edge of an economic precipice. Since then it's taken a giant leap forward. *Michael Cullen*

The Maastricht Treaty has been dealt, at least temporarily, a fatal blow. *Des O'Malley*

If you wake up one morning with the vision that you want to become Taoiseach you should have yourself signed in to a mental hospital immediately. *Harry McGee*

Politics is show business for ugly people. *Ivan Yates*

In constituencies like Clare it is an absolute that you must turn up at the opening of an envelope. *Brian Meaney*

Politics is the chloroform of the Irish people — or rather the hashish. *Oliver St John Gogarty*

I'm thinking of running for government. I learned to count up to eleven in prison. I reckon that qualifies me to be a TD. If I go back in again I'll learn to count to twelve. Who knows, I might make it as Taoiseach. *The late drug baron Martin Cahill*

My family was in politics while de Valera's was still bartering budgerigars in the back streets of Barcelona. *James Dillon*

Russia has just announced a contest for the best new political joke. First prize is twenty years in Siberia. *Sean Kilroy*

Liberals are enamoured of existing evils. Conservatives wish to replace them with others. *W. B. O'Carolan*

Due to government cutbacks, the light at the end of the tunnel has just been cut off. *Ed Byrne*

# THE POPE

The Pope has made a fortune out of his new book, *The Pill's Grim Progress*. *Frank Carson*

The only way you could get me back into the Catholic Church is to have a Chinese Pope. Can you imagine receiving Holy Communion from him? You'd kneel down and he'd go, "Are you going to have this here or do you want a takeaway?" *Dave Allen*

Pope Benedict isn't too keen on women. He should kick off his red socks, settle down with a nice brandy and watch a porn film. *Peter O'Toole*

The last time I visited the Vatican I suggested in the suggestion box that my father should be Pope. *Ian Paisley Jr*

I'm sure the Pope is a lovely man. It's a shame he hasn't got a nice wife and family to keep him company. *Sinead O'Connor*

Pope John Paul II visited Ireland and said Mass to a million people in the Phoenix Park. There was an awful crush at the gates when 100,000 of them tried to leave after Communion. *Donal O'Dea*

The dog will return to its vomit, the washed sow will return to the mire, but by God's grace Northern Ireland will never return to Popery. *Ian Paisley*

Irishmen don't necessarily believe in God but they're convinced of the infallibility of the Pope. *Henry Spalding*

Fr Dougal: "I never met a celebrity."
Fr Ted: "You met the Pope."
Fr Dougal: "Did I?"
**Father Ted**

Pope Benedict looks as if one could not remove his rictus of a smile except with a jemmy and a crowbar. *Hugh Leonard*

Pope John Paul II had the manner of a politician you'd see glad-handing during an election, always looking at the next person while shaking hands with somebody else. His were actor's gestures, offhand but emphatic. *John Doyle*

Apart from having children, the thing I'm most proud of in my life is ripping up a picture of the Pope on live TV. *Sinead O'Connor*

Remember when Sinead O'Connor tore up that picture of the Pope on *Saturday Night Live*? Think about it. A little bald guy in a dress is attacked on national television by another little bald guy in a dress. *Sib Ventress*

# PORNOGRAPHY

If the makers of porn films would like to get women interested they should put in a scene at the end where, after the man takes his thing out of the woman's ear, he goes, "You know, I really love you." *Michael Downey*

Have you heard about the new Irish porn magazine for farmers? It's called *Ploughboy*. *Mike Murphy*

No one ever lost money by underestimating the human race's appetite for watching other people having sex. Even Neanderthal man probably got bored one day and decided that he could make an extra rabbit skin or two by convincing the girls from two caves down to put on a bit of entertainment for the lads, while he took 20 per cent of their earnings. *Padraig Kenny*

I don't like Dutch porn. I can never follow the plots. *Ed Byrne*

I met a male porn star in the San Fernando Valley and get this: he's *married*. Can you imagine that in Ireland? Back from a hard day at the orifice and the wife asks you "How was the traffic?" and "Did you ride anyone nice today?" *Hector O'hEochagáin*

People ask me if I'd do a porn movie and I think: Making love to two women at once and getting paid for it? Where's the catch? *P. J. Gallagher*

It'll be a sad day for sexual liberation when the pornography addict has to settle for the real thing. *Brendan Francis*

I sometimes get quite romantic about porn movies I've watched. I find myself wondering if Veronica is still seeing those four German guys, or if Hans found his watch. *Sean Hughes*

# POTATOES

O'Malley complained to the tourist board about his hotel. "For dinner we had two potatoes," he said. "One of them was hard and the other was an onion." *Hal Roach*

I've heard the preferred Irish seven-course meal is a six-pack and a potato. *Kenny Everett*

Tony Blair apologized for the Famine after 160 years. It's a pity he didn't send over a few potatoes to show he meant it. *Mick O'Kane*

A Texan visited an Irish farm and was disgusted by how small everything was. He picked up a potato and said, "We grow them eight times this big in Texas." The farmer replied, "We only grow them to match the size of our mouths." *Tom O'Connor*

The proliferation of soccer on this island is the best thing that's happened since the potato. *Con Houlihan*

The teacher asked Murphy how he'd divide twelve potatoes among three people. "I'd boil them and mash them, sir," he piped up. *Paddy Crosbie*

# POVERTY

Money talks. Mine said goodbye. *Hugh Malone*

The Irishman's faith in his own perennial poverty is as deep and unshakeable as his belief in the foreigner's eternal wealth. *J. P. Donleavy*

Very few people can afford to be poor. *George Bernard Shaw*

One of the strangest things about life is the fact that the poor, who need money the most, are the very ones that never have it. *Finley Peter Dunne*

Rich people are just poor people with money. *Bridget O'Donnell*

The more he earned, the less he had. *Brian Behan on his brother Brendan*

I'm not saying they're poor, but I believe she used to try and polish the window with the kitten. *Paul Ryan*

It has long been said that the people of Ireland only became poor when the devil invented Scotch whiskey. *Sean Desmond*

# PRAYER

Going to Limerick and not having a drink is like going into a church and not saying a prayer. *Richard Harris*

Flying is where I always rediscover my faith. All those prayers you learned as a child suddenly come in very useful on take-off, or when turbulence rears its ugly head at 30,000 feet. *Eamonn Holmes*

Why is there so much about trespassing in the Lord's Prayer? Was Jesus writing it going, "If those kids don't get out of my fucking garden . . ." *Dara O'Briain*

When I prayed in the US we pronounced every word. Then I came to Ireland and it was like a competition to see who could get out of the church first. I felt as if I was at a Dutch auction. *Des Bishop*

When the gods wish to punish us, they answer our prayers. *Oscar Wilde*

I'm a good Christian. I pray not only for my enemies but to have enemies to keep me alive. It's our friends we should guard against. *George Russell*

My mother came to the Irish Snooker Masters with me one year but she couldn't bring herself to step inside the auditorium. She spent the whole match sitting in the car with a pair of rosary beads. *Ken Doherty*

Many people believe that prayer is more powerful than electricity or a nuclear bomb. Personally I think there's more energy in a half-eaten ham sandwich. *Tom Reilly*

God grant me the senility to forget the people I never liked, the good fortune to run into the ones I do, and the eyesight to tell the difference. *Terry Wogan*

The only time kids go down on their knees these days is when they're giving blowjobs. *Fr John Kerrane*

When I was young I always thought "Blessed Art Thou Amongst Women" was "Blessed Art Thou A Monk Swimming". *Malachy McCourt*

They still pray for me in the convent. *Edna O'Brien*

# PRECAUTIONS

Why do the Irish wear two contraceptives? To be sure, to be sure. *Kevin McAleer*

When I was in Mexico for the World Cup I saw a sign in a hotel that said "When there are earthquakes, please use the stairs". *Con Houlihan*

Catholics are the worst drivers in Ireland. They always pull out at the last minute. *Dusty Young*

Peter McGovern was suing a motorist for knocking him into a drain. The judge asked him if it was dark at the time. He said he could see pretty well. The Justice asked, "Were you wearing any reflectors or had you a light?" McGovern replied, "I had two loaves of bread under me arms." **Roscommon Herald**

The Irish Navy asked for all the lighthouses to be turned upside down so their submarines wouldn't get lost. *Peter Hornby*

# PREDICTIONS

Some years ago I went to an astrologer and she told me what age I was going to die at. The day after that's supposed to happen I'll throw a big party. *Tommy Tiernan*

If I ever plan to have a piss-up in a brewery, I will not be asking members of our current government to organize it. *Paddy Murray*

It would be easier for a black man to become President of America than for a Fine Gael TD from Castlebar to become Taoiseach. *John Drennan — who was proved wrong on both counts*.

I went to a fortune teller to see how long it would be till I became famous. She said, "Cross my palm with silver." I said, "Who do you think I am, the Lone Ranger?" *Jimmy Cricket*

None of us knows what's coming down the line. We might get struck by an asteroid, a bus, or even a bright idea. *Fiona Looney*

The next nuclear war will be held in London so England won't have to qualify. *Dermot Morgan*

The day will come when books will be sold by weight, like soap, and bear the same relationship to literature as a packet of detergent. *John Broderick*

Seamus: "I bet I can predict your next sentence."
Paddy: "I knew you were going to say that."
*Milo O'Shea*

I shall die like a tree, at the top first. *Jonathan Swift, predicting mental illness*

There was some disappointment for California preacher Harold Camping after he predicted a global apocalypse for six p.m. last Saturday and it failed to happen. No worries. The unsuccessful prophet of doom said it will all go belly-up on 21 October. Ah well, you can't get 'em all right. As one observer noted, it's not the end of the world. *Kim Bielenberg*

I've predicted eleven of the last three recessions. *Herb Kelleher*

The Annual AGM of the Irish Clairvoyants Association was cancelled due to unforeseen circumstances. *Keith Barry*

# PREFERENCES

Far better than sex is the pleasure of drinking at someone else's expense. *Dermot Reilly*

I'd rather have a bottle in front of me than a frontal lobotomy. *Dave Allen*

I'm thinking of taking up meditation. It would beat sitting around all day doing nothing. *Jimmy O'Dea*

Which would you prefer to look at: a movie gangster or a real live one with a shiny tracksuit, some meaty flab, and a set of prison tattoos that look like a monkey went nuts with a biro? *Naomi McElroy*

I'd rather buy a Bob the Builder CD for my two-year-old son than Roy Keane's autobiography. *Jason McAteer*

I'll take three hours in the dentist's waiting room, with four cavities and an impacted wisdom tooth, in preference to fifteen minutes at any airport waiting for a plane. *Patrick Campbell*

I'd rather play an invisible fiddle in the dark and presume you can hear it than succumb to a life of rationality and logic. *Tommy Tiernan*

"Would you like some manure for your rhubarb?"
    "No, we always have ice cream on ours."
*Brendan Grace*

My father said he would rather be put up against a wall and shot than support Fianna Fáil. *Fr Gerry Moloney*

There are times in a woman's life when a good game of golf is more satisfactory than sex. *Rhona Teehan*

Why does any woman give herself the nuisance that husbands are when with less trouble she could buy and train a cat? *Brendan Behan*

Women in childbirth prefer men to women doctors. Maybe they want a hair of the dog that bit them. *Oliver St John Gogarty*

# PREGNANCY

Did you hear about the Irish girl who went home and told her mother she was pregnant and the mother said, "Are you sure it's yours?" *Dennis Taylor*

I looked so fat the day I got married, it was the only time in history the priest suspected the groom was pregnant. *Tom Sullivan*

Mrs Murphy went to the doctor to have her pregnancy terminated. "You're too late," the doctor told her. "He starts school tomorrow." *Noel V. Ginnity*

For a bloke, pregnancy is a weird time. The woman goes through some mad-arse shit and you feel like someone tied you on to the end of a tractor and dragged you across a field. *Fran Cosgrave*

There was once a rather devout young Irish girl who went to a doctor and, after he had declared her to be pregnant, insisted she had never slept with a man. The doctor then went over to the window and looked out. When she asked him what he was doing he replied, "The last time this sort of situation occurred, there was a big star in the sky ..." *T. P. McKenna*

I was on the number 33 bus when I heard a mother and her son talking about how she was pregnant. The mother turns to her son, who was about four, and says, "So what would you prefer, a sister or a brother?" And the son replies, "No, I want a hedgehog." *Overheard in Dublin*

I'm pregnant but there's no need to applaud. I was asleep at the time. *Jeannie McBride*

My husband once said to me, "Surely you're not going to Mass pregnant?" *Monica McEvoy*

What is the main difference between men and women? I cannot conceive. *J. P. Mahaffy*

A Catholic went to confession and said, "I got a twenty-four-year-old girl pregnant." A voice said, "I'm a Protestant minister, why are you telling me?" He said, "I'm ninety-two. I'm telling everyone!" *Gene Fitzpatrick*

Irish maternity hospitals have ten-month waiting lists. *Barry Fitzgerald*

I was in the pub last night with Rosie and I says to her, "Are ye having another, Rosie?" "No," she says, "it's just the way me coat's buttoned." *Paul Ryan*

My wife is stupid. The second time she got pregnant she thought we had to get married again. *Gene Fitzpatrick*

# PRESENTS

I asked my wife what she wanted for Christmas. She said, "Something with diamonds." So I got her a pair of cards. *Brendan O'Carroll*

It's a good idea to tell your friends what you'd like for a wedding present. Otherwise you're going to end up with a lot of casserole dishes. *Robert O'Byrne*

The best way to approach a girl with a past is with a present. *Jack Cruise*

"What can we give our local politician for his birthday?"
  "A book."
  "Ah no. He's got one of them already."
*Myler McGrath*

I always felt sorry for Jesus, being born on Christmas Day and all that. He missed out on a Christmas present. *Michael Redmond*

At Christmas we smell good for a few days because we splash on the latest celebrity-sponsored perfumes and after-shave lotions. We model bumper-pack socks for those who gave them to us, just to show that we care, before passing them on to a local charity. We exclaim with hammy delight when unwrapping slippers in the shape of small furry animals, coffee-table books on the television personalities of the Outer Hebrides, or the *Complete Guide to Thermal Underwear Patterns of the Antipodes*. **David Slattery**

The other day an old friend excitedly dragged me out the back to meet her new puppy. There was something vaguely familiar about the new mutt's bedding. It hit me on the way home: that's the bloody hand-dyed alpaca luxury throw I gave her as a wedding gift. **Aoife O'Brien**

I'm sure Our Lady was delighted the Three Wise Men brought her gold, frankincense and myrrh, but maybe she would have preferred Pampers and some Sudocrem. **Mary Mannion**

The Irish male's idea of a romantic Christmas present is a collapsible monkey wrench or a new carburettor. **Joe O'Connor**

# ELVIS PRESLEY

Sometimes I feel old. I once asked a girl if she remembered where she was the day Elvis died and she replied, "I was in my mother." **Paddy Moloney**

I'm glad Jesus died when he did. Otherwise he'd have ended up like Elvis. He had that big entourage: twelve guys willing to do anything he wanted. If he lived to be forty he'd be walking round Jerusalem with a big fat beer gut and big black sideburns going, "Damn, I'm the son of God — give me a cheeseburger and some French fries." If anyone said, "But Lord, you're overweight," he'd go, "Fuck you, man, I'll turn you into a leper." **Denis Leary**

I played opposite Elvis Presley in *Blue Hawaii*. I was his mother. He was twenty-six and I was thirty-five. I would have had him at nine years of age. **Angela Lansbury**

Elvis Presley can't sing a lick. He makes up for his vocal short-comings with the weirdest animation short of an aborigine's mating dance. **Jack O'Brien, in 1956**

Isn't there something wrong about a world that believes God is dead and Elvis is still alive? *John B. Keane*

Elvis Lives – and they've buried the poor bastard. *B. P. Fallon*

The atmosphere at Graceland was halfway between Lourdes and Disneyland. *Hector O'hEochagáin*

I'm so old I knew Elvis when he was alive the first time. *Noel V. Ginnity*

Death, for Elvis, was a good career move. *Bono*

# PRETENCE

To be natural is such a very difficult pose to keep up. *Oscar Wilde*

When I was an amateur actor I often told people I was "touring" when what I meant was that I'd jumped into a van going to Enniscorthy and played to about twelve people who clapped when the show ended out of a mixture of bewilderment and relief. *Gabriel Byrne*

Dublin is a slum, an extensive and terrible slum hidden behind the shallow facades of the rarely painted shops, banks and shabby offices in its few principal streets. *Oliver St John Gogarty*

While I was at UCD I edited a literary magazine. I wrote a lot of the stories under pseudonyms because we didn't have enough people to fill it. I would make up biographies for these pseudonyms: "Seamus MacChommaraigh was born in the Donegal Gaeltacht in 1953 and is at present serving in a ministerial capacity in Ghana." *Gabriel Byrne*

The waxwork of Simon Cowell in Madame Tussaud's is more real than he is. *Louis Walsh*

It's bad when you're making love to your partner and you fantasize that she's someone else, but what happened to me was even worse. I fantasized that *she* was making love to someone else. *Ed Byrne*

# PRIESTS

Young Irish priests tend to resemble Bing Crosby. When they get older they turn into Barry Fitzgerald. *Frank Gannon*

The main reason for the big security presence at the wedding of Posh Spice and David Beckham was to keep the priests away from the altar boys. *Patrick Kielty*

Maynooth seminary turned me down because of my height: I wasn't able to reach the altar. It was just as well. I could never stand all that early morning drinking. *James McKeon*

I once toyed with joining the priesthood but alas I never got the calling. Which is a bit of a bummer as I look good in black. Of course when you say you're a non-believer they try to convert you. *Sean Hughes*

An Irish exorcism consists of trying to get the priest out of your son. *Jim Kemmy*

Did you hear about the priest who was called to a synod by his bishop but wasn't able to make it because he couldn't find a babysitter? *Maureen Potter*

I once heard of a priest who had an affair with a pretty young woman. She always attended his Masses. Every time he gave her communion, instead of saying "Body of Christ" he used to say, "Christ, what a body!" *Pat Buckley*

There's one big difference between a priest and a stand-up comic. Stand-up comics have to make up different jokes for each gig. *Des Bishop*

I see Sinead O'Connor is to wed. At least she won't have to fork out for a priest to do the ceremony. *Ronan O'Reilly after O'Connor became "ordained"*

Did you hear the one about the gay priest? He always turned the other cheek. *Graham Norton*

In Ireland in the old days we used to grow priests like potatoes. *Tommy Tiernan*

What would you call a sleepwalking priest? A roamin' Catholic. *Jackie Murphy*

I think it's rather unfair on priests that they're not allowed to get married. I think that if a priest meets another priest and they like one another, they should be allowed to spend their lives together. *Dave Allen*

I have the unique distinction of having been a failed priest at fifteen. *Gabriel Byrne*

"What was it Father Jack used to say about the needy? He had a term for them."
   "Shower of bastards."
*Exchange from* **Father Ted**

I have a very clear memory of the local curate coming to my house one evening and saying to my mother, "I've just come to talk to Jennifer about being confirmed." My mother burst out laughing and said, "She hasn't even been christened!" *Jennifer Johnston*

The only real use for priests is for bereavement and dying. *Sinead O'Connor*

# PRIORITIES

First things first. Last things never. *Eamonn Andrews*

I am more interested in Dublin street names than the riddle of the universe. *James Joyce*

# PRISON

The English are wonderful. First they put me in jail and then they made me rich. *Brendan Behan*

An elderly pensioner, on being sentenced to fifteen years' penal servitude, cried, "Ah, my Lord, I'm a very old man and

I'll never do that sentence." The judge replied, "Well, try to do as much of it as you can." *Maurice Healy*

I support capital punishment. Where would Christianity be if Jesus just got eight to ten years with time off for good behaviour? *James Donovan*

Nine months in jail for woman who set Alsatian dog on sergeant, exposed her breasts and mooned her bottom at Gardai. *Headline in* **Waterford News & Star**

If England treats all her criminals the way she has treated me, she doesn't deserve to have any. *Oscar Wilde*

Paris Hilton has been sent to prison for a driving offence. She's going down for forty-five days, which is even longer than she did in her video. *Graham Norton*

You get a longer sentence in Ireland for not having a TV licence than you do for a hit-and-run accident. *Leo Lieghio*

The judge told Murphy his sentence was £10 or a week in jail. "Arrah sure musha I'll take the tenner," Murphy replied. *Mick Lally*

Buckley got put inside for his flat feet. They were in the wrong flat. *Seamus O'Leary*

Never get arrested in a country that doesn't use your own alphabet. If it uses squiggles instead of proper letters you're fucked, mate, you're never coming home. *Noel Gallagher*

There had been a fellow in prison whose lawyer was later known to boast that he had got him a suspended sentence. They hanged him. *Brendan Behan*

When England play away matches in Liechtenstein, authorities worry if they have enough cell space for the travelling hooligans since the country has only one jail, with space for twenty-two people. Such hooligans are often confused since the Liechtenstein national anthem is sung to the exact same tune as "God Save the Queen". *Paul Kilduff*

# PROBLEMS

When the rest of the world would say "This problem is very serious but not impossible", the Irishman would say "This problem is impossible but not very serious". *Donald S. Connery*

A problem shared is a problem doubled. *Marian Keyes*

A problem shared is . . . gossip. *Graham Norton*

The only problem with Seamus O'Sullivan is that when he's not drunk he's sober. *W. B. Yeats*

Northern Ireland has a problem for every solution. *Colin Henry*

I used to go to an analyst who made me blame all my problems on my mother. I now have a new one. He tells me it's all my fault. It's a kind of relief. *Tom Walsh*

A wet dream is when you go to bed with a problem and wake up with a solution. *Shay Kelleher*

# PROCRASTINATION

The Spanish for "tomorrow" is *mañana*. In Ireland we don't have any word with that degree of urgency. *Shay Brennan*

The sixties hit Galway in the seventies. *Mary Coughlan*

The only thing that has to be finished by next Friday is next Thursday. *Maureen Potter*

I should have answered your letter a fortnight ago but I didn't receive it until this morning. *Sir Boyle Roche*

If a builder says a job will be finished in three weeks you know the place will be in rubble when the swallows come back from Capistrano. *Gene Kerrigan*

In Ireland we have two of everything. One is the wrong size and the other is due on Wednesday. *Hugh Leonard*

There's no time like the present for postponing what you don't want to do. *John D. Sheridan*

If procrastination was an Olympic event, I wouldn't even turn up. *David O'Doherty*

Procrastination is a waste of time. *Michael Farrell*

Because of lack of space, a number of births have been held over until next week. **Connacht Telegraph**

# PROSTITUTES

All the prostitutes leave Frankfurt during the Book Fair, because publishers are too mean to pay for sex. *Joe O'Connor*

Penitent in confession: "Bless me Father for I have sinned. I slept with a prostitute."
Priest: "That is a heinous sin, my child. I'm not sure I can forgive it."
Penitent: "Are prostitutes evil, Father?"
Priest: "Prostitutes? That's no problem, my child. I thought you said you'd slept with a Protestant!"
*Joe Lynch*

Can prostitutes claim sexual harassment? *Paul O'Donoghue*

It was Murphy's first time in New York. A lady of the night said to him, "Would you sleep with me for twenty dollars?" "I'm not that tired," he told her, "but I could do with the money." *Joe Cuddy*

Spent too much on Christmas this year? Why not try prostitution? That certainly seems to be the fashionable way to earn money at the moment. We should start a sweepstake to see which special interest group is next reported to be turning to the world's oldest profession to make ends meet. Baggsy I get gay one-legged octogenarian asylum-seekers. *Eilis O'Hanlon*

I'm proud to say I've never paid for sex in my life. Which has pissed off quite a few prostitutes I've slept with. **Sean Hughes**

I was in a hotel in Las Vegas and I dialled the prostitute line. "Hello. I would like to book Misty again. I was with her last night. Tell her to bring her whips and thingies." There was a pause. A voice said, "This is reception. You need to dial zero for an outside line." "OK," I said. "Then just send me up a club sandwich." **Patrick Kielty**

I was coked out of my nut every night, and banging more hookers than you could shake a stick at. **Colin Farrell on the years of his Hollywood indulgences**

At this stage I hear everyone's been up on her apart from the 46A. When she dies she'll be buried in a Y-shaped coffin. **Dermot Mahony**

The main reason women don't like prostitutes is because they're competition. **Ulick O'Connor**

I've never paid for sex in my life. Anyone who did that would need to be really hard up. **Fergus Maher**

# PROTESTANTS

There's something deep in the Irish psyche making people want to convert garages — and Protestants. **Des Bishop**

The Protestant Church looks after you from birth to death. The Catholic Church looks after you from conception to resurrection. **Joe Foyle**

Ireland is a nation of Catholics and Protestants, many of them Christians. **John B. Keane**

Just because I've lost my faith doesn't mean I've lost my reason. **James Joyce after being asked if he would convert to Protestantism**

Wanted: Man And Woman To Look After Two Cows, Both Protestant. *Notice on farmyard wall*

I don't have any religion. I'm an Irish Protestant. *Oscar Wilde*

St Patrick was a Protestant. *Ian Paisley*

God must have been a Protestant. He had only one son. *Colin Healy*

Ireland has been turned upside down. Protestants are calling their kids Fiach and living in semi-ds and Catholics are baking scones and insisting on period furniture only. *David McWilliams*

Being Protestant growing up in 1950s Ireland was almost as bad as being gay. I didn't have one thing wrong with me, I had two. I wasn't sure which was the bigger sin. Whenever I did something wrong afterwards I couldn't figure out which part of my damaged make-up was responsible, religion or sexuality. *Graham Norton*

England is so multi-cultural today, a Protestant is almost regarded as being exotic. *Dara O'Briain*

A Catholic converted to Protestantism on his deathbed. Asked why, he explained, "I'd prefer one of them to be going than one of us." *Luke Kelly*

# PSYCHIATRISTS

A man on holiday in Spain sent a postcard to his psychiatrist. It read: "Having a wonderful time. Why?" *Hal Roach*

My wife is a psychiatrist and she knows nothing about snooker. I'm a snooker player and I know nothing about psychiatry. It's a marriage made in heaven. *Ken Doherty*

If Alex Higgins went to a psychiatrist, the psychiatrist would have to go to a psychiatrist. *Ronnie Harper*

A man went to a psychiatrist. "I think I'm a dog," he told him. The psychiatrist said, "Get up on the couch." The man said, "I'm not allowed." **Niall Toibin**

People ask me what it's like being married to a psychiatrist. I tell them, "Great, except in a fight when he tells you what you really mean." **Fionnuala Flanagan**

# PSYCHOLOGY

A psychologist is a man who watches everybody else when a beautiful girl comes into the room. **James N. Healy**

Psychology which explains everything explains nothing. **Marianne Moore**

Psychology won't work on us. We've got too many psychos in the side. **Joe Kinnear on Wimbledon football club**

Sigmund Freud is regarded by many as the father of modern psychology, and by many others as one mean mother. **Kevin McAleer**

# PUBLICANS

Publicans who used to collapse like a Bateman cartoon if anyone asked for coffee now want to know if you want decaf or cappuccino. **Maeve Binchy on Ireland's new sobriety culture**

Jeremiah had three faults that made him a bad publican: he stocked only the best, he kept too easy a slate, and his best customer was himself. **James Plunkett**

# PUBLICITY

Don't read your publicity. Weigh it. *Albert Reynolds*

When I go for my tea, people break into print about me. The only reason they call me is because I happen to have a reputation. If I was the local milkman, or some poor cunt flogging turf from the back of a donkey's cart, the whores wouldn't even stop to give me a light. *Brendan Behan*

I don't care what they say about me as long as they spell my name wrong. *Hector O'hEochagáin*

There's no such thing as bad publicity except your obituary. *Brendan Behan*

I'm thinking of putting a super-injunction on my tour dates next year. It seems a very effective way of getting the word out. *Dara O'Briain*

I don't need publicity. If I fart I get it. *Sinead O'Connor after being accused of being ordained as a Tridentine priest in order to garner more column inches*

Colin Farrell went to court so his sex tape couldn't be shown anywhere. I don't know why. He's very well endowed. If it was me I'd have used it for publicity. *Des Bishop*

You're never as good as they say you are and you're never as bad as they say you are. *Joe Duffy*

Why did Queen Elizabeth II and Barry Obama come over to Ireland anyway? I haven't seen such naked plugs since the nephew blew up the toaster in 2003. *Mick the Maverick on the 2011 state visits*.

# PUBLISHERS

I'm always wary of intellectual publishers. They offer you patronage instead of hard cash, and swear by high heaven to make you famous by the time you've spent your first decade in eternity. *Christy Brown*

I don't believe in publishers. They love to keep the Sabbath, and everything else they can lay their hands on. *Amanda McKittrick Ros*

All her life to labour/and labour for Faber and Faber. *Seamus Heaney*

The most successful article I ever published was called "How To Dye a Sheepskin Rug". *Tim Pat Coogan*

Publishers are marketing popular fiction in supermarkets today at cost price, aware of the huge sales potential, and authors are also desperate to get their books in with the sliced pans. *Ann Marie Hourihane*

Children's publishing today is dog-eat-dog. Or should I say pup-eat-pup. *Fred Hanna*

Twenty-two publishers read the manuscript of *Dubliners* in France. When it was at last printed, some very kind person bought out the entire edition and had it burned in Dublin. *James Joyce*

# PUBS

When Downey's pub in Ballyfermott was closed for a few weeks in the 1980s, two hundred local men were made homeless. *Joe Duffy*

A man from Manchester told me he once approached a barman in a small village in the west of Ireland at one o'clock in the morning and asked what time the pubs closed. "October," he was informed. *Pete McCarthy*

I heartily enjoyed the opening of the new cocktail lounge in Chicago. They have the nicest tables I was ever under. *Mark Sullivan*

Dinny was standing in the street the other day when an Englishman came up to him and said, "I say old chap, could you show me the way to the nearest boozer?" Says Dinny, "You're looking at him." *James N. Healy*

The pub is the best place to talk, and it's good to talk even when no one is listening. In fact it's *best* to talk when no one is listening. *David Slattery*

People who go into pubs optimistically often leave misty optically. *Hal Roach*

Ireland has a great reputation as a literary nation. Walk into any pub in Dublin and it's full of writers and poets. In most other countries they're called drunks. *Ardal O'Hanlon*

Don't complain about the pint in that pub. You'll be old and weak yourself some day. *Cathal O'Shannon*

The traditional Irish pub is now available in a self-assembly flat-pack that can be shipped all over the world. *David Slattery*

A tavern is a place where madness is sold by the bottle. *Jonathan Swift*

I fell out with Paddy Kavanagh for a while in the sixties but then one day we met on Baggot Street and he asked me would I like a drink. I decided to bury the hatchet so I said, "Will we go into Mooney's?" Paddy said no, that he was barred from there. He suggested Searson's but I couldn't go there for the same reason. I suggested the Clubhouse. No go — it was the same problem with him. He said, "What about Andy Ryan's?" I was barred from Andy Ryan's so we just said, "Good luck, see you again some time." *Ronnie Drew*

A good pub is one that's open. *Dave Allen*

Sheila said, "For years I kept wondering where my husband was all the time. Then one night I came home early from the pub and there he was." *Peter Cagney*

Those who drink to forget, please pay in advance. *Notice in the Hibernian Bar in Cork*

There was a time I used to keep bar bills from Helsinki in my wallet so that if a friend ever went into cardiac arrest and there was no defibrillator nearby, I could just whip it out so the shock of it might restart his heart. *Philip Nolan*

The conclusion to your syllogism is fallacious, being based on licensed premises. *Flann O'Brien*

Up until recently a truly authentic Irish pub was usually a filth-encrusted hovel with a leaky roof, corrugated-iron walls and a hole in the ground as a toilet. *Joe O'Connor*

The population of Irish towns is usually based not on the number of people in them, but how many pubs they have. "What's the population of your home town, Bud?" "Haven't a clue, but it's got nine alehouses." *Jon Kenny*

Literary pubs are usually crowded with 58.6794 per cent of the population that is going to write, or has written, the Great Definitive Work of Irish Literature. *Tony Butler*

# PUNS

Must we disregard the Chopin Liszt after leaving the Czech out? *Senan Molony*

Taking minutes at a meeting puts me to sleep for hours. *Joe Duffy*

Some people think U2 should be hung. We are, in fact, well hung. *Bono*

Angelina Jolie has a fine pair of child-bearing lips. *Paul Byrne*

Frank, you deserve a knighthood, or maybe even a Lord of the Rings. *Des Lynam to Frank Bruno after Bruno won the world heavyweight title at his fourth attempt in 1995*

There used to be a Statoil garage down the road from me but now it's just a shell. *Karl Spain*

Mary Magdalene couldn't handle her gargle. She only had one drink but she still got stoned. *Brendan Grace*

Is the quality of Irish tea getting a little strained? *Godfrey Fitzsimons*

Barry Hearn is only in snooker for the money. He doesn't care if the game goes to pot. *Mark Allen*

Nobody in my family knew I was gay before I entered the *Big Brother* house. I suppose you could say I went in before I came out. *BB2 winner Brian Dowling*

I can't see the point of decimals. *Kevin Murtie*

The drinks are on the house. Someone better go and get a ladder. *Spike Milligan*

We've just heard that a lady prominent in Cork's nightclubs has disappeared and hasn't been obscene since. *James Healy*

I was in a field with my girlfriend. We saw a bull. "I hope he doesn't charge us," she said. "So do I," I said, "I only have two pounds on me." *Brendan O'Carroll*

Northern Ireland was famous for the Troubles. On the one side were the Unionists. They were led by the Reverend Elvis Presley, who campaigned under the slogan "Nose Surrender". On the other side were the Publicans, led by Gerry Addams of the famous Addams Family, who campaigned under the slogan "Bits Out". *Craig Brown*

A pun is the lowest form of wit — unless you thought of it first. *Frank Hall*

Did you hear about the man who won five tons of manure in a crap game? *Keith Law*

Ursula Andress should really have been called Arsula Undress. **Stephen Boyd**

Gay Mitchell is the evil of two lessers. **Michael McDowell**

Custard's Last Stand. **Terry Prone after seeing a custard pie thrown at political candidate Michael Noonan in 2002**

They announced one day that Father Burke was being made a canon. We pretended to believe that the parish priest was going to be turned into some class of an artillery piece. **Gene Kerrigan**

Napoleon wore his heart on his sleeve. **Margaret Dowd**

At least James Joyce can be sure of one thing about Nora Barnacle — she'll stick to him. **Stephen Behan**

# QUALIFICATIONS

I swear on my mother's life. Or rather my *late* mother's life. **Alex Higgins**

Bars in America have introduced a talking urinal to deter drink driving. As you relieve yourself, a voice calls "Hey, big boy" and asks you if you need a lift home. Except in Los Angeles, where that service is provided by George Michael. **Des Ekin**

I'd do anything for Ireland except live there. **Vincent Dowling**

U2 were my father's heroes. But he couldn't stand their music. **Niall Andrews**

Bobby Fischer is a chess phenomenon, it is true. But he's also a social illiterate, a political simpleton, a cultural ignoramus and an emotional baby. **Mary Kenny**

Can you just cut the grey hairs and leave the rest? **Customer to barber Peter Quinn**

The Irish drive on the left-hand side of the road, except at pub closing time. **Richard O'Connor**

# QUASIMODO

Quasimodo ran into an old school chum one day. "I can't remember your name," he told him, "but your face rings a bell." **Brian Morrissey**

Quasimodo has just been made redundant. He got ten weeks' back pay and a lump sum. **Dusty Young**

It's very unfair to ask any man to stand in a human wall during a soccer match. A high-speed leather ball hitting you squarely in the pleasure centre could raise your voice by a hundred octaves and have you walking like Quasimodo for the rest of your life. **Pat Ingoldsby**

# QUEUES

Murphy's Law states that the other queue always moves faster. He forgot to add, "Until you get into it." **Jack Cruise**

I won't say the queue was long, but the guy in front of me had a musket wound. **Joe O'Connor**

# QUOTATIONS

The difference between my quotations and those of the next man is that I leave out the inverted commas. **George Moore**

I rang the insurance company and asked them for a quotation. The man on the other end of the line said, "To be or not to be, that is the question." **Ray D'Arcy**

I often quote myself. It adds spice to my conversation. **Brendan Behan**

No comment. And don't quote me on that. *Mick McCarthy*

When in doubt, ascribe all quotations to George Bernard Shaw. *Hilton Edwards*

A teacher was examining his class for their knowledge of famous quotations. He asked them who said "A small step for man, a giant leap for mankind". "Neil Armstrong!" piped up a little girl in the front row. "Very good," he complimented. "Now, who said 'Ask not what your country can do for you, but what you can do for your country?'" "John F. Kennedy!" said the bright spark. A boy in the second row said, "I wish that bitch would keep her mouth shut." The teacher said "Who said that?" The bright spark chirped, "Bill Clinton!" *Dusty Young*

# RACISM

The first time I met Paul McGrath was in Belfast. I turned round to him and said, "It's bad enough being a Catholic here, but being a black one ..." *Norman Whiteside*

I plan to tackle the shocking increase of racism in Ireland today with my character Mrs Brown by having her tell smutty and mildly racist jokes, and then show her knickers. *Brendan O'Carroll*

A taxi driver said to me, "I'm not racist. I have no problems with black people. It's the Nigerians I can't stand." *Des Bishop*

Support gay whales against racism. *Graffiti*

Barack Obama has told a very powerful story about growing up bi-racial. If he adds the Irish bit, the message gets distorted: "He was secretly born in West Cork to a Muslim leprechaun". *Darrell West*

I was talking to a taxi driver the other day and he even blamed the traffic congestion on the immigrants. "How is that?" I asked. "Well," he said, "doesn't everyone slow down to stare at them?" *Ardal O'Hanlon*

An Irishman who'd spent most of his life in London was asked if he'd ever come across anti-Irish feeling amongst the British. "Not much," he said, "but the day I came off the boat I was arrested for hitting a navvy in the elbow with my eyelid." *Cyril Cusack*

The Irish are the niggers of Europe, Dubliners are the niggers of Ireland, and Northside Dubliners are the niggers of Dublin. *Roddy Doyle*

# RADIO

I once auditioned for a part in *All You Need is Frank*, my autobiographical radio play. But the producer told me I wasn't right for it. *Ian MacPherson*

Aside from the nuclear bomb, live radio is the most dangerous thing on the planet. *Pat Shortt*

I'm OK on the radio but on TV I'm donkey shite. *Gerry Ryan*

I have an ideal face for radio. *Ryan Tubridy*

# RAIN

Limerick had a reputation for piety, but we only went into the churches to get in out of the rain. *Frank McCourt*

I wouldn't mind the rain if it wasn't for the wet. *Din Joe*

It has been raining here for the past two days, which strikes me as being against the rules. *Samuel Beckett*

Rain is difficult to film in Ireland because it's so fine the Irish don't even acknowledge it exists. *Alan Parker*

You know it's summer in Ireland when the rain gets warmer. *Dusty Young*

The owner of Bannon's newsagents in Ballyconnell talks about the weather. "It's what we call the wet season here," he smiles. "That is to say, spring, summer, autumn and winter." *Paul Clements*

I believe that in the oul' tenement they're in, the rain comes down the walls like water. *Paul Ryan*

Dear God, I am writing to you in desperation. Is all this crap weather a wee joke? Last time you at least had the courtesy to tell Noah in advance. If it is a biblical flood then at least warn me. I have started work on the ark and it's coming on quite well. I've made provision for all the animals except wasps, tourists and politicians. Yours in dampness, Grandad. *Richard O'Connor*

A farmer looked out happily at the heavy downpour which broke a summer drought. "An hour of this rain," he declared, "will do more good in five minutes than a month of it would do in a week at any other time." *Tony Butler*

Rainbows aren't optical illusions. They only look like them. *Jimeoin*

If you can't see the hills of Clare from Galway, it's raining. If you can, it's about to rain. *Mary Mannion*

Have you heard about the Irishman who cut a hole in his umbrella? He wanted to know when it stopped raining. *Peter Hornby*

# RATIONALIZATIONS

Jet lag isn't all bad. It's a great excuse to go out and get pure stocious, on the principle that if you're sick and psychotic with a hangover you won't notice it. Or if you were planning a nervous breakdown, now's your chance. You'll be feeling alienated and fearful anyway, so you might as well double up. And my own personal favourite: jet lag affords the perfect opportunity to eat guilt-free Toblerones at two in the morning. Your poor stomach is still on home time; it had to miss its breakfast and it's not best pleased that someone wants to deprive it of its lunch as well. *Marian Keyes*

A stupid man doing something he would otherwise be ashamed of always calls it his duty. *George Bernard Shaw*

It's always the same when I go to bed with women. When they're taking off their clothes they say, "I hope you don't think I'm doing this just because you're George Best." *George Best*

Crying isn't proof of a greater capacity to feel. It's just proof of a greater capacity to cry. *Dylan Moran*

I've decided not to give all my money away because that would only make me a bigger star. I already have a problem with people genuflecting before me. If I did that, they'd find a donkey for me to sit on. *Bono*

No human being believes that any other human being has a right to be in bed when he himself is up. *Robert Lynd*

In India a farmhand was caught having sex with his cow. His excuse was that he had bad eyesight and thought it was his wife. *Spike Milligan*

# READING

Brendan Behan read everything he could as a child. One day his father found him up in bed trying to make out the words on the back of a tram ticket he'd picked up off the floor. *Ulick O'Connor*

If a writer has a great time writing, the reader usually has a bad time reading. *John McGahern*

Sean: "Doc, will I be able to read and write good when I get my glasses?"
Doc: "Yes you will."
Sean: "That's great, because I couldn't before."
*Mary Feehan*

Dylan even read the back of sauce bottles. *Caitlin Thomas*

I get nervous if I find myself without something to read. I read in bed, on the bus, and once even attempted it on the treadmill at the gym. With horrifically embarrassing results. *Anne Marie Scanlon*

Writing in English is the most ingenious torture ever devised for sins committed in previous lives. The English reading public explains the reason why. *James Joyce*

A man told me he had been reading my works all his life. I observed that he must be very tired. *Samuel Beckett*

Tommy Docherty's book is one of those that, when you put it down, you can't take it up again. *George Best*

The modern generation seems to have forgotten the art of page-turning. Did you hear about the little girl who received a book from her daddy one Christmas morning and didn't know what to do with it because there was no place to put the batteries? *Brian Behan*

I've come to realize that my readers would prefer if I died rather than if my character Charlie Parker did. *John Connolly*

The demand that I make of my reader is that he should devote his entire life to reading my works. *James Joyce*

My dog can read. When he saw a sign saying "Wet Paint", he did. *Shaun Connors*

It's fact that more people have read *Harry Potter* than are actually alive on the planet. *Victoria Gallagher-O'Houlihan*

Maeve Binchy has given more pleasure in bed than any other woman ever did. *Michael Cullen*

You can't clobber any reader while he's looking, so what you do is divert his attention and *then* clobber him, so he doesn't know what hit him. *Flannery O'Connor*

Reading Joseph Conrad is like gargling with broken glass. *Hugh Leonard*

Even reading the back of a cornflakes packet is an engagement with the printed word. *John Banville*

I could no more read Bertrand Russell than make love to a bald-headed woman. *W. B. Yeats*

# REALITY

Reality isn't for everyone; it's something only Lutherans enjoy. *Mary McDonnell*

Reality TV shows with fading celebs should be avoided like shadowy figures at the end of darkened alleyways twirling iron bars and whistling. *Naomi McElroy*

Do not adjust your mind. Reality is at fault. *Bernard O'Shea*

Reality is for people who can't cope with drugs. *Liam Gallagher*

# THE RECESSION

Now that the boom is over, Ireland is finally starting to do something reasonable with its money, like setting fire to millions of it to save a bank that doesn't exist. *Declan Lynch*

The recession hit me hard. In the middle of the boom I was collecting me dole in fifteen offices. Now I'm down to ten. *Katherine Lynch*

For Sale. One slightly used country. *Brian Abbott*

Ireland is in a recession at the moment, or so they say. It's one of those "I can't go on three holidays this year" recessions. I remember the real ones back in the eighties when entertainment consisted of sitting in a puddle with your best friend. *Jason Byrne*

I've never gone in for stocks and shares or any of that malarkey. Now that the people who do have fucked it up, I find I now own my bank. **Ed Byrne**

A group of builders and developers who were at the Galway Races were overheard playing "Who Used to be a Millionaire". **Peter Quinn**

The reason Ireland fucked up the economy was because we're not comfortable being in charge of ourselves. It took us eight hundred years to get rid of the Brits, and another eighty-five to tell the clergy to stop lecturing us. When we got rich we were like teenagers with the house to ourselves, waiting for Mammy and Daddy to come back from Europe. It was always going to end bad. **Tommy Tiernan**

I didn't lose much in the recession, only about £10 million. **Louis Walsh**

Ireland can't say with certainty what currency we'll be using this time next year. It might be sticks and stones. **Fiona Looney at the beginning of 2012**

Dublin is really suffering in the recession. Dalkey, for instance, is down to its last six wine bars. **Michael O'Doherty on the posh suburb**

One of the best things about the recession is that it has enabled Irish people to act silly again without feeling guilty about it, which is one of our favourite pastimes. **Mary McEvoy**

There are enough unsold apartments and offices around Ireland now to accommodate the population of Mexico City. If we're to believe the forecasters, it'll soon be back to patching the knees of our trousers, sending the kids to school with their milk in an old YR sauce bottle and their sambos in a Johnson, Mooney & O'Brien wrapper. There'll be no more of this globe-hoppin' and posh hotels. You'll have to settle for a week freezing your arse off in a caravan in Ballybunion. And half the country will still be living with the mammy until they're forty. **Donal O'Dea**

Before the recession, Ireland was the Keira Knightley of Europe. Now we're more like a transvestite that's just been slapped in the face. I'm wondering if the recent visits of the

Queen, Barack Obama and the Dalai Lama were a case of going to the sick bed to say goodbye. *Keith Farnan in 2011*

The more Ireland fucks things up, the better off we are. At the moment we're only about nine or ten shit decisions away from total freedom. *Tommy Tiernan*

I've never met people happier to be in a recession than the Irish. They're all going round saying, "I told you the boom wouldn't last!" They'd prefer to be right than rich. *Des Bishop*

You can't get blood from a Blarney Stone. *Howard Gold*

The Irish economy has eaten its young. *Eddie Hobbs*

A man loftily informed me he was going to be spending less money next year. Of course he'll be spending less money next year. Because we're all bloody broke. *Ian O'Doherty*

Ireland is now as broke as my Aunt Hilda's dentures after she dropped them into a tub of Alka Seltzers. *Mick the Maverick*

# RECLUSES

The English sense of humour is subtle, and tinged with sarcasm. For example, you get two gentlemen talking to one another and one of them says, "I passed your house yesterday." And the other one says, "Thank you." *Dave Allen*

If Greta Garbo really wanted to be left alone, she should have come to a showing of one of her films in Dublin. *Hugh Leonard*

# REFEREES

If the ref stood still we wouldn't have had to chase him. *Roy Keane*

Referee Norlinger is outstanding in the sense that he stands out. *George Hamilton*

I'd be surprised if all twenty-two players are on the field at the end of the game. One's already been sent off. *George Best*

Collina is the only referee that, when he makes a decision, there's no arms thrown into the air and no gestating. *Niall Quinn*

He didn't get booked for the yellow card. *Frank Stapleton*

I said to David Elleray in the tunnel, "You might as well book me now and get it over with." *Roy Keane*

# REFUSALS

The first six hundred refusals are the hardest. *Christy Dignam*

I would never do *Hello* or *VIP*. It probably helps that I never got asked. *Dara O'Briain*

I nearly bought a watch last week. It was waterproof, shock-proof and fireproof and the salesman said it wouldn't lose a second in a hundred years. I didn't buy it, though — he wouldn't give me a six-month guarantee. *Jimmy Cricket*

I turned *Hamlet* down because it was going to take up too much of my drinking time. *Richard Harris*

# REGRETS

I wish I'd been a mixed infant. *Brendan Behan*

I always used to hate it when my father carried me on his shoulders. Especially when we were in the car. *Ardal O'Hanlon*

I'd prefer to put Tippex over my eyes than look back at 2011. *Naomi McElroy on New Year's Day 2012*

I have no regrets other than a really awful haircut in the mid-eighties which launched a thousand Third Division soccer players. *Bono*

My mum and dad are both dead now and I think of some of the things I wish I'd said to them. Like, "Be careful of that bus." *Kevin Gildea*

I have no regrets in life. Although I am kind of sorry I never got to beat a man to death while wearing a tuxedo. *George Carlin*

People often ask me have I any regrets about my life. I only have one – a penalty I missed against Chelsea once. *George Best*

My only regret is that we went out on penalties, but I have no regrets. *Mick McCarthy after Ireland exited the 2002 World Cup*

My only regret is that I didn't go for his throat. *Bernadette Devlin after she'd been asked if she had any regrets over assaulting the British Home Secretary Reginald Maudling in the House of Commons when thirteen Irish people were shot dead by the British army in Belfast in 1972*

One of the pleasures of ageing is wallowing in regrets. *Mary Kenny*

# REHAB

Can you imagine walking through the Priory and seeing Robbie Williams coming over in a dressing gown? That's enough to drive you to heroin. *Noel Gallagher*

The last time a mosquito bit me it had to sign itself into the Betty Ford Clinic for detox. *Richard Harris*

Ring Irish Alcoholics Anonymous. If you feel like sobering up, someone comes round with a Guinness. *Seamus O'Leary*

Join AAAA. If your car breaks down, they'll tow you to a pub. **Brian Behan**

Did you hear about the hardened drinker who joined AA? He still drinks, but under a different name. **Ronnie Drew**

Ireland is the only country in the world where there are protestors outside AA meetings. **Des Bishop**

Why do people feel they have to get drunk on St Patrick's Day in the US? That's an insult to all the millions of Irish people who don't drink — the ones in AA. **Colin Quinn**

I went to AA the same way you'd go to Weightwatchers. A couple of weeks and I'd be right. An Irish solution to an Irish problem. When I was told I could never drink again I thought, "Get off the stage!" **Frances Black**

# REINCARNATION

Shirley MacLaine is the type of liberal that, if she found out who she was going to be in her next life, she'd make a will and leave all her money to herself. **Colin Higgins**

I didn't believe in reincarnation the last time either. **Shay O'Donoghue**

If I'm reincarnated, I want to come back as Matt Dillon's underwear. **Boy George**

I'm not so sure if I believe in reincarnation. I can't even remember the things I've done in this life. **Richard Harris**

Reincarnation is making a comeback! **Peader Lamb**

If I could come back in another life it would be as Richard Harris with a stronger liver. **Richard Harris**

If I had my life to live over, I'd live over a Chinese restaurant. **John Jordan**

Why is it that born-again people are always the types you wished were never born in the first place? **Brush Sheils**

If I had my life to live again I wouldn't marry young if I lived to a hundred. *Mark Kavanagh*

# REJECTION

Did you hear about the farmer who had a leg transplant? His welly rejected it. *Frank Carson*

I once made a pass at a bisexual but was rejected on both counts. *Michael Maher*

Even if you have been praying that your boyfriend would end things, it is still about as welcome as a shoe full of vomit. *Graham Norton*

I have the dubious honour of being the only person in Ireland to have been thrown out of the Anarchist Party. *Brian Behan*

Do you know the story of the chaste centipede who said to her suitor, crossing her legs, "No, no, a thousand times no." *Samuel Beckett*

When I was young I used to leave Smarties for Marilyn Monroe under my bed, and a little note that said, "I know you're dead but you should try one of these Smarties if you can manage the trip." The next day they would still be there and I got slightly miffed. The jilted Smartie-giver. *Colin Farrell*

I wrote *The Commitments* in six months and sent a copy of it to every publisher I could find. Invariably it came back unopened. So they didn't reject the book, they rejected the notion of someone *sending* them a book. So I published it myself. *Roddy Doyle*

Me friend's fella just left her and she's in absolute bits. If it wasn't for the Valium she'd be on drugs! *Sue Collins*

Things are so bad at the moment, I rang the Samaritans but they hung up on me. *Jimeoin*

Friends of Bryan McFadden are saying being dumped by Delta Goodrem could drive him to meltdown. How will we be able to tell? *Fiona Looney*

When someone is leaving you they always say something like "I need more space". They don't quantify how much but it seems to be just the same height, breadth and depth as yourself. *Dylan Moran*

# RELATIONSHIPS

Mary and Joseph had a stable relationship. *Arthur Mathews*

A line that should never be used for ending a relationship is "I don't think I'm ready for a relationship yet". So what were you doing in this one? *Robert O'Byrne*

I am nearly incapable of not falling out with anyone who isn't as poor as myself. *Patrick Kavanagh*

People always try to bullshit one another at the end of a relationship. "I'm leaving you because you're such a nice person. I'm not worthy. I have to go and live under a bridge." Better to just tell the truth. Grab them by the teeth, hold them to you and say, "I'm leaving you because you are the most boring fucker I've ever met in my whole life. I hate you so much it gives me energy. You remember that crazy sound you used to hear when you were going to sleep? That was me chewing the bed." *Dylan Moran*

Transatlantic relationships always seem to end when the Atlantic is removed. *Graham Norton*

In every question tossed back and forth between lovers who have not played out the last fugue there is one more question and it is this: "Is there someone new?" *Edna O'Brien*

Relationships begin when you sink in his arms. They end with your arms in his sink. *Maureen Potter*

# RELATIVES

The Baggio brothers, of course, aren't related. **George Hamilton**

I'm related to an Alsatian by marriage. **Brendan Behan**

The main trouble with incest is that it gets you all mixed up with relatives. **Donny Keaveny**

Ireland has changed a lot since I was a child. When I was growing up, my relatives had four teeth between them. Now everyone is dating someone called Pegrovia. **Dylan Moran**

# RELIGION

Catholicism is dying. I saw a sign on a church door the other day saying, "We're open on Sundays now." **Deirdre O'Kane**

The tolerance of Hollywood is best expressed in the burial of Mark Hellinger, a Jew who was buried as a Protestant with a Catholic medal around his neck. **Pat O'Brien**

The closest I've ever got to a communal religious experience kicked off at three p.m. on a Saturday in Old Trafford. **Paul Flood**

If religion is the opium of the masses, I'm a junkie. **Andrea Corr**

Do I believe in the supernatural? Well, I saw Al Greene once. That was pretty close to it. **Elvis Costello**

My religion? I'm an alcoholic. **Brendan Behan**

I'm not a very spiritual person. I've never believed anyone who told me about UFOs or channelling or past lives. I don't even believe Shirley MacLaine exists. **Frank Gannon**

The clerical life in Ireland's past was less *Song of Bernadette* than *Scarface*. **Eamonn Sweeney**

A Jehovah's Witness knocked on the door of a man's house in the country and was invited in for tea and sandwiches. As he was pouring the tea he said, "Now tell me all about Jehovah." The Jehovah's Witness replied, "I'm afraid I know nothing about him. I've never got this far before." *Noel V. Ginnity*

My housekeeper is a Baptist. My doctor is a Jew. My lawyer is a Congregationalist. My secretary is a Presbyterian. My wife is a convert. I have four Catholic kids and six Catholic grandchildren. I'm looking for some atheist friends. *Pat O'Brien*

Religion is for people who are miserable in life and want to make sure they're offering it up for something juicy to come. It's like, "You better be up there, God, for me to be taking all this crap." And if he's not . . . fuck! *Dylan Moran*

Religion has become an industry. It has more in common with McDonald's than it does with me. *Bono*

Religion is like a beautiful flower with sharp teeth. The tranquillity is always matched with moral goose-stepping. Once people have rigid beliefs they inevitably tend to look down on others and act like they've got God in their handbag. *Boy George*

My uncle got a job driving a cab. He had it parked right in front of Grand Central Station and an Episcopal bishop got into it. He said, "Take me to Christ Church." My uncle took him to St Patrick's Cathedral instead and the bishop got mad. He said, "I said Christ Church." My uncle said, "Look, if he's not here, he's not in town." *Jimmy Joyce*

The only good thing ever to come out of religion was the music. *George Carlin*

# REPARTEE

A fella asked me recently if I'd found my karma. "No," I said, "but how much does it cost and how far can it go?" *David Feherty*

"South London." *Andy Townsend after being asked what part of Ireland he came from*

"In a vagina." *Jimmy Carr when asked where he lost his virginity*

I said to my daughter one day, "How come you know everything?" She replied, "How come you know nothing?" *Gabriel Byrne*

"Any tomatoes today, Sadie?"
   "No, luv, I'm afraid they're as scarce as hobby horse manure."
*Paul Ryan*

"I agree." *George Bernard Shaw's response to an ambitious actress who said she was "crazy" to play Saint Joan*

"Not while I've got a hole in my bum." *Mick McCarthy after being asked if he thought Wolves player Nenad Milijas deserved a red card given to him in December 2011*

"Their brains." *Dolores O'Riordan when asked what was man's most useless invention*

"Get married again then." *Taoiseach Charlie Haughey to a woman who told him she was having problems making ends meet on the widow's pension*

When Ma told Brendan she'd like to see Paris before she died, he shot back, "Your chances of seeing it afterwards aren't too good!" *Brian Behan on his famous brother*

"Yes, I'm into the rosary and I talk to Our Lady." *Keith Duffy on being asked if he was a ladies' man.*

"Stringfellows." *George Best after being asked what club he would like to manage*

"Loss of hair, sir." *Pupil to teacher Bryan McMahon after he asked him what caused baldness*

"Yes, but what if he has your brains and my looks?" *George Bernard Shaw to a woman who wanted to have his baby so it could have his brains and her looks*

"I didn't know James Joyce was a question." *Ian MacPherson after being dubbed "Comedy's answer to James Joyce"*

"No problem, sir, I can cut it badly for you." *Barber Peter Quinn to a customer who said he needed his hair cut badly*

The optician asked me if my eyes were ever checked. I said, "No, they've always been this colour." *Jimmy Cricket*

"Faith, I believe I am between both." *R. B. Sheridan to two dukes alongside him who asked him if he was a fool or a rogue*

Cheryl Cole: "How do you see yourselves in fifteen years' time?"
Jedward: "Older."

"No, if you had a gun you'd pawn it." *Luke Kelly to a drunk who said to him one night in a pub, "If I had a gun I'd join the IRA."*

"I have to shave in the morning." *Derek Nally after being asked what he thought differentiated him from the other candidates for the Irish presidency in 1997 – who all happened to be women*

"Half time." *George Best after being asked what was the nearest to kick-off that he ever made love*

"Certainly not – it's done other things as well!" *James Joyce to a woman who wanted to shake the hand of the man who wrote* **Ulysses**

"Negotiating with him is like picking up mercury with a fork." *David Lloyd George on the difficulty of engaging in political discourse with de Valera. De Valera riposted: "Why doesn't he use a spoon?"*

Gay Byrne: "What would you say to God if you died and went to heaven?"
Colin Farrell: "I wouldn't have to say anything. He'd be able to read my mind."

"No, dear, do you?" *Drag artiste Danny La Rue to a woman who asked him if he enjoyed dressing up in female garb*

"That's surprising because I've been practising all night." *John Philpott Curran to a doctor who told him he had a bad cough*

"With a camera." *John Ford to a reporter who asked him how he liked to shoot Monument Valley*

"Well, then it will just have to digest in its waistcoat." *R. B. Sheridan after being informed by his doctor that alcohol couldn't digest in the "coat" of his stomach*

# RESEARCH

New research shows that the more sex a man has, the more he wants. And also that the less sex a man has, the more he wants. *Conan O'Brien*

Researchers have found that women are so concerned about putting on weight, they get on the scales an average of 4,543 times in their adult life. Surely that can be classed as a form of "step aerobics". *Eamonn Holmes*

A survey has discovered the average married couple converse for twenty minutes every week. What do they find to talk about? *Dave Allen*

Robert Powell was asked what preparation he did for the part of Christ in *Jesus of Nazareth*. He said, "I watched every film version of the story of the Bible and all the actors who played Christ blinked, so I wanted to play a Christ who didn't blink." And I thought, "*That's* research?" *Aidan Quinn*

For my friends a party means fun and glamour. For me it means research. *Novelist Marissa Markle*

Research shows that the number of magazines in any society is directly proportional to the amount of cocaine being hoovered up by the chattering classes. *Brendan O'Connor*

# RESENTMENT

There's no way I would want to buy Manchester City. Why would I want to give every penny I've earned to some horrible little chav footballer so he can buy his wife dresses to wear at Aintree. I'd rather piss it up the wall. *Noel Gallagher*

Hugh Leonard had more chips than Burdock's on a busy Friday. *Gay Byrne*

I begrudge Manchester United their success but I am not inconsistent. I begrudged them their failure too. *Tom Humphries*

A woman looked at a book of mine one day and said, "I could do that." "Maybe you could," I replied, "but I did it." *Maeve Binchy*

How many works of the imagination have been goaded into life by envy of an untalented contemporary's success? *Brian Moore*

An Irishman considers any other Irishman who achieves success to be a traitor. *Henry Spalding*

If there's ever a Begrudgery Olympics held in Dublin, Paddy Kavanagh will clear the board at every event. *Brendan Behan*

The Irish always seem to me like a pack of hounds dragging down some noble stag. *Johann Wolfgang von Goethe*

In America they look up at the mansion on the hill and say, "One day that could be me." In Ireland they look up at the mansion and go, "One day I'm gonna get that bastard." *Bono*

# RESOLUTIONS

My New Year's resolution is to give up drinking ... out of damp glasses. *Brendan Grace*

I'm giving up marriage for Lent. *Brian Behan*

My New Year's Resolution is to stop making New Year's Resolutions. *Clara Byrne*

# RESOURCEFULNESS

Jack Charlton's philosophy of soccer was, "If Plan A fails, try Plan A". *Mark Lawrenson*

McDougall found a pair of crutches in the attic so he went downstairs and broke his wife's leg. *Des MacHale*

I was on *Desert Island Discs* and Sue Lawley asked me what two books I'd take to a desert island. I said the first one would be a great big inflatable book and the second one would be *How To Make Oars Out of Sand*. *Ardal O'Hanlon*

Our fire safety warden at work sent around a survey of what we would do in case of fire. One of the questions was, "What steps would you take if a fire broke out?" Some witty so-and-so replied, "Very big ones." *Overheard in Dublin*

There was once a parish priest who suspected his housekeeper was helping herself to his sherry so he decided to dilute it with urine. Weeks later, the level of the decanter was still going down so he decided to tackle her about it. She said, "Oh Father, I put a drop in your soup every day." *Edna O'Brien*

Sean O'Shea learned to cut his fingernails with his left hand in case he ever lost his right. *Hal Roach*

What would you do if an epileptic had a fit in your bath? Throw the washing in. *Sean Hughes*

# RESTAURANTS

You mean you made all that noise for nothing? **R. B. Sheridan to a waiter who dropped a tray without breaking a dish**

The changes in the liturgy are just one more example of emptiness, like restaurant owners who redecorate after losing business. **John McGahern**

There's a new topless restaurant in Dublin. It has no roof on it. **Eamon Morrissey**

It's the food! It's the food! **A terminally ill Richard Harris as he was being wheeled from the restaurant of the Savoy Hotel to an ambulance**

A restaurant is the only place in the world where people are happy to be fed up. **Jack Cruise**

No matter what you ask for in an American restaurant they'll say, "Do you want cheese with that?" One day I lost my temper. "I asked for a fucking newspaper!" **Tommy Tiernan**

The only problem with the restaurant in the National Art Gallery is that you have to go through the gallery to get to it. **Paul Durcan**

In this posh new restaurant they have a menu with *Poulet à la Chevrolet* on it. That's a chicken that was run over by a truck. **Hal Roach**

From experience I know that anything ending in "os" on a restaurant menu is pronounced "heartburn". **Hugh Leonard**

I told her we were going to *La Traviata*. "No we're not," she said. "None of that foreign muck for me. It gives me diarrhoea." **Frankie Blowers**

All guests are advised that all water served in this establishment has been passed by the management. **Restaurant notice**

Gone To Lunch. Back In Five Minutes. Signed, Godot. *Sign spotted in Mayo café*

While impatiently waiting for a table in a restaurant, Mrs O'Brien said to Mrs Clancy, "If they weren't so crowded here all the time they'd do a lot more business." *Hal Roach*

The key to a successful restaurant is dressing girls in degrading clothes. *Michael O'Donoghue*

Upon ringing a restaurant to ask if they had wheelchair access, I was told that they accepted all major credit cards. *Pat Fitzpatrick*

In most Dublin restaurants the service would embarrass a Prague taxi driver. The prices are insulting and the atmosphere has all the warmth of a pioneer's wake. *Trevor White*

Never eat in a restaurant with a multi-lingual menu. Never eat in a restaurant with pictures of the food on the place mats. Never eat in a restaurant with numbered dishes on the menu. Never eat in a restaurant with a written definition of a rare, medium and well-done steak. Never eat in a restaurant largely populated by Japanese tourists. *Paul Kilduff*

It is not so long since good Irish restaurants were as rare as an unautographed copy of a Ulick O'Connor book. *Hugh Leonard*

I brought a woman to a restaurant. She said, "I guess I'll have a steak." I said, "Guess again." *Brendan O'Carroll*

# RETALIATION

Which side went out to retaliate first? *Danny Blanchflower*

There was a bit of retaliation there, though not actually on the same player. *Frank Stapleton*

I think in retaliation for the Holocaust, the Jews should be allowed to kill six million Germans. It's only fair. With sixty years of compound interest, that would come to about 110 million Germans. That ought to put a dent in bratwurst consumption. *George Carlin*

The worst thing about the game was that there wasn't even a row. *Colm O'Rourke*

# RETIREMENT

Kylie Minogue has said she's removing her bottom from public view but her bottom doesn't seem to have been informed about this. It must have been in the dark about its early retirement when it cheekily reared up during Kylie's recent London gig. *Moira Hannon*

I'm retired, but it's an Irish retirement. I have to work to be able to afford it. *Dave Allen*

Anna Kournikova's retirement from tennis is on a par with Bono giving up acting. She probably has a future as a great Russian novelist. *Brendan O'Connor*

I don't want to retire. I have an image of myself following my wife around a supermarket as she fills a trolley and saying to her hopelessly, "Why are you buying this?" *Terry Wogan*

Retiring from boxing made me miss the camaraderie of the gym but I don't miss being smacked in the mouth every day. *Barry McGuigan*

I'm a retired Christian with a capital C. I was brought up Catholic and educated by nuns whose hands had never felt a man. All I believe is that a number 11 bus goes along the Strand to Hammersmith, but I know it isn't being driven by Santa Claus. *Peter O'Toole*

The IRA are retired now. They've all been presented with gold timing devices. *Patrick Kielty*

On the morning of your first day in your new job you should plan for your retirement. Meet your pension representative to make sure your payments will be in place so you can retire as soon as possible. While it is acceptable to look happy on your first day, thereafter you should exhibit as many symptoms of clinical depression as possible and participate in the communal mourning. *David Slattery*

The reason I retired from politics was because I had four children and none of them knew who I was. *Ivan Yates*

I'll probably retire around the age of 104. *Bill Cullen*

# REVULSION

I wouldn't give him the itch for fear that on a cold day he'd scratch himself and get warm. *David Fitzgerald*

I can't stand Beckett's plays. If I happen to be at one I'm ready to applaud, clap, anything — providing it stops. *Tom Murphy*

I'd prefer to lick wet tar or to suck spit from the mouth of a dead pig than let a teaspoon of Monaghan milk pass my lips. *Kevin Myers*

When a band is as big as U2, it gets to be a pain in the arse for people who have to put up with that all the time. The reaction is, "Ah, fuck off". So now people just hate our guts, which suits us fine. *Bono*

James Joyce is a living argument in favour of my contention that it was a mistake to establish a separate university for the aborigines of Ireland, the corner-boys who spit into the Liffey. *J. P. Mahaffy*

How many cunts are there in Oasis? I'll give you a clue. It's more than zero and less than two. *Liam Gallagher*

A man said to me once in a bar, "I think you're crap as a broadcaster, and so does my wife. And she knows fuck all." *Mike Murphy*

I hope they catch AIDS and die. *Noel Gallagher on Blur in 1996*

You could dip a broom in brake fluid, shove the other end up my arse, stick me on a trampoline in a moving lift — and I would still write a better song than Rockafeller Skank. *Dylan Moran*

Bono drives me mad. He's always sniffing around someone who's in office. Shut your face and fucking sing. *Sharon Osbourne*

With the single exception of Homer, there is no eminent writer, not even Sir Walter Scott, whom I despise so entirely as I despise Shakespeare when I measure my mind against his. It would positively be a relief to dig him up and throw stones at him. *George Bernard Shaw*

# RICHNESS

At the height of Ireland's boom, helicopters hired out for the day blocked out the sun at the Galway Races and any man who was doing well for himself thought it a mild extravagance to present his wife with an anniversary gift of a new SUV with a ribbon around it. The ribbon showed that he'd really made an effort this time. *Declan Lynch*

Bono is so wealthy he once employed Salman Rushdie to pose as a gnome at the bottom of his garden. *Paul Howard*

The rich you will always have with you. *Brian Behan*

I'd like to be rich enough to throw the soap away after the letters wore off. *Andy Rooney*

Money is sex for the rich. *Edna O'Brien*

Kid: "Grandad, do your frog impression."
Grandad: "What are you talking about?"
Kid: "Well, Mom said when you croak we'll all be rich."
*Hal Roach*

I am a millionaire. That is my religion. *George Bernard Shaw*

They say Madonna was worth £50 million when she was married to Guy Ritchie. If you include Guy Ritchie's earnings it meant that overall she was worth . . . £50 million! *Graham Norton*

I love the fact that I've managed to generate an extraordinary amount of cash, because it allows me to interrupt people. *Noel Gallagher*

Ken Dodd is one of the richest men in show business. He has Swiss money in Irish banks. *Roy Walker*

Whether you're rich or poor, it's nice to have money. *Cyril Cusack*

After the rich, the most obnoxious people in the world are those who serve the rich. *Edna O'Brien*

It's easy to recognize a rich farmer. He's always pleading poverty. *Spike Milligan*

If the rich could pay people to die for them, the poor would make a marvellous living. *Sean Desmond*

I hear Neil Diamond hires private jets to take his dogs on holiday. That's what I call rich. *Barry Egan*

Bono is now officially richer than God so let's hope the U2 frontman can finally bring himself to stop auditioning for the deity's job. *Liam Fay*

# RIDDLES

Why did the dog with three legs walk into the saloon? To find out who shot his paw. *Maureen Potter*

Q. What's got five hundred legs and no pubic hair?
A. The front row at a Westlife concert.
*Liam O'Mahony*

Why did Ronan Keating cross the road? To get to the middle.
**Mary Carr**

Q. Why do children change garments in shops?
A. Because their parents like them.
**Foggy Spellman**

What's the difference between a Spice Girl and a Big Mac?
I've never shat on a Spice Girl and given it to a homeless
person. **Ed Byrne**

Why did the Kerry girl wave her hair for the St Patrick's Day
Parade? She couldn't afford a flag. **Mary Feehan**

How many soccer players does it take to change a lightbulb?
Eleven. One to stick it in and ten to hug and kiss him afterwards. **Tom Humphries**

# RIVERS

A town without a river is like a plaice without a sole. **Bryan
McMahon**

Teacher: "The river Lee flows into Cork harbour so we call
that its mouth. Can you tell me where the source is?"
Niall: "At the other end, sir."
**Duncan Crosbie**

Why does the Foyle run through Derry? Because if it walked
it would be mugged. **Michael Cullen**

# ROADS

There's more tar in a packet of fags than there is in all the
roads of Mayo. **Padraig O'Connor**

You can always tell when you're leaving a Protestant area in Northern Ireland and entering a Catholic one. The roads deteriorate. *Polly Devlin*

An American tourist stopped in a village and said to a young boy, "Can you tell me where this road goes to?" The boy said, "It doesn't go nowhere. It stays right where it is." *Hal Roach*

Save petrol. Make roads shorter. *Kevin Murtie*

Ireland is officially bilingual, a fact that's reflected in the road signs. This means you can now get lost both in Irish and English. *Frank McCourt*

Road sign noted in Cork: "When this sign is under water, the road is closed for traffic". *Peter Cagney*

# ROBBERY

The darkest hour is before the dawn, which makes it a very good time to steal your neighbour's milk. *Seamus O'Leary*

A toilet bowl was stolen from Blanchardstown today. The guards have nothing to go on. *Frank Hall*

I once stole a chair from a Newcastle comedy club. I wrapped it in a black bin-bag to transport it but the train was busy so I sat on it all the way back to London. *Dara O'Briain*

Did you hear about the travelling salesman who died and left an estate of five hundred hotel towels and two hundred keys? *Hal Roach*

A set of traffic lights were nicked in Sligo yesterday. The police said some criminals will stop at nothing. *Paul Malone*

I am a gentleman. I live by robbing the poor. *George Bernard Shaw*

He that cries "Stop, thief" is often he who has stolen the treasure. *William Congreve*

People never value anything unless they have to steal it. Even an alley cat would rather sneak an old bone out of the garbage than come up and eat a nicely prepared chop from your saucer. *James Joyce*

Thieves broke into a chemist's shop and stole everything but contraceptives and Brylcreem. The police are on the look-out for a bald-headed Catholic. *Frank Carson*

A man was trying to explain the theft of his bicycle to the local friendly Garda sergeant. "I went into the post office to buy a stamp and when I came out, there it was up against the wall, gone." *Clare Boylan*

A government which robs Peter to pay Paul can always depend on the support of Paul. *George Bernard Shaw*

# ROMANCE

Romantic Ireland is sprawled across the couch in a fug of football and beer since some time back in the late 1990s. Where once the former knights in shining armour laid down capes for their women in muddy puddles, these days they can barely bring themselves to lift the quilt in bed to break wind. *Joe McNamee*

Romantic Ireland is dead and gone. Its resting place has been bought on the cheap by a consortium that includes two tax exiles, a bent solicitor and a former politician with business interests in Eastern Europe. *Gene Kerrigan*

I'm not surprised there's so much paedophilia in the Catholic Church. You can't put candles and all that red wine together and not expect romance to flourish. *Patrick Kielty*

Safe sex to a Dubliner is doing it when your wife's gone to the bingo. Romance means taking your socks off before you jump into bed. *David Kenny*

A nervous six-footer named Bridget
Would wiggle and squirm, twitch and fidget.
But she knew perfect peace
And a psychic release
When she found true romance with a midget.
*Old Irish limerick*

# ROUNDABOUTS

Last week I observed a woman negotiating a roundabout with a phone in one hand and a take-out coffee in the other, while steering with her elbows. *Sarah Carey*

When Ireland was poor the Church told us we'd see the devil at midnight at the crossroads if we didn't practise our religion. But then we became rich and got roundabouts. *Jon Kenny*

Irish drivers approach roundabouts like drunken donkeys. *Eddie Cunningham*

Ireland's roundabouts are a kind of vehicular Pamplona. *David Monaghan*

# ROYALTY

Does anyone really believe Prince Harry will be within a country mile of danger in Afghanistan? The closest he'll come to taking a risk is skipping the queue for grub in the canteen. *Colette Fitzpatrick*

The Queen Mother's greatest achievement in 101 years was not choking on a fishbone. *Ian O'Doherty*

I hate name-dropping, as I told the Duke of Edinburgh recently. *Frank Carson*

Wills 'n' Kate declared they would accept wedding presents from close family (so that's the mortgage taken care of) but all other guests were encouraged to make confidential donations to chosen charities. Why do I have a picture of the Duke of Westminster (Britain's richest man) guffawing after giving Coutts the order to transfer a quid to the Distressed Corgi Fund? *Aoife O'Brien*

I went to Buckingham Palace to see the Changing of the Guard. What I can't understand is, if these guards are so good, why do they keep changing them? *Jimmy Cricket*

The Queen Mother's visit to the Vatican was spiritual fornication and adultery with the Antichrist. *Ian Paisley*

Why do people refer to Kate Middleton as a commoner? I don't think she ever went to an ATM machine and worried. *Ian O'Doherty*

I doubt Prince Harry will marry a girl like Kate. He'll probably go to Las Vegas and come back with a whore. He'll run up to Charles and go, "This is Tiffany. She's pregnant but it isn't mine. But then I'm not yours either." *Neil Delamere*

Eddie had a very engaging way of getting your attention. Teaching history, he startled all by coming into class announcing, "Henry the Eighth was a bastard. Queen Elizabeth was a bastard. Mary Tudor was a bastard. In fact the whole Tudor dynasty was a litter of bastards." *Niall Toibin*

Buckingham Palace looks like a vast dolls' house that some bullying skinhead big brother kicked down from the mall. *Joe O'Connor*

The British aristocratic look is either that of an elegant and etiolated horse or a beery, red-faced workman. *Patrick O'Donovan*

In 1977, when Queen Elizabeth celebrated her Silver Jubilee, the Sex Pistols put a safety pin through her nose and rocketed up the charts with a song that proclaimed her a moron and a potential H-bomb. A quarter of a century on, the music world gathered respectfully at her home to celebrate her fifty years on the throne. *Dave Fanning*

I did a fun run with Prince William once. Before it started I thought: Paddy from Northern Ireland, future king of England, gun. A few years ago I might have gone for it. *Patrick Kielty*

Milesius was the legendary king who founded the Irish race. Luckily for him he didn't exist since he has a great deal to answer for. *Terry Eagleton*

The Queen is the most highly paid prisoner in the world. *Lynsey Dolan*

# RUGBY

The motto of Irish rugby has always been "Kick ahead". Any head. *Fergus Slattery*

Our tactic in the match against Romania in 1980 was to kick the proverbial shit out of the opposition in the first half to soften them up. It worked so well we repeated the courtesy in the second half as well. *Willie Duggan*

Horrocks-Taylor came towards me with the ball. Horrocks went one way, Taylor went the other, and I was left holding the hyphen. *Mick English*

A training session in rugby in the 1970s consisted of running around Barry McGann twice. *Tony O'Reilly*

A farmer could make a tidy living if he owned the amount of ground it takes Moss Keane to turn. *Danny Lynch*

Colin Meads is the kind of player you expect to see emerging from a ruck with the remains of a jockstrap between his teeth. *Tom O'Reilly*

Tony Ward is the most important rugby player in Ireland. His legs are more important to his country than Marlene Dietrich's were to the film industry. *C. M. H. Gibson*

Rugby people. Can't live with them, can't shoot them. *Tom Humphries*

Scotland are the nymphomaniacs of world rugby. *George Hook*

That culture of hair-pulling, flesh-biting, stud-raking, testicle-squeezing and head-butting is a closed one where you take your punishment and buy the perpetrator a drink afterwards. *Tom Humphries*

I played rugby once. I gave it up when I discovered you had to run with the ball. *Garret Fitzgerald*

Spread out in a bunch. *Noel Murphy to the 1980 Lions*

Twice around Barry McGann and you qualify as a *bona fide* traveller. *Tony O'Reilly*

Prop forwards don't get Valentine cards for religious reasons. God made them ugly. *Tony O'Reilly*

I can offer no tenable theory as to why the fate of a piece of inflated bladder should occasion displays of woe more suitable to the wholesale assumption of the population of Kerry into heaven. *Hugh Leonard*

Your best attacking move today will be to shake your jowls at your opposite number. *Willie John McBride to an ageing Tony O'Reilly in 1991*

# RULES

Don't learn the rules. Then you can't be accused of breaking them. *Mary Robinson*

Muzzle the rules. They bite. *Patrick Campbell*

If I were asked to rewrite the rules of golf, I'd add just one new one: Players may be allowed to tackle their opponents. *David Feherty*

The first rule for a young playwright to follow is not to write like Henry Arthur Jones. The second and third rules are the same. *Oscar Wilde*

# SADISM

At school I was Minister of Torture. I put dustbin lids over kids' heads and banged them for half an hour. I got stinging nettles and rubbed their balls with them, tweaked their nipples and generally abused them. That was before I read the Marquis de Sade. Sadism is a fairly normal condition. *Shane MacGowan*

Bob Dylan sang the backing vocals to Leonard Cohen's "Don't Go Home With Your Hard-On" and probably thought, with some glee, "Well, there's another rival's career fucked." *Eamonn Sweeney*

When you win the Lottery, do a radio interview to say you're staying on in your job. Then buy a giant Bentley, spray "Losers!" on the rear window and dump it in the car park. As regards begging letters, keep on writing them. *Pat Fitzpatrick*

Golf is a game designed by a sadist for millions of masochists. *Brian Barnes*

The gigs I most enjoy are the ones where I hate the audience and feed off that. *Shane MacGowan*

What would really cheer one of my acquaintances up would be if I were to tell her I was in bad form. *Maeve Binchy*

Masochist to sadist: "Hit me."
Sadist: "No."
*Joe Cuddy*

# SAINTS

When they said he had a face like a saint, they must have meant a St Bernard. *Joe McCarthy*

In the fifty years of its existence, all the Irish Institute for Advanced Studies has done is to show that there were two St Patricks and no God. *Patrick Murray*

In heaven a saint is nobody in particular. *George Bernard Shaw*

St Patrick banished the snakes from Ireland, though a number still survive, disguised as county councillors. His success in converting fragmented pagan kingdoms to Christianity is celebrated each year on 17 March by Irish and pretendy Irish people all over the world, wearing giant Styrofoam pastiches of him on their heads, drinking twelve pints of green beer and then puking into their chicken curry. *Donal O'Dea*

Would she could make of me a saint, or I of her a sinner. *William Congreve*

The Catholic Church is for saints and sinners. For respectable people the Anglican Church will do. *Oscar Wilde*

Ireland's patron saint, St Patrick, has the following draw-backs: We don't really know who he was. We don't really know where he came from. There may have been two of him. And he may not have existed at all. *Terry Eagleton*

# SANTA CLAUS

Everyone pretends to believe in Santa Claus to get their children to bed early so we can get pissed in peace on Christmas Eve. *David Slattery*

Santa's nationality is North Polish. *Mary Feehan*

The main difference between God and Santa Claus is that there really is a Santa Claus. *Dylan Moran*

There are basically three stages in life. You believe in Santa Claus, you don't believe in Santa Claus, you *are* Santa Claus. *Cathal O'Sullivan*

# SCHOOL

When I was in primary school we had a drawing of Northern Ireland on the wall with blue around it. I thought it was an island until I was twelve. *Anne Dunlop*

The biggest influence in my life was the Tech in Ballyfermot, which is the school I didn't go to. *Joe Duffy*

When I was at school the teacher used to ask me was I paying attention. I used to tell him, "Yes, but not to you." *Tommy Tiernan*

# THE SEASONS

I find if I don't die in autumn, I always seem to survive until Christmas. *R. B. Sheridan*

In the spring a young man's fancy turns to things he's been thinking about all winter. *Hal Roach*

I spent five years in LA. There are no seasons there, which means time gets warped. *Gabriel Byrne*

The only times a woman is difficult to live with are: spring, summer, autumn and winter. *Brian Behan*

An Irishman was once asked to define winter. "It's the time of year," he explained, "when it gets late early." *Tom McIntyre*

There are two seasons in Ireland: June and winter. *Eamonn Kelly*

I wonder what day summer is going to fall on this year? *T. P. McKenna*

Long hot summers in Ireland are rare enough to be guaranteed entry into the folk memory. *Anthony Bluett*

# SECRETS

Zsa Zsa Gabor has discovered the secret of perpetual middle age. *John Huston*

A secret in Dublin means just telling one person at a time. *Ciaran MacGonigal*

# SELF-CRITICISM

There's a luxury in self-reproach. When we blame ourselves we feel no one else has a right to blame us. *Oscar Wilde*

I'm no angel, even if I'm named after one. *Gabriel Byrne*

I don't know if I'm the best drummer in Ireland. I don't even know if I'm the best drummer in U2! *Larry Mullen*

I'm a geriatric novelty with a brogue. *Frank McCourt*

I have the hand-to-eye coordination of a cross-eyed drunk. *Anne Marie Scanlon*

I have no football skills to speak of. I played a charity match a month ago and I was rubbish. I disguised this rather well by running around the pitch a lot. The team soon had me playing to my strengths by ignoring me. *Sean Hughes*

When I started out I honestly thought I'd be selling CDs from a suitcase at the end of every gig. *Imelda May, Ireland's biggest musical export since Westlife*

I have an advanced case of spiritual hardening of the arteries. *J. G. Farrell*

I'm so self-critical I could almost sue myself for defamation of character. *Tommy Tiernan*

I'm an acquired taste a lot of people would prefer not to acquire. *Gavin Friday*

The last time I performed on stage, my name was so low on the programme I was getting orders for the printing. *Frank Carson*

I set up a shelter for distressed women. If they weren't distressed coming in, they certainly were going out. *Brian Behan*

I believe in sacrifice, but not yet. *Patrick Bergin*

I don't give a shite if nobody likes me. I'm not a cloud bunny or an aerosexual. I don't like aeroplanes. I never wanted to be a pilot like those other platoons of goons who populate the airline industry. I'm probably just an obstinate little bollox. Who cares? The purpose is not to be loved. The purpose is to have passengers on board. *Ryanair boss Michael O'Leary*

# SEX

Foreplay is a waste of good riding time. *Katherine Lynch*

People accused me of being promiscuous but sometimes I went to bed with men just for the exercise. *Nuala O'Faolain*

Dennis Rodman claimed to be bisexual so he could marry himself. *Brian O'Connor*

Hippocrates recorded the case of a man dying after over-indulging in sex and wine. He complained of "stiffness, vomiting, insomnia, palpitations, delirium and incoherent speech". And that was just the sex. *Declan Lynch*

The age of consent is now lower than the legal age for smoking in Ireland. It gives a whole new meaning to the old gag: "Do you smoke after making love?" "I don't know — I never looked." *Sean Hughes*

And I thought they were only wrestling. *Shay Healy after being told the facts of life*

The one thing they never told us about sex when I was in school was that the reason people did it was because it felt fantastic. *Gerry Ryan*

As a teen you're told to try and make sex last as long as possible. "Think of footballers," I was told. Every time I found myself in bed with a lover I was straining to remember the Crystal Palace first eleven. *Sean Hughes*

Sex is the only game that becomes less exciting when played for money. *Damien McDermott*

My wife said to me, "Why do you never talk when we're having sex?" I said, "I don't like to waken you up." *Frank Carson*

Mrs Clarke: "My husband left me for another woman, though it was my fault I suppose. The sex was getting a little boring and I did nothing to spice it up."
Fr Ted: "Isn't that always the way?"
Mrs Clarke: "Near the end I tried a few things. I used to dress up in very revealing lingerie and when he came to the door I leapt on top of him and had sex right there in the hall."
Fr Ted: "So you had a good sleep then."
**Father Ted**

One of the Legion of Mary's most spectacular actions in its early days was closing a red light district in Dublin. I think they'd have their work cut out today. *Tony Whelan*

Wayne Rooney has slept with more dogs than Roy Keane's Triggs. *Oliver Callan (Triggs was Keane's dog)*

"Will ye still love him when he's no longer able to satisfy ye in bed, Josie?"
    "Oh I do, luv, I do."
*Paul Ryan*

I'm an Irish Catholic so my father never discussed women or sex with me. We talked about sandwich meat instead. *Conan O'Brien*

Casanova's memoirs say he courted 122 ladies in his life. Sadly he died from a venereal disease — and also possibly from exhaustion. *Paul Kilduff*

Practise Safe Sex. Go Fuck Yourself. *T-shirt slogan*

The Church sees your sexual bits like library books on loan from God. But you're not allowed to fold the pages. *Des Bishop*

The naive Irish lad didn't know what to do on the wedding night so he phoned his dad. "Put the hardest part of yourself where she pees," he advised. A few hours later the dad got another phone call, this time from the bride. "Could you please tell your son to get his head out of the toilet bowl," she asked. *Damien Tiernan*

Sex before marriage is a good idea — mainly because there's so little after it. *Brendan O'Carroll*

In Ireland it is well to remember that sex is an eight-letter word spelt m-a-r-r-i-a-g-e. *Tony Butler*

A week before Abraham Lincoln was shot he was in Monroe, Maryland. A week before John F. Kennedy was shot he was in Monroe, Marilyn. *John Scally*

It was an expensive fucking fourteen minutes. Or vice versa. *Colin Farrell on a sex tape he paid to have repressed*

I once lived with three women in Australia but they were all from Cork so the answer to your questions are, respectively, no, no, and no. *Keith Farnan to an interviewer*

Women love being on top because they can look around the room as they jump up and down on you. They go, "I must bring that downstairs," or "I don't like the curtains, Pascal." *Tommy Tiernan*

I was making love to a Swedish woman. She said, "What's your favourite position?" I said, "Corner back." *Neil Delamere*

Q. Why is Gaelic football different from sex?
A. One involves sensuality, passion, emotion, commitment, selflessness, the speechless admiration of sheer heart-stopping beauty, rushes of breathtaking, ecstatic excitement followed by toe-curling, ecstatic pleasure. And the other is sex.
*Pat Spillane*

Sex is nowadays a dour-faced symbol of liberation instead of, as it once was, the form of physical exercise most acceptable to the lazy. *Hugh Leonard*

Paddy was filling in a form to get a passport. Under "Name" he wrote "Paddy Murphy" and under "Address" he put "Kerry". The next box he had to fill in was "Sex". Paddy thought about this for a minute and then wrote down "Once in Ballybunion". *Peter Canavan*

A wife's right to choose not to have sex with her husband is enshrined in law. This is intricately balanced by the man's right not to feed her. *Kevin McAleer*

At my sexual peak I was having more one-night stands in a week than there were nights in a week. *Colin Farrell*

The main problem with vibrators is that you can't cuddle them afterwards. That's why I need a man. *Sinead O'Connor*

# SEXISM

If men can pinch bottoms, why can't women? *Edna O'Brien*

My name is Ian and I have a confession to make. I'm a bloke. *Ian O'Doherty*

It's difficult for women over a certain age — say nineteen or twenty — to secure decent roles in Hollywood today. *Donald Clarke*

Political correctness has now reached such a stage that it will soon be deemed sexist to refer to a woman as "she". *Hugh Leonard*

There's only one thing worse than a male chauvinist pig and that's a woman who won't do what she's told. **Short Back and Sides**

A woman asking for equality in the Church is equivalent to a black person demanding equality in the Ku Klux Klan. *Mary Daly*

If men were shouted down for being sexist when they used the word "postman", asking if there was any chance of a quick shag seemed like a bit of a non-starter. *John O'Farrell*

Equality on the fairways in golf never carried quite the same urgency with Ireland as the vote, the pill or a seat on the jury. *Mary Kenny*

How I wish Adam had died with all the bones in his body. *Dion Boucicault*

The conservative establishment has always treated women as nannies, grannies and fannies. *Teresa Gorman*

Thought does not become a young woman. *R. B. Sheridan*

Life's a bitch – and then they call you one. *Mary Connelly*

I think, therefore I'm single. *Sinead Flynn*

My husband said that if I became a politician it would be grounds for annulment. *Liz O'Donnell*

The next time a man says you have a great pair of legs, take off your tights and strangle him. *Nell McCafferty*

My mother believes there should be more women in male-dominated jobs. I thought she would be pleased I got a post as a petrol pump attendant but I think she would have preferred brain surgery. *Katy Hayes*

If Robert de Niro gains weight for a role it's called "artistic dedication". If I do it's called letting yourself go. *Brenda Fricker*

A little wit is valued in a woman, as we are pleased with a few words spoken plain by a parrot. *Jonathan Swift*

If you pee standing up, you're worth an extra fifth in the salary department. *Eddie Hobbs*

Give women the vote and in five years there will be a crushing tax on bachelors. *George Bernard Shaw*

When I was growing up in Ireland in the sixties the function of women was to marry, breed a succession of little Catholics, stay at home, wear their best clothes to Mass and bake buns for parish sales of work. *Mary McEvoy*

# SEXUAL DEVIANCE

If you read your spam emails, the person who sent them to you — an old lady running a highly profitable porn business from her living-room in Utah — will presume you're interested and continue to bombard you with offers of discounted Viagra, penis enlargement and lesbian sex. *Robert O'Byrne*

I was once propositioned by an elderly plumber of about seventy with emphysema who offered me two and sixpence for a look at my privates. *Gabriel Byrne*

When it comes to how good sex can be, it doesn't really matter what state of mind you're in or how much preparation has gone on. It is and always will be about the chemistry between two people — or six if you're open-minded. *Sean Hughes*

The first time a man told me he was going to "crack a cold one" I thought he was making a reference to necrophilia. *Michael Mee*

A Canadian cop has suggested that women could prevent sexual attacks if they stopped dressing like sluts. Who knew rapists were so picky? I've never heard of a woman on the brink of being assaulted before her assailant realized skinny jeans were doing nothing for her. *Grainne McGuire*

Sleeping with George Michael would be like having sex with a groundhog. *Boy George*

There was no rustle of silk negligee draped on a chaise longue ... it was more like a crotch rub in the kitchenette of a two-room flat in Phibsborough, or beer spilt down a blouse, then pawed at in pretend apology. *Gerry Stembridge*

Paedophilia doesn't count if you're a woman. *Sharon Horgan*

Jack and Jill went up the hill
To fetch a pail of water.
Jack came down with half a crown ...
He must have met Uncle Frank.
*Ian MacPherson*

You can find out your baby's sex before it's born now. The hard part is finding out what sex they're going to be later on. **Kevin Nealon**

I'm not saying he's oversexed, but I'd watch the drawers on me dresser when he's around. **Paul Ryan**

The closest I've come to tying the knot was during a bizarre bonding session with an incredibly attractive but completely psychotic Swiss girl called Lucia in an Amsterdam hotel. **Olaf Tyaransen**

Our sex lives would be a lot simpler if men's genitals were attached to our index fingers, and women's to their shoulders. In order to initiate an interest in a woman, all a man would have to do would be to go up to her and tap her on the arm. **Spike Milligan**

If you tie somebody to a bed, it is quite important that you do not then go down to the pub and forget about them. **Joe O'Connor**

When I was a teenager I wasn't allowed any sexual freedom, so I had to settle for bondage. **Sinead Murphy**

Mike Flynn was fed up with the monotony of things so one night he said, "Come on, Nadia, let's try it a different way." So they moved the bed away from the recess and put it opposite the fireplace. **Peter Cagney**

Liam Brady's been playing inside Platini's shorts all night. **Jimmy Magee**

Murphy told me the difference between kinky and erotica. "If Paddy tickled you with a feather," he said, "that's kinky, but if he used the whole chicken, that's erotica." **Noel V. Ginnity**

I know a woman who truly believes that the radiator in her bedroom is trying to seduce her with throaty gurgles. "It only talks to me when my husband has gone to the toilet," she said. You sometimes get that. **Pat Ingoldsby**

People who knock incest usually have very ugly relatives. **Mick Gorman**

Never have sex with your best friend because it's always a mistake. I did that last week. The next morning I was so embarrassed. I couldn't look at him. I couldn't talk to him. I couldn't bring him for walks . . . *Kevin Gildea*

# SHEEP

You have to have a good yarn to pull the wool over a sheep farmer's eyes. *Noel V. Ginnity*

Bo Peep did it for the insurance. *Graffiti*

Wordsworth was a half-witted sheep who bleated articulate monotony. *James Stephens*

An accountant was having trouble sleeping so he went to his doctor. The doctor advised counting sheep. "That's the trouble," the accountant told him. "Every time I make a mistake I spend hours trying to locate it." *Paul Malone*

What would you get if you crossed a sheep with a kangaroo? A woolly jumper. *Des Bishop*

Many New Zealanders look like sheep, I've decided: their mouths are very near their chins. *J. G. Farrell*

The Faroe Islands only has a population of 172, and nine of those are sheep. *Pat Dolan*

Then there was the socialist farmer whose philosophy was: Shear and shear alike. *Noel Purcell*

The best knitting is done after dark because the sheep are asleep. *Sean Desmond*

Sheep really are pretty dumb. They're not even aware they're of great use for making woolly jumpers, or when they're dead making sheepskin coats for second-hand car dealers. *Bono*

Visit the west of Ireland where men are men and sheep are nervous. *Graffiti spotted in Connemara pub*

Mick: "Did you know it takes twelve sheep to make a jumper?"
Paddy: "I didn't even know sheep could knit." **Dusty Young**

How did Ireland's worst shepherd count his sheep? "One sheep, two sheep, three sheep, another one, another one, another one . . ." **Terry Adlam**

# SHOES

I once won a pair of sneakers off Kurt Cobain when we were playing Russian Roulette. **Sean Hughes**

My book *Emily's Shoes* was about shoe fetishism but the reviewers preferred to see it as a novel about urban realism. I'd prefer to be remembered as a shoe fetishist than an urban realist. **Dermot Bolger**

You know you've got a problem with shoes if you've just bought them but refuse to wear them because you don't want to damage them. **Marian Keyes**

Murphy was trying on a new pair of shoes but he wasn't feeling very comfortable in them. "You have them on the wrong feet," the salesman told him. Murphy wasn't having any of it. "They're the only feet I have," he insisted. **Noel V. Ginnity**

Large Boots Reduced. **Sign on shoe shop window**

She was about as moving as Imelda Marcos pleading for a new pair of shoes. **Michael Redmond on Madonna's efforts to portray a missionary in Shanghai Surprise**

"Nolan, do you think I'm getting crow's feet?" asked Nora as they prepared to go out for the evening. "You might be," said Nolan, "but just keep your shoes on and no one will notice." **Terry Adlam**

How would you recognize a Kerryman at a board meeting? He's the one wearing the pin-striped wellingtons. **Hugh Leonard**

I saw this sign on a cut-price shop: "Shoes For Sale. One Owner Only". *Cathal O'Shannon*

Many a man that could rule a hundred million strangers with an iron hand is careful to take off his shoes in the front hallway when he comes home late at night. *Finley Peter Dunne*

# SHOPPING

I once went to a furniture shop with my wife to buy a coffee table. We couldn't find one we both liked so we compromised and bought one we both hated. *Michael Redmond*

Remember, Tesco shoppers, every Lidl helps. *Michael Cullen*

Dunnes Stores introduced Ireland to the concept of the supermarket with the opening of its store in Cornelscourt in 1961. There are now two supermarkets for every person in the country. *Donal O'Dea*

"Hey missus, are you selling them oranges?"
    "No, luv, I'm going to give them their civil rights and liberate them this afternoon."
*Paul Ryan*

An Irishman goes into a chip shop and says, "Fish and chips twice." The guy behind the counter says, "I heard you the first time." *Jack Cruise*

I like going into newsagent's and saying, "Excuse me, is that Mars bar for sale?" When they say yes, I say, "OK, I might be back later but I have a few other ones to see." *Michael Redmond*

The biggest cultural annoyance in Ireland today is supermarket trolleys that won't go straight. *Maria Doyle Kennedy*

Most of the time I love Amazon. I like the fact that they don't bombard me with emails offering me everything from bowtie stretchers with inbuilt coal scuttles to the back catalogue of *Hannah Montana*. Instead they only send me emails about stuff they think I might actually be interested in. Earlier this year they alerted me to the fact that they were selling box-sets of television drama serials for half nothing and I managed to pick up the entire run of *The Sopranos* and three seasons of *Mad Men* for less than £40. One day I might even get around to taking the cellophane wrapping off them. ***Fiona Looney***

I buy houses like people buy cans of tuna when they fear an impending food shortage. If the *Big Issue* deals with the problems of the homeless, I need a magazine called *Tiny Issues* which deals with the problems of the chronically over-housed. ***Graham Norton***

Shopping centres are the new churches. But maybe in the next generation churches will be the new shopping centres. ***John Waters***

Don't run out of milk in LA. The nearest shop is half an hour away. ***Deirdre O'Kane***

If shopping is the new religion, as a working woman you need to be an atheist. ***Terry Prone***

I suspected I was suffering from shopping bulimia. It seemed like I was always splurging on stuff and then trying to return it. ***Marian Keyes***

Closed For Altercations. ***Notice on Belfast shop***

If men liked shopping they'd call it research. ***Twink***

"Get out of my shop." The manager of FCUK is angry. Funny how you can touch a nerve just by pointing out a simple spelling mistake in a shop sign. ***Kevin McAleer***

Shelley and I fly to San Francisco and there are amazingly long queues in all the stores. People are shoplifting to save time, not money. ***Joe O'Connor***

I remember going into Terry Brady's shop in Fairyhouse some years ago to buy some of his delicious buns. I came out with a motorized buggy. On another occasion I went in for an ice cream and came out with a chainsaw. ***Sean Boylan***

# SHOUTING

I shout a lot. It might be a load of bollocks I'm shouting but it's a funny thing about shouting a lot of bollocks: it makes people respond. *Mick McCarthy*

I don't like watching golf on TV. The players can't hear you shout. *John O'Neill*

If you want your girlfriend to scream while you're having sex, ring her up and tell her. *Martin Tierney*

# SILENCE

There are very few people who don't become more interesting when they stop talking. *Mary Lowry*

Let this be a silent protest that will be heard throughout the country. *Tim Leddin*

The three hermits had lived together for four years when one of them spoke up. "That was a fine black horse that went by." Three years later one of the others said, "It was a white horse." Ten years afterwards the third member had his say: "If there's going to be bickering I won't stay." *Joan Larson Kelly*

Sean quit as a mime artist. It's only now he can talk about it. *Michael Cullen*

I believe in the discipline of silence and could talk for hours about it. *George Bernard Shaw*

I need a thousand years of silence, my own above all. *Samuel Beckett*

Research on male attitudes to oral sex found that 70 per cent of men find it sexually stimulating, 20 per cent find it relaxing, and one in ten enjoy the peace and quiet. *Michael Cullen*

Men are like bagpipes. No sound comes from them until they're full. *Éilis Ní Dhuibhne*

Arthur Griffith was that rare phenomenon: a silent Irishman. *Winston Churchill*

We should silence anyone who opposes the right to freedom of speech. *Sir Boyle Roche*

When we were walking past the Bailey it reminded her that we were twenty-three years married today. "What do you propose?" she asked. "Three minutes' silence," said I. *Oliver St John Gogarty*

An IRA man appeared on *Mastermind* once but came away with a zero score. On his way out of the studio he was beaming. "Relax, lads," he assured his friends, "they didn't get a thing out of me." *Bernard O'Sullivan*

# SIMILARITIES

I know this man who's dating a twin. "How do you tell the difference?" I asked him. "That's easy," he said. "Her brother has a moustache." *Joe Cuddy*

Yesterday I thought I saw my brother on the street and he thought he saw me, but when both of us got up close we realized it was neither of us. *Shane McCarthy*

What do clitorises and anniversaries have in common? Men always miss them. *Deirdre O'Kane*

Male genitalia roughly resemble bagpipes with hair. *Dylan Moran*

A girl told me I reminded her of the sea. I said, "What do you mean — rough and rugged?" She said, "No — you make me sick." *Jimmy Cricket*

Even in a frock I look like Fred Flintstone. *Bono*

# SIN

If you think about it, some of the first sins we ever committed were probably the lies we were forced to invent in the darkness of the confession box for our first confession. *Róisín Ingle*

I think of my body as a sort of tabernacle of sin. This preoccupation makes for a greater excitement in the act of love. *Edna O'Brien*

The Blessed Virgin conceived without sinning. I'd like to sin without conceiving. *Stephen Behan*

"Father," I'm often asked, "is it a sin to sleep with someone?" I always answer, "No, it is not. It's only a sin when you stay awake." *Fr Pat Buckley*

The major sin is the sin of being born. *Samuel Beckett*

When I was a child we were terrorized by the idea of "mortallers", mortal sins. If you had one of these lads on your soul when you died it was enough to keep you in hell for all eternity. Which, as the man said, is a long time to be waiting for a bus. *Lee Dunne*

An Irish person sees a sunny day and goes, "It'd be a sin to go to work on a day like this." Only Irish people can turn the word "sin" to their favour. *Des Bishop*

Have you heard about the ultra-modern church with a special quick confessional for people with six sins or less? *Sean Kilroy*

That's not a sin, my child, it's merely a mistake. *Bray's Fr Healy to a plain girl who confessed the "sin" of vanity to him after looking at herself in a mirror*

# SINGING

A Canadian club offered me $1,000 to sing. For doing the same thing in Dublin I get thrown out of pubs. *Brendan Behan*

Why does Ronan Keating persist in a style of singing that suggests someone is pinching his nose? *Michelle Dwyer*

I don't normally sing, and when I sing I don't sing normally. *Danny Cummins*

Last night I was asked to sing solo — so low I couldn't be heard. *Jimmy Cricket*

Rory Gallagher sang like a guitar. *Gerry McAvoy*

When you're in the last ditch, the only thing left is to sing. *Samuel Beckett*

Never try to teach a pig to sing. It wastes your time and annoys the pig. *Seamus O'Leary*

If women's genitalia could sing, they'd sound like Enya. *Dylan Moran*

Terry Griffiths sings like a sheep with a sore throat. *Dennis Taylor*

Beyoncé bellows out her songs like a bad-tempered bull who's caught his behind on some barbed wire. *Mick the Maverick*

Daniel O'Donnell once worked as a dishwasher but he didn't last long because he sang too much while he worked. Surely that qualified as incredible foresight on the part of the kitchen staff. *Dave O'Connell*

The reason I close my eyes when I'm singing is because I have the words of the songs written on the inside of my eyelashes. *Christy Moore*

# SLEEP

I once bought a device to stop me drinking. It was a tape you played while you were asleep. It worked. I stopped drinking while I was sleeping. *George Best*

I've been pressing the flesh so much over the years I now do it in my sleep. *Gerry Ryan*

"Does he snore in his sleep, luv?"
    "I don't know yet. We've only been married three days."
*Paul Ryan*

I use our songs to wake myself up. It's like sticking a needle into your leg after it's gone to sleep. *Bono*

Getting up in the middle of the night to appear on morning TV isn't easy. One suggestion I was offered to save time was to sleep in my clothes. *Eamonn Holmes*

I only sleep rough when I'm too drunk to care. Sober, I become terrified by thinking of how accomplished rats are at climbing park benches. *Paul McGrath*

Sleep is an excellent way of listening to an opera. *James Stephens*

Britney Spears was never smacked as a child. Well, maybe one or two grams to get her to sleep at night. *Michael Cullen*

Then there was the Irishman who used to snore so loud he woke himself up. But he cured himself. He sleeps in the next room now. *Peter Hornby*

Many are called, but few get up. *Maureen Potter*

I spent a third of my life drunk, a third with a hangover and a third sleeping. *Richard Harris*

I have no objection to long, tedious plays. I always feel fresh when I wake up at the end. *John B. Keane*

There were so many in my family I never slept alone until I was married. *Brian Behan*

Call it superstition if you like but I just won't sleep thirteen to a bed on a Friday night. **Sean Kilroy**

One of the many things they don't teach you in school is how to sleep in a tree. Nine times out of ten, with the Irish weather, you can also manage a shower. **Kevin McAleer**

# SLIPS OF THE TONGUE

If Europe stays still it will start going backwards. **Paddy Ashdown**

It was a bit like Einstein explaining his theory of evolution. **Mary Coughlan**

The Taoiseach has determined that during the lifetime of this Dáil there will be an abortion on the referendum issue. **David McCullough**

John Bruton is a convicted politician – I mean a politician of conviction. **Nora Owen**

Zidane is about to be given a house with a swimming pool and a gardener thrown in. **Good Morning Ireland**

You just hit the nail on the hammer. **Dick Roche**

# SMILES

Terry Wogan has a bionic smile. My guess is that the BBC built him in their workshops under licence from General Dynamics. Unfortunately they had to skimp slightly on the brain. **Clive James**

It was an Irish proverb to "Beware of an Englishman's smile", but I've learned that an Irishman's smile can be a damn sight more dangerous. **Sean O'Casey**

If you want to wake up smiling, go to bed with a coathanger in your mouth. *Cecil Sheridan*

The first time I ever saw Queen Elizabeth smiling in all the years I've been in England was when she went to Ireland. Then a week later Barack Obama was smiling during his visit there. The day after that, the Queen met Obama in London and neither of them were smiling. We have an anti-authority undercurrent when it comes to pomp. *Dara O'Briain*

When Irish eyes are smiling ... watch your step. *Gerald Kersh*

I don't know Phil Mickelson but I've seen him smile and that's quite enough to put me off wanting to know him. *David Feherty*

Janet Jackson has the sort of smile you just know she's rehearsed and rehearsed. Think of a second-hand car dealer trying to beat an NTC deadline. And then add about a thousand watts. *Paul Byrne*

Robert Peel's smile was like the silver plate on a coffin. *John Philpott Curran*

Raquel Welch has a smile like a razorblade and a personality to match. *Terry Wogan*

Melanie Griffith is just about bearable now that her face has been so worked over by plastic surgeons she can't stretch to a smile any more. *Martina Devlin*

When Frank Stapleton wakes up every morning, the first thing he does is race to the bathroom, look in the mirror and smile. Just to get it over with. *Tony Cascarino*

Jeffrey Archer smiles like a man who's had emergency corrective facial surgery in a Third World country. *Joe O'Connor*

When Donal O'Grady smiles, you can hear the cello in *Jaws*. *Keith Duggan on the former Cork hurling manager*

# SMOKING

I love to smoke so much I'm going to have a tracheotomy so I can have two at a time. *Denis Leary*

Dear Mammy, I'm glad to hear you've given up sweets for Lent. I was going to start smoking so I could give up cigarettes. I hear they're really bad for you. I read somewhere that nine out of ten guinea pigs subjected to cigarette smoke died. Well they should have just taken away their cigarettes in the first place. *Jimmy Cricket*

When I die I want to be buried in the No Smoking section of the cemetery. *Spike Milligan*

I heard a joke that goes, "Did you hear Daniel O'Donnell got a girl into trouble? He told her mother she was smoking." *Daniel O'Donnell*

I like to sit in the Smoking section of restaurants and go up to non-smokers and say, "Excuse me, do you mind, this is the Smoking section." *Michael Redmond*

I have two very expensive vices. I smoke cigars and I live in Ireland. *Ronnie Drew*

I was blowing smoke-rings out of my cigarette one night in a pub when a Red Indian came up to me and said, "What did you just say?" *Jimeoin*

Smoking shortens your cigarettes. *Shane MacGowan*

I've decided to give up women and cigarettes for Lent. I know it's not going to be easy because I'm a twenty-a-day man. And I like cigarettes too. *Fergal Dwyer*

It is now illegal to buy or sell packs of ten cigarettes, so any child who used to buy a ten-pack will now buy a twenty instead. Congratulations, legislators, on your incredible bid to increase under-age smoking. *Richard O'Connor*

Over a cigarette my friend warns me that if I could see my lungs I'd quit smoking. I point out that if I could see my lungs

I'd have approximately three seconds to live — just enough time to light up. *Sean Hughes*

If you eliminate smoking and gambling you'll be amazed to find that almost all of an Englishman's pleasures are mostly shared by his dog. *George Bernard Shaw*

I once knew a woman who had her husband cremated and then mixed his ashes with grass and smoked him. She said it was the best he'd made her feel in years. *Maureen Murphy*

Paddy the Irishman, Paddy the Englishman and Paddy the Scotsman all got five years in prison, but they were each given a wish before they were sentenced. The Englishman decided he wanted a big sexy blonde, the Scotsman opted for a hundred bottles of whisky, and the Irishman said he'd like ten thousand cigarettes. Five years later they all came out one by one. The Englishman was utterly knackered from his romantic entanglements, the Scotsman was staggering all over the place hiccuping and belching, and then came Paddy, looking rather frustrated as he whispered through dry lips, "Anybody got a light?" *Joe Lynch*

# SNOBBERY

Yeats is becoming so aristocratic he's evicting imaginary tenants. *Oliver St John Gogarty*

Dublin snobbery — fur coat and no knickers. *Noel Purcell*

An Irish snob is a man who goes to the opera with a copy of the script, a packet of chewing gum and two sleeping pills. *Peter Cagney*

The great quest of his life was to find the perfect butler. He used to send wine back even if it came from his own cellar. *Jared Harris on his father Richard*

There was a lot of snobbery in the drug world. Dopeheads looked down on cokeheads, cokeheads looked down on smackheads, and smackheads looked down on everyone. **Boy George**

I'm not a snob but I wear a bowler hat in the bath because you never know who might call. **Spike Milligan**

# SNOOKER

Steve Davis is so boring, he takes valium as a *stimulant*. **Dennis Taylor**

The beauty of Alex Higgins is that he's magnificently ignorant. **Dennis Taylor**

I love Sheffield. It's full of melancholy, happy-go-lucky people. **Alex Higgins**

Sometimes the deciding frame's always the toughest to win. **Dennis Taylor**

There's more charisma in my little finger. Frankly, I'd prefer to have a drink with Idi Amin. **Alex Higgins on Steve Davis**

The win has made him so conceited he's now going to night school to learn how to spell his name. **Frank Carson on Dennis Taylor after Taylor won the 1985 World Snooker Championship**

Dennis Taylor looks like Mickey Mouse with a welding shield. **Eddie Charlton**

During snooker's heyday I took the game up. I remember entering my first hall. I went over to the cue rack and picked up what I later realized was an extension cue. I was told to break off and I ran towards the table with what felt like a pole vault. I missed the ball completely. I was gutted. It has to be pointed out that I'm a dreamer and when I take up something new I expect with patience and work to become world champion. Unfortunately after my first shot the owner of the club banned me for life. Anyway, I look stupid in a waistcoat. **Sean Hughes**

Did you hear about the man who threw a petrol bomb at Alex Higgins? He drank it. *Dennis Taylor*

The best advice I can give anyone approaching a tense match is to wear brown trousers. *Ken Doherty*

There's no way he can't go into the final session behind. *Dennis Taylor*

On the eighth day God created Alex Higgins. *T-shirt logo*

I played so bad I was lucky to get nil. *Ken Doherty after being beaten 5–0 in a match*

The balls don't forgive. *Fergal O'Brien*

The only way he can beat him is to stay level, or one frame behind. *Dennis Taylor*

I haven't played as well as that since London Bridge was a lighthouse. *Pat Houlihan*

My last cue had more tips than a head waiter. *Dennis Taylor*

Shane Filan said his highest break was 47 but he didn't specify if it was for snooker or darts. *Ken Doherty*

When I potted that last black against Steve Davis to win the world title in 1985, I heard various Protestants converted to Catholicism on the spot. *Dennis Taylor*

# SOBRIETY

After *Camelot* I sobered up. I found it better to wake up feeling a success than clawing hungover through a fog of self-disgust wondering if I, or some other fellow, still had the same number of teeth we went to bed with. *Richard Harris*

One knows where one is with a drunk, but teetotalism in an Irishman is unnatural. If it's not checked he becomes unpredictable. *Hugh Leonard*

Years ago the order would go, "Four pints, two gin and tonics, three large Paddies and a Cidona for your man." "Your man" was thereby marked as being outside the tribe. Nowadays it's just as often the reverse. *Maeve Binchy*

I'm a strict teetotaller, not taking anything between drinks. *James Joyce*

Now must I look as sober and demure as a whore at a christening. *George Farquhar*

St Stephen's Night down the country is the biggest night of the year. Negotiating it when you're not drinking is a test Navy Seals should have to undergo. It makes Glastonbury and Electric Picnic look like the baby room in a crèche. *Colette Fitzpatrick*

Irishmen take the pledge not to drink at the age of twelve . . . and every four years thereafter. *Henry Spalding*

I hear he's giving up the drink. Well fancy that. I'd say his lips will start to put on weight for the lack of exercise. *Paul Ryan*

A bride held up a sozzled groom at the altar. "Take him away," said the priest, "and bring him back when he's sober." "But please, your reverence," the bride pleaded, "when he's sober he won't come." *Sean McCann*

Who would want to discuss immortality when he's sober? *Joseph Brady*

When St Patrick first came to Ireland there was no word in the native language to express sobriety. *Oliver St John Gogarty*

I was sober enough to know I was drunk. *John B. Keane*

During the 1960s and 1970s I don't think I was ever sober when I appeared on TV. *Mary Kenny*

While it has never been adequately proven that sobriety harms the creative faculty, it's hardly worth the risk of finding out. *Ian MacPherson*

He'll probably never write a good play again. *George Bernard Shaw on Eugene O'Neill after he heard he'd given up drinking*

# SONGS

The eyes close and you know you're screwed. Another perfectly good night in the pub is ruined because some tone-deaf culchie is going to sing "The Fields of Athenry". The First World War didn't last as long as this song. The culchie whines through his nose and you think what you wouldn't give right now to be bayoneted to death by a platoon of livid Germans. *Pat Fitzpatrick*

Apparently it was against the law to release an Elvis Presley picture without songs. *Philip Dunne*

The first twenty-five verses are the best. *Hugh Malone on an old Irish air*

Even today, no Irish celebration is complete without a rendition of "Danny Boy", the words of which describe a woman saying goodbye to a war-bound lover, foreseeing her own death before he returns and looking forward to a time when he can join her in the grave. Of course not all Irish songs are as cheerful as this. *Frank McNally*

The theme song from *A Streetcar Named Desire* should be "The Lady is a Tram". *Hugh Leonard*

My first attempt at getting rid of house mice proved futile. I played Cat Stevens repeatedly. It seems it works on humans but not rodents. *Jacqueline Kavanagh*

I have yet to record an album. I do have photo albums but I rarely listen to them these days. Who has the time? *Karl Spain*

"Away in a Manger" is a song so sickly and revolting, no self-respecting adult should be able to reach the second verse without feeling an uncontrollable urge to vomit. *Eilis O'Hanlon*

# SPECULATIONS

If all economists were laid end to end, they would not reach a conclusion. *George Bernard Shaw*

If God had really been in favour of decimalization, there would only have been ten disciples. *Sean Gaffney*

If that shot had been on target it might have troubled the keeper. *George Hamilton*

If the Dutch lived in Ireland it would be the richest country in the world. If the Irish lived in Holland they would surely drown. *Tadhg Hayes*

Have you ever seen a hairdresser with a decent haircut? *Sean Hughes*

If Ireland had scored more goals they would have won the match. *Jimmy Magee*

If God didn't want me to have any more children he wouldn't let me drink on Saturday nights. *Hal Roach*

If I hadn't written *Angela's Ashes* I would have died begging. *Frank McCourt*

If the Three Wise Men arrived here tonight, the likelihood is that they'd be deported. *Proinsias de Rossa on Ireland's strict immigration regulations in 1997*

If Watergate happened in Ireland, we'd all know who Deep Throat was but Nixon would still be in power. *Mark Little*

If God wanted us to believe in him, why did he invent logic? *David Feherty*

# SPEECHES

The brain is a wonderful thing. It never stops working from the time you're born until the moment you stand up to make a speech. *Dan O'Dowd*

My one claim to originality among Irishmen is that I never made a speech. *George Moore*

The most popular speaker is the one who sits down before he stands up. *J. P. Mahaffy*

Someone once quipped, "Give an Irishman an inch and he'll park his car on it." It may equally be said that if one gives an Irishman – or woman – sixty seconds, he or she will squeeze a twenty-minute speech into it. *Hugh Leonard*

Speeches are like babies: easy to conceive but hard to deliver. *Pat O'Malley*

She asked me if the speech was over. "Yes," I replied, "but he's still talking." *Niall Toibin*

I hold the record for the world's shortest speech and I don't want to ruin my reputation. Good night. *William Trevor after receiving the PEN Literary Award in 2002*

The most important thing in a wedding speech is for the best man not to use the word "motherfucker". Unless it's an Irish wedding. *Ed Byrne*

One of the most enjoyable weddings I was at was the one where the father of the bride selflessly had a heart attack during the soup course. The rest of the dinner was cancelled, along with the speeches. We were profoundly grateful. *David Slattery*

I now want to talk about something very close to my heart. My liver. *Sean Hughes*

# SPEED

A few of them moved faster than they ever did on the pitch. *Former Republic of Ireland Football Manager, Brian Kerr, reminiscing on a night he spent in a Dublin hotel in November 2003 when his squad were roused by a burglary and a bullet fired into the ceiling*

They say the new striker I'm marking is fast. Maybe, but how fast can he limp? *Mick McCarthy*

Casey: "I know I was speeding, officer, but I wanted to get home before I ran out of petrol." *Hal Roach*

I'm not quick. If I go out running, women with prams pass me out. *Mick McCarthy*

The foreman loaded Fitzpatrick's wheelbarrow to the brim with lead piping. Fitzpatrick scratched his head. "Would you mind, sir," he said, "tying a few concrete blocks to my ankles?" "What for?" the foreman asked. "To stop me breaking into a run," Fitzpatrick told him. *Joan Larson Kelly*

Last night I ate in a French restaurant. I had snails. It took me three hours to walk home afterwards. *Jimmy Cricket*

A lady driver was stopped by a motorcycle cop. She said to him bitterly, "If I was speeding, so were you." *Hal Roach*

In philosophy, if you aren't moving at a snail's pace you aren't moving at all. *Iris Murdoch*

The Koreans were quicker in terms of speed. *Mark Lawrenson*

He's not fast but he's quick. *Tommy Smith*

# SPITTING

A learned old schoolmaster in Cork was once described to me as a man who could spit in nine languages. *Maurice Healy*

The Irish postal system dropped its proposed series of stamps depicting famous Irish lawyers after they found people were confused as to which side they were supposed to spit on. *Michael Cullen*

Kerry cornerboys are most renowned for their habit of competing with one another to see who has the longest spit. *John B. Keane*

"Hey Paudge, do I hear you spitting in the vase on the mantelpiece?"

   "No, Brigid, but I'm gettin' closer all the time." *Doug Anderson*

# SPORT

If you can't make it as a sporting star you become a coach. If you can't coach you become a journalist. If you're not able to be a journalist you introduce *Grandstand*. *Des Lynam*

Advice to kids: Get high on sport, not drugs. But if there are no sports in your neighbourhood, get high on drugs. *George Carlin*

Try to hate your opponent. If you're playing your grandmother, try to beat her fifty to nothing. If she already has three, try to beat her fifty to three. *Danny McGoorty*

There were a number of reasons my sporting career was cut short. Lack of time, a disinclination to practise, and the fact that I was totally and utterly crap. *Michael O'Driscoll*

You can say what you like about the servicemen amputees from Iraq and Afghanistan, but we're going to have a fucking great Paralympic team in 2012. *Jimmy Carr*

While the state of British sport may be mostly serious but never hopeless, the state of Irish sport, although usually hopeless, is never serious. *Noel Henderson*

Early yesterday morning Sky TV informed us that Colin Montgomerie played hockey in his youth. Two words: "mind" and "boggles". *Mary Hannigan*

# STAMINA

I read that when Sting has sex it goes on for, like, five hours. In my book that means he mustn't be very good. *Ross O'Carroll-Kelly*

Golf is popular because it's like sex. You can go on for ever. Older people prefer it to tennis because in tennis there's no love after forty, much less a ride. *David Feherty*

Sometimes I could make sex last up to forty minutes. Mind you, that was including the bus journey to her house. *Sean Hughes*

# STATISTICS

Eighty-four per cent of statistics are made up on the spot. *Mick Glynn*

If only 60 per cent of people believe all statistical statements presented to them are true, does that mean only 60 per cent will also only believe this one I'm writing now? *Fran Dempsey*

They say you only use 10 per cent of your brain. What about the other 10 per cent? *Sil Fox*

Thirteen out of every ten women prefer chocolate to maths. **Steven Scally**

I only know 25 per cent of Bertie Ahern's mind, and that's 24 per cent more than anyone else. **Charlie McCreevy**

The people I work with live, breathe, eat, drink, shit and fuck ratings. **The late TV broadcaster Gerry Ryan**

I read recently that someone has sex in Ireland every seven seconds. He must be an awful randy bastard. **Colin O'Shea**

In the most recent census, 27 per cent of Monkstown's eighteen- to twenty-five-year-old males listed kite-surfing as their full-time occupation, while 32 per cent listed it as their religion. **Ross O'Carroll-Kelly**

Never run anything or anyone down to a person you don't know. Statistics show that nine times out of ten the person you're speaking to will be the mother/sister/best friend of the one you're bitching about. This is very bad for your health. Especially if they deck you. **Anne Marie Scanlon**

Statistics state that during a normal day a bus conductor will walk twenty-six miles. Why doesn't he catch a bus? **Peter Cagney**

I only want three children because I heard every fourth one born in the world is Chinese. **Fidelma Mooney**

# STATUES

Dublin's O'Connell Street contains statues of Daniel O'Connell, Charles Stewart Parnell and Lord Nelson, three of history's best-known adulterers. **W. B. Yeats**

Anyone that got money out of a priest ought to have a statue put up to them. **Frank O'Connor**

The only way to deal with Daniel O'Connell is to hang him and then erect a statue under the gallows. **Sydney Smith**

# STOMACHS

When you get to my age and you suck in your stomach, a second one appears under it. "Hello, I'm Jeff, your pointless second stomach. I'm a present from death." *Dylan Moran*

I developed a fair old beer belly from spending too much time on the high stool. Hyacinth put her hand knowingly on my stomach and boasted, "If that was on my mam, she'd be pregnant." "It was," I replied, "and she is." *James McKeon*

The only reason I have a reputation as a strong silent type is because I find it difficult to talk while I'm trying to hold my stomach in. *Michael Redmond*

The beer belly is one of our most ubiquitous national symbols, and growing your own is very fashionable. A beer belly can be achieved by drinking beer. However, chips, curries, bacon rolls, Taytos, Cadbury's chocolate, ice cream and big feeds of hairy bacon will also help. A beer belly is handy because you can, for example, rest a can of beer on it, leaving your hands free for scoffing fish and chips or to operate the remote control for the telly. The ideal beer belly should stick straight out at a right angle to your body. If it hangs pendulously above your belt you can make it firmer by stuffing in more beer and curries. Your beer belly should prevent you from seeing anything below your navel, which is essentially a valve to prevent you from actually bursting. Sex becomes impossible for the beer belly couple, thereby allowing them more time for eating and drinking. *David Slattery*

These days I could wear my stomach as a very attractive kilt. *Joe O'Connor*

There's no freedom as sweet as the freedom of a belly released. *John B. Keane*

# STRENGTH

Any team is only as strong as its weakest link and that's been our strength throughout — there hasn't been a weakest link. *Mark Lawrenson*

His strength, or strengths, are his strength. *Boxing commentator Mick Dowling*

# SUCCESS

It took Ireland thirty years to become an overnight success. *Bertie Ahern*

Success is killing me. I think a man should be allowed fame for a month and then be given a pension and allowed to retire. *Brendan Behan*

The James Joyce centenary was so successful we're going to have one every year. *Sean Kilroy*

Success and failure on the public level never mattered much to me. In fact I feel much more at home with the latter, having breathed deep of its vivifying air all my writing life. *Samuel Beckett*

When people wrote me off after Boyzone broke up I used to say to them, "I'll be successful, pal, even if it's only to piss you off." *Keith Duffy*

People have always loved the Irish because we're underwhelmed by success and hugely entertained by shouting abuse in the street. Which only goes to show you what a collection of shallow arseholes the rest of the world is. *Fiona Looney*

"Art for art's sake" means, in practice, "Success for money's sake". *George Bernard Shaw*

Peter O'Toole has been nominated for more Academy Awards than anyone else in Ireland but has won none of them. This endears him to the Irish since they get uneasy when people enjoy too much success. There's a tradition in the country of regarding high achievers as suffering from some rare mental disorder. *Terry Eagleton*

Success to me meant not having to set up my own drums any more. *Larry Mullen of U2*

# SUFFERING

If suffering brings wisdom I would wish to be less wise. *W. B. Yeats*

When Mel Gibson was asked how he got the actor playing Jesus in his film *The Passion* to convey so much suffering, he said, "I forced him to watch *Lethal Weapon 4*." *Conan O'Brien*

# SUGGESTIONS

CBBC Television asked me to contribute to their "Do Something Different" campaign to stimulate the imagination of the young viewer. I've suggested that they smile. *Terry Wogan*

There'd be less litter in Ireland if blind people were given pointed sticks. *Michael Cullen*

When you're trying to find something, it's always the last place you look. So look in the last place first. *Michael O'Keeffe*

A pedestrian ought to be legally allowed to toss at least one hand grenade at a motorist every day. *Brendan Francis*

We can radically reduce carbon emissions by joining al-Qaeda. Who else can save the planet from airlines, oil companies and overpopulation? *Abie Philbin Bowman*

I don't approve of people going on rants. I'd much rather see them putting all that energy into making a piece of art. How brilliant it would be if your boss wanted to have a go at you about how you're always late and instead of burning your ear off he had to put in the hard hours at the canvas. Pubs could be the new galleries. Instead of trying to shout over the din of other ranting drunks, everyone would arrive down with their paintings entitled "Why I Hate Noel Edmonds" or "Why No Girl Should Ever Wear Ugg Boots". You could wander round appreciating everyone's point of view while an old man in the corner did a piece of interpretive dance called "I Blame the Foreigners". *Jarlath Regan*

Many hands make light work, so put them all up to the bulb in the event of a power failure. *Michael Sheridan*

Last year the London Underground lost £40 million in unpaid fares. All they have to do next year is cut the fares in half and they'll save £20 million. *Dave Allen*

It would be easy to eliminate binge drinking in Ireland. Just run a poster that says "Binge drinking – it's very English, isn't it?" *Dara O'Briain*

Life is moving too fast for the mind today and the mind is going nowhere. Maybe we should evolve backwards. *Alice Taylor*

# SUICIDE

Drink and sex killed my father. He couldn't get either so he shot himself. *Dusty Young*

I was going to kill myself by taking a bottle of aspirin but after the first two I felt much better. *Seamus O'Leary*

Pat Murphy tried to commit suicide by hanging himself with a length of elastic. He died of concussion. **Hal Roach**

Russian novels go on for about 942 pages. On page 920 Boris the peasant decides he wants to commit suicide and you find yourself wishing he did it on page 4. **Frank McCourt**

Suicide bombers are promised seventy-two virgins. One would have done me. **Ardal O'Hanlon**

My favourite optimist is the man who threw himself off the Empire State Building. As he passed the forty-second floor, a window washer heard him saying, "So far so good." **John McGahern**

Commit suicide the Irish way. Slip arsenic in your tea while you're not looking. **Seamus O'Leary**

Different marriages work in different ways. Adolf Hitler and Eva Braun got one day of married life together in a bomb shelter and then committed suicide. Fine if that's what they found worked best for them. **John O'Farrell**

Did you hear about the Irishman who killed himself to get revenge on the Samaritans for taking him off the danger list? **T. P. McKenna**

I went to Australia to get away from suicide bombers. You'd never get a suicide bomber in Australia. They'd all get jet lag and just want to lie down. **Sean Hughes**

Suicide bombers would never take off in Ireland. He'd be there with a bale of briquettes in his jacket looking for a light. **Tommy Tiernan**

# SURGERY

In New York when someone puts a knife in your chest you give them money. In LA when someone puts a knife in your chest you give them money and then say, "Thanks, doc, now I can buy a bigger bra." **Deirdre Sullivan**

When it comes to sushi or plastic surgery, never be attracted by a bargain. *Graham Norton*

There's a sign outside the Drogheda hospital that says "Guard Dogs Operating". Personally I think that's taking the medical cutbacks a bit far. *Gene Fitzpatrick*

This month the question on our voxpop was, "If you were having plastic surgery, what would you get done?" One G. Nolan of Malahide said he would become an actual dickhead. *Trevor White*

Before Botox, if I frowned, staff cowered in corners and whimpered softly. For several months after, I can't frown at all. Makes for much better workplace relationships. *Terry Prone*

Kenny Rogers has had more tucks than a Jury's Inn bedsheet. *Michael Cullen*

Charlie Finley's heart operation took eight hours, and seven of those were spent looking for it. *Steve McCatty*

Never lend anyone money for plastic surgery. You won't be able to recognize them when it comes time to collect. *Shaun Connors*

Murphy liked drinking so much he got his toes amputated so he could stand closer to the counter. *Joe Cuddy*

The day after a facelift you look as if someone inserted your face in the middle of a car tyre instead of the hubcap and inflated it. *Terry Prone*

I performed some surgery on my wife last Christmas. I cut up her Visa card. *Frank Kelly*

It has become so acceptable for people to inject botulism into their foreheads, pump collagen into their lips and filler into their cheeks to look younger, that nobody even remarks on it. The trout pout has become a fact of life. Foreheads so smooth you could land a small aircraft on them are par for the course. *Mary McEvoy*

# SUSPICION

My wife is difficult. If I come home early she thinks I'm looking for something. If I come home late she thinks I've already had it. **Brendan Grace**

I began to get worried about the fact that my wife might be having an affair when we moved from Dublin to Donegal and ended up with the same milkman. **Conal Gallen**

A police force should be above the suspicion of Caesar's wife. **Good Morning Ireland**

My wife is great at doing bird imitations. She watches me like a hawk. **Kevin Marron**

Morality consists of suspecting other people of not being legally married. **George Bernard Shaw**

# SWIMMING

I can't swim. I can't drive either. I was going to learn to drive but then I thought: What if I crash into a lake? **Dylan Moran**

If one synchronized swimmer drowns, do they all have to? **Milo O'Shea**

I can't help noticing that nobody blesses themselves any more before getting into the water. I think this has happened since the introduction of lifeguards. **Pat Ingoldsby**

A friend of mine swims off the coast of Waterford. He was telling me recently he was swimming back to the harbour when he saw two American tourists. So he gets back to the harbour wall just below the Yanks and shouts out, "Is this Wales?" To which they reply, "No, this is Ireland." "Oh no," he says, "I must have missed it." And he kicks off the harbour and swims out to sea. **Short Back and Sides**

While vacationing in Africa I got to swim with sharks — which didn't scare me after Riverdance. *Michael Flatley*

I learned to swim early. I had to sleep with five bedwetters growing up. *Noel V. Ginnity*

Shouldn't a swimming pool be called a swimming 'ool? The "p" is silent. *Sean Kilroy*

Should a mighty whale swallow you, keep right on swimming because the hole down the far end is just as big and you'll be out again in no time. *Pat Ingoldsby*

My friend is a wonderful swimmer. He used to be a postman in Vienna. *Joe Cuddy*

# TALENT

If you have it and you know it, you have it. If you don't have it and you think you have it, you have it. But if you have it and you don't know you have it, you don't have it. *Jackie Gleason*

When I discovered I had absolutely no talent or vocation for any job I joined the Civil Service. *Moss Keane*

There are only half a dozen people in the world with that kind of talent. In my estimation he was a one-off. *Danny La Rue*

You can't buy talent like Robbie Keane, and even if you could it would cost you a lot of money. *Mick McCarthy*

The problem with Ireland is that it's a country full of genius but with absolutely no talent. *Hugh Leonard*

# TALKING

"Isn't he a marvellous conversationalist?"
  "That he is. Faith, I could sit and listen to him for minutes."
**Henry Spalding**

In Ireland a writer is looked upon as a failed conversationalist. **George Moore**

I see people in terms of dialogue. People *are* their talk. **Roddy Doyle**

I once asked a girl for oral sex. She thought that meant just talking about it. **Frank Carson**

From my earliest days I have enjoyed an attractive impediment in my speech. I have never permitted the use of the word "stammer". I can't say it myself. **Patrick Campbell**

My mother wasn't very complimentary about my writing career. After seeing my first play, her reaction was, "Too much oul' talk." **Hugh Leonard**

Poor Lord Montlake. He had only two topics of conversation – his gout and his wife. I could never quite make out which of the two he was talking about. **Oscar Wilde**

I once worked with a journalist who wanted to get an interview between Jack Charlton and the Behan family for the sole reason that he could use the heading "Jack and the Behans Talk". **Liam Mackey**

My wife talks through her nose. Her mouth is worn out. **Joe Cuddy**

When first learning to speak Dutch it's best to cough violently and produce as much phlegm as possible. **Paul Kilduff**

I talk to Bono every day. He calls me from the Vatican looking for racing tips or greyhound results. **Christy Moore**

# TATTOOS

Pamela Lee said her name is tattooed on her husband's penis. Which explains why she changed her name from Anderson to Lee. *Conan O'Brien*

The only thing I have left from my marriage is the tattoo of my wife's name. *Colin Farrell*

When I was in London I lived near an estate where a pit bull was as *de rigueur* as a criminal record. Every time I left my flat to buy a paper the place was overrun with tattooed thugs — and that was just the women. *Marian Keyes*

The school I went to was so rough, even the arms of the chairs had tattoos on them. *Brendan O'Carroll*

# TAX

I once asked Alun Owen what the tax advantages of living in Ireland were for a writer. "None," he said. "What you save on tax you spend on drink." *Spike Milligan*

The Minister for Finance has simplified tax forms. They now have only two questions. One: "How much do you earn?" and Two: "Send it to us." *Myler McGrath*

When an Englishman is totally incapable of doing any work whatsoever, he describes himself on his income tax form as a gentleman. *Robert Lynd*

# TAXIS

As the taxi driver dropped me at the House of Commons one day he said only two honest people had ever entered it — myself and Guy Fawkes. *Bernadette McAliskey*

New York taxi drivers try to live up to the reputation all taxi drivers have, that of being wits. As I'm in the wit business myself, I object to the competition. *Brendan Behan*

She asked me to call her a taxi. I said, "Hello, taxi." *Frank Hall*

One night a drunk man got into a taxi and said to the driver, "Take me to the Gresham Hotel." The driver said, "This *is* the Gresham." He got out, handed him £20 and said, "Next time don't drive so fast." *Hal Roach*

I don't like going out in London. Taxi drivers keep telling me if you're tired of London you're tired of life. I don't know. Maybe I'm just tired of taxi drivers. *Sean Hughes*

Rain makes flowers grow — and taxis disappear. *Hal Roach*

In Germany if you see a gleaming cream Mercedes you know it's a taxi. In Ireland if you see a filthy bald fifteen-year-old Datsun with 100,000 miles on the clock you know it's a taxi. *Paul Kilduff*

Did you hear about the Irish millionaire who always takes a taxi when he sleepwalks? *Foggy Spellman*

# TEACHERS AND TEACHING

Everybody who is incapable of learning has taken to teaching. *Oscar Wilde*

Long ago I discovered that teaching is an easy way of earning a living provided that one doesn't make the mistake of actually teaching. *George Ryan*

Teacher: "Who was unhappy at the return of the Prodigal Son?"
Pupil: "The fatted calf, sir."
**Danny Cummins**

"What have you taught the pupils to date?" the inspector asked me. "I've taught them to date girls," I replied. **George Ryan**

I had a job training dogs before I became a teacher. It was a good preparation. **Frank McCourt**

Teacher: "Did you write this by yourself?"
Dublin boy: "Yes."
Teacher: "Well I'm glad to meet you, Mr Yeats — I heard you died years ago."
**Mary Feehan**

I was a teacher's pet. That's why he kept me in a cage at the back of the room. **Tom O'Connor**

A good teacher leaves the print of his teeth on a parish for three generations. **Bryan MacMahon**

Never having anyone to teach me, I learned only by pretending to know. **Frank O'Connor**

# TECHNOLOGY

My mother is determined to master the new technology. She typed an email to me on the computer, printed it out, popped it in an envelope and posted it to me. **John O'Farrell**

CDs can never compete with the physical thing of the needle in the groove. It's like sex. **Bono**

The latest thing the Health Nazis have produced to deter smoking in pubs is a device placed in toilets that detects a cigarette being lit. It would be better if they invented something to detect a paedophile unzipping his trousers. **Richard O'Connor**

They have phones for the deaf now. They light up instead of ringing. The deaf person can pick it up and say hello. Isn't that wonderful? *Dave Allen*

It was the Irishman's first time in the city and himself and his rural brother went into a shop where they saw their first ever dishwasher. They stood transfixed as they watched the dishes whirring round inside and then coming out spotlessly clean. "Whoever invented that contraption was a clever man," said the first brother. "Aye," agreed the second, "and a lazy bastard." *Joe Lynch*

It's impossible for the youth of today to imagine the darkness that reigned over the permanently offline abyss of pre-1990 before home computers and the internet made life on earth almost bearable. The only way to glimpse the horrors now is to Google "boredom" and check out the eighties online. *Kevin McAleer*

If any of you have trouble using the computers, please email me. *Overheard in Dublin*

# TEENAGERS

My last book involved a man being dragged to hell. It was easy for me to write. I live with two teenagers. *John Connolly*

Teenagers know all about sex but they think money comes from God. *Maureen Potter*

I have two teenage children. One is twenty-one and the other twenty-five. *Caller to Gay Byrne's radio show*

My teenage daughter is at the stage where she's all skin and phones. *Hal Roach*

# TEETH

You know you're getting old when the smile that greets you from the bedside isn't she who you went to bed with but your teeth in a jam-jar. *Brendan Grace*

Chelsea Clinton has more teeth than a Ferrari gearbox. *Patrick Kielty*

May your troubles be as few and as far apart as my grand-mother's teeth. *Cecil Sheridan*

If Kelly Rowland is a black beauty, it's only as in the horse. Have you seen her teeth? If you grabbed her by the legs you could plough a field with her. *Katherine Lynch*

What has thirty-six legs and no teeth? The front row of a Daniel O'Donnell concert. *Big O*

The Pogues have done for Irish music what Shane MacGowan did for dentistry. *Roy Guillane*

Never do anything to a clitoris with your teeth that you wouldn't do to an expensive waterproof wristwatch. *P. J. O'Rourke*

When Boyzone started out, I was generally known as the big fella at the back with the broken teeth. *Keith Duffy*

And then there was the woman who gave her dentures back to the dentist because she said they were too big. They wouldn't fit in the glass on her bedside locker. *Noel Purcell*

"How are the new false teeth?" one Irish woman asked another. "They're not bad," she sighed, "but I'm leaving them out till I get used to them." *Terry Adlam*

I don't have a problem with dental tourism. If dentists want to go on holiday, they should have as much of a right to as the rest of us. *Frank Tuohy*

I've got a tooth that's driving me to extraction. *Charlie McCarthy*

# TELEVISION

TV likes young, slim, good-looking, yummy, blonde, vivacious, bubbly presenters – and that's just the fellas. *Joe Duffy*

I was happy that I could get sixty-five channels on my TV at four in the morning but I wished there was something to watch other than re-runs of *I Love Lucy* and "infomercials" selling vegetable juicers and sadistic exercise devices. *Mark Little on a trip to America*

*Tallafornia* is the new reality telly programme in which scantily clad, orange-skinned attention-seekers share a house, bicker and snog. This would have been confusing for Eamon de Valera, whose idea of a good time was a Rich Tea biscuit after Mass. *Patrick Freyne*

There were three programmes my father allowed me to watch when I was growing up: *The News*, *The News* and *The News*. *Pat Shortt*

TV3 insists *The Apprentice* will be back next year, thereby proving that as long as there's a chance to throw good money after bad, they'll keep stuffing it down the jacks. The fact is that the programme slowly deflated like a paddling pool stabbed with a fork. *Naomi McIlroy*

I found it embarrassing watching sex on the television with my parents. I wasn't even aware they knew how to use a camcorder. *Jimmy Carr*

There seems to be a wave of all sorts of Irish performers on British TV at the moment but that could change. Maybe in five years or so, British TV will be full of heavy-set Ukrainian farmers. *Tommy Tiernan*

A Jesuit at Belvedere once asked his religion class what they thought about sex on the television. One boy replied, "I don't know about you, Father, but I find it very uncomfortable." *Tom Doorley*

I've just bought a video machine but I had to sell the TV to pay for it. *Sean Kilroy*

It's more difficult than you can imagine to say no to television offers, so don't be surprised if I turn up in a pile of shite. *Chris O'Dowd*

I refused to do the New Year's Eve broadcast on RTE because people watching TV on this night are grumpy. They think everyone else is out drinking champagne and having a wonderful time. Meanwhile they're stuck at home because their mother-in-law has measles. *Gay Byrne*

Watching *EastEnders* made me too frightened to go out in case I encountered any of them. *Sean Hughes*

There's a programme on Channel 4 tonight that might be of interest to parents with children. *Joe Harrington*

Reality television today means some "creative" type going, "Let's get some ugly cunts to live with beautiful people ... It's going to be fucking amazing!" *David McSavage*

When I was young my whole family used to sit around the television for hours. Eventually my grandfather would say, "Will we turn it on?" *Kevin McAleer*

I'm thinking of suing RTE for dislocation of my lower face. The condition was occasioned by fifty-five minutes of exposure to the programme *Trouble in Paradise*, through which I sat so open-mouthed in astonishment that I developed lockjaw and had to be rushed to A&E, where I was forced to lie on one of Mary Harney's trolleys for seven hours before a kindly Malaysian doctor administered a muscle relaxant. *John Boland*

There's nothing on TV these days except Swedish truck-racing, pro-celebrity shove ha'penny live from Slovakia and documentaries about ice roads in Alaska. The other day I was ogling the box and became so desperate I almost had a conversation. If things get any worse I might even read a book. *Mick the Maverick*

Because of satellite TV, the modern Irishman spends a lot of time watching documentaries about either monkeys or Nazis. On the basis of this, he has concluded that mankind basically consists of chimps in jackboots. *Pat Fitzpatrick*

Professional television watchers generally die from lockjaw after yawning, or from haemorrhoids. Gay Byrne will assure you we're safe from coronary trouble on the grounds that you can't suffer from what you haven't got in the first place. *Kevin Marron*

As an effective means of communicating complex arguments, the television discussion programme ranks somewhere between smoke signals and interpretive dance. *Liam Fay*

An old TV man once told me there was just one unbreakable law about talk shows: No jockeys. *Declan Lynch*

Moses had a TV. He saw God in a burning Bush. *Dave Allen*

Becoming famous has made me suspicious of homeless people. I'll be walking along and they'll say to me, "You're that bloke off the telly." How homeless are they? Did someone leave a television set in the box they're sleeping in? *Graham Norton*

An editor admitted to me recently that a TV critic's function is merely to confirm viewers in their prejudices. *Terry Wogan*

I wouldn't be into throwing TVs out the window of my hotel room like some of the rock stars you read about. These things are heavy and you have to lift them up. It's a waste of energy. *Daniel O'Donnell*

There was no sex in Ireland before television. *Oliver J. Flanagan*

Have you heard about the new Irish video recorder? It records programmes you don't want to see and shows them when you're out. *Kevin Marron*

There's no point running to the newspapers if you lose a TV show. It makes you look like a whinger. Instead you play the game and wish whoever takes over the replacement show the best of luck. Even though, human nature being what it is, you might just want to kill them. *Dave Fanning*

My grand-daughter Bethany was asked by one of her primary school teachers, "Have you ever seen Grandpa on the television?" Bethany thought this over. "No," she replied, 'I've seen him on the sofa." *Val Doonican*

# TEMPTATION

We cannot go about telling everybody about the temptations we have resisted. As a result, people judge us by the ones to which we yield. *Robert Lynd*

I can resist everything except temptation. *Oscar Wilde*

I never resist temptation because I have found that the things that are bad for me never tempt me. *George Bernard Shaw*

# TENNIS

I'll give you the definition of endless love: Ray Charles and Helen Keller playing tennis. *Conan O'Brien*

Henman Hill is now called Murray Mount, which sounds like a Presbyterian sex position. *Andrew Maxwell*

I like to think we're Saint and Greavesie with completed sentences. *Des Lynam on his BBC partnership with Gerry Williams at Wimbledon*

Generally speaking, South Dublin women don't work but they do keep busy, many of them enjoying hobbies such as tennis, golf, and having lunch. *Paul Howard*

I had tennis elbow for so long I finally had to take up the game. *Gene Ferret*

# TERRORISM

Fighting terrorists is like trying to kill a wasp with a fridge. **Dara O'Briain**

Gerry Adams in Armani from Macy's with all the New York society babes chasing after him as he makes his US victory lap this week . . . Now Washington, New York and Hollywood are all caught up in Irish terrorist chic. **Maureen Dowd on the Sinn Féin leader's visit to America in 1998**

The main difference between wives and terrorists is that you can negotiate with a terrorist. **Frank Carson**

I've heard people say "Terrorism works. Look at Gerry Adams and Martin McGuinness. They used to be in the IRA and now they're in government." True, but the government they're in is Her Majesty's one, as junior partners to the DUP. That's like Osama bin Laden leaving al-Qaeda to become Sarah Palin's running mate. **Abie Philbin Bowman**

# TEXTING

My mother has just learned to text and has taken to it like a duck to . . . text messaging. She puts all her messages in capital letters, which means she's still, effectively, shouting at me. Some things never change. **David O'Doherty**

The last text I sent was to my best friend Eamon, letting him know I'm not talking to him. **Holly Carpenter**

# THEATRE

The Queen's is the only theatre I've ever known where the fleas were so big they drove out the rats. *Vincent Dowling*

The other night I went to a play in the West End. I left after the first act but I'm going back next week because it said on the programme that Act Two takes place a week later. *Jimmy Cricket*

I am a timid man except before a piece of paper, or rioters at the Abbey. *W. B. Yeats*

The SFX Centre had none of the things we expect to see in a good theatre – like young men and women dressed in black, talking meaningful shite during the interval. *Roddy Doyle*

People are always saying how cultured Dublin is but that really is a load of bollox. There's not much theatre in Dublin if you don't want to play a drunken priest in a fucking John B. Keane play. *Stuart Townsend*

I meet Shakespeare on his own terms. His people are real. You can smell their breath. They piss against the wall. *Peter O'Toole*

First nights are a modern form of bear-baiting. *Peter O'Toole*

I'm fed up of people telling me the Abbey isn't what it used to be. It never was. *Lennox Robinson*

All the world's a stage and most of us are desperately unrehearsed. *Sean O'Casey*

Christopher Marlowe was a kind of cross between Oscar Wilde and Jack the Ripper. *Seamus Heaney*

There are some who kick the dressing-room door to splinters. Some go home and savage a spouse, a lover, a domestic pet. Others quit their stage doors with all convenient speed, find themselves holes wherein they may safely skulk, and there get as pissed as rats. *Peter O'Toole on how actors wind down after performances*

I suspect that Samuel Beckett was a confidence trick perpetrated on the twentieth century by a theatre-hating God. **Sheridan Morley**

A man may surely be allowed to take a glass of wine by his own fireside. **R. B. Sheridan as he watched his beloved Drury Lane Theatre burn down in 1809**

Why would you need to go to the theatre when you can stay home in your room and watch great dramas like *The Sopranos* and *Mad Men*? **Declan Lynch**

They're talking about naming a bridge after Samuel Beckett. Apparently he wrote a bunch of plays concerning confused tramps and lunatics in giant jars. Who wants to watch that sort of claptrap? Come back to me when you've conceived a film franchise that can knock *Transformers* from the top of the box office charts. **Donald Clarke**

The only theatre I was ever in was the operating room of the Blackrock Clinic after tearing my rotator cuff muscle in a friendly rugby match against the Presentation College in Bray. **Ross O'Carroll-Kelly**

# THINNESS

He's that skinny, you could push him up a flute and he wouldn't stop the music. **Jim Craig**

I don't know how I stay thin. The closest thing I have to a nutritionist is the Carlsberg Beer Company. I just have the appetite of a pigeon. **Colin Farrell**

Mrs Mullarkey, me husband is thin and I'm thin, but me sister is as thin as the two of us put together. **Remark overheard by Tony Butler**

Didn't Madonna do very well to get her figure back? It's only been a few months since she bought her baby. **Graham Norton**

Thin people are beautiful but fat people are adorable. *Jackie Gleason*

Mary, you're so skinny. If you drank tomato juice you'd look like a thermometer. *Bridget O'Donnell*

00 is now Hollywood's dress size of choice. *Sophie Haslett*

She was so thin, after she swallowed a pea, six men immediately went for paternity tests. *Hugh Malone*

I'm not just as thin as a pipe-cleaner; you'd find more meat on a butcher's apron. *Ryan Tubridy*

Even when I was at my thinnest, there was always a fat woman inside me waiting to get out. *Marian Keyes*

Davina McCall claims it was a strict Brazilian boot camp which helped her get the figure of a five-year-old boy, only with smaller boobs. I'm trying to talk her into getting her money back but she keeps falling asleep due to lack of food. *Roisin Gorman*

I know a woman who was so thin, the one eye would have done her. *Jon Kenny*

# TIES

I bought a tie last week but I ended up giving it back. It was too tight. *Noel V. Ginnity*

Don't worry about my soul. Just make sure you get my tie right. *James Joyce to a portrait painter who said he wanted to capture his soul*

What's ten inches long and hangs from a wally? Daniel O'Donnell's tie. *Internet joke*

A well-tied tie is the first serious step in life. *Oscar Wilde*

Murphy got his tie caught up in a fax machine. He ended up in Tokyo. *Noel V. Ginnity*

A bloke arrives at a nightclub and the bouncers say he can't come in without a tie so he goes to the boot of his car and gets a set of jump leads, wraps them around his neck and goes back to the bouncer. "Can I come in now?" he asks. "Yeah," says the bouncer, "but don't start anything." *Jason Byrne*

# TIGHTFISTEDNESS

I saw a Cavan man stripping wallpaper one time. "I see you're decorating," I said to him. "No," he replied, "moving." *Niall Toibin*

Did you hear about the Scotsman who had a hip replacement operation? He asked the surgeon if he could have the bone for the dog. *T. P. McKenna*

Roger Corman could negotiate the production of a film on a pay phone, shoot the movie in the booth and finance it with the money in the change slot. *Mick Molloy*

Eamon de Valera is so mean, if he owned the Atlantic Ocean he wouldn't give you a wave. *W. T. Cosgrove*

Scrooge Murphy was so mean, he found a plaster one day and went straight home and cut his finger. *James McKeon*

I once knew a man who was such a skinflint he was afraid to sneeze in case he gave something away. *Clare Boylan*

The man was a secular version of the Immaculate Conception. He became an alcoholic without ever buying a drink. *Niall Toibin*

He'd offer you an egg if you promised not to break the shell. *Eamon Kelly*

That fellow is so mean, he'd live in one of your ears and rent out the other as flats. *Patrick O'Keeffe*

# TIGHTS

My mother was seven hours in labour. They forgot to take her tights off. *James McKeon*

Seamus: "Is knickers a curse?"
Paddy: "No, but tights are."
*Noel O'Gorman*

Why do women wear tights? Look what they do to bank robbers' faces. *Michael Cullen*

# TIME

Next week is another day. *Peadar Clohessy*

My hairdresser spends more time digging hairs out of my ears than off the top of my head. *Des Lynam*

Makes of men date like makes of cars. *Elizabeth Bowen*

As of today, Dessie's Thursday column will be appearing on Mondays. **Cork Examiner**

I lost so many years through drink, it was 1972 before I learned John Kennedy had been assassinated. *David Kelly*

That was Brendan Howlin, the Labour Party spokesman, speaking to me a little later on. *Ryan Tubridy*

With regard to Michael Flatley's reputation for having sex two or three times a day, you have to remember that he operates on a nine-day week. *Martin Flitton*

Cynics may point to the past but we live in the future. *Bertie Ahern*

Life is a cheap *table d'hôte* in a rather dirty restaurant, with time changing the plates before you've had enough of anything. *Tom Kettle*

After a hellraising binge with Michael Caine once, Peter O'Toole and himself woke up in a strange flat. "What time is it?" Caine asked. "Never mind what time it is," O'Toole replied, "what fucking day is it?" It was two days later. *Paul Whittington*

Men talk of killing time while time quietly kills them. *Dion Boucicault*

I recently woke up jetlagged in Melbourne at 11.30 from a planned twenty-minute snooze that turned into an unexpected eight-hour sleep. It was dark outside but my watch said 11.30 so I concluded that Fukushima reactor number two had exploded, civilization had ended and I was the only surviving human. *David O'Doherty*

The further west you go in Ireland, the greater the time lag. In fact in parts of Galway it's still yesterday. *Frank McNally*

Everybody is born too late. *Con Houlihan*

Note to milkman in Donegal: "No milk today. By today I mean tomorrow as I wrote this yesterday." *Kevin Murtie*

I once had a psychic girlfriend but she left me before we met. *Jimeoin*

The reason for the delay to the kick-off is because it's not kick-off time yet. *Jimmy Magee*

# THE *TITANIC*

I'm proud of anything the Irish built except the *Titanic*. That was the work of Protestants. If Catholics built it, it would have eaten the iceberg. *Tommy Tiernan*

The Last Supper in the *Titanic* dining-room was a lavish affair, consisting of something in the order of twelve courses. No wonder it sank so quickly. *Dan Buckley*

I'm so dumb that if I escaped the *Titanic* I'd probably climb aboard the *Marie Celeste*. **Danny Cummins**

Everyone is talking about peace in the North now, and building a future. I don't mean to worry anyone but the last thing we built in Belfast went down with Leonardo DiCaprio and Kate Winslet hanging off the back of it. **Patrick Kielty**

My grandfather had an unfortunate history. After he got shipwrecked he was picked up by the *Titanic*. **Joe Cuddy**

What did the last diner on the *Titanic* say? "I know I asked for ice, but this is ridiculous." **Joe Lynch**

The movie *Titanic* was a perfect example of how America views the Irish. We're basically third-class passengers, but Jesus didn't we dance well at the start of the film. My God, Paddy, if you could just breast stroke as well as you can jog you'd be laughing now. **Dara O'Briain**

If you're going to travel on the *Titanic* you may as well go first class. **Sean Kilroy**

Two Irishmen are on an iceberg. Paddy says to Murphy, "We're saved, we're saved!" Murphy asks, "How do you know that?" Paddy says, "Here comes the *Titanic*." **Mr O'S**

# TOILETS

Men go to toilets to piss. For women a toilet is a community centre. **Brendan O'Carroll**

My next work shall be on rice paper wound about a spool with a perforated line every six inches and on sale in Boots. The length of each chapter will be carefully calculated to suit, with the average free motion, and with every copy there will be a free sample of some laxative to promote sales. The Beckett Bowel Books. Jesus *in farto*. All edges disinfected. One thousand wipes of clean fun. **Samuel Beckett in 1936**

In Irish pub toilets, incoming traffic has the right of way. **Hugh Leonard**

My entire involvement with the Irish Literary Revival consisted of standing beside W. B. Yeats in the urinal during an interval at the Abbey theatre where I remember he was having great difficulty with his waterworks. **Eoin O'Mahony**

I went to the toilet recently on a plane and it had frosted windows. Who's going to be looking in — a seagull? **Brendan O'Carroll**

There were forty-five people at Bob Geldof's last concert in Rome. You'd get more people than that in the loo at a Westlife gig. **Louis Walsh**

This year we thought we'd do something different for the kids for Christmas. We bought them fuck all and locked them in the toilet. **Brendan O'Carroll**

I envy children their determination.
  "Where are you going?"
  "I'm going to get my harmonica."
  "What are you going to do with it?"
  "I'm going to put it down the toilet."
**Dylan Moran**

George Moore leads his readers to the latrine and locks them in. **Oscar Wilde**

The truly modern man is he who has never used anything but toilet paper to clean his bottom. **John B. Keane**

I figured Portugal's economy had to be in trouble when I went on holiday there and outside the door of the local toilet there was an old woman with a single toilet roll, looking me up and down to see if she'd condescend to give me a sheet. **Keith Farnan**

Toilets Out Of Use. Use Floor Below. **Notice spotted in Dublin pub**

My mother couldn't afford laxatives when we were young. Instead she used to put us sitting on the toilet and tell us ghost stories. **Brendan O'Carroll**

# TOUGHNESS

Tales of my toughness are exaggerated. I never killed an actor. *John Huston*

I'll give you my heart and soul on a plate if you need it but if you take a hair on my head without asking, I'll take your life. That's how I am. *Boyzone's Mikey Graham*

It was rough where we lived. They stole hubcaps from moving cars. *Bill Kelly*

Humphrey Bogart wasn't really tough, only "movie" tough. Jimmy Cagney used to call him "the Park Avenue tough guy". *Pat O'Brien*

You have to be tough to work in a frock for thirty years. *Drag artist Danny La Rue*

The nuns didn't care whether you went to heaven or hell or married a Protestant as long as your handwriting was clear. If you were weak in that department they'd bend your thumbs back till you screamed for mercy and promised a calligraphy that would open the doors of heaven. *Frank McCourt*

It's said that Finglas is so tough, even the Alsatians walk around in pairs. *Fergal Keane on the Dublin suburb*

Jim Sheridan is a tough little bastard. I love him. *Aidan Quinn*

There's a waiting list to be mugged at my local ATM machine in Ballymun. *Ciaran Dempsey*

The school I went to was so tough, the only people who mitched were the teachers. *Mannix Flynn*

# TRAFFIC

I love traffic even though everyone complains about it. They say things like, "Ten years ago there was no traffic in Ireland." They're right. That's because there was nowhere to fucking go. **Des Bishop**

When you get to my age, the first thing you think of when you get stuck in a traffic jam is, "Thank God I don't need to pee." **Richard O'Connor**

There are more cars on the road in Ireland on car-free days than anywhere else in the world. Everyone says, "Jaysus, there'll be nothin' on the road today. I'll drive to work." **Neil Delamere**

# TRAFFIC LIGHTS

Orange traffic lights in Dublin mean "Go", whereas red ones mean "Stop" if you feel in the mood and fancy a breather. **Terry Eagleton**

A green man at a pedestrian crossing in Athens means "Cross If You Think You Can Make It". It's best to ignore all street crossing signs and walk alongside the locals so at least you can all die together. **Paul Kilduff**

Traffic signals in Dublin are just rough guidelines. **Lee Dunne**

When I was a kid, once you left Dublin there were no traffic lights till you got to Cork. **Pete McCarthy**

They're making a new film about Cork's traffic lights. It's called *Forever Amber*. **Ted Bonner**

# TRAGEDY

Being Irish, he had an abiding sense of tragedy which sustained him through temporary periods of joy. *W. B. Yeats*

All women become like their mothers. That is their tragedy. No man does. That's his. *Oscar Wilde*

The tragedy of Northern Ireland is that it is now a society where the dead console the living. *Jack Holland*

# TRANSVESTITES

Humour anoraks tell us the main joke in *Some Like It Hot* comes from watching men in dresses. If that's funny, how come nobody's written a sitcom based on Margaret Thatcher? *Pat Fitzpatrick*

"Daddy, I want to wear a bra."
   "You're not old enough, darling."
   "Even if you forbid me I'm still going to do it."
   "Now, Seamus, don't be difficult."
*Joe Lynch*

How long have I been wearing a feather boa? Ever since my wife found it in the glove compartment of my car! *Tommy Makem*

The latest thing in women's clothes is men. *Milo O'Shea*

Some of my best friends are women. Some of my best friends dress up as women too. *Bono*

# TRAVEL

Ireland is the only country in the world with two M1 motorways. The one in the North goes west to avoid the south and the one in the South goes north to avoid the price of drink. **Paul O'Sullivan**

It is unfortunate that most travel books are written by people whose only talent is for travel. **John Broderick**

Want to know what the world will be like after the Apocalypse? Five pounds on National Express gets you to Glasgow. **Jimmy Carr**

Whoever said "It's better to travel than to arrive" should get his head examined. To travel is awful and to arrive lovely. The only time it's not entirely unbearable to travel is when you're on the Orient Express and your daily champagne allowance would fell an elephant. **Marian Keyes**

Reilly was packing his bags when Mary Kate came home from work.
   "Where are you going?" she enquired.
   "To Fiji," he replied. "I've heard the women out there pay you a fiver every time you make love to them."
   "Hang on a minute and I'll go with you."
   "Why?"
   "Well I want to see how you can live on a tenner a year."
**Frank Carson**

I went to England for a fortnight and stayed for life. **Sean O'Casey**

Although there's no place like home, you have to go away and come back again to realize how dull it really is. **James McKeon**

Dublin Airport, off to Portugal on holidays with the lads, my mate next in line for passport control. "Ever been abroad before?" the passport controller asked. "No," came the reply, "I've always been a man." **Overheard in Dublin**

I've been to almost as many places as my luggage. *Olivia Tracey*

Once the Dublin government realizes it can no longer export bombs along with its social problems to England, it will become as helpful as a Tory backbencher in search of a knighthood. *Former Ulster Unionist Party leader David Trimble advocating travel restrictions between Ireland and the UK in 1996*

Where were you going when I saw you coming back? *James Young*

I have allowed the best part of two days to explore Vaduz. Upon early inspection I have overestimated matters by possibly forty-seven hours. *Paul Kilduff*

I brought my wife on a world cruise. Next year she says she wants to go somewhere else. *Brendan Grace*

# TRIUMPHALISM

We can do no wrong in Ireland now. Our writers, even the most emptily careerist of them, are simply wonderful, and if you doubt that for a second, why, their bank balances will prove you wrong. Our international soccer team isn't a motley crew of dogged plodders lacking both skill and flair but instead is emblematic of all the courage, determination, fighting spirit and everything else that's admirable about a gang of guys whose grannies come from the oul sod. Our pop bands are producing the finest music that you'll hear anywhere, and if you don't believe me turn on that great arbiter of taste, MTV, at any hour of the day. *John Boland*

Oasis aren't arrogant. We just think we're the best band in the world. *Noel Gallagher*

My specialty is omniscience. *Charles Haughey*

I enjoyed Eric Clapton more before he went on to be God. *Fran Dempsey*

The awful trait the Irish have is the power thing. The fella who thinks he's a policeman when he's just the caretaker, who turns into a Nazi when he's given the responsibility of opening and closing the door. *Pat Shortt*

# TROUSERS

At the Channel 4 prize-giving ceremony I wore a sort of glittering Nehru jacket affair and some trousers that were so tight my legs looked like satin sausages. *Graham Norton*

Sports Jackets May Be Worn Here, But No Trousers. *Sign spotted in club*

I once tried to take my trousers off over my head after a feed of drink. I really thought it was possible. My only worry was how I was going to get them on again. *Richard Harris*

# TRUST

He's as good as his word, but his word is no good. *Seamus McManus*

Never trust a woman who tells you her age. A woman who tells you that will tell you anything. *Oscar Wilde*

Trust everyone, but cut the cards. *Finley Peter Dunne*

Because of the rejection I had for so many years before *The Ginger Man*, I can't trust acceptance now. *J. P. Donleavy*

I wouldn't trust some of these people to walk my dog. *Roy Keane on Sky Sports' football commentators*

When you shake hands with an Irishman, always remember to count your fingers afterwards. *Frank McNally*

I distrust acts of kindness. They shake my lack of faith in human nature. *John Banville*

My grandfather used to claim that the reason the British had an empire so extensive that the sun never set on the whole of it was because God wouldn't trust the buggers in the dark. *Tom Doorley*

# TRUTH

Nobody speaks the truth when there's something they must have. *Elizabeth Bowen*

Man is born a liar. Otherwise he wouldn't have invented the proverb "Tell the truth and shame the devil". *Liam O'Flaherty*

Half the lies our opponents tell about us are untrue. *Sir Boyle Roche*

I was only whipped once as a child – for telling the truth. *J. P. Mahaffy*

If one tells the truth one is sure, sooner or later, to be found out. *Oscar Wilde*

# TYPECASTING

I once played God in a play and my wife said it was typecasting. *Vincent Dowling*

My mother was so religious she wouldn't talk to me for six months because I was playing Judas in *Jesus Christ Superstar*. *Colm Wilkinson*

I've played so many priests in films, when we sit down to eat, our entire family discusses everything in Latin. *Pat O'Brien*

I have made seventy movies in my life and been miscast only twice – as a husband. *Richard Harris*

# UGLINESS

On my wedding day the priest said, "Do you take this woman to be your wife?" I said, "I do." He took a look at her and said, "I'll ask you again . . ." *Joe Cuddy*

Peter Crouch looks like the love child of Peter O'Toole's cadaver and a drainpipe that's been kneecapped. *Kevin Myers*

Irish people drink a lot because they're so ugly it's the only way they can have sex with one another. *David McSavage*

I've never gone to bed with an ugly woman but I've sure woken up with a few. *Patrick Kielty*

No one wants to wake up feeling as if they're sharing their bed with an extra from *Gorillas in the Mist*. *Graham Norton*

Ugliness is a point of view. An ulcer is a wonder to a pathologist. *Austin O'Malley*

He was so ugly when he was born, the doctor slapped his mother. *Frankie Blowers*

# *ULYSSES*

*Ulysses* cost me thirty-five shillings and I'm stuck on the first page. I think that's disgusting, don't you? *Cilla Black*

*Ulysses* is the most unread classic of our time and *Finnegans Wake* the most unreadable one. *Denis Donoghue*

I've put so many enigmas and puzzles into the book that it will keep the professors busy for centuries arguing over what I meant. That is the only way to guarantee one's immortality. *James Joyce*

The trouble with *Ulysses*? The covers are too far apart. *Michael Cullen*

# UNANIMITY

Gentlemen, it seems unanimous that we cannot agree. **Charles Stewart Parnell**

Then there was the county council who were unanimous that they couldn't agree because they heard a totally garbled version of what never took place. **Myler McGrath**

# UNDERTAKERS

An undertaker is the last man to let you down. **Micheál O'Muircheartaigh**

My uncle is an undertaker. He says it's a marvellous business. It's quiet, steady and profitable, and in thirty years he's never had a customer ask for a refund. **Hal Roach**

An undertaker called to a client's house on the day of a funeral and asked his widow, "Excuse me, ma'am, but would this be where the dead man lives?" **Pat O'Brien**

# UNDERWEAR

One of the Chippendales told me a G-string was a pair of boxer shorts gone on vacation. **Hector O'hEochagáin**

There's probably something good that can be said about corsets but I just can't think what it is. **Maureen Potter**

Rose's are red, Violet's are blue. In fact everyone is wearing multi-coloured underwear these days. **Sean Kilroy**

Why does the Pope wear underpants in the bath? He doesn't like to look down on the unemployed. **Nuala O'Faoláin**

The life expectancy of a pair of underpants should be about a decade or so. *Kevin Myers*

There are certain garments from a man's past that he should never seek to wear again: a thin leather tie, rainbow-coloured braces, and those little underwear briefs with cartoon super-heroes printed on. *Kevin Murphy*

Male underwear never caught on, probably because of the nature of male genitalia. There's a limited amount you can do with something that looks like what you might find hanging out of a shark's mouth. *Dylan Moran*

They've found a woman in India with five legs. Her knickers must fit her like a glove. *Frank Carson*

A policeman stopped me as I was driving home. "You're not wearing your seatbelt," he said. I said, "That's not the only thing I'm not wearing." The lovely man let me go. *Deirdre O'Kane*

# UNEMPLOYMENT

Unemployed man seeks work. Very honest. Will take anything. *Ad spotted in trade magazine*

Help fight unemployment. Commit suicide. *Martin Reid*

The only way to solve the unemployment problem in this country is to raise the school-leaving age to sixty-five. *Sean MacDonnell*

If you tell people you're a Social Networking New Media life coach they'll just assume you're unemployed. *Pat Fitzpatrick*

I've just come from the Job Centre. Think it must be some-body's birthday in there — the window's full of cards. *Jimmy Cricket*

There are rules governing unemployment. You have to watch Jeremy Kyle on the telly in the mornings, from bed. *David Slattery*

U2 saved my life because I'm unemployable. There's nothing else I can do. *Bono*

I read on the web about a twenty-five-year-old waitress who turned down a job offer in a brothel in Berlin and so faced cuts to her unemployment benefit. *Paul Kilduff*

I read an article in *Time* magazine about a new phenomenon: funemployment. If you've recently lost your job and are secretly quite pleased about it you're funemployed. *Trevor White*

A man fell into a river and another man jumped in after him to save him. "I don't want to be saved," the drowning man said, "I fell in on purpose." The second man said, "I'm not trying to save you. I just want to know where you used to work." *Big O*

I spent eight years on the dole, wearing bad polo-necks and sipping black coffee. I looked on it as my Arts Council grant. When I finally signed off, they gave me a Dole Gold Card. *Tommy Tiernan*

I'm looking for a plane to Jeopardy. I heard on the news today that two hundred jobs were in jeopardy. *Joe O'Shea*

# UNIVERSITIES

I firmly believe that if university education were universally available and availed of, the country would collapse in one generation. *Flann O'Brien*

Dublin University contains the cream of Ireland — rich and thick. *Samuel Beckett*

University is a wonderful place to attend if you want to do something else. I would often fantasize about the amount of writing I could get done by the simple expedient of avoiding lectures. *Ian MacPherson*

Most colleges trample whole fields of wheat trying to put salt on a sparrow's tail. *Austin O'Malley*

There once was an old man of Esser
Whose knowledge grew lesser and lesser.
It at last grew so small,
He knew nothing at all,
And now he's a college professor.
*Ancient Irish limerick*

Academics teach for about ten minutes a week and then go off and write unreadable books about things like Chaucer's use of the semi-colon. *Frank McCourt*

If you want to be cool you have to understand the difference between being an undergraduate student (which is not cool), being a graduate student who attends lectures in a prosaic topic such as Accounting (which is also not cool), and being in the seventh year of your MA in Experimental Music and Development Studies at Trinners, where you have completed two field trips exploring the therapeutic value of bongo rhythms amongst HIV populations in Laos, but have not actually attended any lectures (which is very cool). *David Slattery*

How do you know they haven't? *Samuel Beckett after a critic of* Waiting for Godot *said the tramps spoke as if they'd been to university*

I studied English at university. A bit of an obvious choice really – we spoke it at home. *Ian MacPherson*

Everywhere I go I'm asked if university stifles writers. My opinion is that they don't stifle half enough of them. *Flannery O'Connor*

"How's your son Tomas doing?"
  "He's at university taking medicine."
  "Is it doing him any good?"
*Duncan Crosbie*

During Ireland's golden age, between AD 500 and 800, its monastic settlements were considered the Harvard and Yale of their day, the key difference being that the students didn't have yellow sweaters with the sleeves tied across their shoulders, or drive Porsches. *Donal O'Dea*

What's the first thing a PhD graduate says after leaving college? "Would you like fries with that?" *John Olahan*

# UNPUNCTUALITY

If an Irish plumber says he'll fix your drain on Tuesday he may turn up on Friday. Friday is pretty close to Tuesday after all, even if your kitchen flooded and drowned your kids in the meantime. *Terry Eagleton*

One of the nice things about Irish people is that they never mind you being late for an appointment. Because they're not there either. *Des Bishop*

We should never tell latecomers they're in perfect time when the meal is stuck to the roof in the oven and the other guests are legless with pre-dinner drinks. *Maeve Binchy*

I once taught English in Bilbao. I was about thirty-five years too late for the Spanish Civil War but that's actually what I was going there for. *Gabriel Byrne*

"You were very late for work this afternoon, Mary."
"Yea, the fella that was folleying me was walking very slow."
*Paul Ryan*

I remember a time when the curtain never went up on time in a Dublin theatre because, the theory went, the Irish were all so busy being witty and wonderful in bars they couldn't do anything as prosaic as coming in and being seated before eight o'clock. *Maeve Binchy*

Better never than late. *George Bernard Shaw*

I have a watch with only one hand to prevent my being reduced to appointments. *Oliver St John Gogarty*

We've been waiting seven hundred years. You can have the seven minutes. *Michael Collins after being chastised for being seven minutes late when accepting the handover of Ireland from the British in 1922*

Fifteen years ago an aircraft left a German airport five minutes after its scheduled departure time. They shot the pilot, all the ground handling staff resigned en masse, the departure gate was permanently closed and shrouded in a black silk awning, and a small bronze plaque was placed on a nearby wall to commemorate the terrible event that blighted the nation. *Paul Kilduff*

When I first went to England it came as an awful shock to me when you invited people to dinner at eight and they arrived at . . . eight. I'd be there shaving as they circled the house to kill time. The Irish are different. They arrive late but stay for ever. *Terry Wogan*

Irish train stations don't use timetables. They use calendars. *Percy French*

# UPBRINGING

To have been well brought up is a great drawback nowadays. It shuts one out from so much. *Oscar Wilde*

My mother brought me up to believe that I was a god. For that I am eternally grateful to her. *John Banville*

I was a young lad while I was growing up. *David O'Leary*

I came up through the people system. *Bertie Ahern*

# URINATION

My brother Dom pissed on people selectively. *Seamus Behan*

It annoys me when my husband pisses with the door open. Particularly when I'm trying to drive. *Mary Bourke*

All this drink will be the urination of me. *Cyril Cusack*

The toilets at Buckingham Palace were lovely. It's nice to feel you've been able to leave something behind. *Gloria Hunniford*

People who make a practice of keeping one foot in the past and one in the future wind up pissing in the now. *Brendan Behan*

Jack Charlton taught me that it was more important to be inside the tent pissing out than outside pissing in. *Mick McCarthy*

I was the kind of youngster who, if he sneaks up a dark laneway to pee, discovers that he's doing it on the boot of a lurking policeman. *Hugh Leonard*

Little Seamus was told by the doctor that he had sugar in his urine, so every morning he peed on his cornflakes. *Hal Roach*

When you're ten and a half, the main excitement of sleeping in the back bedroom is the fact that you can piss out the window without being seen. *Jon Kenny*

I go to the toilet every morning at 7.30. The only problem is, I don't get up until 10.30. *Joe Cuddy*

Word reaches me that Enda Kenny is calling for random drug testing in secondary schools. The man isn't just taking the piss, he also wants to sample it. *Olaf Tyaransen*

I'm not afraid of old age. I'm looking forward to sitting in a pub with my children and saying, "I just pissed myself. Deal with it." *Dylan Moran*

# VACUUMS

A hole is nothing at all, but you can break your neck in it. *Austin O'Malley*

I keep an empty seat at every concert for my dead grandmother. *Michael Flatley*

Nothing is more real than nothing. *Samuel Beckett*

People who had never visited the Louvre to see the Mona Lisa came to see the space on the wall from which it had been stolen. *Robert Lynd*

Whenever young writers say to me "I have something to express", I say, "No, you have *nothing* to express. That's what writing is about." *John Banville*

I was disappointed Beckett didn't achieve the ultimate in drama: a play about thirty minutes in duration on a bare stage, with no players. *Con Houlihan*

# VANITY

I look at myself in the mirror 247 times a day. No, make that 248. *Shay Healy*

I'm so vain I even smile at speed cameras. *Katy French*

Diana Ross personally contacted the Channel 4 office to say how much she had enjoyed appearing on my show. The reason she felt moved to call us was because she thought her skin had looked nice. *Graham Norton*

I often wonder how Bono manages to comb his hair without scratching his halo. *Tom Kenny*

Some people have a lot of vanity. They say things like "I only wear glasses when I drive". Hey, if you only need glasses when you drive, then drive around with a prescription wind-shield. *Brian Regan*

Anyone who needs 50,000 people a night to tell them they're OK has to have a bit missing. *Bono*

# VARIETY

Variety is the life of spies. *Dave Callan*

Henry VIII liked to chop and change. *Cecil Sheridan*

# VASECTOMIES

I heard about this guy who had a vasectomy by mistake. He went in to hospital to have his tonsils out and someone turned the trolley round. *Dusty Young*

Vasectomies aren't expensive any more. They're just a snip now. *Gerry Ryan*

The definition of macho: jogging home from the vasectomy. *John Feeney*

# VEGETARIANS

I don't mind vegetarians if they've fallen down the stairs as children and now can't chew. But not on principle. *Noel V. Ginnity*

German food is so bad, even Hitler was a vegetarian. *Dylan Moran*

If vegetarians only eat vegetables, does that mean humanitarians only eat people? *Seamus Carmody*

Most vegetarians I ever saw looked enough like their food to be classed as cannibals. *Finley Peter Dunne*

I make a lot of jokes about vegetarians in my act but most of them don't have the strength to protest. *Ardal O'Hanlon*

I'm a vegetarian but not a serious one. I eat meat, for instance. But only because I like the taste. Morally, I object to it. **Dylan Moran**

# VIAGRA

Viagra is freely available now. These days you can get it over the counter. **Fran Dempsey**

I have to stop taking Viagra because I can't zip up my trousers. **Richard Harris**

Did you hear about the man who mixed up his Viagra with his constipation pills? He didn't know if he was coming or going. **Ted Fitzpatrick**

# VIOLENCE

If you strike a child, take care that you do so in anger, even at the risk of maiming it for life. A blow struck in cold blood neither can nor should be forgiven. **George Bernard Shaw**

The next person who tells me I should take up golf will see me forced to suppress the urge to rip out their intestine and feed it up and down their nasal passages before twirling it into a delightful handlebar moustache. **Dan Buckley**

We've had thirty years of violence in Northern Ireland simply because one group likes bright churches and the other wants to wear condoms. **Jeremy Clarkson**

Ninety-five per cent of crime fiction nowadays has extreme violence against women. This is its attraction. Most of us will never see any violence throughout our entire lives, apart from people waving their fists at each other after their cars collide. **John Banville**

Well I suppose that's the knighthood fucked. *George Best after assaulting a policeman in 1984*

The government will never accept an acceptable level of violence. *Patrick Donegan*

I'll throttle the next person who accuses me of being violent. *Alex Higgins*

Anyone responsible for depicting violence on television should be kicked in the head, have his eyes gouged out, and shot in the left hip. *Gregory McDonald*

Last week I saw a woman flayed and you will hardly believe how much it altered her person for the worse. *Jonathan Swift*

I'm not a fighter, I'm a bleeder. My best chance is to drown the other guy in my own blood. *Dylan Moran*

# VIRGINITY

They used to say that if you lost your virginity in Cork, someone would be sure to find it and bring it back to your mother. *Maeve Binchy*

The town I come from was so conservative, the local hooker was a virgin. *Tom Murtagh*

I didn't lose my virginity. I know exactly where I left it. *Pat Ingoldsby*

The Latin teacher said to his class, "What's an *avis raris*?" "A rare bird, sir," piped up a bright spark. "Very good," said the teacher. "And now can anyone tell me what *virgo intacta* signifies?" The bright spark ventured, "Another rare bird, sir?" *Sean Kenny*

I once knew a girl called Virginia. We called her Virgin for short – but not for long. *Richie Kavanagh*

Patience is a virgin. *John Broderick*

Attracta and Fidelma were coming out of a family planning clinic in Galway. "Are you a virgin?" Fidelma asked. "Not yet," Attracta replied. **Niall Toibin**

The Catholic Church offers women the choice of perpetual virginity or perpetual pregnancy. **Dave Allen**

The US state of Virginia is reputedly named after Queen Elizabeth I, the Virgin Queen. The town of Fukyu in China is also named after her. **Donal O'Dea**

I lost my virginity just to get rid of it. **Mary McEvoy**

# VOICES

My singing voice is like an aural fart. **Graham Norton**

If irate listeners were to rise up in anger every time a voice on the radio irritated them, Joan Burton would be under permanent house arrest. **Miriam Lord**

If Rice Krispies could talk, they'd sound like Padraig Harrington. **Michael Cullen**

I was a wild fucking woman with a vocabulary like the backside of a loo door and a voice like bleeding cherries. **Mary Coughlan on the early years of her musical career**

Bob Dylan's voice sounds like a malfunctioning cistern. **George Byrne**

His vibrato sounded like he was driving a tractor over ploughed fields with weights tied to his scrotum. **Spike Milligan**

The only way I could do Brian Cowen's voice was by having my mouth full of chicken tikka. **Impressionist Mario Rosenstock**

Ronnie Drew has a voice like Tom Waits' grandfather. **Waterford Today**

# VOMITING

If you want breakfast in your room, ring the front desk. This will be enough to bring your food up. *Sign spotted in Kerry hotel*

Murphy threw up on the plane and the air hostess was outraged. "There's a bag in front of you," she said, "why didn't you use that?" "I don't even know the woman," Murphy replied. *Conal Gallen*

Vomiting is the true mark of an Irishman because when you've puked about fifteen times the last thing to come out is always green. And aren't we Irish like puke ourselves? People have tried to keep us down for years but we wouldn't fucking stay down. Every time I see a puddle of vomit on the floor I think of 1916 and the Rising. *Denny O'Reilly*

Just as there is joy to be had from a French film about a housewife trapped in a lift, so there is a certain fun to having your boyfriend hold your hair back while you vomit outside a Slug and Lettuce. *Graham Norton*

Bryan Ferry sings like he's throwing up. *Andrew O'Connor*

Think teenage girls and Justin Timberlake, but with basso profundo yelling – and less vomiting. *Miriam Lord on youthful golf fans*

And then there was the ignoramus who vomited in the church because he saw a box marked "For the Sick". *Jim O'Halloran*

# VOTES

A vote of confidence is a sure sign you're in trouble. *Patrick Hillery*

An electric vote isn't worth the paper it's written on. *Paul Delaney*

Charlie Haughey would unhesitatingly roller-skate backwards into a nunnery, naked from the waist down and singing "Kevin Barry" in Swahili if it would help him gain a vote. *Hugh Leonard on Ireland's former Taoiseach*

There's no city in the United States where I get a warmer welcome – and fewer votes – than Columbus, Ohio. *John F. Kennedy*

# WAITING

Samuel Beckett was sipping a coffee outside Bewleys. The waiter asked him, "Are you waiting for *gateau*?" *Michael Cullen*

The last time I was in Dublin Airport I spent hours waiting for two bags. My wife and my mother. *Brendan Grace*

Two men were in hiding, waiting to ambush Lord Leitrim, who was renowned not only for his brutality but also his punctuality. "He's late tonight," said one of them. The other replied, "I hope to God nothing's happened to the poor gentleman." *Sean McCann*

Why, after two thousand years on the planet, do we still believe women when they say they're ready? *Brendan Grace*

# WAR

Making peace, I have found, is much harder than making war. *Gerry Adams*

The last war Liechtenstein fought was in 1866. Eighty soldiers went off to fight and a few months later eighty-one returned because a guy joined their army along the way. *Paul Kilduff*

Most of us were happy about being neutral during World War One, though some were more neutral towards Germany. *Vincent Dowling*

In a prison camp during the Spanish Civil War where IRA prisoners were housed, there were said to be three factions on the subject of the war: pro-Franco, anti-Franco, and Brendan Behan. *Terry Eagleton*

I'm against the war in Iraq but I love the smell of petrol so I'm torn. *Sean Hughes*

Two IRA men are chatting. One says to the other, "Isn't it a terrible war?" "Indeed," says the other, "but sure 'tis better than no war at all." *Eamonn Mac Thomáis*

# WATER

I had to give up drinking. It wasn't the whiskey that did me in but the water I had with it. *David Norris after contracting hepatitis from tainted water in 2009*

An American tourist at the Sheen Falls in County Kerry rings the reception desk late one night complaining that he can't sleep and could they turn off the waterfall. *Peter Quinn*

An American lady was visiting a country village and met Doolan, the blacksmith. She said to him, "Is the water safe to drink here?" Doolan said, "Oh it is. First we filter it, then we boil it, and when we've done that we throw it out the window and drink beer." *Hal Roach*

# WEATHER

The only profession where you can consistently be wrong and still get paid is a weather forecaster. *David Feherty*

The Irish climate would be wonderful if it wasn't for the weather. *Tony Butler*

Weather and sport were invented to allow Irish family members to converse at great length with each other without saying anything dangerous. *David Slattery*

The only thing you can say for sure about the Irish weather is there's nothing you can say for sure about the Irish weather. *Mary Mannion*

I wouldn't go quite that far. *Samuel Beckett in response to a friend who said that the weather was so nice on a particular day, it made him feel good to be alive*

It would skin the balls off a brass monkey. *Familiar Irish description of a sharp wind*

The weather here is great. Today was so hot it was a shame I didn't have a job because I could have taken the day off. *Jimmy Cricket*

I said, "It is most extraordinary weather for this time of year." He replied, "Ah, it isn't this time of year at all." *Oliver St John Gogarty*

"Isn't the weather awful, Mrs O'Dowd?"
   "It is an' all, but sure it's better than nothin'." *Kevin Murtie*

O'Leary: "How did you find the weather when you went to Limerick?"
Rafferty: "I just opened the door and there it was." *Duncan Crosbie*

Weather reminds me of being a kid. Wednesday was the day the Gaelic fixtures for the weekend would appear in the evening papers. It was the day the Dublin Corporation would begin decreeing whether its pitches would be playable. Generally the urine of an incontinent cat was sufficient disaster for one to be declared waterlogged. *Tom Humphries*

As a barber, I find that talking to the customers about the weather breaks the ice. *Peter Quinn*

The vagaries of the Irish weather dictate that any fine spell will be short-lived. To any positive comments announce, "It will never last." You will find that a bad summer is inevitable so on any fine spring or summer's day, comment, "I suppose this will be our summer." *Tadhg Hayes*

The Irish weather tells people to go indoors, sit on a sofa, watch TV non-stop, and become an alcoholic. *Des Bishop*

In Ireland, if there's a rumour of snow we all ring in sick to work, sit in ten-mile tailbacks and stockpile food and water. In Finland when there's two foot of snow they hop into their cars and do ninety miles an hour down the motorway on snow chains to purchase a pint of milk. *Paul Kilduff*

# WEDDINGS

Two aerials on a roof fell in love and got married. The wedding wasn't great but the reception was fantastic. *Jimeoin*

We had a quiet wedding. Her father had a silencer on the shotgun. *Sean Kilroy*

My wedding to Kerry Katona wasn't real. We were getting married to get loads of money for it. I was too young to understand what having kids meant. Having a child was like getting a dog. *Bryan McFadden*

The most difficult years of marriage are those following the wedding. *Tom O'Connor*

I've sat in the lobbies of the more popular wedding hotels waiting for the brides-to-be to turn up at reception. You can tell who they are because when they arrive they look significantly more miserable than any of the normal guests. They are usually accompanied by an even more worried-looking older couple, who are tightly holding an arm of the bride-to-be in case she tries to make a run for it. These turn out to be her parents. *David Slattery*

A wedding planner is the wedding equivalent of debt consol-idation. Rather than dealing with one arsehole you put all your arseholes into one stone-cold eighteen-carat easy-to-manage fuckface. *Ed Byrne*

I'd say Jesus was great crack. Anyone who goes to a wedding and changes water into wine has a sense of humour. *Pat Ingoldsby*

I love golf so much I played last week instead of attending a wedding. Mine. *Joe O'Donovan*

The moment I said "I do", I was transformed from a snivelling, guilt-ridden, self-conscious, randy single man into a raving sex maniac with a game licence who was exhorted to procreate henceforth like bunnies in Ballybunion. *Mick Doyle*

I have so little regard for myself I didn't even invite myself to my own wedding. *Colin Farrell*

It's the law that "Sweet Caroline" must be played at every Irish wedding. *Kevin Courtney*

# WEIGHT

She said she was forty-seven. She should have added "stone".
*Katherine Lynch*

No, that skirt doesn't make you look fatter. How could it?
*Maureen Potter*

I'm an avid weight watcher. I keep it all in front of me where I can see it properly. *Derek Davis*

I think the term "morbidly obese" is very offensive for overweight people. As if they haven't enough on their plate.
*Jimmy Carr*

Joining a gym class isn't easy. The weighing-in process is more traumatic for your body than a triple bypass, or having twins without an epidural. *Dan Buckley*

I'm not saying she's fat, but whenever she gets on to one of those "I Speak Your Weight" machines, a card comes out saying "One at a time, please". *Frankie Blowers*

According to a doctor I consulted, the singer Enya is quite an effective emetic and is responsible for acute episodes of nausea, vomiting and diarrhoea, often attributed to some blameless bacterium. If you want to lose weight, put on those CDs now. *David Slattery*

My mum always says to my dad, "Do these jeans make my arse look big?" And my dad says, "No, it's your fat arse that makes your jeans look big." *Bryan McFadden*

I hope George Clooney will stop hanging around with skinny young ones half his age and realize that a sturdy Westmeath woman with a farm behind her is a far better bet. *Westmeath farmer and occasional actress Mary McEvoy*

On airplanes I'm usually told it's not possible for the left and right sides of my body to sit together, so one half of me is in 11B and the other in 23E. *Marian Keyes*

Jumping to a conclusion is a great way of losing weight. *Liam Fay*

My wife is the double of Liz Hurley. Liz Hurley weighs nine stone. *Dusty Young*

If you jog backwards, do you put on weight? *John McBain*

If you are rich, serious about losing weight and you really want results, try liposuction. It works every time, if you regain consciousness. *David Slattery*

I'm not saying she's the biggest woman in Ireland but last week she bent over in Wexford and they had an eclipse in Kerry. *Terry Adlam*

# WHISKEY

The true Irish cocktail is made by adding half a glass of whiskey to three quarters of another. *Tony Butler*

God invented whiskey to stop the Irish ruling the world. *Ed McMahon*

There is no such thing as a small whiskey. *Oliver St John Gogarty*

Give an Irishman lager for a month and he's a dead man. An Irishman is lined with copper and the beer corrodes it. But whisky polishes the copper and is the saving of him. *Mark Twain*

If a man tells you he has mastered whiskey, you may be certain it is the whiskey that is doing the talking. *John B. Keane*

Did it ever occur to you that the bottom of a bottle of whiskey is much too near the top? *Sean O'Faolain*

It takes two glasses of whiskey to bring an Englishman up to the functional level of an Irishman. *Fr Denis Faul*

Getting hitched up to a rich woman is about the only way a poet can remain true, and keep up an adequate supply of whiskey. *Patrick Kavanagh*

The reason whiskey kills more people than bullets is because bullets don't drink. *Richard Harris*

I fantasize about whiskey the way other men fantasize about women. *John B. Keane*

Irish whiskey is not to be confused with Scotch, which is spelt differently, or American, which tastes like turpentine. *Richard O'Connor*

Timothy O'Mahony was fined £200 at the local court for drunken driving. He tried to overtake a row of cars but collided with another vehicle. He was found to have a small quantity of whiskey in his car. He explained to Justice Wallace that he didn't normally drink whiskey but rather used it for calves with pneumonia. *The* **Corkman** *newspaper*

Whiskey bottles have narrow necks to stop Irishmen from knocking off the contents in one go. *Sean Desmond*

# WIFE-SWAPPING

We always hear about wife-swapping parties. Why aren't there any husband-swapping ones? *Peg Bracken*

Did you hear about the two Irish guys in bed together? One says to the other, "D'ye know what it is, Mick, this wife-swappin' lark isn't all it's cracked up to be." *Joe Donaghy*

# WILLS

The only sort of man most women want to marry is the fella with a will of his own — preferably made out in her favour. *Brendan Behan*

Where there's a will, there's a relative. *Michael Boylan*

Spendthrifts make their heirs prematurely grey. *J. P. Donleavy*

My eldest daughter came to me recently and said she wanted to borrow against my will. Then she tried to convince me it was a short-term loan. *Brendan Grace*

"And have you made your will, Shamuseen?"
   "Indeed I have. All me fortune goes to the doctor that saves me life."
*Doug Anderson*

# WINDOWS

I'm not into throwing plasma TVs out of the windows of hotel rooms. Besides, plasma screens are really heavy, and most hotel windows are reinforced. *Ronan Keating*

A man was walking down the street carrying his front door. His friend said, "What's wrong?" "The lock is broken," he told him, "I'm going to have it fixed." "How will your wife get in?" his friend asked. "It's OK,' he said, "I left the window open." *Noel V. Ginnity*

Alex Higgins' autobiography is called *Alex Through the Looking Glass. Through the Plate Glass Window* would have been more appropriate. *Nick Hancock*

Marriage is an alliance entered into by a man who can't sleep with the window shut and a woman who can't sleep with it open. *George Bernard Shaw*

# WINE

Abstain from wine, women and song. Mainly song. *George Best*

The English have the miraculous power of turning wine into water. *Oscar Wilde*

I don't think Jesus should have turned water into wine at the wedding feast of Cana. He should have paid for his round like everyone else. *Jack Cruise*

There's more to life than wine, bitterness and food – but not much. *Boy George*

Larry Gogan: "Complete the phrase 'Wine, women and . . .'"
Contestant: "Sex!"
*Exchange on Gogan's* **Just-a-Minute Quiz**

# WIVES

He told me his wife was an angel. I said, "You're lucky. Mine is still alive." *Jimmy O'Dea*

I can't find any thread of consistency in my marriages. My wives were a mixed bag: a schoolgirl, a gentlewoman, a motion picture actress, a ballerina — and a crocodile. *John Huston*

Here's to our wives and mothers — may they never meet! *Old Irish toast*

If you saw an Irishman out with his wife you might easily get the notion that he didn't like her. You might even think he didn't know her. *John D. Sheridan*

To avoid coveting my neighbour's wife I desire to be coveted by her instead — another thing entirely. *William Congreve*

My wife is the sort of woman who gives necrophilia a bad name. *Patrick Murray*

I don't tell my wife anything. I figure that what she doesn't know won't hurt me. *Danny Cummins*

My wife and myself were blissfully happy for twenty years. Then we met. *Joe Lynch*

Murphy came home from work and got a terrible shock. His wife said she wasn't leaving him. *Noel V. Ginnity*

I'm not saying my wife is cold but when she opens her mouth a light comes on. *Joe Cuddy*

Bigamy is having one wife too many. Monogamy is the same thing. *Oscar Wilde*

I've had bad luck with all my wives. The first two died from poisoning and the third wouldn't take it. *Frank Carson*

My wife was a bag of nerves the day we got married. Now she's just a bag. *Big O*

I love to praise my wife. She's gorgeous. She's wonderful. She's listening. *Brendan O'Carroll*

# WOMEN

A woman would talk intimately with a lamp-post. *Gerry Ryan*

Women are a mystery to man because they only understand lovers, children and flowers. *George Moore*

Even if a man could understand women, he still wouldn't believe it. *Niall Toibin*

Women love Glenda Gilson because she's a horse. *Ben Frow*

A wise woman will always let her husband have her way. *R. B. Sheridan*

Women who can't bear to be separated from their dogs often send their children to boarding schools quite cheerfully. *George Bernard Shaw*

I'm constantly fighting the deep-seated sense that women come from another planet. *Gerry Ryan*

One of the things that has contributed to the idea that women do not exist in Ireland is the fact that when they were first discovered, no one knew what to do with them. *Tony Butler*

Women see things that men don't: dirt, relatives, bargains. *Dylan Moran*

I don't have much luck with women because they're never as interested in me as I am. *Tommy Tiernan*

Women are the stronger sex because of the weakness of the stronger sex for the weaker sex. *Graham Buckley*

Irish son: "What part of speech is woman, Da?"
Irish father: "The whole of it, son."
*Peter Cagney*

I would happily dispense with the company of women if I could find a sheep who'd do my washing for me. *Big O*

Anyone who really thinks women are the weaker sex should try pulling the covers of the bed over to their side some night. *John D. Sheridan*

When I was growing up, women were strapped down in case anybody would think they had breasts. They had lead at the end of their frocks in case anyone would catch a glimpse of their knees. **Ronnie Drew**

No woman can be a beauty without a fortune. **George Farquhar**

I have been surrounded by women all my life. I swim in oestrogen. **Bob Geldof**

# WORDS

Did you ever notice that the word "engaged" has "gag" in the middle of it? **Rosie O'Donnell**

The words "husband", "wife" and "spouse" are falling into desuetude nowadays, replaced by the all-purpose "partner", a term once reserved for the business arrangements between Marks and Spencer or Rolls and Royce. **Mary Kenny**

The first two-syllable word I ever learned growing up was "discretion". **Eamon Dunphy**

I've never understood the expression "casual sex". Sex is only casual if one of you is eating an omelette and the other is doing the crossword. **Noel V. Ginnity**

There's a new word for a bastard today: love child. I can't see it catching on at football matches: "That referee is a love child!" **Brendan Grace**

The reason there are so many Irish jokes is because they have a quaint way with words. Like the patient who hobbled into the surgery's waiting-room and said, "I hope to God the doctor finds something wrong with me because I'd hate to feel like this if I was well." **George Coote**

Is there any other word for synonym? **T. P. McKenna**

Women should reclaim the C word. Just as homosexuals took possession of "queer" from the straight community and

African-Americans now have sole rights to the word "nigger", so we should rise up and take control of "c***". We have nothing to lose but our asterisks. *Fiona Looney*

# WORK

A Dublin drayman once pleaded that he was unfit for work because he'd been to a christening the day before and the baby was the only one there that took water. *Sean Desmond*

If you really care about your work you shouldn't be able to cope. The ideal is to die from a burst blood vessel two rungs from the top of the ladder. You'll be guaranteed a company funeral where your employees will do their utmost to pretend they're unhappy you're dead — because this is in their contract. *David Slattery*

The only really dirty four-lettered word is "work". *Brendan Kennelly*

Whenever I told people I was a musician, they used to say, "And do you work as well?" *Donal Lunny*

Could anyone please tell me what Paris Hilton actually does for a living? *Dickie Rock*

A country gentleman admonished a man for begging when there was plenty of work in the hayfields. "Ah, we can't all work," the beggar said. "If we did, there'd be nothing for the rest of us to do." *Sean Desmond*

There's no more dignity in labour than there is in not working. I never felt ashamed to be out of work. I just felt broke. *Bob Geldof*

I knew a man who was so industrious he went on his honeymoon alone, leaving his wife at home to mind the shop. *Jack Cruise*

All work and no play makes Jack's wife a very rich widow. *Brian Behan*

Hard work never killed anybody, but why take a chance?
**Charlie McCarthy**

If play interrupts your work you're healthy. If work interrupts your play you're broke. **James O'Hara**

Young lad in court for minor offence. Judge asks him, "Are you working at the moment?" Lad replies, "Yes." Judge asks, "Who do you support?" Lad answers, "Man United." **Overheard in Dublin**

Superstitious Irishmen refuse to work in any week that has a Friday in it. **Paul Malone**

# WORRY

An Irishman can be worried by the thought that there's nothing to worry about. **Austin O'Malley**

Poems are written by young men who are dreaming and by old men who have lived. The men in between are too busy surviving and worrying. **Michael Longley**

People should never worry. If you're well there's nothing to worry about. If you're sick there are two things to worry about: either you'll get well or you'll die. If you get well there's nothing to worry about. If you die there are two things to worry about: you'll either go to heaven or you'll go to hell. If you go to heaven there's nothing to worry about and if you go to hell you'll be so damn busy shaking hands with your friends you won't have time to worry. So why worry? **Traditional Irish philosophy**

The best way to make an Irishman worry is to tell him not to. **Seamus O'Leary**

# WRITERS AND WRITING

The success of the Patricia Cornwell novels has had many young women declaring that their greatest ambition in life is not to be air hostesses but to be performing post-mortems. *Declan Lynch*

James Joyce's ambition was to forge within the smithy of his consciousness the uncreated conscience of his race. And then, hopefully, have it reproduced in plastic. *Frederic O'Neill*

To be a real Dublin writer it's not necessary ever to have written a line or had anything published. The sign "Work in Progress" can be seen adjoining the walls of many Dublin snugs as the Fair City's writers wrestle with syntax and a pint glass while discussing the Great Irish Novel they're working on. Most of these writers harbour dreams of being found dead, semi-naked, with a bottle of crème de cacao in one hand, a copy of *La Mouche* in the other, and a coked-out gerbil asleep on the pillow beside them. *David Kenny*

There's nothing new to say about Oscar Wilde, yet people will go on saying it. *John Broderick*

Writing is a curious business. The true believer can find more excitement in creating a oneliner or a metaphor or even a pun than in getting a message from Meryl Streep that she wishes to share the rest of her life with him. *Con Houlihan*

I'd be a goner long ago if I did everything I wrote about. *Edna O'Brien*

Writing is turning one's worst moments into money. *J. P. Donleavy*

George Moore wrote brilliant English until he discovered grammar. *Oscar Wilde*

Wilfred Owen is a revered sandwich board. He's all blood, dirt and sucked sugar stick. *W. B. Yeats*

Sometimes when things are going really well I back away from the desk and wander around and fill the fridge, or I go down to the shops for a bottle of milk that I don't need. **Roddy Doyle**

I've written every possible kind of sex scene except a couple doing it standing up in a hammock. **Lee Dunne**

My dad's a writer. His favourite expression is "The pen is mightier than the sword", which I believed for a long time until I moved to the city and I got into a fight with this guy and he cut me up real bad. I drew a moustache on his face and then I wrote him a nasty letter. **Kevin Brennan**

To be a Dublin writer you first need to find a grotty little bedsit. Then you need to block up the bath and windows and stay indoors for two weeks living on Easi Singles, cornflakes and chocolate raisins. Then when you're starting to smell like a kipper that's been left in a sock under a radiator since Christmas, unleash yourself on the nearest pub carrying a wadge of dog-eared foolscap. **David Kenny**

Writing is like getting married. One should never commit oneself until one is amazed at one's luck. **Iris Murdoch**

The public is largely influence by the *look* of a book. It is the only artistic thing about the public. **Oscar Wilde**

Writing is like jumping from a plane. The worrying thing is that you don't know if you're going to come out with a parachute or a grand piano. **Joe O'Connor**

I find writing very difficult. The only time I manage to say what I want is when I'm not aware of it. **Marianne Moore**

The best thing I ever wrote was a cheque for £50,000 that didn't bounce. **Patrick Kavanagh**

Some people think James Joyce was the greatest Irish writer, some think he was writing in Albanian, and others think he was dyslexic. **Terry Eagleton**

All good writing is swimming under water and holding your breath. **F. Scott Fitzgerald**

# XENOPHOBIA

You're still a blow-in if you've been living somewhere in Ireland for twenty years. *Alice Taylor*

An Irish farmer, to avoid the possibility of unexpected visitors, can often be found eating his dinner out of a drawer. *Niall Toibin*

I'm a kranky [sic] man and I don't like anyone. *Samuel Beckett*

# YOUTH

In my youth I didn't think I had a prayer of becoming an atheist. *Tom Reilly*

When I was young I used to think I was indecisive but now I'm not so sure. *Eoin Carey*

Young people today spend their time bullying each other on Facebook and drinking alcopops before becoming morbidly obese teenagers. *Ian O'Doherty*

# ZOOS

I asked a man what was the weirdest place he was ever thrown out of. He said, "A zoo." I said "Why?" "Because ducks don't eat Tictacs," he told me. *Neil Delamere*

To keep down the rising birth rate among animals, Belfast zoo has shot all the storks. *Peter Cagney*

A zoo is a place of refuge where wild animals are protected from people. *Hal Roach*

Have you been to the zoo? I mean as a visitor. *Noel Purcell*

I went to the zoo in Regent's Park and had a row with one of the keepers. I was looking round the Reptile House and he ran up to me and said, "What are you sticking your tongue out at that snake for?" I replied, "He started it." *Jimmy Cricket*

When I saw the zebra in the Dublin zoo I thought it was one of my father's donkeys in pyjamas. *James McKeon*